MRN no 4/2/18

THE CAUSES OF WAR: 1400 CE TO 1650 CE

This is the third volume of a projected five-volume series charting the causes of war from 3000 BCE to the present day, written by a leading international lawyer, and using as its principal materials the documentary history of international law, largely in the form of treaties and the negotiations which led up to them. These volumes seek to show why millions of people, over thousands of years, slew each other. In departing from the various theories put forward by historians, anthropologists and psychologists, Gillespie offers a different taxonomy of the causes of war, focusing on the broader settings of politics, religion, migrations and empire-building. These four contexts were dominant and often overlapping justifications during the first four thousand years of human civilisation, for which written records exist.

The Causes of War

Volume III: 1400 CE to 1650 CE

Alexander Gillespie

·HART·
PUBLISHING
OXFORD AND PORTLAND, OREGON
2017

Hart Publishing
An imprint of Bloomsbury Publishing Plc

Hart Publishing Ltd
Kemp House
Chawley Park
Cumnor Hill
Oxford OX2 9PH
UK

Bloomsbury Publishing Plc
50 Bedford Square
London
WC1B 3DP
UK

www.hartpub.co.uk
www.bloomsbury.com

Published in North America (US and Canada) by
Hart Publishing
c/o International Specialized Book Services
920 NE 58th Avenue, Suite 300
Portland, OR 97213-3786
USA

www.isbs.com

**HART PUBLISHING, the Hart/Stag logo, BLOOMSBURY and the
Diana logo are trademarks of Bloomsbury Publishing Plc**

First published 2017

British Library Cataloguing-in-Publication Data
A catalogue record for this book is available from the British Library.

ISBN:	HB:	978-1-84946-646-2
	ePDF:	978-1-50991-766-2
	ePub:	978-1-50991-765-5

Library of Congress Cataloging-in-Publication Data
A catalogue record for this book is available from the Library of Congress.

Typeset by Compuscript Ltd, Shannon
Printed and bound in Great Britain by CPI Group (UK) Ltd, Croydon CR0 4YY

To find out more about our authors and books visit www.hartpublishing.co.uk. Here you will find extracts,
author information, details of forthcoming events and the option to sign up for our newsletters.

This book is dedicated to those who are trying to make sense of the past for the benefit of the future.

Contents

I

Introduction

1. THE CONVERSATION ON SUNDAY AFTERNOON

T HE TOPIC OF this book is the causes of war. It is the third volume on this topic, covering the years between 1400 CE and 1650 CE. The complementary volumes I have written around this subject deal with the customs and laws of war, covering the methods by which humans have fought and killed each other for the last 5,000 years.[1] This book and its accompanying volumes are different: they are about why people fight, not how.

My interest in the causes and practices of warfare began with a discussion I had with my mother over 15 years ago, towards the end of the twentieth century, on whether humanity was better or worse than in the past. Simply put, was humanity making progress or not? Whilst I argued in the affirmative, my mother argued in the negative. As with many such lunchtime discussions on Sunday afternoons, trying to find robust benchmarks was (and is) very difficult, if not impossible. Although the conversation on this particular Sunday afternoon moved on to other topics, this question of 'progress' caught my attention. It has remained on my mind for the last decade, during which time I have gone from moments of optimism to pessimism. My supposition is that the causes of warfare have changed for the better—that is, progress has occurred, with the reasons by which we justify killing becoming more acceptable than in the past. To prove this point requires a great deal of research to show what the causes were and how they have changed. This means that this volume, which covers the years between 1400 and 1650, is a stepping-stone towards my final answer.

2. UTOPIA

There are many philosophical discussions around the idea of 'progress'.[2] These are often linked to various forms of Utopian thinking.[3] This is especially so as regards the

---

[1] Gillespie, A (2011) *A History of the Laws of War*, Vol 1: *Combatants*; Vol 2: *Civilians*; and Vol 3: *Arms Control* (Oxford, Hart Publishing).

[2] Doren, V (1969) *The Idea of Progress* (NYC, Praeger); Hiderbrand, G (ed) *The Idea of Progress: A Collection of Readings* (Los Angeles, CA, California University Press); Melzer, A (ed) (1995) *History and the Idea of Progress* (NYC, Cornell University Press).

[3] Manuel, F (1979) *Utopian Thought in the Western World* (NYC, Harvard University Press); Manuel, F (ed) (1969) *Utopias and Utopian Thought* (NYC, Condor); Buber, M (1949) *Paths in Utopia* (London, Routledge); Mumford, L (1962) *The Story of Utopias* (NYC, Viking); Bernini, M (1950) *Journey Through Utopia* (London, Routledge).

question on which I am focusing, as the flipside of any question about the causes of war is the search for enduring peace. I struggle to think how many gallons of ink have been expended in debates on this question, or on suggestions as to the correct path to Utopia, where the difficulties of the past are bypassed and a bright, violence-free future awaits humanity. There is no monopoly on these plans, and libraries are full of variations on themes that run to thousands of miles of shelving, from theology to ideology, cross-referenced to a bewildering collection of historical epochs and philosophical musings.

The idea of a 'Golden Age', in which there was no warfare, can be found in the writings of, amongst others, the scholars of ancient China and India.[4] Such views were mirrored in Greece and Rome: the Roman poet Ovid wrote of a previous time when 'men kept faith and did what was right ... the peoples passed their lives in security and peace, without need for armies'.[5] These dreams later flowered into the eschatology and promises of times to come of religions like Christianity and Islam. They later flowed into the Enlightenment, when Jean Jacques Rousseau argued in the eighteenth century that it was demographic growth, private property, the division of class and state coercion that forced warfare upon an otherwise peaceful species.[6] In the twentieth century, the cultural anthropologist Margaret Mead famously wrote in 1940 that '[w]arfare is only an invention, not a biological necessity'.[7] A similar view was later reflected in the constitution of UNESCO, which was drawn up in the immediate aftermath of the Second World War. Specifically, 'since wars begin in the minds of men, it is in the minds of men that the defences of peace must be constructed'.[8] UNESCO subsequently added to this view with its Seville Statement on Violence, issued to celebrate the International Year of Peace in 1986. This suggested that it was 'scientifically incorrect to say that we have inherited a tendency to make war from our animal ancestors', or 'that war or any other violent behavior is genetically programmed in our human nature'. UNESCO affirmed that 'biology does not condemn humanity to war', and anathematised the 'alleged biological findings that have been used ... to justify violence and war'.

I like this view, especially the idea that humanity can escape its past and what Sigmund Freud saw as an underlying desire for aggression as part of our instinctual endowment.[9] I consider this essential, as I am of the belief that humanity has been

[4] Hsiao, K (1979) *A History of Chinese Political Thought* (Princeton, NJ, Princeton University Press) 299, 308. Bary, T (ed) (1960) *Sources of Chinese Tradition*, Vol I (NYC, Columbia University Press) 99, 128–30, 237.

[5] Ovid, *Metamorphoses* trans Raeburn, D (2004) (London, Penguin) 1.89–100. Note also Hesiod, *The Works and Days* trans Most, L (2003) (Boston, MA, Loeb) 1.146.

[6] Rousseau, JJ *The Discourses* trans Gourevitch, V (1997) (Cambridge, Cambridge University Press).

[7] Mead, M (1940) 'Warfare in Only an Invention' 40 *Asia* 402–05. For contemporary debates about this question, see Livingston-Smith, D (2007) *The Most Dangerous Animal: Human Nature and the Origins of War* (London, St Martins); Fry, D (2007) *Beyond War: The Human Potential for Peace* (Oxford, Oxford University Press).

[8] Preamble, UNESCO Constitution.

[9] Freud, S (1930) *Civilisation and its Discontents* (London, Penguin) 86.

constantly beleaguered by warfare. This is certainly the pattern to be found in the period covered by this book, the third volume on the causes for war, as they appeared between the years from 1400 to 1650.

3. Facts

The methodology of this book is somewhat complicated. The skeleton on which it is built comprises treaties. I place great weight on the bilateral and international instruments of each age, as despite all of the difficulties posed by different languages and different ages, treaties and/or agreements reflect in the clearest way possible how different nations see a shared problem and shared solution. As such, at each point, the law, or at least the settlement by which peace has been reached, has been set out as simply as possible. In places where there were no treaties, the bones are taken from the practice of key players of the period, which often became custom. In each epoch I have attempted to read and quote the original sources. These have often been supplemented by the best monographs I can find on each epoch.

Within this methodology it is important to keep in mind, when reading historical texts, that there is a high risk that mistakes have occurred, that the original sources were wrong, mistaken or have been taken out of context. I was conscious of this risk in writing this book, as at various points only fragments of history are available. In places I think these fragments resemble dinosaur bones in the desert: a huge amount of material is often missing, and what remains can be assembled to make a variety of bizarre species bearing no relation to what actually existed. My interpretations are the way in which I see the evidence. I have no doubt others will see it differently. I particularly urge caution in the areas where numbers of those killed have been included. Nevertheless, despite the uncertainties in this area, I have included such figures to provide the roughest of gauges, by which the impacts of decisions concerning warfare can be seen.

4. *Casus Belli* in Practice

Casus belli is a Latin expression meaning the justification for acts of war. The noun *casus* means 'incident', 'rupture' or 'case', while *belli* means 'of war'. The need for people to have a just cause can be the difference between an act of heroism and an act of murder. For this reason, hundreds, if not thousands, of philosophers and leaders of states listed justifications for why bloodshed was necessary, and why the following loss or acquisition of property was fair. This point about property is an underlying recognition in all of the chapters that follow. That is, the overwhelming majority of all the wars studied in the period covered by this book have the control and/or ownership of resources as their result. No matter which way the causes for violence are cut, the results are nearly always the same—namely, that the control and/or ownership of resources (from physical resources through to the ability to draw tax) can change hands, or be defended. This is the practical result of nearly all of the conflicts, involving the great diversity of cultures operating within the 250 years documented in this volume.

5. THIS VOLUME

Volume 3 of *The Causes of War* is different from the first two volumes. In the first volume, I divided the causes of war from 3000 BCE to 1000 CE into the categories of empire, migratory peoples, politics and religion. In many ways, this worked for the initial period, as, when I looked back on history, although the ideas were of a currency that could be understood in the twenty-first century, most of the regions, empires, actors and countries were not. Within the period of second volume, from 1000 CE to 1400 CE, it became apparent to me that the regions, empires, actors and countries with which I was dealing were very familiar, there was a much greater density of information and some of the patterns discernible in Volume 1 started to disappear. This was particularly obvious in connection with migratory peoples. Politics remained the same, albeit with a greater division between absolute sovereigns, a third force of nobles and/or aristocracy as counterweights, and the development of constitutional mechanisms to limit power. The real change here was in the development of peasant revolutions. An additional difference was the occurrence of wars over dynastic issues, in which both marriages and debates about mechanisms for patrimony became much more common, unlike in first volume of this work. Finally, religion remained a constant cause of war, in terms both of fighting other faiths and of inter-faith warfare. The difference was in Asia, where the Mongols, and the Song and Ming dynasties, managed to diminish religious justifications for warfare.

The wars covered by Volume 3 (between 1400 CE and 1650 CE) that have the greatest resemblance to those that went before them in Europe, were the wars caused either by those wanting to be or to remove the existing monarch and/or by monarchs seeking to expand their realms by military force. The exemplars of these are the Hundred Years' War, the Wars of the Roses, the wars for the expansion of France and the Italian Wars. The dominance of these patterns nevertheless diminished in Western Europe after 1550 CE, when considerations of religion came much more to the fore. Indeed, if there was a notable change in the latter period, it was that wars about religion, and especially inter-Christian wars, dominated the epoch. Although there was an earlier history of discontent and violence against the Catholic Church within Western Europe, by the sixteenth century the writings of Martin Luther were perfectly timed to split not only countries but the whole of Western Europe too. This split was enlarged by temporal rulers, who sought to use religion to advance their own power. Most notably, warfare erupted in the countries we know today as Germany, France, the Netherlands, and then Germany again as the Thirty Years' War reached its climax. Peace was ultimately achieved by the establishment of sovereign independence and/or the abandonment of the ideal of an absolute and universal type of Christianity. Even countries like England, which managed to avoid being directly pulled into the wars of religion, were strongly influenced by them, from which fundamental changes to constitutional governance occurred, with Charles I ultimately losing his head. This type of conflict, in which war was ultimately about different types of political power, succeeded in England to such an extent that for a short period the country was a republic. Similar uprisings for radical constitutional change failed to achieve their goals, while radical peasant uprisings were also crushed. Only Poland-Lithuania achieved, albeit without violence, advanced constitutional structures that restrained the power of monarchs who increasingly had become absolute rulers.

The other noticeable difference in this period was the occurrence of wars in the New World, in the Northern, Central and Southern parts of the Americas. The causes of warfare in this area were founded on the fact that lands already occupied by other peoples had been gifted by the papacy to the Spanish and Portuguese monarchs. Full and absolute obedience was said to be owed by the indigenous peoples to these European rulers and their religious views. Failure to comply would, and did, cause repeated conflicts in Central and Southern America. The colonies in the north, especially as established by the English, Dutch and French, rather adopted a view that the benefits of European civilisation were the fruits the indigenous peoples would reap, religion being seen more as a secondary consideration.

War in Eastern Europe broadly followed the patterns of earlier centuries, with the notable difference that everything was getting bigger, most notably the rise in power and prestige of both Russia and Poland-Lithuania. The Russian justifications for war were that the lands they desired once belonged to them and that they needed to intervene to protect members of the Orthodox Christian faith. Those Eastern European rulers who went the other way and advanced into the core Rus lands asserted that their actions were legitimate as they were made by invitation and/or because they sought to possess the title of *Tsar* in Moscow.

The wars involving Islam discussed in this book are also different from those of earlier centuries. Most notably, inter-Muslim wars became much more frequent, predicated on a drive for dominance but wrapped in justifications such as that a ruler was not fulfilling his duties, for example being a heretic, or failing to persecute heretics or protect pilgrims, as a leader of the faith should do. Muslim wars against Christian forces were much less nuanced. The causes of war, which glossed over the underlying momentum and continual rhetoric of religion, were typically about the inability to control border areas, especially when local rulers were willing to swap allegiance from one side to another, usually in exchange for greater degrees of autonomy in religious and/or economic terms. This was the pattern in Eastern Europe, the Western Mediterranean and North Africa, with the clear trend in all three areas being the advance of Muslim forces.

The last chapter in this book covers war in Asia. The patterns in this part of the world were broadly similar to what had occurred before, with the exception that at the beginning of this period, in 1400, the dominant power in the region was Ming China. At the end of this period it was Qing China. Over the same time, Vietnam became more independent, while Korea came closer to the orbit of China. Japan became unified and for the first time in its history projected its power outwards, invading Korea with a view to conquering China. The external wars were about honour, power and the acquisition of territory. The internal wars were about quests to bring stability, order and virtue back to failing states.

II

Crowns, Dynasty and Territory

1. INTRODUCTION

THIS CHAPTER EXAMINES wars caused either by those wanting to be or to remove the existing monarch, and/or by monarchs seeking to expand their realms by military force. The core countries for consideration are England, France, Spain and Italy. The conflicts covered include the Hundred Years' War, the Wars of the Roses, the wars for the expansion of France and the Italian Wars. These were all about the acquisition of power and territory for monarchs and dynasties. This acquisition would be effected via marriages, alliances, war and/or treaties. In the period covered by this chapter, there was initially minimal consideration of religion in these conflicts, and political counterweights (alternative political management options not based around monarchy) designed to negate the power of absolute monarchs were only barely evident in each country. After 1550, causes based around religion and political control played a greater role in the causes of conflict.

2. THE HUNDRED YEARS' WAR

Although known as the Hundred Years' War, this was a series of conflicts between England and France, starting in 1337 and concluding in 1453. The War is generally divided into three phases separated by truces: the Edwardian War (1340–60); the Caroline War (1369–60); and the Lancastrian War (1415–53). In this section we examine the events that led to the breaking of the *Truce of Paris* (1399) and the third phase of the Hundred Years' War, as overlapping with other considerations and causes for war.

A. The Removal of Kings

The removal of kings was always a prime source for conflict. The dawn of the fifteenth century in Europe saw the removal of two kings, one with little bloodshed, the other accompanied by much. The first instance involved Germany, where Wenceslaus IV was replaced as King of Germany (formally of the Romans) by Rupert III, who was elected Elector Palatinate in 1400. Rupert achieved this deposition by getting three ecclesiastical prince electors to agree (thus achieving a majority vote) that Wenceslaus was not worthy to be King of Germany as he had refused to appear to answer charges against him for failing to maintain public peace or resolve the Western Schism. For these failures, he was deposed on account of his 'futility, idleness, negligence and ignobility'.[1]

The second instance occurred in England and involved the future King Henry IV's taking of the throne, by force, from Richard II. As discussed in the previous volume, Henry Bolingbroke was the son of John of Gaunt (and therefore grandson of King Edward III). After Richard II had exiled Bolingbroke and then refused to allow him to inherit his father's estate, Bolingbroke struck back.[2]

This conflict went much further than the obtaining of raw power by Henry: the deposition of Richard II showed that despite the concept of hereditary right, the monarch was not above the law, and that in England, Parliament (even if in reality only a weak body that could be manipulated) could depose a king if he became a tyrant. Parliament subsequently agreed to the legitimacy (as opposed to treason) of Richard's cousin, Henry Bolingbroke, becoming the next King of England, after he had put his case to them of what a good king should be (Richard II, who was a bad king, being justifiably deposed). Henry explained:

> I am descended by the right line of the blood coming from the good lord Edward III, and through that right that God of his grace has sent me, with the help of my kindred and my friends to recover ... [the] ... realm ... [which] ... was on the point of being undone for default of governance and undoing of good laws.[3]

Henry explicitly undertook to eschew the arbitrary ways of his predecessor, and to govern not according to 'his will' but 'by the common advice, counsel, and consent' of Parliament.[4] These words were well received, and in October 1399, Henry Bolingbroke was crowned King Henry IV, Richard II being held to have forfeited his right to be monarch due to his absolutism and abuse of office. Richard II was imprisoned first at Leeds Castle and then at Pontefract. He died in 1400, probably of starvation.[5] At the same time, Henry (and later his son, Henry V) sought to achieve full control over the Church in England, and to appease the papacy in Rome by strengthening traditional values and seeking to extinguish heresy in the kingdom.[6] Such supplementary power,

---

[1] Stubbs, P (1908) *Germany in the Later Middle Ages* (London, Longmans) 152.

[2] Gillespie, A (2017) *The Causes of War*, Vol 2: *1000 CE to 1400 CE* (Oxford, Hart Publishing) 213–16.

[3] Speech of Henry Bolingbroke, crowned as Henry IV, recorded in Jones, D (2012) *The Plantagenets: The Kings Who Made England* (London, Harper) 587. Also Anon, 'The Succession of Henry IV', as reproduced in Baker, D (ed) (1982) *England in the Later Middle Ages* (London, Academica) 47–49; Genet, J (2013) 'The Problem of Tyranny in Fifteenth Century England', *Moreana* 50 (192), 43–66; Theilman, J (2004) 'Caught Between Political Theory and Political Practice', *History of Political Thought* 25(4), 600–19; Fletcher, C (2004) 'Narrative and Political Strategies at the Deposition of Richard II', *Journal of Medieval History* 30, 323–41.

[4] Henry, as cited in MacKinnon, J (1906) *A History of Modern Liberty*, Vol I (London, Longmans) 304. Also Wilkinson, B (1939) 'The Deposition of Richard II and Accession of Henry IV', *English Historical Review* 54 (214), 215–39.

[5] Fletcher, C (2004) 'Political Strategies at the Deposition of Richard II', *Journal of Medieval History* 30 (3), 323–41.

[6] 'The Burning of Heretics Act, *De heretico comburendo* 1401' as reprinted in Baker, D (ed) (1982) *England in the Later Middle Ages* (London, Academica) 124. Dahmus, J (1981) 'Henry IV of England: An Example of Royal Control of the Church', *Journal of Church and State* 23 (1), 35–48;

through both Parliament and the Church, meant that when revolts occurred against Henry's rule, on the grounds that Richard did not abdicate of his own free will, inter-linked with claims of greater autonomy for some of the regions, they were relatively easy to put down, as both Parliament and the Church supported Henry IV's occupying the throne of England.[7]

B. The Regional and International Context

The situation was more complicated for Henry IV when dealing with his Welsh, Scottish and French neighbours, all of whom ended up harbouring considerable numbers of supporters of Richard II. Many of them believed that despite what Parliament and the Church had said, Henry had wrongfully usurped the Crown of England, giving them legitimate cause to oppose him.

Henry IV first decided to keep Scotland in check. Soon after taking power, the King of England sent a letter to Robert III, the King of Scotland, and his nobles, informing them that he expected them to meet him at Edinburgh to do homage to him, according to ancient tradition. The fact that Robert III was dealing with internal difficulties in Scotland, and that a number of supporters of Richard II had fled to Scotland, made this an ideal time for Henry to strike. When Robert III addressed his reply to Henry as the Duke of Lancaster, rather than as the King of England, Henry decided he had sufficient cause to act. Not only would such an effort threaten the Scots, it would also, he hoped, provide a display of national unity by bringing together all of the forces of England under his lead, as the sole and legitimate king. Henry crossed the border with over 13,000 men and marched north. The English found no opposition until they reached Edinburgh, which Robert had no intention of surrendering. Not willing to getting bogged down besieging the city, Henry marched back to the border, preferring to concentrate on making sure that his own crown was secure, leaving the Scots to brew in their own internal dissension around the Scottish throne.[8]

The relationship between Henry IV and the French was to be seen in the context of the Hundred Years' War, which at this point was frozen at about the half-way point. The current hiatus was due to the *Truce of Paris* of 1399, which was cemented with the marriage of Richard II to the six-year-old Isabella of France, the daughter of the French king, Charles VI. The risk that Henry IV faced after Richard's death was that, although Henry allowed Isabella to return to France (she having refused to marry Henry's son, the future Henry V), he was concerned that her father might

[7] Walker, S (2000) 'Rumour, Sedition and Popular Protest in the Reign of Henry IV', *Past and Present* 166, 31–65.

[8] Curry, A (2010) 'Henry IV's Scottish Expedition of 1400', *The English Historical Review* 125 (517) 1382–1413; Jacob, E (1987) *The Fifteenth Century* (Oxford, Clarendon) 34–35, 47–49, 64–65; Venning, T (2013) *The Kings and Queens of Scotland* (Stroud, Amberley Publishing) 130–39, 142–49.

attempt to invade England, to pursue Isabella's interests acquired by the marriage to Richard (even though the marriage itself had not been consummated as she was not yet of age).

The French king, rather than openly breach the *Truce of Paris*, to which Henry IV had promised to adhere, preferred to cruise on the back of the Welsh Revolt that had started in 1400, discreetly landing some 2,500 French troops in 1401 to support the efforts of Owain Glyndwr, Prince of Powys. Glyndwr was particularly disgruntled over confiscated estates in the Welsh Marches (border zones shared with England), for which he could find no redress in the English Parliament. Owain was also annoyed over English demands for Welsh soldiers to fight in English wars. In Owain's first battle at Mynydd Hyddgen, some 500 Welshmen faced, and defeated, an English force of three times that number. This success then grew into a large-scale rebellion, for which support was sought from nobles still loyal to the usurped Richard II, as well as soldiers from Scotland, Ireland and, as noted above, France. Collectively, these forces went on to capture large amounts of territory and key strongholds, such as Aberystwyth and Harlech. However, the revolt against Henry IV as wrongful King of England found little long-term success. The downward spiral began when two opposing armies, of perhaps 14,000 men each, faced each other at Shrewsbury in 1403. The leader of the opposition, Henry Percy ('Hotspur'), son of the Earl of Northumberland, who was initially a close supporter of Henry IV but had latterly allied himself with Owain Glyndwr, accusing the English king of 'tyrannical government', lost his own life along with 3,000 of his men, after being defeated by Henry IV. All of the rebellious areas within Wales were slowly reclaimed after the loss of perhaps another 15,000 Welsh at the Battle of Usk in 1405. By 1412, the rebellion had petered out, and Glyndwr died an outlaw a few years later.[9]

The other significant reason why the Welsh rebellion failed was because the French, after 1403, lost interest in supporting it, and by 1404 both France and England were again on a stronger footing of peace. The reason why France recommitted itself to the spirit of the *Truce of Paris* was the lack of leadership of the French king, Charles VI, who was mentally unable to govern for long periods, leading to turmoil within the country. In the periods when Charles was unable to govern, his brother, Louis, the Duke of Orleans, ruled in his place. However, Louis was at loggerheads with the Dukes of Burgundy (first Philip the Bold and then John the Fearless, both of whom were descended from the French king, John II). The disagreements soon developed into a civil war, after John the Fearless ordered the assassination of Louis. Both sides would appeal to Henry IV of England, making offers of both land and/or subsidies for his support, and Henry would, after growing weary of the fragile nature of the *Truce of Paris*, at different times support both sides with men and/or money. Henry IV also explored alliances with the Dukes of Brittany and individual Flemish cities, both of

[9] Allmand, C (1997) *Henry V* (London, Yale University Press) 18, 24–37; Tanner, J (ed) (1958) *The Cambridge Medieval History: Decline of Empire and Papacy*, Vol VII (Cambridge, Cambridge University Press) 525; Grant, R (2011) *1001 Battles* (London, Penguin) 212.

which sought greater independence from the French Crown, and/or Burgundy.[10] Such a descent into civil war and the fragmentation of France, with the active engagement of outside participants, as Christine de Pizan argued in 1414 in her *Book of Peace*, not only constituted an unjust war (as it was designed to usurp the lawful authority of the sovereign of France) but it could only end in disaster for the nation. She was correct in her forewarning of the disaster to come, as it was the civil war in France that would allow Henry V to advance further than any other English monarch in obtaining the French Crown.[11]

C. Henry V

King Henry V began his reign in April 1413, just over two weeks after the death of his father Henry IV, with Parliament agreeing to Henry's succession before the old king had died.[12] He inherited a realm that was relatively peaceful. The constitutional relationship between king and parliament was a cooperative and non-revolutionary one, in which the representatives took office entirely at the king's will, to give effect and authority to royal policies, producing revenue from taxes, legislating as directed and supporting the goals of the monarch.

Henry V was now on good terms with his immediate neighbours, Wales and Scotland, despite having personally fought in both countries when his father was on the throne and having been struck in the face with an arrow in the course of battle in Wales. However, Henry held no personal grudge against the Welsh, and when the Welsh Revolt ended, he skillfully wove the Welsh nobility and soldiers into his campaigns in France. With regard to Scotland, thanks to the fortuitous capture of the young Scottish monarch James I, who had been sent to France for safekeeping but was captured en route in 1406, Henry V managed to hold many of the Scots in check for the 18 years of James's captivity, during which time James became a friend and ally of the English king.[13]

With Wales and Scotland in hand, Henry V could now turn his attention to France and go on to forge his reputation—and the basis of a new, more cohesive, national identity for England—as subsequently penned by Shakespeare. Henry began this process by crossing the Channel after making a secret alliance in 1414, as a result of which the

[10] Dumolyn, J (2008) 'Privileges and Novelties: The Political Discourses of the Flemish Cities, 1385–1506', *Urban History* 35 (1), 5–23; Phillpots, C (1998) 'The Fate of the Truce of Paris', *Journal of Medieval History* 24(1), 61–80.

[11] Christine de Pizan, 'The Book of Peace' in Blumenfield, R (ed) *The Selected Writings of Christine de Pizan* (NYC, Norton) 229–48; Christine de Pizan, *The Book of Deeds of Arms and of Chivalry* trans Willard, S (2003) (Pennsylvania, PA, Pennsylvania State University Press) 14–17; Walters, L (2005) 'Christine de Pizan', *Journal of European Studies* 35 (1), 29–45.

[12] See the 1406 'Act to Regulate Succession', reproduced in Adams, G (ed) (1947) *Select Documents of English Constitutional History* (London, Macmillan) 173–74.

[13] Chapman, A (2015) 'Welsh Archers at Agincourt: Myth and Reality', *Historian* 127, 12–16.

Duke of Burgundy agreed to help Henry defeat the French king, Charles VI, and pay homage to Henry as the King of both England and France. In return for his support, Henry promised Burgundy considerable autonomy. In an open letter to all parts of the English kingdom, Henry explained that he was going to France, 'for the recovery of his duchy of Aquitaine'. He added that he set himself with all devotion, in his cause of war, to achieve

> [t]hose things which make for the honour of God, the extension of the Church, the freeing of his country and the tranquillity of kingdoms, and especially of the two kingdoms of England and France that they might be more coherent and united, which from long and unhappy times past had damaged each other and caused deplorable effusion of human blood.[14]

Henry V was much harder to placate than his father regarding the English relationship with France. He was continually annoyed about the failure of the French to adhere to the terms of the 1360 *Treaty of Bretigny* between France and England, with regard both to the return of territory and non-payment by the French of the ransom for their former king, John II.[15] Henry took this so seriously that he ordered authenticated copies of the *Treaty of Bretigny* to be distributed in all of the areas he controlled, just before he crossed the Channel with his army and successfully besieged the town of Harfleur. When Henry heard that Charles VI's army was approaching, he left some men in occupation of Harfleur and marched some 1,000 men-at-arms and 5,000 archers to meet the French force, comprising at least 6,000 men-at-arms and 6,000 archers. The two forces met in battle at Agincourt on 25 October 1415. The result was an unmitigated disaster for the French, who lost over 5,000 men. The following year, 1416, the Holy Roman Emperor, Sigismund, agreed in the *Treaty of Canterbury* that the claims of Henry were robust, and that he would provide men to help the English war effort and support the king. However, Sigismund never supplied the troops to assist his ally, and Henry realised that if he wished to push his claim to the French throne further, support would have to come from within France itself.[16]

The support that Henry V found for his quest for the French crown came from the civil war in France and his explicit military alliance with the Duke of Burgundy. Although Henry had earlier lent assistance to the Burgundians in their conflict, they proved difficult allies, refusing to commit, oscillating in their loyalties between the French and English Crowns. This changed when Duke John the Fearless was treacherously killed while meeting the French Dauphin (later Charles VII). This was the turning point, as now Duke John's son, Philip the Good, was ready to commit to the English

---

[14] Henry V, as cited in Jacob, E (1987) *The Fifteenth Century* (Oxford, Clarendon) 115 and 161, 167–69, 422–25; Hunt, C (2007) 'The Origins of National Identity in Shakespeare's Henry V', *Perspectives on Political Science* 36 (3), 133–40; MacKenzie, C (2005) 'Henry V and the Invasion of France: The Moral Justification', *The Upstart Crow* 25, 65–80.

[15] Gillespie, A (2017) *The Causes of War*, Vol 2: *1000 CE to 1400 CE* (Oxford, Hart Publishing) 204–07.

[16] Honig, J (2012) 'Reappraising Late Medieval Strategy: The Example of the 1415 Agincourt Campaign', *War in History* 19 (2), 121–51; Allmand, C (1997) *Henry V* (London, Yale University Press) 48–49, 54–58, 66–67, 108–09; Gabriel, R (2005) *Empires at War*, Vol III (NYC, Greenwood) 978–82; Tanner, J (ed) (1958) *The Cambridge Medieval History: Decline of Empire and Papacy*, Vol VII (Cambridge, Cambridge University Press) 381–87.

cause in their fight against the Dauphin, whom he held responsible for the killing of his father. Or, as was traditionally explained when the damaged skull of John the Fearless was later shown to subsequent French monarchs, 'this is the hole through which the English made their way into France'.[17]

(i) The Treaty of Troyes

Henry consolidated his success at Agincourt by landing a further 10,000 English troops in Normandy. In 1417 the forces of England and Burgundy combined and overpowered most of the opposition. This larger force systematically overran the province, taking Caen, Cherbourg, Evreux and then Rouen. All of Normandy was taken by the end of 1419, and Paris was under threat. At this point, the French, rather than risk total destruction, sued for peace with their enemies, as a result of which the 1420 *Treaty of Troyes* was agreed. Under this treaty, Charles VI was allowed to retain the crown in his lifetime, but the English king was given charge of the government of France, and upon the death of Charles VI, Henry would be granted the French crown. Despite one king holding two crowns, the idea was that the two kingdoms would remain separate and France would not be anglicised. Henry also attempted to bolster the support of the French institutions, by providing that the oaths of fealty would be required not only from the great lords, but also from the Estates, spiritual and temporal, and the cities and communities of the kingdom. That is, Henry V saw France as a multilayered society in which all citizens had direct interests and responsibilities. Moreover, Henry promised that he would govern France (and England) with the advice and consent of the Estates.

This was a radically different approach on two fronts. First, attempts to strengthen the French *Parlement* at this point had been very weak, and initiatives such as the 1413 *Ordinance Cabochienne*, with its 258 articles of detailed reform, had failed to make any headway in Paris. Henry was trying to turn this around and create a greater form of constitutional governance in France, not unlike that in England. Secondly, unlike the *Treaty of Bretigny* of 1360, with which the English had tried to regulate a long-standing feudal dispute concerning territory in south-western France, the *Treaty of Troyes* effected an absolute dynastic settlement, in which the English dictated very clear terms.[18] Henceforth, there would be only one monarch ruling over both England and France. To secure the deal, Henry agreed to marry the daughter of Charles VI, Catherine. This marriage would make Henry V the French king's son-in law and heir, thus repudiating Charles's own son, the Dauphin Charles. The treaty specified:

> Since the marriage agreement between ... king Henry, and our most dear and beloved daughter, Catherine, he has become our son ... Our son, the king Henry, will not disturb nor disquiet us nor prevent us, while we live, from holding and possessing the crown and royal

[17] 'Words of the Charterhouse at Dijon', as in Cohen, M (ed) (2004) *History in Quotations* (London, Cassell) 303.
[18] See Butterfield, A (2013) 'Fuzziness and Perceptions of Language in the Middle Ages: Three Treaties and a Funeral', *Common Knowledge* 19 (1), 51–64.

dignity of France, as we now hold and possess them ... Immediately after our death, the crown and kingdom of France, with all their rights and appurtenances, shall be and remain, permanently the possession of our son, the king Henry, and of his heirs ... the two kingdoms [England and France] shall be governed under one person who shall be, for the time, king and sovereign lord of both kingdoms; saving always to each kingdom its rights, liberties and customs, usages and laws, not subjecting in any way one kingdom to the other ...[19]

Following this agreement, Henry V, together with Charles VI, entered Paris after the Estates General agreed to the peace. The Dauphin Charles, now linked to the murder of Duke John the Fearless, was banished from the kingdom and denied his right to the throne, due to what the *Treaty of Troyes* recognised as 'the horrible and enormous crimes and misdeeds, perpetuated against the kingdom of France'.[20] The Dauphin would not accept this, and continued to oppose Henry with his Armagnac supporters. Thus, whilst the English were in charge of areas to the north-west of Paris, and Burgundians controlled the region to the south-west of the city, the forces of the Dauphin, with the assistance of thousands of men from Scotland and Castile, continued to hold sway to the south and east of Paris. This last point about the Scots is notable, as although Henry and King James of Scotland had become friends, thousands of Scotsmen still left for France to fight the English, as part of the *Auld Alliance* with France, which the Scottish Parliament had reactivated whilst James was being held in England.[21]

D. Henry VI and Charles VII

Henry V and Charles VI both died in 1422. Initially their deaths did not change matters, as the alliance between England and Burgundy remained strong. It was reinforced with the 1423 *Treaty of Amiens*, whereby the Dukes of Burgundy and Brittany acknowledged the English (infant) Henry VI, the son of Henry V and his French wife Catherine (the daughter of Charles VI), as the lawful king of France. Accordingly, they agreed to continue to oppose the Dauphin, now the uncrowned Charles VII. For his part, Charles argued that his fight was legitimate and that he was the rightful king of France, as although his father had promised the kingdom to Henry V, because Henry died before Charles VI, he had therefore never acquired the crown and thus could not bequeath it. Accordingly, Charles VII would not accept that the infant Henry VI, his nephew, had any valid claim to rule France. Despite his resolution, Charles continued to lose both ground and men. At the Battle of Auxerre in 1423, in which Charles was defeated, he lost perhaps 4,000 men, whilst at Verneuil in 1424, another defeat for Charles, a further 10,000 men were killed.[22]

---

[19] Arts 1, 2, 6 and 24 of the Treaty of Troyes 1420, as in Laffan, R (ed) (1929) *Select Historical Documents: 800–1492* (New York, Holt) 166–67.

[20] Art 29 of the Treaty of Troyes.

[21] Allmand, C (1997) *Henry V* (London, Yale University Press) 80–90, 132, 151–55; Meron, T (1993) *Henry's Wars and Shakespeare's Laws* (Oxford, Oxford University Press) 182–90; Jacob, E (1987) *The Fifteenth Century* (Oxford, Clarendon) 177–83; Knecht, R (2007) *The Valois* (London, Hambledon) 52–60, 62.

[22] Jones, M (2002) 'The Battle of Verneuil: Towards a History of Courage', *War in History* 9 (4), 375–411.

The tide only began to turn in 1425, when Burgundian forces attacked the village of Domrémy, where Joan of Arc lived. At this time, Joan said that she had heard the voices of saints, ordering her to go to the king (Charles VII) and save the kingdom. She later explained in a letter to the English that she

> [had] come on behalf of God to reclaim the blood royal. She is ready to make peace, if you are willing to settle with her by evacuating France and making restitution for whatever you have stolen ... I have been sent here by God, king of heaven, to chase you completely out of France.[23]

Four years later, in 1429, Joan was finally taken before Charles VII, whom she persuaded to be formally anointed as king at Rheims. Thereafter, Charles began to act like a king in the traditional French style of absolute power. He stopped calling national gatherings, reverting back to local or regionally based assemblies. Whilst he was content to listen to comment on such local or regional matters, he declared that all national matters, such as tax and foreign policy, were his alone.[24] With this strengthened approach and renewed belief in himself, Charles found that after forcing the English to lift the siege of Orleans, with an army led by Joan of Arc, subsequently dubbed 'the Maid of Orleans', success followed success, such as at the Battle of Patay, where a force of 1,500 French defeated 5,000 English, leaving half of them dead or captured. With such results, the morale of the English drooped, Paris was almost recaptured by the French and the English hold on Normandy began to waiver, although their confidence rose when Joan was captured in 1430 by the forces of Burgundy and then sold to the English. The University of Paris provided the charges of heresy, idolatry, superstition and schism for which Joan faced trial before an ecclesiastical tribunal. Faced with the spectre of being burned alive, she abjured. When she then retracted her abjuration, she was deemed a relapsed heretic and burned at the stake in Rouen's market square. Although her reputation was later redeemed, this act of killing Joan of Arc was a rallying point that gave the French a saint, an icon, a hero, and the impetus they needed to push harder against the English.[25]

(i) The Treaty of Arras

Philip of Burgundy, despite having secured full control of Flanders and having a large degree of autonomy in Burgundy from the English king, warned the regents of the infant Henry VI in 1430 that 'I cannot continue these military operations without

---

[23] Letter to the English, reproduced in Rosenwein, B (ed) (2006) *Reading the Middle Ages: Sources from Europe, Byzantium and the Islamic World* (Ontario, Broadview) 517.

[24] Carlyle, AJ (1910) *A History of Medieval Political Theory in the West*, Vol VI (Blackwood, London) 159–65; MacKinnon, J (1906) *A History of Modern Liberty*, Vol I (London, Longmans) 129–31.

[25] Taylor, L (2012) 'Joan of Arc, the Church and the Papacy', *The Catholic Historical Review* 48(2), 217–40; Freeman, J (2008) 'Joan of Arc: Soldier, Saint, Symbol', *The Journal of Popular Culture* 41 (4), 601–34; Wolffe, B (2001) *Henry VI* (London, Yale University Press) 54–57; Grant, R (2011) *1001 Battles* (London, Penguin) 222.

adequate provision in the future from you ... and without payment of what is due to me'.[26] The tensions between the English and Burgundy escalated to the point that Duke Philip began negotiations with Charles VII, in which, in exchange for Philip's agreement to swap sides, Charles promised to make him the Premier Duke in France. This agreement was recorded in the 1435 *Treaty of Arras*. This treaty brought the Anglo-Burgundian alliance to an end and sealed the fate of the English in France. Although the promise of Philip's being the Premier Duke in France was not fulfilled, Philip was still satisfied with a number of other concessions. First, Charles promised he would ensure that the murderers of Philip's father would be brought to justice. Secondly, Charles agreed that the

> Lord Burgundy shall not be held to do homage or service to the king for the lands and lord-ships he now holds in the kingdom of France, nor for those which he shall have by this present treaty ... but after the king's decease, the Lord of Burgundy shall do to his son and successor in the crown of France, the homages ...[27]

The English relationship with the Scots collapsed at the same time as that with the Burgundians. Although James of Scotland had become a friend of Henry V, and his freedom was eventually achieved by agreement in 1423 for a ransom (of 60,000 *marks*), despite James's marrying Joan Beaufort, the half niece of Henry VI, the ongoing peaceful relationship with Henry VI did not hold. Although a truce for seven years had been agreed between England and Scotland (in tandem with James's release), the ransom payments to England stopped, and negotiations for a renewed *Auld Alliance* between Scotland and France commenced. The generous overtures from England for a full peace treaty with Scotland in 1433, including a return to the Scots of Berwick and Roxburgh, were subsequently refused by the Scottish advisers, overruling James I who personally supported the peace treaty. In 1435, as England was deep in the quag-mire that was France, James I, in accordance with the renewed *Auld Alliance*, besieged Roxburgh Castle, although when English forces arrived to relieve the siege, James fled. Despite this failure, the following year, the son of the French king, Charles VII, the future Louis XI, was married to Margaret of Scotland, James I's daughter. James had little time to celebrate this diplomatic achievement, as in 1437, following an attempted coup, he was assassinated on the orders of his uncle.[28]

The Hundred Years' War entered its final stage when the Scots advanced on England and the French restarted their offensive on the Continent. Paris was recovered by Charles VII in 1437. English efforts to win back the favour of Burgundy failed to produce any fruit, and four years later the English were driven out of Pontoise, part of a

---

[26] 'Letter of Philip the Good to Henry VI', as reproduced in Cohen, M (ed) (2004) *History in Quotations* (London, Cassell) 305.

[27] Re Arts 2, 10 and 24 of the 1435 Treaty of Arras, as reproduced in Laffan, R (ed) (1929) *Select Historical Documents: 800–1492* (New York, Holt) 167–68. Also Knecht, R (2007) *The Valois* (London, Hambledon) 68–70.

[28] The 1423 'Treaty of London', as in Dickinson, W (ed) (1958) *A Sourcebook of Scottish History*, Vol I (London, Nelson) 157; Macrae, C (1939) 'The English Council and Scotland in 1430', *The English Historical Review* 54 (215) 415–26.

pattern of slow retreat. In 1444, a truce was agreed in the *Treaty of Tours*. This was supported by the marriage of Margaret of Anjou, the niece of Charles VII, to Henry VI. In exchange, Maine was meant to be returned to France. Despite this marriage, in 1449, when England tried to persuade Brittany to become an ally once more, Charles VII invaded Normandy on three fronts. The area in English hands shrank rapidly, despite Henry's sending over thousands of reinforcements. A further loss at Formigny in 1450, where 4,000 out of 4,500 soldiers fighting for the English were either killed or captured (by an equal number of French), continued the slide, which was underlined with the loss of Cherbourg.[29]

In the spring of 1453, Charles VII, probably aware of the civil tensions that were begin to appear in England between Henry VI and Richard, Duke of York, opened the last campaign of the Hundred Years' War. He rejected Henry VI's offer to renounce his title to the kingdom of France, if he (Henry) could keep Normandy and Gascony. Instead Charles ordered three armies, of over 30,000 men each and 300 cannon, into Bordeaux from the south-east, east and north-east. The region, defended by half that number, was overwhelmed and surrendered to the French. Only Calais and the Channel Islands remained in English hands. There was no treaty to mark the losses, which represented the end of most of English holdings in France, with Aquitaine, Gascony and Normandy disappearing from the control of the English monarch. In all of these areas, the inhabitants had to 'recognise and affirm the King of France as their sovereign lord'.[30] Accordingly, peace was ultimately achieved by the absolute defeat of the English in these locations.

3. The Wars of the Roses

A. Richard, Duke of York

In 1455, two years after the end of the Hundred Years' War, a series of dynastic civil wars erupted in England, between the supporters of the House of Lancaster (with the red rose in their heraldry) and the House of York (with the white rose), which lasted for the next three decades. As Shakespeare wrote, 'a thousand souls' would be sentenced to 'death and deadly night'.[31] This was an underestimate, for as Thomas More suggested, this dynastic struggle in England, 'cost more English blood than hath twice the winning of France'.[32]

---

[29] Jacob, E (1987) *The Fifteenth Century* (Oxford, Clarendon) 260–63, 475–90.

[30] Serchuk, C (2007) 'Cartography and National Identity in France at the End of the Hundred Years War', *Journal of Medieval History* 33 (3), 320–38; Wolffe, B (2001) *Henry VI* (London, Yale University Press) 16–17, 52–59, 81, 146–49, 163–73, 198–205, 211.

[31] Shakespeare, *1 Henry VI*, Act 2, Scene 4. Also Hay, D (1996) *Europe in the Fourteenth and Fifteenth Centuries* (London, Longman) 138.

[32] More, T, *History of King Richard the Third* in Campbell, W (ed) (1931) *The English Works of Sir Thomas More*, Vol 1 (London, Dial Press) 441.

The conflict started to take root when King Henry VI, having presided over the liquidation of England's first overseas empire between 1444 and 1453, followed by uprisings in England against those who had lost assets in France, suffered a mental breakdown. His fragile mental state was worsened by his poor relationship with the English Parliament, which began to refuse his tax demands and take revenge on Henry's advisers for the losses in France. Into this vacuum stepped Richard, Duke of York, Henry's cousin and great grandson of Edward III, who acted as Lord Protector and Defender of the Kingdom during the King's incapacity between 1453 and 1455. His appointment in 1453 followed three years of tension with Henry VI, during which Richard expressed his dissatisfaction both with the loss of territories in France and with the continual mismanagement of affairs in England and Ireland. As Lord Protector, Richard did what he believed was required to help govern the realm, but when he targeted some of the King's friends at the end of 1455, he overstepped the mark. When Henry was recovering, his wife, Margaret of Anjou, called for a Great Council that excluded the Yorkist faction headed by Richard. Richard was then dismissed from his position, whilst charges that he was trying to usurp the throne were brought. Richard then rose in revolt against Henry.[33]

The first Battle of St Albans, in 1455, saw Duke Richard, with perhaps 7,000 men, defeat and capture the English king, who was supported by a mere 2,000 men. Richard then undertook his first Protectorate. This unravelled when Henry temporarily recovered and Margaret of Anjou attempted to overturn all of the Lord Protector's earlier appointments and confirm her son's right to inherit the throne. As the situation deteriorated and physical conflict threatened, Richard returned to Ireland as its Viceroy. When Richard returned to England, joined by the armed forces of other disgruntled nobles who had also been subsequently disenfranchised, he found military success at the Battle of Northampton in early July 1460, at which point King Henry VI was captured. Subsequently, resistance largely crumbled, allowing Richard to enter London and Parliament uncontested, the *Act of Accord* being passed a few months later at the end of October. With this legislation, it was settled that Richard of York would again be Lord Protector, the king's closest adviser, and would accede to the throne on Henry's death, rather than Henry's own son, Edward of Westminster, due to Richard's strong claims based on primogeniture (as a great grandson of King Edward III through his father, and a great-great grandson of the same king through his mother).[34]

Although King Henry was in Yorkist hands, Queen Margaret fled first to Wales and then to Scotland, in search of support to continue the fight, in defiance of the *Act of Accord*. There was no point in appealing to the Irish, as the Irish Parliament, supporting the House of York, passed a *Declaration of Independence*, strongly leaning towards Duke Richard.[35]

---

[33] Griffiths, R (2012) 'Richard, Duke of York and the Crisis of Henry VI's Household', *Journal of Medieval History* 38 (2), 3–19; Hicks, B (1999) 'From Megaphone to Microscope: The Correspondence of Richard Duke of York with Henry VI', *Journal of Medieval History* 25 (3), 243–56.

[34] See the 1460 'Recognition of the Duke of York as Heir to the Throne', as in Adams, G (ed) (1947) *Select Documents of English Constitutional History* (London, Macmillan) 198–200. Also, Curtis, E (1932) 'Richard, Duke of York, as Viceroy of Ireland', *The Journal of the Royal Society of Antiquaries of Ireland* 2 (2), 158–186.

[35] The 1460 'Declaration of Independence of the Irish Parliament', as in Curtis, E (ed) (1943) *Irish Historical Documents 1172–1922* (London, Methuen) 72–73.

Scotland made a different choice, as the Scottish King James had dynastic linkages by both blood and marriage that made Henry VI's faction (the House of Lancaster) his logical ally. This was especially so since, in the months before his capture, Henry had tried to make a permanent peace with James, offering him Northumberland, Cumberland and Durham in return for aid to fight Richard. James joined the conflict with an army of Scots and anti-Yorkist Englishman, invading northern England. James was so much at the forefront of these efforts that when a cannon misfired at the siege of Roxburgh Castle, he was accidentally killed. Despite this disaster for the Scots, the Lancastrian forces advanced, gathering resources and men. The next decisive battle was at Wakefield in December 1460, when perhaps 18,000 men loyal to the king overcame the forces of the Duke of York. The youngest son of Duke Richard was killed along with his father, whose body was then quartered, so that his head, wearing a paper crown, could be displayed on the walls of York.[36]

B. Edward IV

The year 1460 ended well for the Lancastrians. After the deaths of Richard, Duke of York, and his youngest son at the Battle of Wakefield, Queen Margaret followed up her success by routing the Earl of Warwick at St Albans in February 1461 and advancing upon London. Thereafter, the tide turned in favour of the House of York. Although the Lancastrian forces, led by the Queen, Margaret of Anjou, recorded a victory at the second Battle of St Albans, freeing Henry VI in the process, they could not gain momentum, nor could they secure London. Although Richard, Duke of York, was dead, he left behind two sons, both destined to be future kings of England—namely, Edward IV and Richard III. Edward was the first to take up the gauntlet, continuing his father's claim to the throne of England. Edward achieved victory at Mortimer's Cross at the beginning of 1461 and at Towton in March 1461, when opposing armies of perhaps of 30,000 men clashed. The *Chronicle* of the period recorded:

> [The Lancastrian] ranks being now broken and scattered in flight [the Yorkist] army eagerly pursued them, and cutting down the fugitives with their swords, just like so many sheep for the slaughter, made immense havoc among them for a distance of ten miles, as far as the city of York ... [T]he blood of the slain, mingling with the snow which at this time covered the whole surface of the earth, afterwards ran down in the furrows and ditches along with the melted snow, in a most shocking manner, for a distance of two or three miles.[37]

To conclude the victory, execution of the leaders occurred on the battlefield, and confiscation of property and estates followed for many of the losers. The Lancastrians'

---

[36] Wolffe, B (2001) *Henry VI* (London, Yale University Press) 15, 239–43, 275–86, 293; Neillands, R (2006) *The Wars of the Roses* (London, Phoenix) 12–15, 20, 32–35, 49–53, 89–93, 100, 143–45, 167; Venning, T (2013) *The Kings and Queens of Scotland* (Stroud, Amberley Publishing) 159–63.

[37] The Crowland Chronicle, as noted in Cohen, M (ed) (2004) *History in Quotations* (London, Cassell) 311. Also Ransome, C (1889) 'The Battle of Towton', *The English Historical Review* 4 (15), 460–66.

lack of success, coupled with the fact that Henry had now joined his wife in opposing the *Act of Accord* to which he had previously agreed, led many to believe, both in the wider community and in Parliament, that the Lancastrians lacked legitimacy to sit on the throne of England.[38] Parliament now took the view that Edward was now the legitimate king, and recognised his hereditary right to the throne, while the Lancastrian Henry was declared a usurper.[39]

Following the Lancastrian defeat at Towton and Edward of York's recognition as king by the English Parliament, Henry VI spent four years in exile in Scotland and lived as a fugitive in northern England, supported by Lancastrian allies in Northumberland and Yorkshire, whilst Margaret of Anjou fled to France, hoping that her cousin, the new French king, Louis XI, who had acceded to the throne in 1461, would support her. However, Louis had other ideas. Louis was relatively progressive for a French king, taking advice from the Three Estates on broad constitutional questions, such as whether the Duchy of Normandy should be separated from France, and allowing them to nominate members to the King's Council. This progressive approach was also reflected in Louis' willingness to support the new English king, Edward IV, not Henry VI and his wife, Margaret of Anjou. In 1463 Louis and Edward agreed that they would not assist each other's enemies (and especially not Margaret).[40]

With France out of the picture, Edward turned on those who had supported Henry VI, with executions, despite earlier pardons, following. Henry himself was captured in 1465 and imprisoned in the Tower of London. Edward's early intention was to destroy Scotland by dividing it up and changing its leadership, in revenge for Scottish support of Henry VI, although he later changed his mind, agreeing instead to a 15-year peace in the *Treaty of York*, in exchange for the Scots' not supporting or giving shelter to further dissidents (Lancastrians). For their part, the English promised not to assist dissidents against the Stuart regency in Scotland. This peace allowed the young Scottish king, James III, to mature, and Scotland to diplomatically settle outstanding issues with Denmark and Norway, whereby The Orkneys and the Shetland Islands were handed over to Scottish rule, thus setting Scotland's final boundaries, as they would largely exist thereafter.[41]

The peace that Edward IV and Louis XI had earlier secured unravelled towards the end of the decade, when Edward, who feared that Louis was plotting against him, decided to allow his sister Margaret to marry Charles the Bold, the Duke of Burgundy,

---

[38] Kleineke, H (2014) 'Robert Bale's Chronicle and the Second Battle of St Albans', *Historical Research* 87 (238), 740–50.

[39] See the 1462 'Act Declaring Valid Acts of Lancastrian Kings', as in Adams, G (ed) (1947) *Select Documents of English Constitutional History* (London, Macmillan) 202–03; Richmond, C (1999) 'The Nobility and the Wars of the Roses: The Parliamentary Session of January 1461', *Parliamentary History* 18 (3), 261–69.

[40] Jacob, E (1987) *The Fifteenth Century* (Oxford, Clarendon) 510–15, 534, 569. Also Fawtier, R (1974) *The Capetian Kings of France* (Macmillan, London) 13, 53–55.

[41] See Grohse, I (2014) 'Medieval Maritime Diplomacy: The Case of Norwegian–Scottish Relations', *The International Journal of Maritime History* 26 (3), 512–28. See also the 1461 'Treaty of Westminster-Ardtornish', in Dickinson, W (ed) (1958) *A Sourcebook of Scottish History*, Vol II (London, Nelson) 53–55; and the 'Acquisition of Orkney and Shetland', ibid, at 55–57.

who was Louis' enemy.[42] Louis responded to the marriage, and thus Edward's support of Charles the Bold, by becoming an active supporter of the ousted King Henry VI. This yielded quick results, Edward IV being deposed in a coup and fleeing London, after hearing that between 2,000 and 3,000 men on loan from the King of France were marching on him. Henry VI was then restored to the throne after being freed from the Tower of London in late 1470. Henry rewarded Louis for his assistance, quickly declaring war on Charles the Bold in support of the King of France. Charles the Bold, in return, championed the exiled Edward IV. With support from both inside and outside of England, and at a time when revolts were breaking out independently over the failure of good government to protect both citizens and property, in 1471, Edward returned to reclaim the throne of England. Edward's Yorkist army met the Lancastrians, led by Margaret of Anjou, at Tewkesbury. In the following battle, 2,000 Lancastrians were killed, including Edward of Westminster, the son of Henry VI. Margaret was captured and held prisoner. Henry VI was recaptured, but this time, within one month of incarceration in the Tower of London, he was dead, thus ending the Lancastrian line of kings.[43]

Edward's first action against Louis for supporting Henry VI was to deepen his alliance with Charles the Bold, as a result of which the latter said that he would recognise Edward as the King of France. However, Edward changed his mind, and rather than getting dragged further into the alliances that were building in Europe between Burgundy and France, he opted to remain neutral, agreeing to the 1475 *Treaty of Picquigny*. This created a seven-year truce between England and France, under which Edward was to leave France peacefully after receiving 75,000 crowns from Louis. Neither king was to form an alliance without the knowledge of the other. Margaret of Anjou was ransomed by the French king, Louis XI's son (Charles) was to marry Edward's daughter (Elizabeth of York) and both monarchs were to cooperate in crushing rebellions. Remaining differences, such as whether Edward really did have a valid claim to be the King of France, were to go to arbitration. As it turned out, the arbiters never met and no decision on the matter was ever handed down.[44]

Edward IV's principal supporter, other than his brother, Richard, Duke of Gloucester, was Richard Neville, Earl of Warwick ('Warwick the Kingmaker'), head of the most powerful family in England in the 1460s. By 1464, however, friction was simmering between the King and Warwick, for two reasons. First, in that year, Warwick was sent to France to look for a wife for the King. His diplomatic skills resulted in a promised marriage for Edward with a member of the French royal family, but when he returned to England, Warwick found that on 1 May, Edward had secretly married Elizabeth Woodville, the widow of a Lancastrian knight killed at the second Battle of St Albans

[42] See pages 25–26.

[43] Leigh, A (2003) 'Royalty, Virtue and Adversity: The Cult of King Henry VI', *Albion* 35 (2), 187–209; Lee, P (1986) 'Reflections of Power: Margaret of Anjou and the Dark Side of Queenship', *Renaissance Quarterly* 39 (2), 183–217; Richmond, C (1970) 'Fauconberg's Kentish Rising of May 1471', *The English Historical Review* 85 (337), 673–92; Grant, R (2011) *1001 Battles* (London, Penguin) 232.

[44] Hicks, M (2009) 'Edward IV Treatise and the Treaty of Picquigny of 1475', *Historical Research* 83 (200), 252–65.

in 1461 and a commoner. Secondly, Edward was showering his new wife's ambitious family with honours and arranging advantageous marriages for them. If the Wood-villes' new-found prominence at court and their grasping behaviour were not reason enough to engage the enmity of Warwick and other nobles, and that of Edward's own family, he compounded the error by allowing them to dominate his council and influence the young Prince of Wales (later Edward V). In 1469, open conflict erupted between the king and Warwick, when Warwick and the king's brother, the Duke of Clarence, who had secretly married Warwick's daughter, Isabel, declared that Edward was no longer fit to rule. For more than a year, battles raged between the two sides, first one side prevailing, then the other. Early in 1470, Warwick realised that he could not be victorious without further help, and he fled to France, to plot with Margaret of Anjou to return the Lancastrian King Henry VI to the English throne. Henry's brief restoration collapsed in 1471 when the Lancastrian forces were comprehensively defeated, and Warwick killed, at the Battle of Barnet. Edward IV returned to the English throne. However, he handled the power vacuum left by the deaths of Warwick and other nobles by granting their titles and lands to the Woodvilles and their allies—a decision that would have far-reaching consequences.

C. Richard III

Edward IV died in 1483. His son, Edward, was residing at Ludlow on the Welsh border at the time, and his mother's family rushed to his side, prior to escorting him to London. His father's brother, Richard, Duke of Gloucester, whom Edward IV had named Protector of England during his son's minority, intercepted them at Stony Stratford and took the young king into his care, before proceeding to London to arrange the coronation.

According to the Tudor chroniclers who came to record the history of Richard III (and justify Henry Tudor's later seizing of the throne), Richard was a tyrant who achieved power by usurping the throne meant for his nephew.[45] He allegedly achieved this, once he had the young king in his hands, by persuading Edward V's mother to give up her other son—the young Duke of York—from the sanctuary of Westminster Abbey, where she and her children had been living since shortly after Edward IV's death, into his custody as Protector. The two young brothers were then taken to the Tower of London—the royal residence where Kings of England would lodge prior to their coronations. What happened to them thereafter is not known, although it is said that they were not seen in public after Easter 1484; what is certain is that their

---

[45] Davies, C (2012) 'Information, Disinformation and Political Knowledge Under Henry VII and Henry VIII', *Historical Research* 85 (228), 228–54; Slotkin, J (2007) 'Sinister Aesthetics in Shakespeare's Richard III', *Journal for Early Modern Cultural Studies* 7 (1), 5–32; Markham, C (1891) 'Richard III: A Doubtful Verdict', *The English Historical Review* 6 (22), 250–83; Gairdner, J (1891) 'Did Henry VII Murder the Princes?', *The English Historical Review* 6 (23), 444–64.

Woodville uncles and other supporters were executed for treason against the Protector shortly after the Duke of Gloucester took the young king into his care in 1483.

Throughout May 1483, preparations for Edward V's coronation seemingly went ahead. In June, however, a rumour started, apparently substantiated by Robert Stillington, Bishop of Bath and Wells, that Edward IV's sons were bastards because his marriage to Elizabeth Woodville was invalid in canon law, Edward IV having been precontracted to marry the Lady Eleanor Butler. Parliament agreed that Edward's IV's marriage was not a true marriage and that Richard, Duke of Gloucester, was the lawful heir, his place on the throne being 'just and lawful, as grounded upon the laws of God and nature, and also upon the ancient laws and laudable customs of this said realm'.[46] Richard accepted the crown, promising to uphold the traditional laws and customs of old, and to protect the rights of the Church.[47]

D. Henry VII

Despite support from the Church and Parliament, Richard III's enemies were quick to seize on his acts as those of a tyrant, which gave them their cause for war. Richard faced rebellions almost as soon as his short reign began. The Woodvilles and former servants of Edward IV rose up first, before the unrest spread into a general revolt against the rule of Richard III and the House of York. Henry Tudor, son of Edmund Tudor, Earl of Richmond (and the grandson of Owain Tudor, a young Welshman of no particular prospects, who won the heart of the widow of Henry V, Catherine of Valois, and secretly married her in 1430), half-brother of King Henry VI, and the Lady Margaret Beaufort, daughter of the Duke of Somerset, took part in the uprising. However, Henry Tudor was not at the forefront of the rebellion against Richard III. That honour went to the Duke of Buckingham, who was captured and beheaded for treason in October 1483. Henry fled to the safety of the court of the French king, Charles VIII.[48]

Charles VIII's advisers relished the opportunity provided to them when Henry Tudor arrived in France. When he returned to England two years later on 7 August 1485, it was with the support of some 3,000 to 4,000 troops supplied by King Charles. The forces of Henry Tudor and other exiles (some 5,000 men) met those of King Richard (around 8,000 men) in battle on Bosworth Field near Leicester on 22 August 1485. In the ensuing melee, Richard was unseated from his horse and hacked to death by

---

[46] The 1484, 'Confirmation of Richard's Title' in Adams, G (ed) (1947) *Select Documents of English Constitutional History* (London, Macmillan) 207–10.

[47] Wolffe, B (2001) *Henry VI* (London, Yale University Press) 215, 219–29; Allmand, C (1997) *Henry V* (London, Yale University Press) 374–84; Jacob, E (1987) *The Fifteenth Century* (Oxford, Clarendon) 18–22, 28–29, 53, 87, 406–07, 542, 620–21, 632; Mackie, J (1985) *The Early Tudors* (Oxford, Clarendon) 12–13, 51–54.

[48] Meyer, G (2011) *The Tudors* (NYC, Bantam) 20–21, 34–38.

Tudor supporters, the last English king to die in battle. The final toll is estimated at 1,000 dead on the field. It is said that Richard's crown was found under a hawthorn bush and placed upon the head of Henry Tudor. With this coronet and the acclamation of his soldiers, Henry was pronounced king. Despite the obvious fact that he had usurped the throne, it was seen as justified given Richard III's purported acts as a tyrant. This justification was believed to be stronger than Henry's right to rule based upon either conquest or any form of diluted hereditary right.[49]

Henry subsequently had his title to the throne confirmed by Pope Innocent VIII, whilst the English Parliament, displaying its malleability in the face of a ruler who quickly began stripping nobles who were not to his liking of power, added:

> [B]e it ordained, established and enacted by authority of the present parliament, that the inheritance of the crowns of the realms of England and France ... be, rest, and remain and abide in the most royal person of our new Sovereign Lord King Henry VII.[50]

Despite this proclamation, rebellions continued against Henry Tudor. Before these could extend to the north of the country, Henry (whose mother, Margaret Beaufort, was related to Joan Beaufort, wife of King James I of Scotland) agreed a three-year truce, in 1486, under which Henry would help King James III to deal with internal discontent in Scotland. This suited James on two fronts, as his relationship with both King Edward IV and Richard, Duke of Gloucester, had been poor, after the two brothers had crossed the border and advanced on Edinburgh when the 15-year peace with Scotland under the *Treaty of York*[51] came to an end. Although Edward and Richard returned to England, they decided to keep the border town of Berwick upon Tweed, after its castle finally surrendered in 1482. Nevertheless, although the Scots were now out of the picture because of Henry's agreement with James, a surprising number of Anglo-Irish nobles had declared themselves for Richard III, and these made up a significant number of the some 20,000 soldiers (of whom 12,000 fought for the Tudors) at the Battle of Stoke Field in 1487, the final battle in the Wars of the Roses.[52]

Following his victories in England, Henry VII decided to pardon the surviving rebels who still lingered on after the death of Richard III. He incorporated many of them into his own military forces, and rewarded local magnates with land taken from those who had died, after they took the oath of allegiance to him. Although the role of Parliament was weak and dissent was limited, Henry brought improvements to the land, via the centralisation of law enforcement and finance, and the creation of a new legal body, the Star Chamber, with a greater degree of flexibility to deal with difficult cases than the law courts could traditionally offer. He then set about controlling the reins

---

[49] Thornton, T (2005) 'Henry Tudor's Understanding of the Meaning of Bosworth Field', *Historical Research* 78 (201), 436–22; Ross, C (2005) *Richard III* (New Haven, CT, Yale University Press) 200–10.

[50] The 1485 'Recognition of the Title of Henry VII', as reproduced in Adams, M (ed) (1947) *Select Documents on English Constitutional Law* (London, Macmillan) 213.

[51] See page 20.

[52] Lenman, B (2001) *England's Colonial Wars, 1550–1688* (London, Longman) 26–27; Mackie, J (1985) *The Early Tudors* (Oxford, Clarendon) 130–35; Ross, C (2005) *Richard III* (New Haven, CT, Yale University Press) 44–47; Jacob, E (1987) *The Fifteenth Century* (Oxford, Clarendon) 531, 539, 542, 642–47.

of power in Ireland, by ensuring that no parliament could meet in that land unless it was given leave by the English king, and it was also made clear that any laws made in England were equally applicable in Ireland. Although Henry's rule was challenged by further uprisings in England between 1485 and 1489, these were based more on political anger over tax and authority than on dynastic issues. Nonetheless, dynastic challenges against Henry VII did continue, the last occurring at the end of the century, when the last Yorkist pretender (Perkin Warbeck, who claimed to be Richard, Duke of York, the younger of the two princes who had disappeared in the Tower of London) was killed with 8,000 of his men.[53]

4. THE WARS FOR THE EXPANSION OF FRANCE

A. Charles the Bold

Although the Hundred Years' War had, in theory, ended in the middle of the fifteenth century, for the next five decades, the histories of France, Burgundy, Brittany and England continued to be closely intertwined regarding questions of conflict and war. Nonetheless, despite the renewed interventions of the English in the Continent at the end of the century, they could not stop the clear trend that saw France expanding in terms of both territory and the absolute power of the king.

The expansion of France was facilitated by the agreements of the Kings of England and France not to meddle in each other's affairs, despite their overlapping dynastic concerns. In reality, neither could resist the opportunity to cause trouble for the other. Thus, whilst Edward IV originally agreed to keep the peace with Louis XI and not interfere in France, he took a different view with regard to Brittany and Burgundy, as the proposed marriage of his sister to Charles the Bold reflected, after he feared the Louis was plotting against him. Charles the Bold was the son of Philip the Good, the man whose support had allowed Henry V, temporarily, to become King of France.[54] Charles, like his father, also saw the benefit of alliances with the English. This was especially so since the autonomy of Burgundy, as promised by the French Crown, had not eventuated. Accordingly, Charles adopted the goal of a fully independent kingdom of Burgundy, of which he would be ruler, for which he was willing to explore alliances with whomever he needed.[55]

[53] Tucker, P (2009) 'Henry VII's Contribution to the Emergence of Constitutional Monarchy in England', *Historical Research* 82 (217) 511–25; Cavill, P (2006) 'Debate and Dissent in Henry VII's Parliaments', *Parliamentary History* 25 (2), 160–75; Bennet, M (1990) 'Henry VII and the Northern Rising of 1489', *The English Historical Review* 105 (414), 34–59; Lehmberg, S (1961) 'Star Chamber: 1485–1509', *Huntington Library Quarterly* 24 (3) 189–214.

[54] See page 13.

[55] Boehm, L (1979) 'Burgundy and the Reign of Charles the Bold', *The International History Review* 1 (2),153–62.

Charles had already opposed Louis XI with the *League of the Public Weal* in 1465, in which over 30,000 men, divided between his leadership and a collection of feudal nobles, fought the French king while pursuing the goals of restoring good kingship, respecting ancient rights, bringing an end to over-taxation, and protecting both the Church and the poor. It was, in essence, a constitutional struggle, 'to be able to show the king by force the corruption of his administration of the commonwealth'.[56] Neither side was wholly victorious, meaning that the war came to an end with a mosaic of peace treaties—Saint-Maur (with a collection of individual princes), Conflans (with Burgundy) and Caen (with Brittany). Each was concluded individually with the French Crown, with promises, in the words of the *Conflans Treaty*, of 'good peace, love and tranquillity'.[57] The treaties included concessions by the French Crown involving the movement of titles, estates and territories between the opposing sides. A committee of 36 was also established to reform the abuses of government. A reciprocal part of the deal was that the key areas, notably Burgundy and Brittany, were not to engage in dynastic relations that could destabilise the area. However, as Louis failed to deliver on his commitments, Charles the Bold did just what he was meant not to do, marrying Margaret of York in 1468, the sister of the English king, Edward IV (and the future Richard III), despite the disapproval of the French king, Louis XI, who could see a regional alliance developing before him. Charles then proceeded to purchase Upper Alsace from Sigismund the Archduke of Austria in 1469, whilst simultaneously putting down all dissent in the Low Countries.[58]

By 1473, Charles was in direct negotiations with the Habsburg Emperor, Frederick III, about the possibility of Burgundy becoming an independent kingdom. The French king, Louis XI, formally declared war on Charles, on the grounds that he was perpetuating violence with the realm. He then declared that Charles's French lands and titles were forfeit. Charles responded by forbidding his subjects in Burgundy to appeal to the *Parlement* in Paris, as he no longer considered himself the vassal of the French Crown. He also continued his negotiations with Frederick, although these were a failure and Charles was offered less than full independence.[59]

B. Switzerland and the Alliance with Louis XI

It was in the fifteenth century that a new and fully independent power, Switzerland, emerged in Europe. War between the Swiss and Emperor Frederick III broke out

---

[56] As per Philippe de Commines, in Bakos, A (1990) 'The Historical Reputation of Louis XI in Political Theory', *The Sixteenth Century Journal* 21 (1), 3–32.

[57] The Treaty of Conflans, as in Gilmore, M (1952) *The World of Humanism* (NYC, Harper) 78. Also Tanner, J (ed) (1958) *The Cambridge Medieval History: Decline of Empire and Papacy*, Vol VII (Cambridge, Cambridge University Press) 385–86, 692; Knecht, R (2007) *The Valois* (London, Hambledon) 17, 29, 79, 89–91, 99, 110–12; Hay, D (1996) *Europe in the Fourteenth and Fifteenth Centuries* (London, Longman) 110–12.

[58] Clarke, P (2005) 'English Royal Marriages and the Papal Penitentiary in the Fifteenth Century', *The English Historical Review* 120 (488) 1014–26.

[59] Baumgartner, F (2007) 'Declaring War in Sixteenth Century France', *Journal of the Historical Society* 7 (1), 85–110.

in 1461, ending when the Habsburgs relinquished many of their remaining holdings in Switzerland. This was furthered in 1474 with the *Treaty of Perpetual Accord*, in which Austria agreed to respect the Swiss territories, the Swiss promised not to support dissent within Austria, and arbitration would be their preferred method to solve disputes between them. Any suggestion that they were still part of the Holy Roman Empire with some residual obligations came to a dramatic end in 1499, when Maximilian I, the next Holy Roman Emperor, attempted to force the Swiss to provide money or men for his military campaigns. The Swiss used these attempts to control what they saw as their sovereign rights as their final excuse to quit the Empire, after Austrian and German troops were sent to try to force them to accept Maximilian's demands. The Swiss not only rejected them, but also attracted other rebel provinces, like Basel, to their cause. After a further military defeat of Maximilian, at a total cost of 20,000 dead and the destruction of 200 castles and villages, was the conclusion of peace by the 1499 *Treaty of Basel*. Apart from the recognition that Basel was now part of the Swiss confederation, there were no significant territorial changes. There were, however, significant changes in political relationships, as in essence, peace was only achieved when Maximilian renounced all the rights of suzerainty that the Emperor had over the Swiss. Henceforth, the Swiss were fully independent of all imperial power, although in reality this had been the case for decades, with Swiss military forces offering their skills for sale to foreign rulers in both France and Italy.[60]

Evidence of the earlier independence of the Swiss and their military alliances was clear from their relationship with the French king, Louis XI, who had carefully prepared for the war with Charles the Bold by making an agreement, 'that in every war of ours [the Swiss], especially against the Duke of Burgundy, ... shall afford us help, support and protection'.[61] The Swiss forces, following a series of local disturbances that were the justification for war, then swept into Picardy, Burgundy and Luxembourg, and Charles suffered defeats at Grandson and Murten, although he did strike back and conquer Lorraine. The Emperor Frederick III then joined the fight against Charles the Bold, whom he accused of 'never being content with your own territories. You lead armies, ravage the lands of others, and either massacre of subjugate free peoples ... [O]ur intention is of wiping you out with might and main, both in Upper Germany and in the coastal areas of the Channel'.[62] However, Frederick could not crush Charles, whose forces advanced deep into the heart of the Rhineland, besieging the town of Neuss, north-west of Cologne. At this point, Frederick and Charles both sued for peace, and in a treaty in 1475 it was agreed that Mary, Duke Charles's daughter, would marry Frederick's son, Maximilian (which occurred in 1477). This was a very significant event, as not only did it breach the spirit of the 1435 *Treaty of Arras*, it meant, in essence,

---

[60] Tanner, J (ed) (1958) *The Cambridge Medieval History: Decline of Empire and Papacy*, Vol II (Cambridge, Cambridge University Press) 202–04, 260–61, 298–314.

[61] 'The 1474 Treaty between Louis XI and the Swiss' and 'Letter of Louis XI on the Recovery of Normandy', as in Laffan, R (ed) (1929) *Select Historical Documents: 800–1492* (NY, Holt) 175, 176–78.

[62] 'The Manifesto of Frederick III, 1474', in Cohen, M (ed) (2004) *History in Quotations* (London, Cassell) 307,

that the Burgundian possession would pass into the Habsburg Empire. The French king, Louis XI, responded quickly by making peace with the English under the 1475 *Treaty of Picquigny*,[63] which left Louis and his Swiss allies free to deal with Charles of Burgundy. Louis then struck, his forces overrunning the southern part of Burgundy, to the Somme, most of Artois and all of the Boulonnais. At the first major battle, of Morat in 1476, Charles lost 7,000 men, as did the similarly sized enemy. However, whereas the opposition could replenish its forces with troops and arms quite easily, Charles could not, and at the following Battle of Nancy in 1477, a much smaller Burgundian army of 8,000 was cut in half by a much larger French/Swiss force of 20,000 men.[64]

C. Mary of Burgundy

Charles the Bold, Duke of Burgundy, died on the battlefield in 1477, leaving an empire that was greatly desired by others. Charles's only offspring, his daughter Mary, acted quickly, as French jurists argued that she could not legitimately hold such lands of her father, as they belonged to the French Crown, and that she, as a woman, in accordance with Salic law, had no standing to hold such assets (or rule). Mary acted contrary to the jurists' rulings. First, she agreed to celebrate the marriage her father had planned for her to the Archduke Maximilian, son of the Emperor, Frederick III. Secondly, Mary ensured the loyalty of the citizens of the Low Countries through promulgating the *Great Privilege* of 1477. The *Great Privilege* was the *Magna Carta* of the Netherlands. In this foundational document, Mary confirmed a number of liberties and privileges to towns and provinces in the Low Countries, including the right to assemble when they desired and manage their own grand court, which would allow considerable degrees of self-governing independence. She also promised an end to arbitrary and corrupt rule, and sought to guarantee certain civic rights. The sovereign could not marry, declare war or raise taxes without their consent. Importantly, it was agreed that disobedience was permissible if the Crown refused to uphold these liberties.[65]

D. The Archduke Maximilian

The Archduke Maximilian, who married Mary of Burgundy eight months after her father had been killed on the battlefield, was the son of Frederick III and his wife, Eleanor of Portugal. This marriage, in accordance with an earlier agreement between

---

    [63] See page 21.
    [64] Knecht, R (2007) *The Valois* (London, Hambledon) 101, 110–18; Jacob, E (1987) *The Fifteenth Century* (Oxford, Clarendon) 575–79; Grant, R (2011) *1001 Battles* (London, Penguin) 233.
    [65] Saenger, P (1977) 'Burgundy and the Inalienability of Appangages in the Reign of Louis XI', *Society for French Studies* 10 (1), 1–26; MacKinnon, J (1906) *A History of Modern Liberty*, Vol I (London, Longmans) 235–39.

Mary's father, Charles, and Maximilian's father, Frederick, linked the Burgundian inheritance to the Habsburg star, and secured a pathway for the formation for one of the most powerful dynasties in European history. The French king, Louis XI, recognised the threat and sought to seize control of Burgundy. Maximilian managed to repel Louis' attacks, culminating at the Battle of Guinegate in 1479, where 27,000 men under the direction of Maximilian defeated Louis XI and his Flemish allies (numbering only 11,000 men). Despite this victory, following the accidental death of his wife Mary in 1482, Maximilian, as regent for their son Philip, made a deal with the French when Ypres, Ghent and Bruges began to contest his rule after the French king offered them improved conditions whilst encouraging their rebellion against their Habsburg master. Unprepared to get sucked into a war over such areas and to settle the conflict with France, Maximilian agreed to the new *Treaty of Arras* in 1482, whereby he ceded large areas, including most of Burgundy and the County of Artois, to France. Maximilian also agreed that Philip would do homage for Flanders to the French king. This agreement reversed the 1435 *Treaty of Arras*, which in theory had given Burgundy great degrees of independence. Brabant, Holland and other parts of the Burgundian state were left to the German princes, and Lorraine and Alsace went to Austria. Peace was secured via an agreement that Margaret of Austria, the daughter of Maximilian and Mary, would marry Louis XI's son, the future Charles VIII.[66]

E. Charles VIII

Charles, the son of Louis XI, inherited the French throne as King Charles VIII in 1483 as a sickly 13-year-old boy. His regents distanced the monarchy from any of the progressive traits of his father in terms of governance in France, shaking off all forms of supervision and/or support from the Estates General, who were no longer summoned. Henceforth, there were only occasional regional assemblies with poorly defined powers, within a France that was divided into four alienated parts. Not content with the subdued nature of the four parts, as recently supplemented by his father with large parts of Burgundy, Charles decided he wanted to make France even bigger, and set his eyes upon the Duchy of Brittany, which had been largely autonomous from Paris for the previous 500 years.[67]

The trigger for the war that followed was that the previously loyal Duke of Brittany stopped paying homage and sought full independence from France. Henry VII of England had been trying to persuade Brittany to follow this route since the mid-1480s.

---

[66] 'The Treaty of Arras, 1482', as in Laffan, R (ed) (1929) *Select Historical Documents: 800–1492* (NY, Holt) 177–80; Curtis, B (2013) *The Habsburgs* (London, Bloomsbury) 34–46; Haemers, J (2009) 'Factionalism and State Power in the Flemish Revolt', *Journal of Social History* 42 (4), 1009–30; Holmes, G (2000) *Europe: Hierarchy and Revolt* (London, Blackwell) 222; Stubbs, P (1908) *Germany in the Later Middle Ages* (London Longmans) 206–07.

[67] Hay, D (1967) *The New Cambridge Modern History: The Renaissance*, Vol I (Cambridge, Cambridge University Press) 224, 236–38, 298–99.

Charles responded by making deals with barons exiled from Brittany under the 1487 *Treaty of Chateaubriant*, under which the barons agreed that the French king could invade and take control of Brittany, on the promise that Duke Francis II would not come to personal harm. The French forces then swarmed over the border the following year, destroying an opposing Breton-led army of 10,000 men, taking Orleans and then, at the Battle of Saint-Aubin-du-Cormier, destroying another Breton force, of whom at least 5,000 were killed. The result was fatal for Francis II. Before he died a few months later, he was forced to conclude the 1488 *Treaty of Sable*, under which he acknowledged himself to be a vassal of the King of France. He ceded various territories, promised to remove all foreign troops from his lands and lost the right to summon further troops from abroad. Finally, Francis promised that his daughter and heir, Anne, would not marry without the consent of the French Crown.[68]

F. Anne of Brittany

Upon her father's death, Anne (aged 12) did not follow the obligation to obtain French consent to her marriage, marrying (by proxy) Maximilian I, whose first wife, Mary of Burgundy, had died in an accident in 1482. The French saw this not only as a breach of the *Treaty of Sable*, but also as a direct threat to France, as it risked introducing foreign rulers into the region. France immediately prepared to invade Brittany. Anne sought to deflect this threat and secure Breton independence from France with military aid from Castile, as well as from England under the 1489 *Treaty of Redon* with Henry VII. With this treaty, Anne accepted the protection of English troops, maintained at Breton expense, in exchange for Henry's having the power of veto over any dynastic or political alliances she might make, and to surrender strategic towns to the English as security for payment of the English troops.

Henry buttressed the *Treaty of Redon* with the *Treaty of Medina del Campo*, which linked Spain and England into a common policy against France. As a measure of its importance, a marriage alliance was agreed between the elder son of Henry VII (Prince Arthur) and Princess Catherine, the daughter of Isabella of Castile and Ferdinand of Aragon. Henry then published a proclamation pertaining to the formation of a confederation between England, Spain and the Empire, for mutual security against France, and for the independence of Brittany.[69]

King Henry VII of England justified going to war against France in support of Brittany 'to defend another man's rights' and also 'to recover our own'.[70] The reality was not that Henry believed he could recover the lost rights and legacy of the Plantagenets, but more that an expanded France and the loss of an independent Brittany would be

---

[68] Mallett, M (2012) *The Italian Wars: 1494–1559* (Harlow, Pearson) 7–8.
[69] Currin, J (1991) 'Henry VII of England and the Breton Plot of 1492: A Case Study in Diplomatic Pathology', *Albion* 23 (1), 1–22; Meyer, G (2011) *The Tudors* (NYC, Bantam) 45.
[70] Francis Bacon, as recorded in Mackie, J (1985) *The Early Tudors* (Oxford, Clarendon) 106.

detrimental to the national interests of Tudor England. However, Henry's hopes of forming an alliance with Castile and the Holy Roman Empire to defend Brittany from the French came to nothing, despite sending some 4,000 English soldiers to help defend Brittany and promising 6,000 more. Archduke Maximilian was distracted fighting in Hungary, whilst Castile failed to help at all. In such an atmosphere, the Bretons lost the will to keep fighting, as Charles's armies slowly overran the region, with Rennes being the last stronghold to fall, after a siege of two months.[71]

After being defeated militarily, Anne of Brittany agreed to marry Charles VIII and thus become Queen of France. Just to ensure that there was no lingering questions about the marriage's validity, in 1492 Pope Innocent VIII annulled Anne's marriage to Maximilian and approved of her marriage to Charles. With this, the idea of a Brittany independent from France disappeared from history. The English accepted this situation in the *Treaty of Étaples* of 1492. Under this treaty, Henry VII did not have to renounce Plantagenet claims. He also received 1 million gold crowns. Due to a carefully worded treaty, Henry could read this payment as tribute, whereas Charles could read it as payment for all English debts in the region. Both sides promised that they would not support insurrection against the other. The Holy Roman Empire accepted the overall situation with the 1493 *Treaty of Senlis*. These two treaties ended the conflict between France and the 17 provinces in Burgundy, whereby the disputed territories were divided, with Artois and Flanders being annexed to the Holy Roman Empire, whilst France retained legal claims to both provinces, and the Duchy of Burgundy remaining in French hands. Brittany was also now part of the kingdom of France. Similarly, peace was made with the Crown of Aragon in the 1493 *Treaty of Barcelona*, under which the French returned all the disputed territory of Navarre, which they had occupied a few decades earlier as collateral for a loan that was not repaid. In return, the Crown of Aragon promised to remain neutral in the event of any future French invasions of Italy. Thus, aside from the remaining English stronghold of Calais, all the territory from the base of the Pyrenees to the Atlantic seaboard now belonged to the French, and they had now made peace with all of their traditional enemies.[72]

5. THE ITALIAN WARS

A. The Paradigm

The Italian wars raged through Europe for 65 years (from 1494–1559), burning for most of the first half of the sixteenth century. This was a conflict in which the powers

---

[71] Currin, J (2000) 'Henry VII and the Breton Wars, 1489–1491', *War in History* 7 (4), 379–412; Currin, J (1998) 'Persuasions to Peace: Anglo-French Relations, 1489–1490', *The English Historical Review* 113 (453), 882–904.

[72] Meyer, G (2013) *The Borgias* (NYC, Bantam) 192; Mallett, M (2012) *The Italian Wars: 1494–1559* (Harlow, Pearson) 8–11; Knecht, R (2007) *The Valois* (London, Hambledon) 119–21; Fernandez-Armesto, F (2011) *1492: The Year Our World Began* (London, Bloomsbury) 136–39; Hay, D (1967) *The New Cambridge Modern History: The Renaissance*, Vol I (Cambridge, Cambridge University Press) 77, 250–55, 302.

of Spain and France would battle for and against the papacy to control the independent parts of Italy, of which Naples, Milan, Venice and Florence were at the forefront. The wars consumed tens, if not hundreds, of thousands of lives, and resulted in Italy remaining divided for more than three centuries.

These wars unfolded as the two greatest scholars of the early decades of the sixteenth century, namely Niccolo Machiavelli (1469–1527) and Desiderius Erasmus (1466–1536), came of age, who in a way expressed two diametrically opposing views of what world order could look like. On the one hand, Erasmus called upon all Christian princes to stop fighting for reasons of 'ambition, anger and the desire for plunder'.[73] He urged them to settle matters of dispute by arbitration, and to avoid enforcing their theoretical rights 'to the great detriment of the whole world', encouraging them to pursue the kind of glory that was bloodless and involved no harm, to avoid marriage alliances and to prevent the 'riches of all the people being concentrated in a few hands'.[74]

Machiavelli, on the other hand, did not engage in debates about arbitration or universal peace within Christendom. He accepted what the world was, rather than what it should be. For Machiavelli, there was nothing more important for a leader than to concentrate on war.[75] Although Machiavelli emphasised the importance of virtue, good faith and diplomacy, there was no substitute for arms and money when it came to the security of the state, for which *raison d'état* would become the guiding principle and traditional patterns of integrity could be departed from, if necessary. Within his political thinking, although Machiavelli pointed towards democracy and republics, he was highly sceptical of their effectiveness in an age of corruption, and of their tendency to succumb to anarchy. Accordingly, he was willing to accept dictatorships to ensure the survival and prosperity of republics, and for political leaders to be willing 'to enter into evil, when necessity commands'.[76]

[73] 'The Complaint of Peace' in Dolan, J (ed) *The Essential Erasmus* (NYC, Omega) 188–91,196–97; Idris, M (2014) 'Erasmus on Peace, Speech and Necessity', *Theory and Event* 17 (4), 1–30; Dallmayr, F (2006) 'Erasmus on War and Peace', *Asian Journal of Social Science* 34 (1), 232–48; Herwaarden, J (2012) 'Erasmus and the Non-Christian World', *Erasmus of Rotterdam Society Yearbook* 32, 69–83.

[74] Erasmus, *The Education of a Christian Prince* trans Jardine, L (1997) (Cambridge, Cambridge University Press) 102–07; 'The Complaint of Peace' in Dolan, J (ed) *The Essential Erasmus* (NYC, Omega) 177; Murad, I (2014) 'Erasmus on Peace, Speech and Necessity', *Theory and Event* 17 (4), 1–25; Nathan, R (2014) 'The Peace of Erasmus', *The European Legacy* 19 (1), 24–72.

[75] Machiavelli, *The Prince* trans, Donno, D (1992) (NYC, Quality Paperbacks) 50, also at 20–30 and 87; Yves, W (2014) 'The Prince and His Art of War: Machiavelli's Military Populism', *Social Research* 81 (1), 165–91; Lynch, C (2012) 'War and Foreign Affairs in Machiavelli', *The Review of Politics* 74, 1–26.

[76] Machiavelli, *The Prince* trans Donno, D (1992) (NYC, Quality Paperbacks) 70; Evirgenis, I (2011) 'Wrestling with Machiavelli', *History of European Ideas* 37 (2), 85–93; Berridge, G (2001) 'Machiavelli: Human Nature, Good Faith and Diplomacy', *Review of International Studies* 27 (4), 539–56; Russell, G (2005) 'Machiavelli's Science of Statecraft: The Diplomacy and Politics of Disorder', *Diplomacy and Statecraft* 16, 227–50; Geuna, A (2015) 'Machiavelli and the Problem of Dictatorship', *Ratio Juris* 28 (2), 226–41; Jurdjevic, M (2007) 'Machiavelli's Hybrid Republicanism', *The English Historical Review* 122 (499), 1228–57; Skinner, Q (1980) *The Foundations of Modern Political Thought*, Vol I (Cambridge, Cambridge University Press) 47, 158, 171, 181.

B. The Context

The actual fuse leading to the Italian wars, as operating purely within the paradigm that Machiavelli advocated, was connected to the ownership of Naples. The Kingdom of Naples was held at different times by the French House of Anjou and the Spanish House of Aragon, with the latest holder being Ferrante of Naples, the illegitimate son of Alfonso V of Aragon. Alfonso V, who had earlier arrived in Naples in response to Joanna of Anjou's pleas to help her stay in power, had claimed the throne of Naples on the death of Joanna in 1435, as she had no children and left behind only chaos. The papacy, trying to turn back the clock and re-establish its authority over all of its traditional areas, also claimed Naples as a papal fief, especially since Joanna had repeatedly refused its demands that she contribute to the rebuilding of the papal army of Rome. When Alfonso V expressed his desire to sit on the throne of Naples, for which goal he promised to provide men and materials to the papal army and fight the enemies of Rome as directed, the papacy gave its approval. However, it took seven years of conflict for him to secure his title and establish his authority against disgruntled nobles in the area. When Alfonso then failed to respond to papal demands for a Crusade against the Ottomans, Pope Callixtus III warned him 'Your majesty should know that a Pope can depose kings', to which Alfonso replied, 'Your Holiness should know that, should we wish, we shall find a way to depose a Pope'.[77] Although neither deposed the other, the papacy did refuse to recognise Ferrante (Alfonso's son) as being entitled to inherit the throne of Naples. When Alfonso died, Calixtus issued a papal bull declaring that on Alfonso's death, Naples reverted back to the papacy, as Naples had been granted to him only for his lifetime.[78]

Other than Naples and Rome, three other independent areas of Italy had an interest in the political context and balance of which Naples formed a part. These were the city states of Venice and Florence, and the Duchy of Milan. Venice had become an imperial power following the Fourth Crusade, the capture of Constantinople and division of the Byzantine Empire.[79] By the thirteenth century, Venice was the most prosperous city in all of Europe. Although the Venetian hold on Constantinople lasted only for a few decades, its acquisitions in the Mediterranean resulted in ongoing commitments in terms not only of holding these, but also of keeping them out of the grip of the Ottoman Empire. The city was governed broadly on a system that was similar to the republic of ancient Rome, by the Great Council, which was made up of hereditary members of noble families. This Council elected a Senate of a few hundred individuals, a Council of Ten, who was responsible for much of the administration of the city, and a Doge, or Duke, who was the chief executive of the Council. The city was fiercely independent, continually seeking to preserve and extend its privileges wherever

[77] Calixtus and Alfonso, as noted in Meyer, G (2013) *The Borgias* (NYC, Bantam) 45; see also ibid, 12, 22–23, 37, 77.
[78] Clough, C (1992) 'The Kings of Naples: A Study in Fifteenth Century Survival', *Renaissance Studies* 6 (2), 113–72.
[79] Gillespie, A (2017) *The Causes of War*, Vol 2: *1000 CE to 1400 CE* (Oxford, Hart Publishing) 90–92.

it could.[80] Florence, which Leonardo Bruni in 1440 saw as a land of 'equal liberty [that] exists for all—the hope of gaining high office and to rise is the same for all',[81] was at that time governed by Cosimo de' Medici who was, according to Pope Pius II, 'king in everything but name'.[82] This man and his family, as well as encouraging vibrant civic humanism and renaissance creativity, established a type of power that brought both social and financial stability, as well as clear identity, to the community.[83]

In northern Italy, Francesco Sforza had slowly taken over Milan, after being employed by the Duke of Milan to defend it. After gaining military control, Sforza married the daughter of the Duke in 1441, and then assumed full power upon the latter's death. The problem for Sforza was that large parts of the population of Milan, and most of the other regions in Italy, disliked him and his pathway to power. Venice and Naples then attacked Milan, whilst Florence, with strong links to the Medici, came to Milan's aid. Sforza could not be toppled, and to make matters even more complicated, in 1452 Sforza agreed a treaty with France, under which King Charles VII promised to recognise Sforza as Duke of Milan and defend the duchy. In exchange, the French king was assured that if he decided to move against Naples, there would be no interference from Milan.[84]

The four regions were all jostling one another when Constantinople fell in 1453. This event, emphasised by the papacy in Rome, made them wake up to the fact that they had to work together if they too were not to be overrun by the Ottomans. Accordingly, following the *Treaty of Lodi* between Venice and Milan ending the war surrounding the succession to the Milanese duchy in favour of Francesco Sforza the five states that dominated the Italian peninsula—Venice, Milan, Naples, Florence and the Papal States—agreed a supplementary mutual defensive pact, the *Italian League*. This was built around maintaining the existing boundaries and a common and shared defensive arrangement. Although this treaty of 1454 did not prevent all war in the region, it gave expression to the conviction that the common interests of all of the primary city states required peace, cooperation and unity within Italy, if the larger threats that hung over the whole country were to be kept at bay. To help maintain this cohesion, it was promised that the status quo of existing territories would stand, and all forces would join together to punish any state that broke the peace. This agreement broadly held together for the following quarter of a century, until Pope Sixtus IV, in the 1470s, decided to unravel the peace in Italy.[85]

[80] Bouwsma, W (1984) *Venice and the Defence of Republican Liberty* (London, California University Press) 14–22; Hay, D (1996) *Europe in the Fourteenth and Fifteenth Centuries* (London, Longman) 178–80.

[81] Bruni, as reproduced in Cohen, M (ed) (2004) *History in Quotations* (London, Cassell) 272.

[82] Pius II, as in Hibbert, C (1980) *The House of Medici* (NYC, Morrow) 63; Bouwsma, W (1984) *Venice and the Defence of Republican Liberty* (London, California University Press) 47.

[83] Vivienne, K (2005) 'Illegitimate and Legitimating Passions in Fifteenth Century Florentine Political Discourses', *Current and Social History* 2 (1), 49–52; Jurdjevic, M (1999) 'Civic Humanism and the Rise of the Medici', *Renaissance Quarterly* 52 (4), 994–1020; Padgett, J (1993) 'The Rise of the Medici, 1400–1434', *American Journal of Sociology* 98 (6), 1259–99.

[84] Hibbert, C (1980) *The House of Medici* (NYC, Morrow) 78–85.

[85] Ilardi, V (1959) 'The Italian League, Francesco Sforza and Charles VII', *Studies in the Renaissance* 6, 129–66; Lesaffer, R (2002) 'Amicitia in Renaissance Peace and Alliance Treaties, 1450–1530', *Journal of the History of International Law* 4 (1), 77–99; Gilmore, M (1952) *The World of Humanism* (NYC, Harper) 141–43.

Pope Sixtus IV came to power in 1471, succeeding Pope Paul II, who had developed forthright ideas about absolute papal monarchy. Paul II disliked Ferrante of Naples and his continual insubordination, for which reason he would openly encourage the House of Anjou to pursue its claim to Naples. Sixtus IV followed the same pattern. During the 13 years of his rule until his death in 1484, he sought to advance the primacy of the papacy in every area, from the glorification of Rome through to the reaquisition of or increased influence in Church territories throughout Italy. This quest led Sixtus to clash head-on with a number of the leading figures of the day, most spectacularly with Lorenzo de' Medici (the grandson of Cosimo) of Florence. Both Florence and the papacy laid claim to a series of towns, and a dispute over ecclesiastical appointments in Florence led to an attempt by the papacy to usurp power within Florence. Although Pope Sixtus did not explicitly authorise the assassination of Lorenzo in an attempted coup in 1471, he assured the plotters of 'every assistance by way of men-at arms or otherwise as might be necessary'.[86]

The assassination attempt failed. The conspirators were caught, tortured and confessed. This resulted in large-scale public reactions against the papacy and its supporters in Florence. These reprisals led to the Pope's ordering the arrest of all of the Medici bankers in Rome, and then demanding that Lorenzo should be handed over to papal justice. The bull of excommunication against 'that son of iniquity and foster-child of perdition' pronounced Lorenzo de' Medici and his accomplices 'culpable, sacrilegious, excommunicate, anathematised, infamous, unworthy of trust and incapable of making a will'.[87] If these men were not forced out of Florence within two months, the entire city was to be placed under interdict. When the authorities of Florence did not do as Sixtus demanded, the Pope declared war against them, and had no difficulty in persuading the King of Naples to follow suit. The King, Ferrante I, was happy to oblige, as Pope Sixtus had decided to recognise his value, despite his predecessor's refusing to do so, preferring Ferrante as a better option in Naples than any direct French or Spanish candidate, even though Ferrante had grown into one of the most ruthless and cruel men in Italy. The Signoria (Council) of Florence replied:

> You say that Lorenzo is a tyrant and command us to expel him. But most Florentines call him their defender … [T]he Keys of St Peter were not given to you to abuse in such a way … Florence will resolutely defend her liberties, trusting in Christ who knows the justice of her cause; trusting in her allies who regard her cause as their own; especially trusting the most Christian king Louis of France.[88]

After a year of small-scale battles, Lorenzo personally went to Naples to make peace with Ferrante, following which a treaty was agreed. Florence agreed to pay some of

---

[86] Sixtus, as noted in Hibbert, C (1980) *The House of Medici* (NYC, Morrow) 133, also at 78–85; Dover, P (2008) 'Pope Paul II and the Ambassadorial Community in Rome', *Renaissance and Reformation* 31 (3), 3–34; Blondin, J (2005) 'Power Made Visible: Sixtus IV', *The Catholic Historical Review* 91 (1), 1–25.

[87] The Interdict of Sixtus IV, as in Chambers, D (ed) (2001) *Venice: A Documentary History, 1450–1630* (London, University of Toronto Press) 219.

[88] The Reply of the Signoria, as in Hibbert, C (1980) *The House of Medici* (NYC, Morrow) 148–49, 154, 160.

the costs of the war, release prisoners and give up a series of territories in southern Tuscany. In reply, Naples relinquished all of the Florentine territory it had acquired. Lorenzo also persuaded the Pope that, with all of Christendom in peril from the Ottoman threat, this was no time for the Italian states to be quarrelling amongst themselves. Florence apologised to Rome, Rome lifted its interdict on Florence and in 1480 the *Treaty of Lodi* was renewed for another 25 years.[89]

C. The French Invasion of Italy

Although Sixtus had made peace with Florence, he continued to cause difficulties elsewhere, before turning his anger back on the kingdom that had made peace with Florence (Naples) and thus sidestepped him. Sixtus took three considerations into account: first, he believed that Naples was a papal fief, free to dispose of as he saw fit; secondly, he wanted the support of the French Crown for other matters, such as a crusade; and lastly, the French king arguably had legitimate dynastic interests in Naples, to which he had a theoretical claim.[90] Sixtus wrote to the French king in 1482, suggesting, 'now is the acceptable time … This realm belongs by hereditary right to his royal Majesty … The pope's will is that his Majesty or the lord dauphin be invested with this kingdom'.[91] To the delight of Louis, the next Pope, Innocent VIII, followed the same path as Sixtus, with the addition that he actually attempted to depose Ferrante, the King of Naples, for failing to recognise the historic rights of the papacy to jurisdiction in his kingdom and inciting rebellions in other papal states.

The following Pope, Alexander VI (Rodrigo Borgia), who came to power in 1492, had a different view on France. Although he wanted to expand papal power, he preferred the friendship of Spain to that of France. Alexander did not want the King of France, now Charles VIII, to have Naples, to which Charles believed he was entitled. In response, Charles started to offer sanctuary to those fleeing the power of Pope Alexander, who argued that Rodrigo Borgia was not a legitimate pontiff due to his overt corruption. When the old King of Naples, Ferrante, died early in 1494, matters came to a head, as Pope Alexander wanted Ferrante's much more compliant son, Alfonso II, to retain power in Naples and the French king to concentrate on attacking the Ottomans. Charles VIII had other ideas and decided to press his claim. He made it clear to the summoned representatives of his kingdom's Three Estates that he intended to

---

[89] Holmes, G (1997) *Art and Politics in Renaissance Italy* (London, British Academy) 147–51; Hay, D (1967) *The New Cambridge Modern History: The Renaissance*, Vol I (Cambridge, Cambridge University Press) 343–50.

[90] In theory, the inheritance of Joanna II of Anjou had mistakenly been given to Alfonso V of Aragon. The original title was bequeathed by Joanna to Charles III, the last Angevin Count of Provence, who in turn bequeathed all his land and titles, including the kingdom of Naples, to the King of France, Louis XI.

[91] Sixtus, as noted in Fernandez-Armesto, F (2011) *1492: The Year Our World Began* (London, Bloomsbury) 137; Bonney, R (2012) *The European Dynastic States* (Oxford, Oxford University Press) 80; Hay, D (1996) *Europe in the Fourteenth and Fifteenth Centuries* (London, Longman) 187.

depose the Pope, and he threatened Pope Alexander with a General Council for this purpose. When the more experienced of Charles's counsellors threw up their hands at the impracticality of trying, in essence, to conquer Italy and topple the Pope, he ignored them.[92]

King Charles VIII of France crossed the border into Italy with 40,000 men in the middle of 1494, beneath white silk banners embroidered with the arms of France and the words *Voluntas Dei* (God's Will). The will of the independent regions of Italy to oppose Charles, despite much rhetoric, came to very little, allowing Charles to progress easily down the peninsular. Pope Alexander recognised that Charles was not going to change his mind, and rather than try to fight him, surrendered Rome into the hands of the king, saying mass before 20,000 soldiers of the French army. Charles abandoned all thought of deposing Alexander, and Pope Alexander VI publicly endorsed the power of Charles VIII.

For Florence, long under the sway of the Medici, this was a chance to reinvigorate its republic and get rid of its de facto monarchy. This was achieved in 1494, after the Medici successor (Piero) was chased from the city, when the Florentines agreed to seek peace with the French who were now outside the city walls. When the Medici and the old oligarchy fled, the city reorganised itself, with its new French protectors, on republican grounds. Part of a new process of selecting the members for the Signoria was imposed by the new French overlords and a payment of 120,000 florins was made to the French king.

In addition, the radical preacher Savonarola, who was an arch critic of Pope Alexander VI and his nepotism and corruption, declared that Charles VIII was sent by God to cleanse wicked Italy.[93] With such views, Savonarola found himself in a position of authority in Florence. The problem was that he was not a democrat. He had no faith in popular government, and accordingly implemented a strict theocratic regime, under which everything from carnivals to the vanities of fashion were either banned or burned. In addition, although Charles had reconciled with Pope Alexander, Savonarola had not, and progressed to denying the authority of the Church in Rome and Alexander's right to wear the papal crown.[94]

The following year, 1495, Charles entered Naples. Alfonso II abdicated and fled to a monastery, where he died later that year. However, the departure of Alfonso II did not ensure peace in Naples. The Neapolitans discovered that one foreign oppressor was very much like any other, and the other Italian powers feared what an entrenched French invader could do. Later that year, the *Holy League of Venice* was formed by Pope Alexander VI. The ostensible purpose of the League was the defence of Christianity against the Turks, but its real target was the French. Those allied in the League included the Papal States, Venice, Naples, Milan and Florence, as well the Emperor

---

[92] Meyer, G (2013) *The Borgias* (NYC, Bantam) 172–77, 191, 208–09.

[93] Savonarola, 'The Sermon on the Revocation of the Church' in Elmer, P (ed) (2000) *The Renaissance in Europe: An Anthology* (London, Yale University Press) 286.

[94] Knecht, R (2007) *The Valois* (London, Hambledon) 123; Hibbert, C (1980) *The House of Medici* (NYC, Morrow) 183–85, 190–91, 193–200.

of the Holy Roman Empire, Maximilian I. The Emperor decided that it time for him get involved in Italian matters, despite his earlier *Treaty of Senlis* with France, as he had married Bianca Sforza, the niece of Ludovico Sforza, in 1494 and was thus now thinking of his own claim to Milan. The Spanish, who had stayed quiet as the French king progressed through Italy, enjoying the rewards of the *Treaty of Barcelona*,[95] also joined the *Holy League*, fearing that Charles might overrun all of the Papal States; they demanded the return of some territories to the Pope. When Charles replied that he had no intention of complying with the Spanish request, the *Treaty of Barcelona* was declared null and void. Even the English, who had made peace with the French in the *Treaty of Étaples*, decided to join the *Holy League of Venice* to help defeat an expansionist France, due to their fear of what they called the French king's 'unbridled rage for domination'.[96]

It was at Fornovo, en route to Milan in northern Italy, in mid-1495 that the first significant efforts to defeat the French in Italy occurred. Nineteen miles south-west of Parma, 10,000 French soldiers came up against a force of triple that number, mainly made up of men from Milan and Venice. The battle left 3,500 men dead on the field. Although the French had nominally won the day, with 3,000 of the dead being soldiers from the *Holy League*, they realised that they could not easily replenish their lost men or materials. Accordingly, they concluded the *Peace of Vercelli*, which allowed the remaining French forces to exit Italy peacefully. Once the French forces had left Naples, the question of ownership of this kingdom again came to the fore, at the very point that Spanish troops were being moved in substantial numbers to the Neapolitan mainland. Pope Alexander then sent a note to the Spanish commander, requesting him to come and take command of the military situation, following which Ferdinand II of Naples (the son of Alfonso II) returned to take the throne.[97]

The reclamation of territory that followed throughout most of Italy happened quickly, as the areas that had been deferential to the French were quick to eject their French-imposed overlords. For example, when the French, who had a nominal control over Florence, left Italy, the Pope demanded that Savonarola come to Rome to explain himself, which he refused to do. He was then excommunicated for having 'disseminated pernicious doctrines to the scandal and great grief of simple souls'.[98] All Christians were then forbidden to associate with him. Savonarola replied that the Church had become a satanic institution. The problem for Savonarola was that his apocalyptic teachings and strictly theocratic rules were wearing thin in Florence. Accordingly, when the Papal authorities came in 1498 to arrest him, torture him and then execute him for heresy, there were very few objections.[99]

---

[95] See page 31.
[96] This quote is from the English Chancellor, John Morton, as in Currin, J (2009) 'Henry VII, France and the Holy League of Venice: The Diplomacy of Balance', *Historical Research* 82 (217), 526–46.
[97] Mallett, M (2012) *The Italian Wars: 1494–1559* (Harlow, Pearson) 27–28; Mackie, J (1985) *The Early Tudors* (Oxford, Clarendon) 86–88, 102–10, 114–16.
[98] The Excommunication of Savonarola, as noted in Meyer, G (2013) *The Borgias* (NYC, Bantam) 274.
[99] MacKinnon, J (1906) *A History of Modern Liberty*, Vol I (London, Longmans) 77–80, 249, 427.

D. Isabella and Ferdinand of Spain

As the French and Italians were considering their next moves, a new superpower—
Spain—was emerging. For 400 years, three principal areas, Portugal, Castile and
Aragon, had experienced internal civil wars based on dynastic claims and/or political competition from the nobility within the *Cortes*. The principal example of this was
Aragon. At one point in the fifteenth century, the throne of Aragon was the goal of
six competing claimants. From these squabbles emerged King John II of Aragon and
Navarre, who came to power in 1458 and ruled until 1479. He succeeded his older
brother, Alfonso V, holding all of the Aragonese possessions, including original territory in Spain, as well as other acquisitions in southern Italy, including Sicily, Sardinia
and, arguably, Naples. To hold on to power he had to battle his own son, Charles, who
sought an independent kingdom, and the French, who fought to take Navarre from
him as collateral for an unpaid loan.[100]

The new monarchy, and a truly unified Spain as we know it today, came into being
with the union of Ferdinand of Aragon and Isabella of Castile. Ferdinand was the son
of John II of Aragon and his second wife, Juana Enriquez. Isabella was the daughter
of John II of Castile and his wife, Isabella of Portugal. Ferdinand married Isabella in
1469. Although the ideal was to create two linked but separate realms, with Ferdinand
promising to 'preserve and maintain the ruling councils of these kingdoms [Castile
and Aragon]',[101] the reality was that, for the first time since the eighth century, a single
political unit referred to as *Espana* (Spain) emerged. Royal officials, designed to ensure
the will of the monarchy and to centralise and control corruption, were appointed in
every city in Spain. Ferdinand and Isabella summoned the *Cortes* only rarely, its advice
being reserved to minor decisions, and the *Cortes* was virtually neutralised as an independent estate.[102]

The security of their territories was bolstered by their victories in the Castilian War
of Succession, in which the daughter of the late King Henry IV of Castile, Joanna,
who was married to the King of Portugal, Alfonso V, fought Henry's half-sister Isabella
for control over Castile, with a view to merging it with Portugal. The victory of Isabella
and Ferdinand at Toro in 1476 secured them Castile, but their losses in naval battles
with Portugal in 1478 meant that they had to settle for peace with the 1479 *Treaty of
Alcacovas/Toledo*. This treaty involved the return to established borders, and mutual
renunciation of dynastic claims to either Portugal or Castile.[103]

---

[100] MacKay, A (1977) *Spain in the Middle Ages* (London, Macmillan) 110, 137.

[101] Ferdinand's Marriage Concessions, in Cowans, J (ed) (2003) *Early Modern Spain: A Documentary History*
(Philadelphia, PA, Penn State University Press, 2003) 8–9.

[102] Elliot, J (2002) *Imperial Spain* (London, Penguin) 40–42, 82; Maltby, W (2002) *The Reign of Charles
V* (London, Palgrave) 14–15; Marvin, L (1982) 'Governing the Cities of Isabella the Catholic', *Journal of
Urban History* 9 (1), 31–55.

[103] Ferdinand's Marriage Concessions, as in Cowans, J (ed) (2003) *Early Modern Spain: A Documentary
History* (Philadelphia, PA, Penn State University Press, 2003) 8–9; Gilmore, M (1952) *The World of Humanism*
(NYC, Harper) 88–102; Hay, D (1967) *The New Cambridge Modern History: The Renaissance*, Vol I (Cambridge,
Cambridge University Press) 324–27, 331–32, 337–40.

When Isabella and Ferdinand were secure in their new and authoritarian Spain, they set about maintaining Catholic orthodoxy in their territories. This process began when Pope Sixtus IV agreed to their request for an Inquisition in 1478. Although the Inquisitions sanctioned by Rome at this time were primarily aimed at witchcraft, in Spain an Inquisition was requested by Isabella and Ferdinand to 'uproot from our kingdoms and domains all abomination, apostasy, and heresy'.[104] The Inquisition in Spain was then extended to Portugal, and over the next 350 years operated through all of their respective colonies in India, the Philippines and parts of Africa, as well as later in North, Central and South America, involving around 300,000 trials in Spain alone. From these, about 12,000 citizens would be condemned to death during the course of the Spanish Inquisition's history. The corresponding figure for Portugal is about 3,000. The numbers of those brought to trial in the colonies was also significant. There were over 16,000 trials in Goa, following which 114 people were burned at the stake.[105]

In Spain, the Inquisition was used not so much against witches and heretics, as against Jews and Muslims. The first people to be condemned under this Inquisition were six men and women in 1481 in Seville, all prominent *conversos*—people who had converted from Judaism to Christianity but who were suspected of reverting to their former faith. The Jews had been under pressure to convert to Christianity in the Christian areas of Spain since the turn of the fifteenth century. Individual cities were prohibiting Jews from living within their walls by the 1480s. Despite the execution of thousands of 'relapsed' souls in the 1480s, Isabella and Ferdinand decided that something further needed to be done at the national (not just the local or regional) level because it was believed that that heresy in Christian circles was being strongly supplemented by Jewish support. The 1492 *Edict of Expulsion* explained:

> [G]reat damage has been done and is being done to Christians by the contact, conversation and communication they have had and have with Jews ... [T]hey always seek by all possible means to subvert faithful Christians and taken them away from our Holy Catholic faith, separating them from it and luring them and perverting them with their flawed beliefs and opinions ... [W]e know that the true remedy for all of this damage and disturbance lies in completely prohibiting communication between Jews and Christians and expelling them from all of our kingdoms ... [W]e order all of the Jews of our kingdoms to leave them, never to return to them.[106]

By the end of 1492, perhaps 150,000 people of the Jewish faith who preferred not to convert to Christianity were forced to leave their property, homes and lands within which their families had existed for centuries. Coexistence with different faiths was no

---

[104] Ferdinand, 'Letter on the Inquisition', as reproduced in Cowans, J (ed) (2003) *Early Modern Spain: A Documentary History* (Philadelphia, PA, Penn State University Press) 10–11.

[105] Murphy, C (2011) *God's Jury: The Inquisition and the Making of the Modern World* (London, Penguin) 65–66, 68, 80, 102, 166; Green, T (2007) *Inquisition: The Reign of Fear* (London, Macmillan) 8–9, 11–12, 24, 32, 36–37, 46, 53, 76–77, 145, 153; Maltby, W (2002) *The Reign of Charles V* (London, Palgrave) 14; Elliot, J (2002) *Imperial Spain* (London, Penguin) 102; MacKay, A (1977) *Spain in the Middle Ages* (London, Macmillan) 195–96.

[106] The Edict of Expulsion, as reproduced in Cowans, J (ed) (2003) *Early Modern Spain: A Documentary History* (Philadelphia, PA, Penn State University Press, 2003) 21–23.

longer deemed possible. Synagogues were converted into churches, almshouses and other public institutions, and cemeteries were commonly turned over to grazing. Jewish communal property was assigned to be held in escrow for settlement of debts to the Crown, whilst all debts owed to expelled Jews were cancelled. Portugal followed suit in 1497, as did Navarre in 1498.[107]

E. Louis XII

Louis XII ascended the French throne in 1498, after the death of Charles VIII. Undeterred by the experience of his cousin Charles in Italy, Louis sought to reinstate the French claims to both Naples and Milan. He realised that before he could do this, he needed to tie up some loose ends. First, to enhance his domestic support, he presented himself as being much more open to consulting the Three Estates of his kingdom than his predecessor had been (especially on questions such as taxes and war). Secondly, Louis had his marriage annulled, and instead married Anne of Brittany[108] in 1499, the widow of his cousin Charles VIII. This was important, as Anne and Charles had no surviving children and therefore Brittany would revert to being an independent state with Anne as its sovereign. Thirdly, in the same year as his accession, he secured new peace treaties with Spain and with the Emperor Maximilian and his son Philip the Handsome, with the latter agreeing not to claim Burgundy (or other contested areas) and to do homage for the county of Flanders, in return for three cities in Artois. Peace with Maximilian and his son Philip was particularly important, as Philip was married to Joanna, the daughter of the emerging superpower of Spain. This cleared the way for Louis to claim Milan without interference from Spain, as prior to the peace treaty the claim of Louis XII to Milan, which came from the Angevin title he inherited from his grandmother, was contested by King Ferdinand of Spain. Lastly, the French king reversed the previous antagonism to Rome and commenced a positive relationship with Pope Alexander VI. This was easy to achieve, as Alexander saw an opportunity to further his own goals in Italy with the help of Louis XII and his large French armies. As part of this reconciliation, Alexander agreed to Louis' request that he nullify the earlier marriage of Charles VIII and Anne of Brittany on the ground that they were both too young at the time, so that he (Louis) could marry Anne and ensure that Brittany stayed within the realm of France.[109]

With such matters settled, in 1499 Louis led a second French army of 30,000 men into Italy. He quickly acquired Milan, after agreeing in advance with Venice that it

[107] Peters, E (1995) 'Jewish History and Gentile Memory: The Expulsion of 1492', *Jewish History* 9 (1), 9–34; Marx, A (1908) 'The Expulsion of the Jews from Spain', *The Jewish Quarterly Review* 20 (2), 240–71.
[108] See pages 30–31.
[109] Monaco, M (1988) 'The Instructions of Alexander VI to his Ambassadors Sent to Louis XII in 1498', *Renaissance Studies* 2 (2), 251–57; Carlyle, AJ (1910) *A History of Medieval Political Theory in the West*, Vol VI (London, Blackwood) 470–72.

would be equitably partitioned between the two of them (Venice being rewarded with Cremona), ousting the Duke of Milan, Ludovico Sforza. Sforza was duly captured by the French in 1500, who imprisoned him for the last eight years of his life. When Ferdinand finally heard of the agreement between Venice and France for the partition of Milan, he recalled his ambassadors.

With regard to Naples, Louis concluded the secret *Treaty of Granada* in 1500 with Spain, to conquer and divide the kingdom, with the northern part of the province going to France, along with the city itself and the actual crown. Ferdinand would receive the territory to the south of the Naples for recognising Louis' title. Pope Alexander VI ratified this pact in 1501, agreeing to crown Louis as King of Naples. The French king, now having all of northern Italy, as well as Milan and northern Naples, firmly in his grasp, held more territory than any French king since 887 CE. None would hold as much again before 1769.[110]

In exchange for this stamp of legitimacy, Pope Alexander VI expected support for his appropriation of all of the former, or lapsed, papal areas in central Italy, to be held by members of the Borgia family, in particular by his illegitimate son, Cesare Borgia. Cesare found that the combination of his military might and his father's papal bulls, alienating those who held the lands he wanted, made success easy. Bologna, in conjunction with a host of other small papal states surrendered to him.[111]

As Pope Alexander came more under the influence of France, the Spanish threatened him with a General Council of the Church, accusing him of simony and nepotism. Alexander replied, declaring that Ferdinand and Isabella were usurpers, with no right to their thrones. Spain's official position, shared by both Portugal and the Habsburg Emperor Maximilian, was that the election of Pope Alexander VI was invalid, and a council must be called to put things right. At the same time, the French were also pulling back from their relationship with Alexander, as they too felt that the Pope's nepotism and wish for territorial expansion in Italy rendered their own recent acquisitions quite vulnerable. As all three sides were cautiously assessing one another, Alexander VI died.[112]

F. Pope Julius II

The new Pope, Julius II, was a man of contradictions. On the one hand, he gave the Vatican its most important Renaissance art and beauty, but on the other hand, his quest to enhance the power and possessions of the papacy was linked to corruption, extortion and illegal acts, as a result of which Erasmus described his tenure as

[110] Mallett, M (2012) *The Italian Wars: 1494–1559* (Harlow, Pearson) 58–59.
[111] Hibbert, C (1980) *The House of Medici* (NYC, Morrow) 201–09; Bouwsma, W (1984) *Venice and the Defence of Republican Liberty* (London, California University Press) 97–100.
[112] Meyer, G (2013) *The Borgias* (NYC, Bantam) 284, 288, 297, 350, 372, 406–07.

'the kingdom and the tyranny'.[113] Foremost amongst the charges against his character was his use of duplicitous diplomacy to achieve his goal of forcing the French out of Italy.

As it was, the relations between France and the other superpower with an interest in Italy—Spain—were tense at the turn of the century. Antagonism was rife between them both over the ownership of certain provinces, for which the *Treaty of Granada* of 1500, covering the division of Naples had not made provision. War broke out, with battles at Cerignola in April 1503, when a Spanish force of 10,000 defeated a French force of 30,000, killing 5,000 French, and then at Garigliano in December of that year, when a Spanish force of 12,000 overcame a much greater French force—with the loss of 8,000 French soldiers—and captured Naples. Fearing that he could lose even more, the French king, Louis XII, agreed to the *Treaty of Blois* with the Emperor Maximilian in 1504, in which he gave up his claim to Naples in exchange for 900,000 florins and retention of several Italian interests. This treaty recognised Naples as a Spanish possession. A marriage alliance was set to seal the deal (but never eventuated).[114]

As the dust was settling from the conflict between Spain and France, Pope Julius II decided to direct an aggressive campaign to consolidate the areas he believed belonged to the papacy. In 1506, in a campaign led by the Pope himself in full armour, he wrested Perugia and Bologna from their petty tyrants and restored their obedience to the Church. His next targets were Rimini, Faenza and Ravenna, which had fallen into the hands of Venice. Venice was an opponent he could not defeat alone, for which reason he created the *League of Cambrai* in 1508. Ostensibly, this was an alliance designed to fight the Ottomans, but in reality it was a weapon that could be aimed in any direction. The secret article of the League was that an attack would be aimed at Venice, to strip her of all of her possessions, except the city itself, and divide her empire. England (Henry VII), France (Louis XII), Spain (Ferdinand) and the Holy Roman Empire (Maximilian) all joined the League and waited while Julius continued negotiations with Venice, to see if the city would make enough concessions that war could be avoided.

When the Venetians would not agree to Pope Julius's demands, he placed Venice under interdict and the members of the Venetian senate were excommunicated. The reasons given for the Pope's actions were that the Venetians occupied property that belonged to the papacy; their continual refusal to allow the Church full autonomy in Venetian territories; and Venice's failure to pay associated resources as levied. The following year, an army of 22,000 won a resounding victory at Agnadello, against a similar number of Venetians, of whom at least 4,000 were killed. By the beginning of 1510, unable to find any allies, Venice surrendered. In the peace that followed, the city's excommunication was lifted, but the Venetians lost nearly all the lands that they had acquired throughout the Italian mainland, including the cities of Cremona, Crema and Brescia, as well as all other traditionally papal lands. Pope Julius also regained control of Church appointments and tithes in Venetian territories.[115]

---

[113] Erasmus, as noted in Dust, P (1980) 'Erasmus' Epigram against Julius II', *Moreana* 17, 99–106.

[114] Gilmore, M (1952) *The World of Humanism* (NYC, Harper) 157–59; Grant, R (2011) *1001 Battles* (London, Penguin) 240; Rogerson, B (2010) *The Last Crusaders* (London, Abacus) 143, 198–99.

[115] Shaw, C (1993) *Julius II: Warrior Pope* (Oxford, Oxford University Press) 14–18, 23–38, 42–50; DeSilva, J (2010) 'Official and Unofficial Diplomacy Between Rome and Bologna, 1503–1513', *Journal*

After defeating Venice, Pope Julius turned his attention to France, which now seemed to be the greatest power in Italy. Using dissension simmering between the erstwhile allies under the *League of Cambrai*, the Pope formed the *Holy League* in 1511. This was built around what Julius said was 'God's will' that the French be driven out of Italy. The primary force in the *Holy League* against France was Spain, Pope Julius noting that the cement meant to hold together the *Treaty of Blois*—a marriage arrangement—had failed to be put in place. Julius built on the Spanish discontent in this matter by promising them that he would guarantee to invest title to Naples and the surrounding territories in Spain. He then made a deal with the Swiss, to ensure that their mercenaries would only fight for him and not the French, following which 6,000 men arrived to serve at the pleasure of the Holy See.[116]

Louis XII was dumbstruck. In response, he organised a French council of churchmen to condemn the Pope's actions. This council, called a General Council, met in Pisa in 1511 to discuss the deposition of Pope Julius II. Julius retaliated by condemning the gathering at Pisa as illegitimate, calling it a *conciliabulum*, not a council, and summoned the Fifth Lateran Council as a countermeasure. This Fifth Lateran Council quashed the decisions of the Council of Pisa and excommunicated the (overwhelmingly French) cardinals involved.[117]

G. The Young Henry VIII

Most pleasing of all to Pope Julius II was that the challenge of the French king, Louis XII, to his right to rule the Vatican meant that he now had reason to strip Louis of his throne and give it to someone else. The person Julius had in mind was the English king, Henry VIII. Henry was the son of Henry VII, who succeeded to the throne of England in 1509. Henry had been second in line to the throne, but his older brother, Prince Arthur, had died prematurely in 1502, only six months after marrying Catherine of Aragon when he was 15 years old. Henry's father, Henry VII, did not wish to lose the vast Spanish dowry brought by Catherine to the marriage, nor did he wish to risk

of Early Modern History 14, 535–57; Bouwsma, W (1984) *Venice and the Defence of Republican Liberty* (London, California University Press) 97–100; Sherman, M (1977) 'French Reactions to the League of Cambrai', *The Sixteenth Century Journal* 96–128; Mallett, M (2012) *The Italian Wars: 1494–1559* (Harlow, Pearson) 87–88, 90–91; Finlay, R (2000) 'The War of Cambrai', *Renaissance Quarterly* 53 (4), 988–1031.

[116] Holmes, G (1997), *Art and Politics in Renaissance Italy* (London, British Academy) 8–9, 19–23, 127–29; Skinner, Q (1980) *The Foundations of Modern Political Thought*, Vol I (Cambridge, Cambridge University Press) 114; Tanner, J (ed) (1958) *The Cambridge Medieval History: Decline of Empire and Papacy*, Vol VII (Cambridge, Cambridge University Press) 29–30.

[117] Britnell, J (1993) 'The Antipapalism of Jean Lemaire de Belges', *Sixteenth Century Journal* 24 (4), 783–95; The 1510 'Complaints Against the Pope', as reproduced in Thatcher, O (ed) (1905) *A Sourcebook for Medieval History* (NYC, Scribner) 336–39; Hay, D (1967) *The New Cambridge Modern History: The Renaissance*, Vol I (Cambridge, Cambridge University Press) 82, 207, 302.

the 1489 *Treaty of Medina del Campo* with Spain. He therefore sought the Pope's dispensation for his younger son to marry his brother's widow. Julius II issued the dispensation in 1503.

Upon ascending to the throne of England in 1509, Henry VIII confirmed his support for the Catholic Church and Pope Julius II in particular. He had pledged England to work with Spain against France in the 1511 *Treaty of Westminster*, and also convinced the Emperor Maximilian to join the Holy League in 1511. Accordingly, it was no surprise when, in 1512, Pope Julius II offered to Henry, in draft form, the 'name, glory and authority' of the King of France, 'for as long as [the English king] shall remain in faith, devotion and obedience to the Holy Roman Church and Apostolic See'. Julius promised to come to Paris to crown Henry personally, once Louis XII had been defeated. The French king was then excommunicated by the Pope, and his subjects were absolved of any oaths of allegiance to him.[118]

All of the allied forces then fell upon the French. The Spanish streamed across the border with France and claimed the southern part of Navarre. In Italy, at Ravenna in 1511, although the French army numbering 23,000 defeated the Spanish and papal troops (numbering 16,000, leaving 9,000 dead), the French could not easily replenish their losses (of 4,000 men). As they then tried to consolidate their forces, the Spanish continued to attack, such as within the city of Prato, which was sacked, with great loss of military and civilian life. The following year, in 1513, at Novara in Italy, the French lost another 7,500 men to a Swiss force (which lost only 2,000). Henry VIII then joined the fight, sending a small force of soldiers to the Low Countries to help the Emperor.[119]

As the English attacked France, the French responded by calling upon the Scottish king to honour the *Auld Alliance*. A decade earlier, in 1502, the Scottish king, James IV, had agreed the *Treaty of Perpetual Peace* with England, promising 'a true, sincere, whole and unbroken peace, friendship, league and alliance, not only for the term of the life of each of our said princes ... but from this day forth in all times to come'.[120] Each king then promised not to make war upon the other directly or indirectly, nor to receive rebels against the other. The treaty was cemented with a marriage between the daughter of the English king, Margaret Tudor, to James.[121] When Henry VIII came to power, one of his first acts, in 1509, was to renew the *Perpetual Peace* with Scotland. However, this pact fractured following Henry's invasion of France, when James of Scotland (due to his prior commitments to France) broke the treaty, citing the refusal of Henry to rein

---

[118] Murphy, N (2012) 'Henry VIII's French Crown', *Historical Research* 85 (230), 617–26; Scarisbrick, J (1997) *Henry VIII* (London, Yale University Press) 33–34.

[119] The Letter of the Cardinal to Julius, as reproduced in Hibbert, C (1980) *The House of Medici* (NYC, Morrow) 214.

[120] The 1502, 'Treaty of Perpetual Peace between England and Scotland', in Dickinson, W (ed) (1958) *A Sourcebook of Scottish History*, Vol II (London, Nelson) 59–60.

[121] Dunlop, D (1994) 'The Politics of Peace-Keeping: Anglo Scottish Relations From 1503 to 1511', *Renaissance Studies* 8 (2), 8–24; Ross, C (2005) *Richard III* (New Haven, CT, Yale University Press) 32–34, 62–84, 97–99, 102–04, 186, 215–26; Grant, R (2011) *1001 Battles* (London, Penguin) 234, 245.

in English privateers and put an end to border disturbances (which James may have been equally guilty of supporting).[122]

Despite Pope Julius II's informing King James IV that he would be excommunicated if he invaded England and helped the French in the process, James crossed the River Tweed to do battle with the English with the largest Scottish army—30,000 men—ever to enter into England. Although the conflict began well for the Scots, with James taking four English castles, the overall campaign was a disaster. After three hours of battle on the field of Flodden (in Northumberland) in 1513, the Scottish army was destroyed. The Scots lost 10,000 men, the English only 1,500. James died on the battlefield, along with one of his sons, the Archbishop of St Andrews, two abbots, 12 earls, 14 lords and representatives of most of the important families of Scotland. The power of Scotland was broken. Better still for Henry, Scotland was now left in the hands of James's widow, Henry's sister Margaret, regent for the child king, James V. Henry VIII's wife, Queen Catherine, who was regent in England for six months during Henry's absence in France, sent Henry the Scottish king's blood-stained coat, suggesting that he should use it as his battle banner.[123]

Although the French king took some consolation in the death of Pope Julius II in 1513, the new Pope, Leo X, followed the same policies as his predecessor with the *Treaty of Mechlin*, whereby England, the Holy Roman Empire, Spain and the papacy were regalvanised in their opposition to France. Henry VIII, in particular, pushed over 10,000 troops into France, in a (failed) attempt to take Aquitaine, as well as sending more troops to the Low Countries to help the Emperor Maximilian. The French king, Louis XII, decided that he could no longer sustain his military campaigns in Italy, for which reason he quit the country, taking all of his compliant cardinals along with his retreating forces. He also gave up all claims to Milan, following which Ludovico Sforza's son, Massimiliano Sforza, returned as Duke.

The Pope's Swiss mercenaries settled for a payment of 400,000 ecus. All of the other members of the *Holy League* then made their separate peace with France. Henry and Louis made peace soon after, in 1514, with the English king keeping the town of Tournai and doubling the pension promised to the English Crown under the *Treaty of Étaples*. The peace was cemented with the marriage of Louis XII and Henry's sister, Mary Tudor, in October 1514, though it was short-lived, since Louis died on 1 January 1515. Louis was succeeded by his cousin, Francis I, who was married to Louis' daughter, Claude. Louis' other daughter, the four-year-old Renée of France, was promised in marriage to the future Charles I of Spain (later the Holy Roman Emperor Charles V) under the *Treaty of Paris* of 1515, in an attempt to secure an alliance between France and Spain, though the marriage was never concluded.[124]

[122] Norwich, J (2011) *Absolute Monarchs* (London, Random House) 280–83; Connolly, S (2012) *Contested Island: Ireland 1460–1630* (Oxford, OUP) 4–10, 60–61, 65–72.

[123] Phillips, G (1999) 'Strategy and its Limitations: The Anglo-Scots Wars, 1480–1550', *War in History* 396–416; Mackie, J (1985) *The Early Tudors* (Oxford, Clarendon) 74–77, 145, 158–59, 270–75, 280–85.

[124] Mallett, M (2012) *The Italian Wars: 1494–1559* (Harlow, Pearson) 97, 123; Scarisbrick, J (1997) *Henry VIII.* (London, Yale University Press) 24–29, 33–34, 54–55; Gilmore, M (1952). *The World of Humanism* (NYC, Harper) 77, 88, 158–59; Grant, R (2011) *1001 Battles* (London, Penguin) 243–44, 248.

H. Francis I

King Louis XII of France died in 1515 without a male heir. He was succeeded by his cousin and son-in-law, Francis I. A year earlier, in 1514, to ensure that Brittany stayed within the French realm, Francis had married Claude, the daughter of Louis XII and Anne of Brittany.

King Francis I was a ruler who believed, fundamentally, in the power of his monarchy. His thinking was supplemented by scholars such as Claude de Seyssel, Guillaume Bude and Charles du Moulin, who would all suggest that due to the outstanding nature of the monarchs in France, they were (in theory) absolute in their power, had no equals and were above all forms of control from any of the Three Estates, or as Bude suggested, 'Kings are not subject to the laws and ordinances of their realm ... divine law alone suffices to command them ... [God] conducts their free will, leading them to divine inspiration'.[125] With such endorsement, Francis took the seal of *Parlement* into his own hands, to ensure all of his orders were carried out exactly as he wished. Policy was to be decided by the king alone, with the advice of his council, unless it was specifically delegated to others. Provincial assemblies were not to meet without his approval, were subject to his agenda and had to be presided over by one of his deputies.[126]

Despite these autocratic beginnings, Claude de Seyssel tried to provide the young king with advice on when war could be just. He suggested that 'it is permissible to declare war according to divine and human law'.[127] However, war was not to be fought for the glory of victory and conquest, nor for any other 'disordered passion', but only to recover what had been unlawfully seized, to gain reparations for injuries inflicted on the prince or his subjects, or to aid friends and allies who had been unjustly attacked. Seyssel then cautioned against foreign conquests, writing:

> In the past and recently [ie the French intervention in Italy] such conquests have proven very expensive both in good and honourable men and in money, and although well based have not lasted long; and ... the kingdom has suffered as much or more shame and harm in losing them that it has acquired honour and profit winning them.[128]

Francis I was not impressed by such advice. He was not happy with the loss of all of the French acquisitions in Italy. He was angry to see Milan back under the control of the Sforzas, Genoa as an independent republic and the Kingdom of Naples belonging to Aragon. The duplicity of the papacy irked him even more. This combination of concerns and their contexts gave him the impetus to seek glory for himself and

---

[125] Bude, as in Greengrass, M (2015) *Christendom Destroyed: Europe 1517–1648* (NYC, Penguin) 286–87.

[126] Knecht, R (2003) 'An Update on the Reign of Francis I' *History Compass* 1 (1), 20–28; Carlyle, AJ (1910) *A History of Medieval Political Theory in the West*, Vol VI (London, Blackwood) 470–72; Elton, G (ed) (1968) *The New Cambridge Modern History: The Reformation*, Vol II (Cambridge, Cambridge University Press) 211, 439.

[127] de Seyssel, C, *The Monarch of France* trans Hexter, J (1981) (New Haven, CT, Yale University Press) 130.

[128] de Seyssel, C, *The Monarch of France* trans Hexter, J (1981) (New Haven, CT, Yale University Press) 143.

France by invading Italy in 1515, on the pretext of renewing French claims to Milan. The Swiss, who were now in the pay of the Milanese, stood fast to defend Milan. Despite the fact that some Swiss cantons could be bought off by Francis, five others could not, and troops from the latter were now blocking Francis' advance. At the Battle of Marignano that followed, 40,000 French (4,000 of whom were lost), armed with reliable artillery that could be reloaded and fired quickly, defeated Swiss army, which lost up to three-quarters of its 20,000 men during a battle that lasted 24 hours. The traditional pike-based squares of the Swiss, which had dominated European practice of warfare for two generations, were ripped apart by the French artillery, and the history of the Swiss Confederacy as a military superpower came to an end. Watching this devastation from a distance were the troops of Pope Leo X (Giovanni de' Medici), who despite, in theory, being allies of Milan, stood to one side and did not engage with the French.[129]

Pope Leo subsequently met the victorious French king at Bologna, after which the *Concordat of Bologna* was issued, under which Leo gave up all the rights of investiture of 620 major Church officials in France, in exchange for the papacy's still being able to collect taxes from France, as well as retaining formal powers of confirmation in that country. All of the Swiss cantons then came to terms with Francis I under the *Perpetual Peace of Fribourg*, whereby Francis agreed to pay them 1 million ecus, plus an annual subsidy of 2,000 ecus to each canton. The Swiss then evacuated the Duchy of Milan and promised not to serve anyone against the King of France. The frontiers between Italy and Switzerland were now set, more or less, as they remain today. Swiss forces were never to be used against France; and the king of France was authorised to enlist up to 16,000 Swiss into his armed forces, for defensive purposes. Milan was confirmed as a French dependency in 1516 under the *Treaty of Noyon* with the young King Charles I of Spain, who had only just succeeded to the throne. Charles was content at this point to make peace with France through his recognition of the French title to Milan, in exchange for which France abandoned its claims to the Kingdom of Naples.[130]

Finally, in 1518, Francis I concluded the *Treaty of London*. This was primarily a non-aggression pact between the major Christian powers in response to the rise of Ottomans, with the goal of a new era of peace within Europe. The papal legate in England, Cardinal Wolsey, included supplementary agreements between France and England, involving a marriage treaty between the Dauphin Francois and Henry VIII's daughter, Princess Mary; the return of Tournai and its territories to the French Crown; and an agreement on the part of both countries to suppress piracy.[131]

[129] Mackie, J (1985) *The Early Tudors* (Oxford Clarendon) 275–80, 306–08; Gagne, J (2014) 'Counting the Dead: Traditions of Enumeration and the Italian Wars', *Renaissance Quarterly* 67, 791, 825–27; Chamberlin, E (1979) *The Sack of Rome* (London, Batsford) 35–40.

[130] Skinner, Q (1978) *The Foundations of Modern Political Thought*, Vol II (Cambridge, Cambridge University Press) 54–62; Mallett, M (2012) *The Italian Wars: 1494–1559* (Pearson, Harlow) 129, 131; Hay, D (1967) *The New Cambridge Modern History: The Renaissance*, Vol I (Cambridge, Cambridge University Press) 208.

[131] The Christian League, as reproduced in Reddaway, F (ed) (1930) *Select Documents in European History*, Vol II (London, Methuen) 32; Bamforth, S (1994) 'The Silva of Bernadino Rincio', *Renaissance Studies* 8 (3), 256–69.

I. The Emperor Charles V

The daughter of Ferdinand and Isabella of Spain, Joanna, married Philip the Hand-some in 1496. Philip was the son of the Holy Roman Emperor, Maximilian I. Philip directly inherited the greater part of Burgundy. Joanna was the personification of the union of Castile and Aragon, with dynastic claims to Navarre. After Joanna lost her mental ability to govern, Philip went on to succeed to the Crown of Castile in 1506. With military force, he sequestered the northern part of Navarre in 1515, as a follow through to the successful taking of the southern half three years earlier in 1512, after creating the fiction that they were about to attack him. However, Philip's real success was not his taking of Navarre but the son he produced with Joanna, Charles.[132]

Charles was the fruit of the Habsburg, Valois-Burgundy and Trastamara (Aragon-Castile) dynasties. He was born in Ghent in 1500. In addition to the Netherlands, Charles inherited a united Spain, as well as the Habsburg possessions of Austria, the Tyrol and parts of southern Germany. He was bequeathed Aragon and other Spanish kingdoms in Italy, Sicily, Sardinia and Naples upon the death of his grandfather in 1516. With his marriage to Isabella of Portugal, his cousin and the daughter of the Portuguese king, Manuel I, his reach was unprecedented. In total, he inherited 72 dynastic titles, 27 kingdoms, 13 duchies and 22 countries. He ruled over some 28 million people in lands that stretched from the New World to Spain, northern and central Europe. Charles may have protested to the papacy that he did not wish to be monarch of the world, but his advisers throughout Europe projected the opposite view after he was proclaimed as Holy Roman Emperor Charles V in 1519 by Pope Leo X, after trouncing the other two contenders, namely the Kings of England and France, who could not successfully compete in an election that was blatantly bought. For many, the dream of a universal Christian empire finally seemed possible; as Charles's Grand Chancellor informed him in 1519, 'God has set you on the path towards a world monarchy'.[133]

The French king, Francis I, had no intention of playing second fiddle to Charles, particularly after Charles V was elected Holy Roman Emperor by the German electors. Charles tried to smooth the matter over, agreeing to pay the French king 100,000 ducats each year in recognition of his rights (but not possession) over the Kingdom of Naples. This soothing of the French king's ego was necessary, as Charles began to reconsider the situation concerning Milan, title to which he was increasingly of the view that Francis had usurped. Francis responded by encouraging the Duke of Sedan to attack Charles V and his possessions in Luxembourg.[134]

---

[132] Hay, D (1967) *The New Cambridge Modern History: The Renaissance* Vol I (Cambridge, Cambridge University Press) 326–30.

[133] Grand Chancellor, as noted in Elton, G (1968) *The New Cambridge Modern History: The Reformation*, Vol II (Cambridge, Cambridge University Press) 301, 341; Aurelio, E (2005) 'The Grand Strategy of Charles V: Castile, War and Dynastic Priority', *Journal of Early Modern History* 9 (3), 239–83; Pagden, A (1995) *Lords of All the World: Ideologies of Empire in Spain, Britain and France* (New Haven, CT, Yale University Press) 42–44, 50–58.

[134] Cohn, H (2001) 'Did Bribes Induce the German Electors to Choose Charles V as Emperor in 1519?', *German History* 19 (1), 1–27.

Before Charles V could fully engage with Francis, he had first to gain full control of Spain. His predecessors had a good reputation amongst the poor in Spain, as they had fought and defeated the nobles of the *Cortes*, who had long held the monarch in check, abolishing the 'six evil customs' relating to serfdom in 1455 and declaring all peasants to be free. The nobles of the *Cortes* had to be made to accept such social changes by force, in an area that was traditionally believed to be their sole prerogative.[135]

The revolt faced by Charles V in 1520 largely resulted from the imposition of new taxes (the *servicio*), which had been voted in, and from the fact that some of the commoners who had traditional rights in town councils were excluded from voting. The fact that Charles himself was not in the country and that it was being governed by Adrian of Utrecht (the future Pope Adrian VI) did not help. The rebellious towns, led by Toledo, formed a league and set up a *junta* that was in effect a revolutionary government. The rebel leader, Padilla, captured Tordesillas and kidnapped Joanna, the insane queen mother. The rebels, known as *Comuneros*, were primarily townspeople, but also included clergy, nobles and commoners. They issued a series of demands for, inter alia, the imposition of local and autonomous controls through the *Cortes*, under which the king would not be able to take certain actions without their consent, such as going to war or imposing new taxes. These demands were not seeking to go much further than restoring rights previously possessed.[136]

After the revolutionaries destroyed some of the commercial centres, and seemed to be fomenting a general revolt against the nobility (the core of the *Cortes*), many of the nobles began to fear that that the movement would encompass their private possessions. Accordingly, they began to move towards reconciliation with Charles. In 1521, the forces of Charles V, in alliance with a majority of Castilian nobles, routed the *Comunero* army. Following their defeat, although Charles had 300 of the surviving leaders executed, the remaining rebels were given a general pardon. The nobles reaped a benefit, being made exempt from any further taxation, whilst the *servicio* tax that had caused so much difficulty in the first place was imposed on all others. The *Cortes* of Castile was maintained, along with the right to petition the king, and Charles interacted with it, to the surprise of many, ensuring that the needs of the poor were not overridden by the wishes of the nobles.[137]

---

[135] MacKay, A (1977) *Spain in the Middle Ages* (London, Macmillan) 110, 137; Elliot, J (2002) *Imperial Spain.* (London, Penguin) 40–42; MacKinnon, J (1906) *A History of Modern Liberty*, Vol I (London, Longmans) 249, 427.

[136] 'The Demands of the Comuneros', as in Cowans, J (ed) *Early Modern Spain: A Documentary History* (Philadelphia, PA, Penn State University Press) 46–48; Solorzano, T (2014) 'The Politics of the Urban Commons in Spain in the Middle Ages' *Urban History* 41 (2), 183–203; Perrone, S (2001) 'Opposition in Habsburg Castile', *European History Quarterly* 31 (3), 323–52.

[137] MacKay, A (1977) *Spain in the Middle Ages* (London, Macmillan) 154–55; Hay, D (1967) *The New Cambridge Modern History: The Renaissance*, Vol I (Cambridge, Cambridge University Press) 196–97, 208–12, 214–19; Maltby, W (2002) *The Reign of Charles V* (London, Palgrave) 27, 43–46, 80–82; Elton, G (ed) (1968) *The New Cambridge Modern History: The Reformation*, Vol II (Cambridge, Cambridge University Press) 320, 440–43. Elliot, J (2002) *Imperial Spain* (London, Penguin) 152–55.

J. The Widening War

With the revolution in Spain under control, the Emperor Charles could turn his attention back to France and deflecting the attacks in Luxembourg manipulated by Francis I. In 1521, Charles enteried into a secret agreement with Pope Leo X once again to drive the French from Lombardy and restore the Duchy of Milan to the House of Sforza. At the same time, with French backing, the locals of Navarre were being encouraged to rebel against their Spanish overlords. The forces of Navarre captured Pamplona, initially by defeating the Spanish garrison, which included Ignatius of Loyola (the founder of the Jesuits). Charles V then moved the conflict back into Italy, where, in combination with papal forces, he fought the French at Bicocca just north of Milan at the end of 1522. Although the French were supplemented by Venetian and Swiss troops, they were defeated, leaving over 3,000 of their number dead on the field, in the first recorded battle in which gunpowder and a hand-held firearm, the arquebus, played a defining role. The Duchy of Milan then passed back into the hands of the Emperor.[138]

Charles V proceeded to secure the help of Henry VIII of England in a treaty of alliance against France. Henry was happy to consider this, as although his holdings in Ireland were relatively secure, his relationship with Scotland had worsened, despite the English gaining the upper hand following the death of James IV on the battlefield at Flodden, with Henry's sister, the Queen of Scotland, Margaret Tudor, initially acting as regent to her son, James V. The problem was that in 1517, the Duke of Albany, now the young Scottish King's regent, signed the *Treaty of Rouen* with France, to renew the *Auld Alliance*, at which point Margaret Tudor fled to England, leaving James V in the care of Scottish nobles. Despite hopes for a broad peace between Scotland, France and England (with Henry VIII and Francis I meeting in the middle of 1520), the hoped for Anglo-French alliance failed to materialise. The following year, France sent 4,000 soldiers to Scotland, who engaged in a series of border raids against England, after the Scottish Parliament agreed to reopen hostilities against Henry in 1521, largely at the behest of France.

It was at this point that Charles V and Henry VIII secretly signed the 1521 *Treaty of Bruges*, under which Charles was to marry Henry's daughter Mary, and both England and Spain were to wage war on France in 1523. This Anglo-Imperial alliance was confirmed in 1522 (although the advance date was put off until 1524) when Charles visited England and the *Treaty of Windsor* was concluded. Henry duly sent 10,000 men to Calais, in preparation to advance on Paris. He then proclaimed his reasons for going to war against France: the French king had allowed dissidents to return to Scotland to foment rebellion; the French had assisted in the uprising in Navarre, hiring foreign mercenaries; Francis I had allowed French pirates to pillage Henry's ships; and the

---

[138] Harvey, A (2006) 'The Pistol on the Battlefield', *The RUSI Journal* 151 (1), 66–70; Cassidy, B (2003) 'Machiavelli and the Ideology of the Offensive: Gunpowder Weapons in the Art of War', *The Journal of Military History* 67 (2), 381–404.

French king had terminated the pension granted under promises made at the end of the Hundred Years' War. The larger reality was that Henry VIII saw this as an opportunity to launch a joint invasion of France, so that the Valois line could be 'abolished, removed and [made] utterly extinct'.[139]

Francis I rejected all of the assertions made by Henry, adding that he had felt for years that the King of England was his mortal enemy, and he would not pay him any money to be used against himself. Fighting broke out soon afterwards, but the English forces could not extend their reach far outside Calais and thus retreated. With the English no longer an immediate threat, Francis felt free to go to Italy to recover Milan. Before he did so, he reorganised the diplomatic chess board, making an alliance with the new Pope Clement VII (Guilio de' Medici), after Francis promised Clement the acquisition of Parma and Piacenza for the Papal States, as well as the rule of the Medici over Florence. Francis advanced and retook Milan, and then moved on to Pavia, some 35 kilometres south of Milan, where he ran into serious opposition. The Battle of Pavia in 1525 was one of most decisive engagements in European history. It was also the first to prove conclusively the superiority of firearms over pikes. When the fighting was over, the King of France had been captured, and his army had largely been destroyed, with the loss of 8,000 men, compared to the Emperor, who lost about 1,000 men. Pope Clement VII now changed sides once more, this time expressing his support for the Holy Roman Emperor, Charles V.[140]

K. The Peace Treaties to End the Italian Wars

Peace came to Italy only after four treaties—Madrid, Cambrai, Crépy and Cateau-Cambrésis—were signed over a 25-year period. Although each of these dealt with a different aspect of the war, they slowly progressed to a settlement which, underscored by much more killing, finally brought this conflict to an end.

(i) The Treaty of Madrid and the League of Cognac

In 1525, Henry VIII agreed the *Treaty of More* with the interim French Government. Under the agreement, Henry would renounce some territorial claims in France in return for a handsome pension. This pension and the 1525 Treaty were subsequently eclipsed by the 1526 *Treaty of Madrid*, under which Francis and Charles agreed to

---

[139] Henry VIII, in Bonney, R (2012) *The European Dynastic States* (Oxford, Oxford University Press) 103; Baumgartner, F (2007) 'Declaring War in Sixteenth Century France', *The Journal of the Historical Society* 7 (1), 85–94, 95; the 1517 'Treaty of Rouen', in Dickinson, W (ed) (1958) *A Sourcebook of Scottish History*, Vol II (London, Nelson) 68–69; Connolly, S (2012) *Contested Island: Ireland 1460–1630* (Oxford, Oxford University Press) 78.

[140] Hibbert, C (1980) *The House of Medici* (NYC, Morrow) 235–39, 238–43; Scarisbrick, J (1997) *Henry VIII* (London, Yale University Press) 8889, 127, 140–42; Grant, R (2011) *1001 Battles* (London, Penguin) 254–55.

make peace, as a stepping-stone to a 'universal peace of all Christians', whereby their energies could be diverted into fighting non-Catholic foes, amongst them 'heretics banished from the bosom of our Holy Mother Church'.[141] The terms of the 1526 Treaty included payment to Henry VIII of 2 million ecus (considerably more than agreed in the *Treaty of More*), and Francis agreeing to surrender the Duchy of Burgundy and renounce all claims to Naples, Milan and Genoa. A marriage was meant to cement the relationship between France and Spain, with Francis promising to marry Charles's sister.[142]

Although the French king had agreed to the *Treaty of Madrid*, and had handed over two of his sons as hostages to secure his word in order to obtain his freedom, once released he broke his oath and refused to honour the agreement, on the ground that it had been made under duress. In an age when such a blatant breach of good faith in a treaty could lead to the Pope's issuing an order of excommunication, this was a radical act. When Charles V recognised that he had been duped, he challenged Francis to single combat, but Francis declined to reply to the challenge, preferring to respond by setting up defensive alliances with England (with Henry VIII) and Hungary (with John Zapolya), binding them to make war on Charles as soon as the Emperor refused to free the French king's sons and/or pay the debts (from the earlier agreement) of the King of England. Francis also created the 1526 *League of Cognac*, whereby Milan, Venice, Florence and France pledged themselves to act as an anti-imperial alliance. Here, for the first time, was an agreement dedicated to the proposition that Milan, and by extension all other Italian states, should be free from foreign domination. Pope Clement then added his weight to the agreement, swapping sides once more, indulging in invective against Charles V and absolving Francis from the oath he had taken to uphold the *Treaty of Madrid*, on the grounds that Francis was not bound in either honour or conscience.[143]

Charles V wrote to Pope Clement, accusing him of failing to protect Christendom. For this failure Charles wanted a General Council for the reform of the Church. In Pope Clement's eyes, Charles's demands were tantamount to a declaration of war against the papacy. The greater difficulty for Clement was that, unlike many others who made such demands, it appeared that Charles was actually in a position to enforce his. This seemed especially so when an imperial army advanced on the remaining papal states, ultimately arriving outside the walls of Rome. Imperial troops in Italy were discontented because they were owed so much back pay. Clement tried to calm their anger by promising to pay their wages. However, when the promise was not fulfilled, the troops mutinied and breached the walls of Rome. In a sack lasting four days, at least 1,000 Swiss guards who tried to defend the Pope and 25,000 citizens of Rome

---

[141] The *Treaty of Madrid*, in Reddaway, F (ed) *Select Documents in European History*, Vol II (London, Methuen) 34.

[142] Mackie, J (1985) *The Early Tudors* (Oxford, Clarendon) 316–18; Knecht, R (2007) *The Valois* (London, Hambledon) 135, 142–43.

[143] Lesaffer, R (2000) 'The Medieval Canon Law of Contract and Early Modern Treaty Law', *Journal of the History of International Law* 2, 178–98; Chamberlin, E (1979) *The Sack of Rome* (London, Batsford) 91–96, 100–05.

were killed, and in the eyes of many, the Renaissance came to an end. Pope Clement took refuge in Castel Sant' Angelo, where his forces held out for one month, promising his defenders that all of the deaths they caused while defending him would be forgiven by God. Despite such encouragement, the defenders could not hold out and Clement was forced to surrender, following which he was held prisoner by Charles V for six months.[144]

Pope Clement VII obtained his release by promising neutrality in Charles's war with the *League of Cognac*, agreeing to the Emperor's occupation of a number of important cities (Ostia, Civitavecchia, Piacenza and Modena) and their removal from papal control, settling the arrears of pay of all the imperial troops in the city, amounting to some 400,000 ducats, and agreeing to hold a council to reform to the Church and extirpate heresy. He also had to look the other way with regard to all of the hostages and the extortion, pillage and destruction that was taking place in Rome. In addition, the commune within Rome, which had allowed an independent type of government, was destroyed. The power of Rome was henceforth to belong to no one except the Emperor Charles V.[145]

(ii) The Peace of Cambrai

Nothing could stop Charles V's advance through Italy, the *League of Cognac* having being defeated step by step and having surrendered over the next two years. In 1529 the *Peace of Cambrai* was achieved. This confirmed Spanish rule in Italy. All French interests in Italy came to an end, with Francis giving up all claims and handing over the towns of Hesdin, Arras, Lille and Tournai, as well as suzerainty of Flanders, Artois and Tournai, which he ceded to the Emperor. In addition, the French king had to part with 2 million gold crowns to obtain the return of his sons, who had been Charles's hostages, of which 1,200,000 were be handed over in a single payment of gold. Francis also had to assume the debt (290,000 crowns) that Charles owed Henry VIII. In return, Charles gave up his imperial claims to Burgundy. Francis married Charles V's sister (Eleanor of Portugal). Francesco Sforza was also permitted to return to Milan. Charles then restored the Medici to Florence, and the Republic was dissolved into the Grand Duchy of Tuscany. Alessandro de' Medici then had the great bell in the Palazzo della Signoria smashed, to symbolise the death of the Republic, and the pieces were melted down and recast into medals representing his family. The title of subsequent Grand Dukes of the Medici line were then endorsed, and bestowed, by the papacy. When all of these matters were concluded, Pope Clement VII crowned Charles V as Emperor

---

[144] Gouwens, K (1997) 'Discourses on Vulnerability: Orations on the Sack of Rome', *Renaissance Quarterly* 50 (1), 38–77; Chamberlin, E (1979) *The Sack of Rome* (London, Batsford) 160–89; Hibbert, C (1980) *The House of Medici* (NYC, Morrow) 242–43, 253–55, 265–69; Grant, R (2011) *1001 Battles* (London, Penguin) 260.

[145] Gillespie, A (2017) *The Causes of War*, Vol 2: *1000 CE to 1400 CE* (Oxford, Hart Publishing) 59-62; Brown, K (1975) 'The Fall of Modena: An Episode in the Campaign of the League of Cognac', *European Studies Review* 5 (4), 357–73; Mallett, M (2012) *The Italian Wars: 1494–1559* (Harlow, Pearson) 165, 234.

of the Holy Roman Empire at Bologna in 1530, in the last ever imperial coronation by a pope. Three years later, Pope Clement organised the marriage of Catherine de' Medici (the daughter of Lorenzo de' Medici) to the future King of France, Henri II (the son of the Francis I).[146]

Despite the 1529 *Peace of Cambrai*, fighting continued to break out. First, in 1535, when Francesco Sforza of Milan (Francesco II) died without an heir, Francis I claimed the duchy for his son. Despite all of the previous deals, Francis firmly believed that Genoa, Milan and Asti were rightfully his. Charles V objected and allowed his representatives to take charge of the duchy. This intensified Francis' desire to reclaim it. He then made a deal with the Ottomans,[147] with the goal of collectively attacking the Emperor Charles in Italy. However, this arrangement never really came to anything. When the Ottoman offensive was blunted, Charles invaded Provence but failed to achieve his goals, subsequently abandoning the attempt. In 1538, Francis and Charles concluded the *Truce of Nice*, under which both sides returned to their earlier agreements and Francis promised that he would help Charles in his wars against the Ottoman Empire. However, conflict broke out again when two French diplomats were murdered in northern Italy in 1541, which Francis decried as 'an injury so great, so detestable … to those who bear the quality and title of a prince that it cannot in any way be forgiven, suffered or endured'.[148]

(iii) The Peace of Crépy

As Henry VIII continued to tighten his grip in both England and Scotland,[149] he was increasingly squeezed out of European relations. Despite trying to stay engaged, even his alliance with Charles V was difficult, since Henry by this time was a schismatic and therefore not technically able to be supported by any Catholic monarch. Moreover, when significant peace treaties were concluded, such as the *Peace of Crépy*, Henry was not included. In large part this was because the major conflicts of the early years of the 1540s took place far from western Europe. For example, the Battle of Ceresole in 1544, where nearly 30,000 men came together in a conflict that left about 6,000 imperial troops dead and a further 3,000 taken prisoner. Although the imperial forces were defeated, the status quo remained the same, as both sides were well entrenched in the region. Nonetheless, the slaughter was sufficient for both sides to conclude the *Peace of Crépy* of 1544.

---

[146] Gilmore, M (1952) *The World of Humanism* (NYC, Harper) 112–15; Maltby, W (2002) *The Reign of Charles V* (London, Palgrave) 37; Mackie, J (1985) *The Early Tudors* (Oxford, Clarendon) 318–20; Norwich, J (2011) *Absolute Monarchs* (London, Random House) 304–07; Elton, G (ed) *The New Cambridge Modern History: The Reformation*, Vol II (Cambridge, Cambridge University Press) 345; Bonney, R (2012) *The European Dynastic States* (Oxford, Oxford University Press) 105

[147] See pages 245–246.

[148] Francis, as noted in Baumgartner, F (2007) 'Declaring War in Sixteenth Century France', *The Journal of the Historical Society* 7 (1), 85, 99; Maltby, W (2002) *The Reign of Charles V* (London, Palgrave) 39; Kinross, L (1976) *The Ottoman Centuries* (NYC, Quil) 174, 219.

[149] See pages 88–90.

Charles, who was keen to make peace with France so that he could concentrate on the rising Protestant challenges in Germany (without Francis interfering), gave up his claims to Burgundy and Francis gave up his claims to Naples, Flanders and Artois, and Savoy. Francis agreed to leave the New World possessions of both Portugal and Spain alone, and not to attempt any discoveries around the Indies. In exchange, he was to be given the right to trade in these regions. Finally, there was to be a marriage alliance, but this never occurred as Francis' youngest son died before the deal could be concluded.[150]

War broke out again in the next decade between the then French king, Henri II, and the then King of Spain, Philip II, and his wife, Mary Tudor, who became Queen of England in 1557.[151] Although this was a disaster for the English holdings in France, it led to success for the Spanish forces of Philip II, which consolidated all Spanish holdings in Italy, with Montalcino, the last relic of republicanism linked to French support in Italy, falling into the hands of Cosimo de' Medici on behalf of the joint imperial forces, in the same year, 1557.

(iv) The Treaty of Cateau-Cambrésis

The grandchildren of the original French and Spanish monarchs who had started the Italian Wars 65 years earlier, eventually brought the conflict to a conclusion with the two parts of the *Treaty of Cateau-Cambrésis* of 1559. Both rulers were about to get deeply engaged in the forthcoming wars of the Reformation, and warfare would go from being about dynastic issues and territory, to being about religion and authority. The first treaty to end the Italian Wars marked an acknowledgement that the English had lost Calais, although the French undertook to return it (which was unlikely) or pay compensation after eight years of occupation. The second treaty, which dealt with the question that had dominated Europe since 1494—which country was the paramount power in Italy—was very favourable to Spain. It was symptomatic of the time that the fate of Italy was decided by the French and the Spanish around a table at which sat not one Italian, not even a representative of the Pope. The only benefits France received were that Metz, Toul and Verdue were transferred to it, but the French could not enjoy full sovereignty over these towns without the Emperor's consent, and this was not granted until 1648. In exchange, the French withdrew all claims to Milan and Naples, for all practical purposes making Italy a Spanish/Habsburg dependency. The peace was sealed with the marriage of the daughter of Henri II and Catherine de' Medici, Elizabeth of Valois, to Philip II. Thus the Italian Wars, that had raged for 65 years, came to an end. King Henri II of France also met his end at the same time, dying from a jousting accident at the celebrations to mark the *Peace of Cateau-Cambresis* and the marriage of his daughter.[152]

---

[150] The 1544 Treaty of Crepy-en-Lanonnois as reproduced in Davenport, F (ed) (1917) *European Treaties Bearing on the History of the United States and its Dependencies to 1648* (NYC, Carnegie Institute) 205–14.

[151] See pages 93–96.

[152] Bonney, R (2012) *The European Dynastic States* (Oxford, Oxford University Press) 128; Wernham, R (1968) *The New Cambridge Modern History: The Counter Reformation* (Cambridge, Cambridge University Press) 149.

6. Conclusion

During the period 1400 to 1560, wars fought for the acquisition of thrones, dynastic succession and/or associated territory were very common. The toppling of kings who were tyrants, incompetent or simply unable to govern was seen in Germany, France and England. None of this was carried out by constitutional agents. Although a Parliament existed in England, the *Cortes* in Spain and shades of the Three Estates in France, none of these bodies had sufficient power to seriously challenge the monarchy and what were becoming increasingly autocratic forms of government. In all three instances the trend was towards greater, if not absolute, power of kings.

Where kings were toppled, it was achieved by other dynastic contenders, typically buttressed by justifications of tyranny or incompetence, and new rulers were always legitimised by the parliament and the Church. In the case of England, Henry VI had health problems, and there were long periods when he was unable to govern. During these periods, Richard, Duke of York, acted as Lord Protector, and eventually claimed the throne of England in what became a prolonged and bloody dynastic struggle between the Houses of York and Lancaster. Although Richard of York would be killed in battle, his sons, Edward and Richard, would be more successful, slowly gaining control over all of England, with both Ireland and Scotland being pulled into the dynastic struggle, until Edward celebrated victory over his enemies and came to the throne as Edward IV, Henry VI being deposed. The intrigues and dynastic struggle only got worse following the death of Edward IV, when his brother—the future Richard III—ascended the throne of England in place of his nephew, Edward V. Rebellion followed, during which Henry Tudor (the grandson of the Welshman Owain Tudor, the second husband of Catherine of Valois, and son of the half-brother of Henry VI) and his supporters prevailed, killing Richard at the Battle of Bosworth in 1485. Henry Tudor, now Henry VII, was much more concerned about avoiding interference in his realm, in order to secure his own position, than engaging in conflict on the Continent, making peace treaties with Scotland and marrying his family into their royal line. At all points, the English Parliament, from the time of Henry V through to Henry VII, remained flexible, providing stamps of legitimacy to whoever had the military power to demand them.

In France, the rebellion that allowed Burgundy to form an alliance with England resulted from to the incompetence and duplicity of King Charles VI. In both England and France, what started out as war between families ended up as war between regions, as each contender brought in support by way of military alliances that were often cemented by dynastic marriages. Such marriages were the common currency for treaties of peace and/or alliance, and although useful good-faith measures in the short term, more often than not they ended up turning national disputes into regional, if not international, conflicts, as each marriage brought with it theoretical rights and entitlements that monarchs believed were worth fighting for. For example, when English Henry VI was threatened, his wife, Margaret of Anjou, appealed to her brother, the French king, Louis XI, for assistance. Louis only agreed to help when it appeared that Edward of York was trying to repeat Henry V's trick, of making an alliance with Charles the Bold, the reigning Duke of Burgundy, who, like his predecessors, was trying to break free from the influence of Paris, in conjunction with Brittany. Charles's first battles were for better governance by the French king and respect for the ancient rights of the regions. He ended up fighting under the banner of autonomy for Burgundy. The difference this time was that, whereas Edward IV won his battles, Charles the Bold lost his, eventually being crushed by the combined weight of French, Swiss and imperial forces.

France's not-so-secret weapon against England was Scotland; England's greatest threat against the French was Burgundy and Brittany. In both instances, as long as Scotland, Burgundy and Brittany were independent, both England and France were at risk. Despite dynastic marriages, Scotland remained a theoretical and/or real enemy of England for most of the fifteenth century and half of the sixteenth century. France was continually at risk from its immediate neighbours. This weakness was made starkly clear when the English king, Henry V, managed to secure the crown of France, through treaty and marriage, after making an alliance with Burgundy. The English grip on the French crown was only loosened when Burgundy was persuaded to rejoin France, albeit with a strong degree of autonomy.

France faced a similar problem decades later, following the death of Charles the Bold, leaving his daughter Mary, like the other great daughter of the age, Anne of Brittany, to become one of the most powerful dynastic chess pieces on the board. Mary ended up married to the heir to the Habsburg line, but not before entrenching all of the great privileges of local autonomy of what became the Netherlands, and Burgundy being split between France and Germany. Conversely, Brittany, after battle, became sequestrated by France, with Anne being married directly to the French king to ensure it would never be separate again. These marriages were the conclusion of wars based around goals of achieving the territorial solidarity of France under the clear rule of one king, trumping those of local autonomy. At the same time, the French monarchy began to move ever closer to autocratic rule, and away from measures that might curtail its powers. The peace that France finally found at the end of the fifteenth century was thus won by destroying any semi-autonomous regions and ridding the Continent of any English influence.

After the English toehold on the Continent had been removed, and Burgundy and Brittany joined fully to France, it became possible for the French kings—Charles VIII, Louis XII and later Francis I—to begin extending their reach outwards. Their target was Italy, spurred on by dynastic claims to both Naples and Milan. In this age, while all rulers studied the higher ethics of Erasmus, they practised the raw politics of Machiavelli. To achieve their goals, they would make agreements both with Popes and with the emerging superpower that was the very conservative Spain, trying to ease transfers, whilst the opposition of traditional counterweights, like the Swiss Confederacy, would first be crushed by the new military technologies and then their loyalty ensured by money and treaties. As it was, the papacy and Spain would both change sides whenever it suited them to do so to expand their own interests. Pope Julius II was the exemplar of this approach, one day negotiating international alliances aimed at Venice and the next day alliances aimed at France. When subsequent pontiffs tried the same tricks, and backed the wrong side, it led to the sack of Rome in 1527. The next two decades followed this pattern, with the Spanish king and (later) Holy Roman Emperor, Charles V of the Habsburg line, acquiring full power over all of Italy, and any vestiges of independent republics disappearing under a succession of treaties—Madrid, Cambrai, Crépy and finally Cateau-Cambrésis. These treaties ultimately reflected the fact that in what had become a competition for dynastic power in Italy between Spain and France, Habsburg Spain was the victor.

III

Religious Wars in Europe: The Beginning

1. INTRODUCTION

THIS CHAPTER IS about the rise of religious wars in Europe. Although there was an earlier history of discontent with and violence against the Catholic Church within Western Europe, the most well-known wars typically occurred in the sixteenth century. My thesis is that the background to these lay in the fifteenth century, when all of the elements of theological challenge, national discontent and a loosely knit Holy Roman Empire were present. Martin Luther built on all of these factors, developing a revised version of the Christian faith that had both theological and political implications. These became evident in Northern Europe and in Switzerland, before conflict erupted in Germany. In all instances, peace was ultimately secured by compromise, where competing Christian faiths were tolerated. This was a particularly difficult point to reach, as tolerance was not on the agenda of many leaders during this period.

2. THE ABSOLUTE POWER OF THE POPE

The wars of religion in Europe were ultimately about rejecting the omnipotence of the Pope and the Catholic Church. Although this rejection had its roots in earlier centuries and led to outbreaks of war,[1] it was only towards the end of the fourteenth century that serious disputes split the Church into different parts with the *Western Schism*. This split was only healed with the Council of Constance, between 1414 and 1418, which finally ended the competing claims to be Pope of three men, all at the same time. These claims and counter-claims rocked Western Christendom to its core, as it was simply impossible to work out who was the legitimate spiritual leader.

The significance of ending this schism cannot be overestimated as, whilst it was in operation, Western Christendom lacked the unity that had previously held it together. The tool that achieved the reconciliation was a council, or assembly, convened by the monarchs of Europe, including representatives of the whole Church. The seeds of this process lay in the 1409 *Council of Pisa*, where, after 15 years of debate within the College of Cardinals, the Popes in both Rome and Avignon were condemned as 'notorious

---

[1] Gillespie, A (2017) *The Causes of War*, Vol 2: *1000 CE to 1400 CE* (Oxford, Hart Publishing) 95-98.

schismatics and heretics',[2] and a third Pope—Alexander V—was elected. However, neither of the deposed pontiffs accepted the result (declaring it heretical and trying to imprison those who spoke of it), and for a period there were three Popes, all claiming supremacy. A council was then called at Constance in 1414. This time, it was an international gathering of thousands, including 22 cardinals and 30 representatives from five nations. The first outcome of this council, the decree *Sacrosancta* of 1415, stated that the General Council 'derives its power directly from Christ, and every one, whatever his state or position, even if it be the Papal dignity itself, is bound to obey it in all those things which pertain to the faith and the healing of the said schism'.[3] This conclusion was reached, and power bestowed, because

> [t]he frequent holding of General Councils ensures an excellent cultivation of the Lord's acre. It cleans out the thorns, brambles and spikes of heresies, errors and schisms, corrects excesses, reforms the deformed and brings the Lord's vineyard to a state of abundant fruitfulness.[4]

By having a public council of hundreds of nationally nominated theologians 'cultivate ... the Lord's acre', the idea that the elected Pope was the equivalent of a king with absolute power, who could not be deposed, no matter what, was shaken to its core. To suggest that a council could depose a Pope was to make the Pope a type of constitutional monarch, a minister or an official of the Church, whose authority was overseen by others was radical. As Nicolas of Cusa stated, 'the universal council ... has supreme power in all things over the Roman pontiff'.[5] The three existing Popes were all deposed and a new Pope, Martin V, was elected and the Papacy resettled in Rome. The difficulty was that Martin V, once in power, showed very little interest in being overseen. This was especially so within Italy, where he went on to direct armies against the deposed Popes and those who supported them.

The Council of Basel that followed Pope Martin's death in 1431 came together to discuss what had occurred, and revisited the idea of papal superiority. The result of this was that when they tried to suspend the next Pope, Eugenius IV, who, despite being correctly elected had become autocratic in his rule, as had Martin V, declaring him a heretic and electing an Anti-Pope, Eugenius IV responded by excommunicating all of those taking part in the Council of Basel part and summoned his own council. From this moment on, the Council of Basel slowly disintegrated, and never again would papal supremacy be challenged from within the Church.

---

[2] The quotation is from Norwich, J (2011) *Absolute Monarchs: A History of the Papacy* (London, Random) 233. The 1409 'Council of Pisa Declaration', as in Thatcher, O (ed) (1905) *A Sourcebook for Medieval History* (NYC, Scribner) 327.

[3] The 1415 Canon 'Sacrosancta', as in Cohen, M (ed) (2004) *History in Quotations* (London, Cassell) 193.

[4] 'Frequens, 1417', as part of the Council of Constance, as in Elton, G (ed) (1968) *Renaissance and Reformation* (London, Macmillan) 12–13; Blasi, A (1989) 'The Sociological Implications of the Great Western Schism', *Social Compass* 36 (3), 311–25; Powers, G (1928) 'Nationalism at the Council of Constance', *The Catholic Historical Review* 8 (2) 171–204.

[5] Nicolas of Cusa, *The Catholic Concordance*, Vol II, trans, Sigmond, P (2003) (Cambridge, Cambridge University Press) 34, no 249. Also Hay, D (1996) *Europe in the Fourteenth and Fifteenth Centuries* (London, Longman) 309; Skinner, Q (1980) *The Foundations of Modern Political Thought*, Vol II (Cambridge, Cambridge University Press) 41–46, 116–17, 202.

The end point of this rejection of any form of constitutional control over pontiffs occurred a few decades later in 1464, when Pope Paul II ruled that there should be a return to pontifical absolutism, condemning any future councils that sought to have power over a Pope as 'erroneous and detestable'.[6] Although some countries, such as England, and France with its *Pragmatic Sanction of Bourges* of 1438, had begun to restrict the matters the Pope could regulate in their countries, within the Vatican the idea that a legitimately elected Pope could ever be subject to checks on the exercise of his power was dismissed.[7]

3. THE HUSSITE WARS

The foremost example of the loss of papal influence directly leading to war in the fifteenth century occurred in Bohemia, where the Hussites, followers of the Bohemian religious reformer Jan Hus (below), entered into a conflict regarding considerations of nationalism and religious autonomy from Rome. Given that the success of Council of Constance, under the careful guidance of the Emperor Sigismund, had brought the Western Schism to an end, it made sense that Sigismund would be at the forefront of implementing its recommendations.[8] One of these recommendations concerned focusing upon the Hussites of Bohemia. Bohemia had a long history of independence and difficult relations with both the Holy Roman Empire and the Church of Rome. Early in the fifteenth century, Jan Hus embodied these problems. Hus was a popular preacher in Prague, who was in continual disagreement with the papal authorities in the region. He was a strong supporter of the work of the English theologian Wycliffe,[9] and believed that Rome was so corrupt that it would be better to support its enemies than profess loyalty to the Pope. He also argued for a decentralised type of democratic control for communities, as opposing to more hierarchical conceptions of authority.[10]

For these views Hus was excommunicated by Anti-Pope John XXIII in 1411. Undeterred, Hus continued to preach, refusing to submit unconditionally to the authority of any of the contending pontiffs who were active during the Western Schism, appealing to

[6] Pius II, *On Papal Authority*, as reproduced in Webster, D (ed) (1969) *Documents in Renaissance and Reformation History* (Sydney, Cassell) 196; Partner, P (1958) *The Papal State Under Martin V* (London, Brown) 78–95, 134, 200–09.

[7] D'Elia, A (2007) 'Porcari's Conspiracy Against Pope Nicholas V in 1453' *Journal in the History of Ideas* 68 (2), 1–17; Schofield, A.(1964) 'England, the Pope and the Council of Basel, 1435–1449', *Church History* 33 (3), 248–63.

[8] Morrissey, T (1983) 'Emperor-Elect Sigismund and the Council of Constance', *The Catholic Historical Review* 69 (3), 353–70; Haberken, P (2011) 'What's at Stake When We Talk About Hussites?', *History Compass* 9 (10), 791–801.

[9] Gillespie, A (2017) *The Causes of War*, Vol 2: *1000 CE to 1400 CE* (Oxford, Hart Publishing) 208–209.

[10] See Jan Hus, 'On Simony', as reproduced in Elton, G (ed) (1968) *Renaissance and Reformation* (London, Macmillan) 7–9; Cook, W (1973) 'John Wycliffe and the Hussite Theology, 1415–1436', *Church History* 42 (93), 335–49; Heymann, F (1962) 'City Rebellions in 15th Century Bohemia', *The Slavonic and East European Review*.40 (95), 324–40; Thompson, H (1933) 'Pre-Hussite Heresy in Bohemia', *The English Historical Review* 48 (189), 23–42.

Christ and conscience instead. Moreover, the authorities in Prague, where Hus preached, were under the wider umbrella of the deposed king of Germany—Wenceslaus[11]—but who was still the reigning king of Bohemia. Thus Hus could not be censored in practical terms. Anti-Pope John XXIII then placed Prague under interdict, but was still unable to resolve the matter. Accordingly, he referred it for consideration to the Council of Constance. The Council preferred to deal directly with the matter of Wycliffe and indirectly with the matter of Hus. The Council of Constance condemned the teachings of scholars like Wycliffe as 'rash', 'contrary to ecclesiastical practice', full of manifest 'error' and unlawful, and called on those who followed them 'to be confirmed as heretics and severely punished'.[12] As Hus was a follower of Wycliffe, he too fell into the trap in both theoretical and physical terms. That is, Hus, who had made an appearance at the Council to debate such matters after believing he was safe due to the personal guarantees given by the King Sigismund of Germany, found that the promises of safety came to naught. Hus was found to be an incorrigible heretic, after he refused to renounce his own writings or condemn Wycliffe's teachings, and was burned at the stake in July 1415.[13]

Sigismund, who had already massacred many Czech citizens following an earlier attack upon himself in Buda on an unrelated matter, found that the execution of Hus (and others associated with him) in violation of the promise of personal protection, was intolerable to Hus's supporters who began to rise in rebellion. Despite his pleas, Sigismund could not curb the growing influence of the Hussite movement, as the Hussite clergy and over 450 barons refused to change their views in support of the teachings of Hus, which were buttressed by an existing, strong regional identity and desire for autonomy, and radical political ideas, including common property. The central pivot of the revolt, however, was not political so much as theological, the movement for reform becoming wrapped up in the so-called *Four Articles of Prague*, which allowed lay participation in the Eucharist and thus interaction with God without the established Catholic Church's acting as intermediary.[14] Matters then went from bad to worse when new Catholic councillors, who had been sent to Prague to try to refute these claims and calm the atmosphere, were thrown out of a window to their deaths. The election of Sigismund to the Bohemian throne in 1419, after the death of King Wenceslaus, was

---

[11] See pages 7–8.

[12] The 'Council of Constance', as in Fudge, T (ed) (2002) *The Crusade Against Heretics in Bohemia, 1418–1437* (London, Ashgate) 17–20. Also Kelly, H (1998) 'Trial Procedures Against Wyclif and Wycliffites', *Huntington Library Quarterly* 61 (1), 1–28; MacKinnon, J (1906) *A History of Modern Liberty*, Vol I (London, Longmans) 158–65.

[13] Hay, D (1996) *Europe in the Fourteenth and Fifteenth Centuries* (London, Longman) 39, 181, 192–93, 237, 240–43; Stubbs, P (1908) *Germany in the Later Middle Ages* (London, Longmans) 168–69, 174–77.

[14] See the 'Four Articles of Prague', referring to freedom of preaching without supervision of ecclesiastical superiors, utraquism (ie communion in both wafer and wine), abolition of excessive clerical wealth and punishment for all who commit mortal sins. These are reproduced in Rosenwein, B (ed) (2006) *Reading the Middle Ages: Sources from Europe, Byzantium and the Islamic World* (Ontario, Broadview) 530. Also Graham, B (2006) 'The Evolution of the Utraquist Mass', *The Catholic Historical Review* 92 (4), 1–9; Fudge, T (1998) 'Neither Mine Nor Thine: Communist Experiments in Hussite Bohemia', *Canadian Journal of History* 33 (1), 25–47; Kaminsky, H (1957) 'Chiliasm and the Hussite Revolution', *Church History* 26 (1), 43–71.

the tipping point. The Bohemian nobles refused to accept Sigismund as their ruler, and instead elected George of Podebrady. This situation was too much for both King Sigismund and Pope Martin V, both who were aghast at the idea that Bohemia might become fully independent in both political and theological terms. Accordingly, a crusade was proclaimed by Pope Martin, and pursued by Sigismund against the heretics of Bohemia in 1420. The authorities behind this crusade confirmed that all those who fought against the Hussites would receive absolution from all of their sins.[15]

These promises did not bring victory, nor did the subsequent attacks against the Hussites from Hungary, Austria, Saxony or Bavaria. The first battle, in 1421, saw crusader losses of around 12,000 out of a force that may have been five times that size. Further losses were recorded in 1422, 1425, 1427 and 1431. The last battle, at Domazlice, in the fifth crusade against the Hussites, saw possibly tens of thousands of soldiers killed on both sides, though the Hussites comprehensively won the day. Taking their survival as a sign from God, the Hussites then went on the offensive, marching through Silesia, Saxony and Bavaria, and finally into Poland in 1433, before fragmenting due to their own internal disagreements. The progress of the Hussites came to an end when they suffered a significant loss at Lipany in 1434, when 13,000 men defeated the Hussite forces. This loss allowed Sigismund to reach peace with the opposition via a negotiated settlement, concluded in 1436. It saw (now) Emperor Sigismund finally accede to the throne of Bohemia as king, but only after he had guaranteed to safeguard the Hussite religion, via the *Four Articles of Prague*. Thus, although the political settlement was good for the king, in terms of bringing Bohemia back into the fold, the theological settlement was a failure for the Church of Rome. That, however, was the price of peace.[16]

4. Albert II, Frederick III and Maximilian I

The war against the Hussites showed many things, including the fact that the Holy Roman Empire, and Germany in particular, was not a coherent and harmonious entity. Rather, there was continual movement, especially in the east, by regions seeking autonomy. This continued after the Hussite wars, affecting rulers such Albert II. Albert, who was married to the daughter of the Emperor Sigismund, came to inherit the Duchy of Austria, and was elected to the thrones of Bohemia and Germany, but in both of these instances he was unable to rule in practice, due to strong disagreements regarding

---

[15] Holmes, G (1973) 'Cardinal Beaufort and the Crusade against the Hussites', *The English Historical Review* 88 (349), 721–50; Betts, R (1952) 'Some Political Ideas of the Early Czech Reformers', *The Slavonic and East European Review* 31 (76), 20–35; Johnson, L (1996) *Central Europe: Enemies, Neighbours, Friends* (Oxford, Oxford University Press) 64–69.

[16] Papajik, D (2012) 'Did Jan Capek Betray the Hussites at the Battle of Lipany in 1434?', *The Journal of Slavic Military Studies* 25 (3), 369–80; Fudge, T (ed) (2002) *The Crusade Against Heretics in Bohemia, 1418–1437* (London, Ashgate) 5–7, 49–51; Betts, R (1947) 'The Place of the Czech Reform Movement in the History of Europe', *The Slavonic and East European Review* 25 (65), 373–90; Grant, R (2011) *1001 Battles* (London, Penguin) 219, 223.

his accession. Albert wished to divide Germany into four parts, alongside a separate Bohemia and Austria. Although this did not come to fruition, it did reveal the deeper underlying malaise within Germany, which was only just holding itself together and which continued to splinter as many of the private rulers, regional and local authorities wanted as much autonomy, or power, as possible. As Machiavelli described the period, each region and its associated leaders had the 'principal intention to maintain their liberty' (as testified to by a number of local treaties seeking to divide and re-divide various areas following conflicts relating to hereditary and/or imperial titles).[17]

The continual drive for autonomy was even more evident in the reign of Frederick III. Frederick, of Habsburg lineage, was elected to the throne of Germany in 1440. Twelve years later he was crowned Holy Roman Emperor by Pope Nicholas V, spending the next five decades defending the eastern part of his realm. The conflicts began with the actions of Matthias Corvinus. Matthias was the son of the famed military leader, the Hungarian noble, John Hunyadi.[18] Matthias became King of Hungary and Croatia in 1458. His rise followed his earlier imprisonment and the execution of his brother by the Hungarian king, Ladislaus V. When Ladislaus died, the Hungarian Estates elected Matthias in his place. Almost immediately, he had to contend with the Holy Roman Emperor Frederick III, who coveted the Hungarian Crown. Peace between the two sides was made in the *Treaty of Wiener Neustadt*, of 1463, under which they agreed to a number of shared initiatives (such as fighting the Ottomans), succession and a type of joint kingship, one in theory and one in practice, although Frederick was the senior monarch.[19]

The peace between the two sides began to wobble in 1467, following the excommunication, and then preaching of a crusade against, George of Poděbrady, the King of Bohemia, by both Pope Paul II and Pope Sixtus IV. Matthias responded to this by invading Bohemia. George of Poděbrady was not only guilty of suspected Hussite sympathies, in 1460 he had also been advocating the revolutionary ideas that the Holy Roman Empire should be dissolved, and in its place a peace agreed throughout Christendom via a multilateral treaty, made up of equal and independent, yet federated, states under a broad European umbrella within a permanent assembly. Matthias was able to conquer Moravia but not all of Bohemia, with critical areas, such as Hussite-infused Prague, remaining out of his grasp. When George of Poděbrady died, his followers chose Vladislaus Jagiellon (Vladislaus II), the eldest son of Casimir IV of Poland, to continue the fight. This only ended in 1478 with the *Treaty of Brno*, which

---

[17] Machiavelli, 'Account of German Affairs', as in Webster, D (ed) (1969) *Documents in Renaissance and Reformation History* (Sydney, Cassell) 59; Stubbs, P (1908) *Germany in the Later Middle Ages* (London, Longmans) 208, 212, 220–50.

[18] See page 239.

[19] Curtis, B (2013) *The Habsburgs* (London, Bloomsbury) 35–36, 42–43, 68–70; Carlyle, AJ (1910) *A History of Medieval Political Theory in the West*, Vol VI (London, Blackwood) 169–72; Tanner, J (ed) (1958) *The Cambridge Medieval History: Decline of Empire and Papacy*, Vol VII (Cambridge, Cambridge University Press) 72–76; Hay, D (1996) *Europe in the Fourteenth and Fifteenth Centuries* (London, Longman) 192–93; Gilmore, M (1952) *The World of Humanism* (NYC, Harper) 92–93, 96–98, 119.

divided the Bohemian territories, Moravia, Silesia and Lusatia going to Matthias, and both Matthias and Vladislaus being able to use the title King of Bohemia.[20]

Following this success, Matthias broke the peace with Frederick III and waged war against him between 1482 and 1487, beginning with the invasion of the Duchy of Styria, followed by the siege and conquest of Vienna. Matthias then occupied Vienna, whilst Frederick III was forced to move his capital to Linz. Matthias offered Frederick (and his son and future king of Germany, Maximilian) the return of the Austrian provinces he had seized, if they would renounce the treaty of 1463 and accept Matthias as Frederick's designated heir and therefore probable inheritor of the title of Holy Roman Emperor. Before this was settled though, Matthias died, in 1490, whilst still in occupation of Vienna.

Frederick III's son, and the future Holy Roman Emperor, Maximilian I, did not favour any idea that would deprive him of power. Maximilian, who also spent his time waging war against France and Switzerland, became involved in the conflicts of his aging father, launching an invasion of Hungary with a mercenary army to stop the Hungarian nobles electing their own king. However, the Hungarian election had already taken place, the nobles having offered the throne to Vladislaus II of Bohemia, after extracting a large number of concessions to protect their privileges. As Maximilian could not succeed militarily against the Hungarian forces, he agreed to the 1491 *Treaty of Pressburg*. Under this treaty, peace was achieved when Maximilian recognised Vladislaus as King of Hungary, in return for recognition that the Austrian provinces were his and the promise of succession for himself or his son, if Vladislaus died without male heirs.[21]

With his eastern border broadly under control, Maximilian attempted to radically reorganise his realm. He did this by prohibiting 'all feuds and private wars throughout the whole empire'.[22] Maximilian wanted the Empire to work like England or France, where internal war was relatively rare, so that peaceful cohesion within his borders for a unified realm could be secured. The solution was to be found in the *Reichstag* (Imperial Diet). Through this, Maximilian attempted to carry out plans for an assembly comprising six electors, 120 prelates, 30 lay princes, 140 counts and lords, and the representatives of 85 towns. This was to be linked to a Supreme Council, through which the Emperor and the assembly would have joint responsibility to govern. At the Reichstag of Worms in 1495, subsidies were granted in exchange for certain reforms, including a new court of justice, the *Reichskammergericht* (to resolve disputes between parts of the Holy Roman Empire). Effective machinery for punishing offenders, administering justice and settling disputes on a common basis was also to be established throughout

---

[20] Bozanic, S (2012) 'Bofinius on the War Between Corvinus and Podebrady', *Istazivanja* 37 (3), 415–25.

[21] Hay, D (1996) *Europe in the Fourteenth and Fifteenth Centuries* (London, Longman) 235–36; Hay, D (1967) *The New Cambridge Modern History: The Renaissance*, Vol I (Cambridge, Cambridge University Press) 372, 387; Johnson, L (1996) *Central Europe: Enemies, Neighbours, Friends* (Oxford, Oxford University Press) 57; Kejr, J (1964) *The Treaty of the Establishment of Peace Throughout Christendom* (Prague, Czech Academy of Sciences) 81–90.

[22] The 1495 'Perpetual Peace', as in Thatcher, O (ed) (1905) *A Sourcebook for Medieval History* (NYC, Scribner, NYC) 427.

the realm. In addition, an expanded administration and a uniform system of tax ('the common penny') was advocated for the servicing of a shared military force, which could answer Maximilian's constant call to the *Reichstag*, 'Unite under your king, defend Germany against France and the Turks, or perish.'[23]

The only problem was that the *Reichstag* would not grant Maximilian the men or money he wanted to fight where he wanted. To make matters even worse, the Diet established an Imperial Governing Council to check the Emperor's dominance in the conduct of foreign policy. Maximilian responded by denying it the powers by which it could become self-autonomous, restoring his own royal court and judges. Germany sank into even greater confusion and disturbance, as Maximilian was restricted to the traditional means (of only calling on his own estates) to collect men and money for war, meaning that he ended up playing a relative minor role in the Italian Wars, in spite of his wish to be more closely involved.[24]

5. MARTIN LUTHER

Martin Luther, once an Augustinian friar, scholar, professor and seminal influence in the Reformation, lived in an age of unparalleled violence, social upheaval and challenge to the status quo, and to the papacy in particular. The foremost critic of the age (who overlapped with Luther) was Erasmus.[25] On the question of religion, Erasmus argued in his *The Praise of Folly* that the greatest admirers of foolishness were the monks, priests and bishops, and especially the Pope, all of whom were bound up in corrupt and abusive practices.[26] For Erasmus, and for Luther who followed him, such criticism was building upon work of emperors and theologians who had challenged the papacy throughout the previous five centuries, which was a rich legacy. In Luther's own time, the teachings of Ockham, Wycliffe and Hus were fresh, whilst the execution of Savonarola in 1498[27] was very recent history, which made an impact upon Luther when he visited Florence. The Western Schism[28] also rocked the credibility of a single universal church. The Borgias Popes, Callixtus III and Alexander VI, had deepened this lack of respect, as they were personally suspected of many crimes, both civil and ecclesiastical, and of the unbridled pursuit of family interests over those of the Church. The next

---

[23] Maximilian, as in Hay, D (1967) *The New Cambridge Modern History: The Renaissance*, Vol I (Cambridge, Cambridge University Press) 198. See also the 1495 'Establishment of a Supreme Court, as in Thatcher, O (ed) (1905) *A Sourcebook for Medieval History* (NYC, Scribner, NYC) 430; Bozeman, A (1994) *Politics and Culture in International History* (NYC, Transaction) 271.

[24] Maximilian, as in Hay, D (1967) *The New Cambridge Modern History: The Renaissance*, Vol I (Cambridge, Cambridge University Press) 203.

[25] See page 32.

[26] 'The Praise of Folly', as reproduced in Dolan, J (ed) (1964) *The Essential Erasmus* (NYC, Omega) 94–174.

[27] See page 37.

[28] See pages 60–61.

Pope, Julius II, although eschewing familial benefits, strove, with all diplomatic and military means available, to restore and extend the powers of the papacy to such an extent that Italy had become the battleground for Europe. Such was the state of the papacy that Machiavelli noted, in 1516, that 'the evil example of the court of Rome has destroyed all piety and religion in Italy, which brings in its train infinite improprieties and disorders ... her priests have become irreligious and bad'.[29]

It was against this world that Luther was reacting. His famous act of nailing up his *Ninety-Five Theses*[30] on the door of the Castle Church at Wittenberg on the Eve of All Saints in 1517, marked the beginning of a process, commonly known as the Reformation, which would completely change the Western world and result in decades of warfare. The genesis of Luther's act was the Church's selling indulgences, that is, remissions from penance in exchange for a financial contribution, to those who confessed their sins. Towards the end of the fifteenth century, following a ruling by Pope Sixtus IV in 1476, the sale of indulgences had been extended, with the assertion that souls in purgatory could be helped by the purchase of indulgences on their behalf. Another variety allowed for the purchase of indulgences for sins not yet committed, for which a credit balance for advance absolution could be purchased for hard cash. Variations on a theme involved the selling of indulgences for eating meat during Lent, or the purchase of an indulgence to avoid having to spend consecutive days at church listening to sermons. The particular indulgences attacked by Luther were the sale of some 2,000 Church positions (at a cost of about 10 times their annual income), offered by Pope Leo X for the rebuilding of the Basilica of St Peter in Rome. Luther considered this a most wicked perversion, as

> [f]or payment of money they make unrighteousness into righteousness, and they dissolve oaths, vows and agreements, thereby destroying and teaching us to destroy the faith and fealty which have been pledged. They assert that the Pope has authority to do this. It is the Devil who tells them to say these things.[31]

Pope Leo X responded with a papal bull in 1518, threatening the excommunication of anyone who denied his right to grant and issue indulgences. Luther was undeterred, taking his condemnation even further, as he saw the problem of the sale of indulgences as just a subset of a much larger problem. Specifically, he stated that there existed

> [a] state of affairs in Rome that beggars description ... they have stolen in all countries, and extorting, by indulgences, bulls, letters of confession, ... [T]his wicked regime is not only

---

[29] Machiavelli, 'On Church and State', as in Webster, D (ed) (1969) *Documents in Renaissance and Reformation History* (Sydney, Cassell) 148–49.

[30] Disputation of Doctor Martin Luther on the Power and Efficacy of Indulgences (1517), available at www.iclnet.org/pub/resources/text/wittenberg/luther/web/ninetyfive.html.

[31] Luther, as noted in Skinner, Q (1978) *The Foundations of Modern Political Thought*, Vol II (Cambridge, Cambridge University Press) 12–13. See also art 32 from his 'Explanations of the 95 Theses', as reproduced in Elmer, P (ed) (2000) *The Renaissance in Europe: An Anthology* (London, Yale University Press) 307. Luther's argument on the abuse of indulgences was not new, see the 1512 'Abuses in the Sale of Indulgences', as reproduced in Thatcher, O (ed) (1905) *A Sourcebook for Medieval History* (NYC, Scribner) 338–39. Also Hillberbrand, H (2003) 'Was There a Reformation in the Sixteenth Century', *Church History* 72 (3), 525–52.

[guilty of] barefaced robbery, trickery and tyranny ... but a destruction of the body and soul of Christendom.[32]

Concern about the selling of indulgences or the abuse of Catholic Church powers was not new. What was unique was Luther's challenge to the assertion that the Catholic Church had such powers at all. The theological core of Luther's thinking was the complete unworthiness of humanity. The papacy argued that through reason, it was possible to understand what God wanted. Luther expressed a very different view, arguing that only faith, not a reason orchestrated by the papacy, could lead to salvation; and only God, not the papacy, could offer spiritual salvation. Luther rejected the entire spectrum of intermediaries and rituals that Catholicism placed between people and God, from the Virgin Mary and the saints, through to the ecclesiastical hierarchy, with the Pope as its supreme leader. In Luther's view, the Church, with its rules and divisions between the spiritual and temporal world was, 'a piece of deceit and hypocrisy'.[33]

Luther believed that each individual could make his or her way to God without any intermediary, especially since only two of the seven sacraments (baptism and communion) were required to become a Christian, and for these, the intervention of the established Church was not necessary. Rather, only the Scriptures were required to serve as a guide for the Christian faithful. As Luther stated in 1520, 'a Christian is a perfectly free lord of all, subject to none'.[34] Further, all Christians were equal by virtue of their equal capacity for faith, or as he explained, 'we are all consecrated priests through baptism'.[35] Thus, 'there is no real difference among laymen, priests, princes [and] bishops'.[36] This idea of a universal priesthood of all believers, as opposed to a clergy that had established itself as a superior and gate-keeping entity, was revolutionary, as was the printing press that allowed over 300,000 copies of Luther's work to be sold between 1517 and 1520 alone, with his theses being read everywhere, from Rome to London.[37]

Pope Leo X issued the edict *Exsurge Domine* in 1520 which condemned as 'heretical or scandalous, or false and offensive to pious ears, or as dangerous to simple minds, or subversive of catholic truth' 41 of the theses extracted from Luther's writings. Luther was given 60 days to recant or face excommunication. Luther responded by publicly

[32] Luther, 'An Appeal to the Ruling Class of German Nationality as to the Amelioration of the State of Christendom', reproduced in Elmer, P (ed) (2000) *The Renaissance in Europe: An Anthology* (London, Yale University Press) 314; Wicks, J (1983) 'Roman Reactions to Luther: The First Year (1518)', *The Catholic Historical Review* 69 (4), 21–62.

[33] Luther, as noted in Skinner, Q (1978) *The Foundations of Modern Political Thought*, Vol II (Cambridge, Cambridge University Press) 11.

[34] Luther, 'The Freedom of a Christian Man', as reproduced in Hillerbrand, H (ed) (2009) *The Protestant Reformation* (NYC, Harper) 3; Luther's 'Invocavit Sermons', ibid, at 29–37. Also Luther, 'The Babylonian Captivity of the Church', reproduced in Elmer, P (ed) (2000) *The Renaissance in Europe: An Anthology* (London, Yale University Press) 323.

[35] Luther, in Skinner, Q (1978) *The Foundations of Modern Political Thought*, Vol II (Cambridge, Cambridge University Press) 13.

[36] Luther, 'Address to the Christian Nobility of the German Nation', in Webster, D (ed) (1969) *Documents in Renaissance and Reformation History* (Sydney, Cassell) 143.

[37] Edwards, M (1995) 'Printing, Propaganda and Martin Luther', *Theological Studies* 56 (1), 188–203.

burning the papal bull and defending his work with the assertion that 'they [the papacy] make monkeys and fools of the world, and define the terms "Christian" and "heretic" to suit themselves'.[38] He added, 'it is time the glorious Teutonic people should cease to be the puppet of the Roman pontiff'.[39] A few months later, in 1521, at the *Diet of Worms*, Luther, in a clear trial of conscience, defended himself further when he was asked if he would revoke his writings:

> I believe neither in popes nor in councils alone, since it is known that they have often erred and contradicted themselves. I remain committed to the passages I have cited from Scripture and my conscience is captive to the Word of God. I cannot and I will not recant anything, for to act against the dictates of conscience is neither right nor safe. Here I stand. I can do nothing else. God help me.[40]

In May 1521, the papal envoy asked the Holy Roman Emperor, Charles V, in accordance with the *Edict of Worms* that followed the debate and Pope Leo's edict, *Decet Romanum Pontificem*, excommunicating Luther, that Luther be outlawed and dealt with like all heretics. Pope Leo expected a positive response from Charles, as the Emperor had promised in his Imperial Coronation oath at Aachen in 1520, to keep and advance the Catholic faith, to protect the Church and show due obedience to the Pope, and he also personally disliked Luther for what Charles saw as his impudent attitudes to tradition and established positions. The problem was that although Charles acted against heresy in the areas he directly controlled, he only indirectly controlled the area in which Luther was active. Charles had walked away from the goals of a unified control of the type his grandfather, Maximilian I, envisaged with the *Reichstag* (Imperial Diet). In this part of the world, Charles would only call diets on an ad hoc basis, and had to accept that he had limited power in some places, such as Saxony, which was governed by Frederick the Wise. The Elector of Saxony was determined to protect the popular Luther, and to save Saxony money by cutting the competition with the local and regional Catholic churches. Frederick thus gave Luther sanctuary, after which Luther returned to wider society in Germany in 1522, having translated the *New Testament* into German, and drafted a program of reforms for churches in Germany.[41]

[38] Luther, 'Defence and Explanation of all the Articles Which Dr Martin Luther Was Unjustly Condemned', reproduced in Elmer, P (ed) (2000) *The Renaissance in Europe: An Anthology* (London, Yale University Press) 317.

[39] Luther, reproduced in Reddaway, F (ed) (1930) *Select Documents in European History*, Vol II (London, Methuen) 44; Luther, 'On Government Authority', as in Hillerbrand, H (ed) (2009) *The Protestant Reformation* (NYC Harper) 43–55.

[40] 'Luther at the Diet of Worms' (1521), as in Reddaway F (ed) (1930) *Select Documents in European History*, Vol II (London, Methuen) 45; Archibald, Y (2003) 'Martin Luther and Thomas More: Two Trials of Conscience', *Moreana* 40, 153, 173–89; Smith, J (1923) 'Concluding Words of Luther's Speech at the Diet of Worms', *Catholic Historical Review* 9, 647–57.

[41] Maltby, W (2002) *The Reign of Charles V* (London, Palgrave) 27, 43–46, 80–82; Elton, G (ed) (1968) *The New Cambridge Modern History: The Reformation*, Vol II (Cambridge, Cambridge University Press) 320, 440–43; Cowie, L (ed) (1970) *The Reformation of the Sixteenth Century* (London, Wayland) 27–28.

6. THE PEASANTS' WAR

Before Luther's work could proceed much further, rebellions by peasants broke out in Germany. These were much more extensive than those in Castile a few years earlier.[42] In Germany, not only there were more pronounced economic and political inequalities but religious discontent was also bubbling. Large numbers of common people were serfs (*servii*), which meant that although they were not slaves, their persons were unfree, being tied to the land. These people and the communities they came from had few recognised rights to representation, petition or legal redress when they were abused. Their discontent, manifested as armed violence, would reappear on an ad hoc basis throughout the sixteenth century in Northern and Eastern Europe. It appears to have begun in the fifteenth century in Swabia and the Upper Rhine in 1449 and 1459, and then broke out again in 1462 and 1478 in the Tyrol and Carinthia. Much of this unrest was stirred by the rhetoric of preachers such as Hans Boheim, who was arrested and burned at the stake in 1476 after arguing:

> Princes, civic and ecclesiastical, ought to possess no more than common folk, and then all would have plenty. The time will come when princes and nobles will have to labour for a day's wage. Everyone would then be his neighbor's brother. The fish in the water and the game upon the land ought to be common ...[43]

In Germany, major uprisings occurred in 1493 in Alsace, and at Spires in 1502, before the actual 'Peasants' War' erupted in 1524, raging across the Black Forest and Upper Swabia, Franconia, Thuringia, Alsace and the Alpine lands (the Tyrol, Salzburg and Austria). Over 300,000 people would be killed, and a further 150,000 or more would flee to Switzerland, in a conflict that would be the largest popular uprising until the French Revolution in 1789. The difference from other uprisings, in either Spain or Hungary, was that in Germany the revolt was not only a reaction against ever more restrictive feudal institutions, it was also anti-clerical.[44]

Although each region had its own particular concerns, there was a considerable overlap between them. This was made evident in the *Twelve Articles of the Upper Peasants of Swabia* of 1525. This document, as drafted by Sebastian Lotzer, which went on to be utilised in a number of interim peace treaties before the rebels were finally defeated, was the blueprint for most of the revolutionary documents prepared throughout the regions.[45] In addition to considerations of religious autonomy, the *Twelve Articles*

---

[42] See page 50.

[43] Hans Boheim, as noted in MacKinnon, J (1906) *A History of Modern Liberty*, Vol I (London, Longmans) 172; Greengrass, M (2015) *Christendom Destroyed: Europe 1517–1648* (NYC, Penguin) 82–85.

[44] Scott, T (2002) 'The German Peasants War and the Crisis of Feudalism', *Journal of Early Modern History* 6 (3), 265–95; Laube, A (1987) 'Social Arguments in Early Reformation Pamphlets and Their Significance for the German Peasants' War', *Social History* 12 (3), 361–78. Also MacKinnon, J (1906) *A History of Modern Liberty*, Vol I (Longmans, London) 169; ibid, Vol II, 98–100.

[45] 'The Territorial Constitution for the Tirol', as in Scott, T (ed and trans) (1991), *The German Peasants War* (NYC, Humanity Books) 265–67, the Treaty of Miltenberg at 281–82, and the Treaty of Ortenau at 284–88; Baylor, G (ed and trans) (1991) *The Radical Reformation* (Cambridge, Cambridge University Press) 95–129.

demanded a number of measures to limit the power of the members of the ruling classes. Specifically:

[3] It has hitherto been the custom for the lords to treat us as their serfs ... [but] ... it is demonstrated by Scripture that we are free and wish to be free. Not that we wish to be completely free and have no authority, for God does not teach that ... [but that] as true and genuine Christians, you will gladly release us from serfdom.

[4] No poor man had been empowered or permitted to catch game, wildfowl or fish ... we consider this quite improper and unbrotherly ...

[5] We are also aggrieved about woodcutting, for our lords have appropriated the woods.

[6] Our grievous burden of labour services, which are increased from day to day in amount and variety, we request a proper investigation in order that we be not so heavily burdened.

[7] Lords should not force or compel [peasants] in any way by asking for more services without recompense.

[8] Lords should fix fair rents.

[9] Punishment should be imposed according to the old written penalties, according to the circumstances, and not with partiality.

[10] Some have appropriated meadows or arable [land] that once belonged to the community. We wish to restore those to common ownership unless they have been properly purchased.[46]

The anti-clerical element present in most of the rebellions in Germany overlapped strongly with the revolutionary attitudes of some of the leaders. Most notably, Thomas Muntzer invoked apocalyptic visions, calling for direct rebellion against all authority, with the goal to create a more just and equitable social order. Before he was captured and executed, Muntzer argued that 'the sword is necessary as a means to destroy the Godless ... Godless rulers, especially the priests and monks, should be killed'.[47]

Martin Luther entered into the debate. Luther, who was keen to support those who gave him protection from the papacy, argued in opposition to Muntzer. Although Luther had a certain sympathy with some of the demands of the peasants, advising the Princes and Lords to treat their subjects with reason, restraint and a degree of equity, he still believed that the peasants had to accept the tyranny of the temporal authorities because '[t]he fact that there are rulers who are wicked and unjust does not excuse the tumult and rebellion, for to punish wickedness does not belong to everyone, but to the worldly rulers who bear the sword'.[48]

---

[46] The Twelve Articles of the Peasants of Swabia, in Elmer, P (ed) (2000) *The Renaissance in Europe: An Anthology*. (London, Yale University Press) 341–47; Scott, *The German Peasants' War* ibid, 65–95.

[47] See Thomas Muntzer, 'Sermon before the Princes', as reproduced in Elton, G (ed) (1968) *Renaissance and Reformation* (London, Macmillan) 166–68. Also Muntzer's, 'A Protest about the Conditions of the Bohemians', as reproduced in Baylor, G (ed and trans) (1991) *The Radical Reformation* (Cambridge, Cambridge University Press) 1–10; his 'Highly Provoked Defence Against Luther' is in the same volume, at 74–94. Also Scott, T (ed and trans) (1991) *The German Peasants' War* (NYC, Humanity Books) 96–114, 238, 251–53, 265–67; Kuenning, P (1987) 'Luther and Muntzer: Contrasting Theologies in Regard to Secular Authority Within the Context of the German Peasant Revolt', *Journal of Church and State* 29 (2), 305–21.

[48] Luther (1525), 'A Friendly Admonition to Peace Concerning the Twelve Articles of the Swabian Peasants', as reproduced in Hillerbrand, H (ed) (2009) *The Protestant Reformation* (NYC, Harper) 73.

Luther added that equality between people was not consistent with the Scriptures, 'for a worldly kingdom cannot stand unless there is in it an inequality of persons'.[49] He stated that whilst it was unlawful for a peasant to rise up against his master, it was lawful for a master to kill a peasant, 'like a mad dog', because

> [i]f the peasant is in open rebellion, then he is outside the law of God, for rebellion is not simply murder, but it is like a great fire which attacks and lays waste a whole land ... [N]othing can be more poisonous, hurtful or devilish than a rebel.[50]

With such support, after the military forces of the establishment finally organised themselves and acted cooperatively, all of the German peasants' uprisings were eventually crushed, along with all of their demands. There was no final peace treaty. Serfdom remained an established practice, at the discretion of each local lord to apply or not, and as the official Diet at Speyer in 1526 warned:

> All subjects shall henceforth conduct themselves obediently, loyally, and peacefully towards their authorities, whether secular or ecclesiastical, perform what is prescribed by their oaths and obligations, and not give cause for their own ruin and disorder.[51]

7. The Influence of Luther

Up until this point, Luther's work had only been a matter of theological debate. After the Peasants' War, it became a matter of political debate. By 1526, Augsburg, Hanover and Frankfurt, and a host of smaller cities, like Nuremberg and Bremen, after arguing over whether uniformity of religion or local autonomy was the best choice, agreed that each prince 'is to live, govern, and bear himself as he hopes and trusts to answer to God and his imperial majesty'.[52] The following year, in 1527, Christian II, the King of Denmark (and brother-in-law of Emperor Charles V) affirmed that 'the Christian faith is free' and that neither Catholics nor Lutherans were to be 'forced to renounce their faith.'[53]

---

[49] Luther (1525), 'A Friendly Admonition' *ibid*, 67–68, 83.

[50] Luther, *Against the Robbing and Murdering Hordes of Peasant* in Cowie, L (ed) (1970) *The Reformation of the Sixteenth Century* (London, Wayland) 31; Luther, 'On Secular Authority' in Hopel, H (ed) (1991) *Luther and Calvin on Secular Authority* (Cambridge, Cambridge University Press) 29, 39; Skinner, Q (1978) *The Foundations of Modern Political Thought*, Vol II (Cambridge, Cambridge University Press) 82; Carlyle, AJ (1910) *A History of Medieval Political Theory in the West*, Vol VI (London, Blackwood) 275–79; MacKinnon, J (1906) *A History of Modern Liberty*, Vol II (London, Longmans) 49, 78.

[51] 'Recess of the Imperial Diet, 1526', as reproduced in Scott, T (ed and trans) (1991) *The German Peasants' War* (NYC, Humanity Books) 314–17, also at 53, 170–96; MacKinnon, J (1906) *A History of Modern Liberty*, Vol II (London, Longmans) 100–03, 106–07; Sea, T (2007) 'The German Princes' Responses to the Peasants' Revolt of 1525', *Central European History* 40 (2), 219–40.

[52] The Declaration of 1526, as noted in Elton, G (1968) *The New Cambridge Modern History: The Reformation*, Vol II (Cambridge, Cambridge University Press) 92, also at 76, 150–59.

[53] Christian II, as reproduced in Elton, G (1968) *The New Cambridge Modern History: The Reformation*, Vol II (Cambridge, Cambridge University Press) 137; Moller, J (2013) 'Lutheran Orthodoxy and Anti-Catholicism in Denmark', *European Studie* 31, 165–89; Sawyer, P (1997) *Medieval Scandinavia* (London, Minnesota University Press) 74–78; Bonney, R (2012) *The European Dynastic States* (Oxford, Oxford University Press) 30, 32, 244.

Charles V's influence at this point, in either the Nordic countries or Germany, was minimal, as he was battling the papacy and the French in Italy on the one hand, and having to deal with the rise of the Ottomans on the other. This meant that many of the key decisions fell to his brother, Ferdinand. The only thing that the Catholics and Lutherans could agree upon was that Anabaptists (re-baptisers)—those who made adult baptism on profession of their faith and argued for a simplified and decentral-ised church, with common property, polygamy and pacifism at its core—were a threat to all and needed to be severely prosecuted. The Anabaptists' early leaders, such as Hans Huth (the role model for the Pied Piper in the German folk legend) and Baltasar Hubmaier, and their followers were all captured and killed, with no fewer than 30,000 Anabaptists being put to death in Holland and Friesland alone.[54]

The emerging Lutherans and associated religious groups were not advocating for freedom of conscience of anyone but themselves. Other Luther-influenced giants, such as Ulrich Zwingli in Zurich and John Calvin in Geneva, strove to create conservative, self-governing, religious theocracies, in which violence would be used to condemn those who challenged the rules or dogma, as the great scholar Michel Servetus found out, paying with his life for his alleged blasphemy, having written against the dogma of the trinity. Likewise, the hunting of witches was the same in both Catholic and Lutheran (soon to become Protestant) regions, as was intolerance towards Jewish communities.[55]

Aside from their mutual hatred of Anabaptists, nothing else could be agreed between the Catholics and the Lutherans. Originally, in 1526, due to the need for German sol-diers to fight the Ottomans, Charles V had agreed to the holding of a general coun-cil to look at many of the questions that Luther was raising, such as dogma, church rites, free preaching and the organisation of the Church. Until this council was held, and as troops arrived from Germany to help on the eastern frontier against the Otto-mans, Ferdinand, Charles's brother, promised that '[everyone] would live, act and rule their subjects in such wise as each one thought right before God and his imperial majesty'.[56] However, when the next Diet was convened in 1529 at Speyer, the major-ity condemned the 1526 idea that each state could determine its own religion, as this would be detrimental to the established order. The minority at Speyer, comprising six princes and the representatives of 14 imperial cities, signed a Protestation against the

[54] For the theologies of the three groups that made up the Anabaptists, see the 1527 'Schleitheim Confession of Faith', as in Hillerbrand, H (ed) (2009) *The Protestant Reformation* (NYC, Harper) 129–37. Also Friedman, R (1940) 'Conception of the Anabaptists', *Church History* 9 (4). 341–65; Smolin, D (1997) 'Anabaptist and Lutheran Perspectives on the Sword', *Journal of Legal Education* 47 (1), 28–38. For the recom-mendation of drowning Anabaptists, see Ulrich Zwingli, 'The Swiss Reformers', in Reddaway, F (ed) (1930) *Select Documents in European History*, Vol II (London, Methuen) 64–65.

[55] Bury, J (2007) *Freedom of Thought: A History* (NYC, Prometheus) 64–65; Levack, B (1995) *The Witch Hunt in Early Modern Europe* (NYC, Longman) 4–5, 20–22, 53–59, 6–63, 102–06, 180–90; Bainton, R (1936) 'Servetus and the Genevan Libertines', *Church History* 5 (2), 141–49; For Zwingli, see *On Church and State*, as in Webster, D (ed) (1969) *Documents in Renaissance and Reformation History* (Sydney, Cassell) 158; for Calvin, *On the Authority of Civil Government*, ibid, at 151–53; and *On Christian Discipline*, at 154–56. Ulrich Zwingli, 'An Exposition of the Faith', as in Elton, G (ed) (1968) *Renaissance and Reformation* (London, Macmillan) 115–20.

[56] Ferdinand, as quoted in Fischer, A (1954) 'Ottoman Imperialism and the Lutheran Struggle for Rec-ognition in Germany, 1520–1529', *Church History* 23 (1), 46, 57–58.

majority view. This stated, 'our great and urgent needs require us openly to protest against the said resolution [to put an end to innovation in religion] … as being … null and void, and, so far as we ourselves and our people, one and all, are concerned, not binding'.[57] They added:

> In matters which concern God's honour and the salvation and eternal life of our souls, everyone must stand and give account before God for himself … [I]n matters of religion … we live [and] govern … ourselves …[58]

The signatories were thereafter called *Protestants*. The Catholic majority remained unmoved, and drew up a resolution in which they insisted that the 1521 *Edict of Worms*, outlawing the Lutheran heresy, should be imposed forthwith. The difficulty for Charles V was twofold. First, the *Augsburg Confession* was agreed the following year in 1530, under which the Lutheran Church settled its theological core, to which a number of German rulers and free cities pledged their allegiance at the Diet of Augsburg.[59] Secondly, it was becoming apparent to the Emperor Charles that a collective Germany was becoming an impossibility, as a result of which he abolished the Imperial Diet in 1530, following which it would remain in abeyance until 1648. Charles's reasoning was that, rather than dealing with the problem collectively, he would deal with it region by region. For example, in the Netherlands, Charles ordered the passing of the 1531 Imperial Edict, which stipulated:

> We decree that no one … shall print or write, sell or buy, distribute, read, preach, teach, maintain or defend, or argue publicly or secretly … with the books, writings or doctrines of Luther, Wyclif, Huss, Marsiglio or Padua … and no-one is to dispute about the Holy Scripture except theologians approved by a famous university. Offenders if relapsed are to be burned; if not, men to be beheaded and women drowned.[60]

As these matters were evolving, war broke out in Switzerland between the Catholics and the leading Protestant reformer, Ulrich Zwingli. Zwingli, who had come to gain control over Zurich and associated regions that were sympathetic to Protestants, decided that the five cantons that had executed Protestant preachers as heretics, should be taught a lesson. He warned, 'we thirst for no man's blood, but we will cut the nerves off the [Catholic] oligarchy. If we shun war, the truth of the gospel … will never be secure

---

[57] As in Cohen, M (ed) (2004) *History in Quotations* (London, Cassell) 358.

[58] The 'Protestants' of 1529, as in Reddaway, F (ed) (1930) *Select Documents in European History*, Vol II (London, Methuen) 57. The full story of this event can be found in Miller, N (2012) *The Religious Roots of the First Amendment: Dissenting Protestants and the Separation of Church and State* (Oxford, Oxford University Press).

[59] The 'Confession of Augsburg', 1530, as reproduced in Reddaway, F (ed) (1930) *Select Documents in European History*, Vol II (London, Methuen) 59; Spitz, L (1980) 'The Augsburg Confession: 450 years of History', *The Sixteenth Century Journal* 11 (3), 3–9; Rupp, G (1980) 'The Augsburg Confession, 1530', *The Expository Times* 91 (4), 127–37.

[60] The 'Imperial Edict in the Netherlands' (1531), as in Reddaway, F (ed) (1930) *Select Documents in European History*, Vol II (London, Methuen) 59; Curtis, B (2013) *The Habsburgs* (London, Bloomsbury) 60–61; Maltby, W (2002) *The Reign of Charles V* (London, Palgrave) 51; Dickens, A (1965) *Reformation and Society* (London, Thames) 35–40, 61, 74–78, 87–88, 158–64.

among us'.[61] Zwingli then directed his forces to erect a blockade around the opposing cantons. The five cantons replied by declaring war on Zurich, and Zwingli found that his devout faith was not enough to save him, or his 2,500 men, from the larger force of 8,000 Catholics. Despite this victory, there was no serious effort at a counter-reformation at this time. The *Treaty of Cappel* that followed anticipated the *Peace of Augsburg* by a quarter of a century, allowing each canton to decide its own religion, except in the reformed areas, where the Catholic minorities were to be protected. Protestant preaching in the Catholic cantons was forbidden.[62]

Fearing that such a conflict could also break out in Germany, the Protestants, following Saxony's lead, agreed to the compact that formed the Schmalkaldic League in 1531, so named after the town of Schmalkalden on the border between Saxony and Hesse where the League assembled. This agreement saw the signatories come together

> solely for the sake of our own defence and deliverance, which by both human and divine right is permitted to everyone ... [W]henever any one of us attacked on account of the Word of God and the doctrine of the Gospel, or anything connected therewith, all others shall immediately come to his assistance.[63]

The shared commitment to a military defence of members of the Schmalkaldic League was significant, as this reflected the fundamental change in Luther's original belief that the use of force against those in authority was not permissible, to one whereby the use of force against established authority might be legitimate in some situations, such as when a ruler became a tyrant, not allowing freedom of conscience, or committed atrocious and notorious injuries against his citizens. Luther, who had earlier spoken in defence of the use of force against rebellious peasants, in 1526 explained to the soldiers, who had to fight in all conflicts, that the use of force was legitimate within his theology. Thus:

> You would not be doing it with the purpose of avenging yourself or returning evil for evil, but for the good of your neighbor and for the maintenance of the safety and peace of others. For yourself, you would abide by the gospel and govern yourself according to Christ's word, gladly turning the other cheek.[64]

Therefore,

> if worldly rulers call upon them to fight, then they ought to and must fight and be obedient, not as Christians, but as members of the state and obedient subjects. Christians therefore do

---

[61] Ulrich Zwingli, as noted in MacKinnon, J (1906) *A History of Modern Liberty*, Vol II (London, Longmans) II: 140.

[62] Dickens, A (1965) *Reformation and Society* (London, Thames) 122–24; Elton, G (ed) (1968) *The New Cambridge Modern History: The Reformation*, Vol II (Cambridge, Cambridge University Press) 102–04; Weart, S (1998) *Never At War: Why Democracies Will Not Fight Each Other* (New Haven, CT, Yale University Press) 95–97.

[63] The 'Schmalkaldic League' (1531) as in Reddaway, F (ed) (1930) *Select Documents in European History*, Vol II (London, Methuen) 59; Ocker, C (2010) 'The Birth of an Empire of Two Churches: Church Property, Theologians and the League of Schmalkalden', *Austrian History Yearbook* 41, 48–67; Gilmore, M (1952) *The World of Humanism* (NYC, Harper) 106.

[64] Luther, as quoted in Miller, G (2007) 'Wars of Religion and Religion in War: Luther and the 16th Century Islamic Advance into Europe', *Seminary Ridge Review* 9 (2), 38, 48.

not fight as individuals or for their own benefit, but as obedient servant of the authorities under whom they live.[65]

Luther later added that opposing 'murderers and blood thirsty Papists'[66] would be acting in lawful and legitimate self-defence. Thus, in as much as Luther came to accept that fighting against the Ottomans was lawful and correct (as it was a war of defence against aggressors who were disturbing the peace), so too was acting in self-defence against those who threatened violence to enforce Catholicism. Luther, in a letter to English king, Henry VIII (with whom he had strong differences of opinion), summed up the situation thus:

> My dogmas will stand, and the pope will fall ... They have challenged me to war: well, they shall have war: they have contemptuously rejected the peace I offered them; they shall have no peace. God will see which of us will soonest cry quarter, the pope or I ...[67]

The Protestants, aware that they shared an enemy with the French, reached out for help in their battle against the Emperor Charles V. The French king, Francis I, despite having no love for the Protestants (he had approved the first burning of a Lutheran in 1523, as a somewhat indifferent persecutor), agreed to support them in Germany, the Protestants in return paid him a subsidy and allowed Francis to occupy the towns of Cambraie, Metz, Toul and Verdun. In light of this emerging coalition, in 1532, at the Diet of Nuremburg, and in need of military support to fight the Ottomans, Charles V agreed to promise toleration for Protestants in Germany and not force the issue until a general council could be held. This promise of imperial peace, 'until the council' (what became the Council of Trent, below) could address the divisive matters, allowed the Protestants to join the fight against the Ottomans.[68]

8. WAR IN GERMANY

As the war against the Ottomans continued, in Europe two trends were developing. First, the theological arm of the Counter-Reformation, as the counter-strike against Luther came to be known, emerged. This began with Pope Paul III, who established a commission in 1536 that was tasked to examine the state of the Catholic Church and questions of theology, with particular regard to how it differed from that espoused by Protestants. The report condemned abuses in the Church and described 'innumerable

---

[65] Luther, as quoted in Miller, G (2007) 'Wars of Religion and Religion in War: Luther and the 16th Century Islamic Advance into Europe', *Seminary Ridge Review* 9 (2), 48.

[66] Luther, as noted in Bonney, R (2012) *The European Dynastic States* (Oxford, Oxford University Press) 33.

[67] Luther, 'Letter to Henry VIII', as in Reddaway, F (ed) (1930) *Select Documents in European History*, Vol II (London, Methuen) 49; Corey, D (2011) 'Luther and the Just War Tradition', *Political Theology* 12 (2), 305–28; Johnson, J (2003) 'Aquinas and Luther on War and Peace: Sovereign Authority and the Use of Force', *The Journal of Religious Ethics* 31 (1), 3–20.

[68] Knecht, R (2007) *The Valois* (London, Hambledon) 149; Elton, G (1968) *The New Cambridge Modern History: The Reformation*, Vol II (Cambridge, Cambridge University Press) 164–67.

scandals and ... contempt for holy orders'.[69] Pope Paul III responded via three mechanisms. First, he initiated a plan to try to revive and rebuild the integrity of the Catholic Church, in addition to clarifying how it differed from the beliefs of the Protestants, by calling a general council of the Church. Secondly, Pope Paul III approved the devout new religious order of the Society of Jesus (the Jesuits), as founded by Ignatius Loyola, a former soldier who had earlier fought against the French. This Society and its members all professed vows of poverty, chastity and loyalty, including a special vow of obedience to the Pope in matters of direction and assignment. Lastly, Pope Paul brought the Inquisition to Italy to help confront the problem of Protestant teaching, although in time the Inquisition also ensnared Jews, homosexuals, people accused of practising witchcraft and many of those who threatened the status quo with new ideas, such as Galileo. No fewer than three grand inquisitors went on to become Pope. Within Rome alone, at least 50,000 formal trials were conducted over the following 300 years, as a result of which, throughout the entire peninsular, some 1,250 citizens would be executed.[70]

The second trend that developed was that the Emperor Charles V found clarity as to what action he believed was needed. This process began with the 1539 *Treaty of Frankfurt*, which agreed a 15-month truce between the Emperor and Protestants, during which period both parties tried to resolve their differences peacefully. The German Protestants were doubly inclined to agree to this process, as by this stage, the French king, Francis I, had ended his alliance with them. However, when the Protestants and Catholics, including the Emperor Charles V, eventually met in 1541 at Regensburg, staunchly opposing theological disputes on the sacraments and papal authority meant that only the most bland of agreements could be reached, and both the Pope and Luther distanced themselves even from this. Whilst discussions over the mass ended in unity, the parties' views on confession, absolution and satisfaction, and Church government remained irreconcilable for both Protestant and Catholic alike. By this stage, Charles V recognised that imperial unity could only be restored by force. Accordingly, he finally moved his armies down the Rhine in preparation for war. The refusal of the Protestants to attend further discussions on theological differences and possible reconciliation in forums (in what became the Council of Trent, below) that were being established by Pope Paul III, reinforced Charles's determination of to use force to end religious differences and restore unit to Germany. He explained:

> If we failed to intervene now, all of the Estates of Germany would be in danger of breaking with the faith ... After considering this and considering it again, I decided to embark on war against Hesse and Saxony as transgressors of the peace against the Duke of Brunswick and his territory. And although this pretext will not long disguise the fact that it is a matter of religion, yet it serves for the present to divide the renegades.[71]

[69] Bonney, R (2012) *The European Dynastic States* (Oxford, Oxford University Press) 57.

[70] Murphy, C (2011) *God's Jury: The Inquisition and the Making of the Modern World* (London, Penguin) 11, 104–05, 131; Gleason, E (1995) 'Who Was the First Counter-Reformation Pope?', *Catholic Historical Review* 81 (2), 173–87.

[71] Charles V, as noted in Bonney, R (2012) *The European Dynastic States* (Oxford Oxford University Press) 118; Mackenzen, H (1958) 'The Diplomatic Role of Gasparo Cardinal Contarini at the Colloquy of

The Emperor then made peace with the French, secured Danish neutrality (through the 1544 *Treaty of Speyer*) and managed to induce one significant Protestant leader (Maurice, Elector of Saxony) to embrace his cause. He then outlawed the remaining Protestant princes for their disputed occupation of land of others. Pope Paul III joined the alliance against the Protestants, for which he sent men and money. Although he justified the use of force to extirpate heresy in Germany, he did not classify it as a Crusade. In reply, the Protestants, as galvanised through the Schmalkaldic League and in the form 50,000 men, 7,000 cavalry and 110 pieces of artillery, declared war on Charles V in 1546. They believed that without recourse to violence, the 'pure doctrine of gospel, our true Christian religion, and the Augsburg Confession'[72] were in danger of suppression. The Protestants claimed the right to self-defence against a force that they claimed was neither lawful nor deserving of obedience. However, their military forces were unable to deliver their religious rhetoric promising victory on the field of battle, as the imperial forces routed the League's forces at the Battle of Mühlberg the following year, with over 7,000 of the League being killed or wounded, and a further 1,000 taken prisoner, compared with the loss of only a few hundred of the Emperor's men.[73]

In the following surrender, 30 different Protestant cities were to return to Catholicism, and the integrity of the core of the Empire in Germany was to be restored. However, two cities, Bremen and Magdeburg, continued to resist. Undeterred, Charles laid down rules for the government of the Christian churches in his dominions, until a free and general council (the Council of Trent) could pronounce on the outstanding theological questions. The rules formed an 'Interim', which made a few concessions to the Protestants but outlawed the Lutheran Church throughout the Empire. Charles's ruling was proclaimed in 1548 at Augsburg, and was meant to remain in place whilst the Council of Trent, which had begun its work in 1545, was in session.[74]

The peace that Charles V hoped would ensue was broken by the new French king, Henri II, the son of Francis I. Henri hated Charles V, as he had been his hostage following his father's capture by the Emperor and after Francis defaulted on his promises in breach of the *Treaty of Madrid*.[75] He schemed incessantly to topple his enemy. When he succeeded to the French throne in 1547, the Venetian ambassador reported, 'not one single province [of France] was uncontaminated [by Calvinism]'.[76] In spite of his

Ratisbon of 1541', *Church History* 27 (4), 312–37; Dickens, A (1965) *Reformation and Society* (London, Thames) 74–75, 82–83, 98–99; Maltby, W (2002) *The Reign of Charles V* (London, Palgrave) 49, 62–65.

[72] As noted in Elton, G (1987) *Politics and Society in Reformation Europe* (Oxford, Oxford University Press) 321.

[73] Skinner, Q (1978) *The Foundations of Modern Political Thought*, Vol II (Cambridge, Cambridge University Press) 201–02; Close, C (2009) 'Augsburg, Zurich and the Transfer of Preachers Duuring the Schmalkadic War', *Central European History* 42 (4), 595–619; Bonney, R (2012) *The European Dynastic States* (Oxford, Oxford University Press) 118, 119.

[74] See 'The Interim of Charles V' (1548), as reproduced in Reddaway, F (ed) (1930) *Select Documents in European History*, Vol II (London, Methuen) 63–64; Kaufmann, T (2004) 'Our Lord's Chancery: Magdeburg and its Fights Against the Interim', *Church History* 73 (3), 566–82.

[75] See pages 52–53.

[76] Report by the Venetian Ambassador (1561), as reproduced in Webster, D (ed) (1969) *Documents in Renaissance and Reformation History* (Sydney, Cassell) 159.

hatred of Protestants, Henri supported Protestant forces in other countries through committing to the *Treaty of Chambord* in 1552 with three German Protestant princes, who jointly agreed to wage war against Charles V. The deal provided military and economic aid, in exchange for the areas of Toul, Verdun and Metz. The French then helped force the armies of the Emperor Charles out of Germany and into Italy, as well as waging war against Charles in the New World by sending naval forces across the Atlantic to attack both Havana and Purto Rico.[77]

9. THE PEACE OF AUGSBURG

Realising he was over-stretched, Charles V opted for peace with the Protestant princes in Germany at Passau in 1552. The freedom of the Lutheran faith was recognised in some parts, and the prisoners taken during the Schmalkaldic War were released. This ended all of Charles hopes for religious unity within his empire. It was particularly important that Charles should agree to this, as by this point, Protestant princes now enjoyed a majority in the imperial electoral system. Charles subsequently left Germany to its fate, leaving his brother, Ferdinand I, to attend the Diet at Augsburg in 1555, to 'act and settle' the overlapping disputes of territory, religion and local power.[78]

Ferdinand, the Archduke of Austria by birth, King of Hungary by election and treaty, and King of Bohemia by marriage, was a man familiar with the concept of having to make deals and compromises to achieve greater goals. In all of the realms he governed, he accepted limits on his power, acknowledging the rights of local authorities as the price for being the recognised ruler. In the case of Bohemia, this meant that he had already accepted the right of these peoples to practise their own Hussite faith, which was in direct conflict with the wishes of the Pope in Rome. These pragmatic views of Ferdinand affected the 1555 *Peace of Augsburg*, which ended the killing in Germany, despite the objections of the papacy to the peace and the fact that Ferdinand's brother, Charles V, did not want to deal with it. This treaty explicitly granted Lutheranism (all other Protestant sects being excluded) official status within the Holy Roman Empire under the principle of *Cuius regio, eius religion* ('whose realm, whose religion'). This meant that, apart from two exceptions,[79] the religion of the ruler defined the religion

---

[77] Elton, G (1968) *The New Cambridge Modern History: The Reformation* Vol II (Cambridge, Cambridge University Press) 11–12; Elliot, J (2002) *Imperial Spain* (London, Penguin) 209–11.

[78] Curtis, B (2013) *The Habsburgs* (London, Bloomsbury) 46–48, 59, 62–64; Knecht, R– (2007) *The Valois* (London, Hambledon) 185–89; the 1552 Treaty between Spain and Portugal is reproduced in Davenport, F (ed) (1917) *European Treaties Bearing on the History of the United States and its Dependencies to 1648* (NYC, Carnegie Institute) 205–14.

[79] The first exception was the *Declaratio Ferdinandei*, which exempted knights and some of the cities of the jurisdiction of a prince if they had practised Lutheranism for some time, came to cause a significant degree of debate in some Catholic areas, but the peace held. The second exception was the *reservatum ecclesasticum*, which meant that if the prelate of an ecclesiastical state changed his religion, the people living in that state did not have to do so. It was expected that the prelate would resign his post.

of the state's inhabitants. The Peace, which in essence granted more autonomy to the cities, stated:

> In order to bring peace into the Holy Empire of the Germanic nation … let neither his Imperial Majesty or the Electors, Princes … do any violence or harm to any estate of the Empire on account of the Augsburg confession, but let them enjoy their religious belief, liturgy and ceremonies … Likewise, the Estates espousing the Augsburg Confession shall let all the Estates and Princes who cling to the old religion live in absolute peace and in the enjoyment of all their estates, rights and privileges … No Estate shall try to persuade the subjects of other Estates to abandon their religion …[80]

Thereafter, in the Habsburg lands in Germany and Austria, the opposing denominations cooperated in relatively peaceful coexistence. Later in the century, Emperor Maximilian II facilitated this relationship, granting benefits and basic rights of equality, ranging from considerations based on tax through to public rights of worship, to the Protestants, if they would continue to provide troops to help fight the Ottomans on the eastern frontier.[81]

10. CONCLUSION

The religious connection as a cause of war was particularly strong in Europe throughout the period on which this volume focuses. Although there was an earlier history of discontent with and violence against the Catholic Church within Western Europe, the most well-known wars typically occurred in the sixteenth century. The background to these wars lay in the fifteenth century, when all of the elements of theological challenge, national discontent and a loosely knit Holy Roman Empire were present. The epicentre of discontent was the papacy, which had, following the Western Schism, shaken itself free of any form of overseeing bodies, thus holding absolute power. The first evidence of disquiet in this area for the period covered by this volume was the Hussite Wars, where direct disagreement with Rome overlapped with a strong drive for national autonomy. The significance of these wars and the peace that followed was that although the Hussites of Bohemia could be brought back within the existing political structure, this could be achieved only by allowing them to observe their own religious practices.

Martin Luther built arrived in this era, at a time when the Italian Wars and the increasingly the extreme nature of the papacy, in both theological and political terms.

---

[80] The 1555 'Religious Peace of Augsburg', as in Reddaway, F (ed) (1930) *Select Documents in European History: 1492–1715*, Vol II (London, Methuen) 64; Chrisholm, M (2008) 'The Religionspolitik of Emperor Ferdinand I', *European History Quarterly* 38 (4) 551–77; Dixon, S (2007) 'Order and Religious Coexistence in the German Imperial City: Augsburg', *Central European History* 40 (1), 117–73; Spitz, L (1956) 'Particularism and the Peace of Augsburg', *Church History* 25 (2), 110–26; Elton, G (1968) *The New Cambridge Modern History: The Reformation*, Vol II (Cambridge, Cambridge University Press) 467, 471, 513–15.

[81] Parker, G (1998) *The Thirty Years' War* (London, Routledge) 4–5.

Luther's teachings—in essence, that the intervention of the Catholic Church between Christians and God was not required—split Western Europe. However, before this split became apparent, the Peasants' War occurred in Germany. This, again, showing the discontent of the age, was driven by a desire to put an end to serfdom and improve the status and rights of the poorest people. The War failed to achieve any lasting success, being most notable for the fact that Luther came to support the established (non-Catholic) leaders, not the peasants. Thus, the revolution fathered by Luther was about changes in theological, not political, leadership.

When the theological and political leaderships were joined, war eventually broke out between the newly emerged Protestants and the traditional Catholics. This was especially evident in Switzerland and Germany. In both cases, peace was achieved not by outright domination, but by learning to tolerate different religious views in different regions, within a united country. This was a particularly difficult point to reach, as tolerance was not on the agenda of many leaders of this period: it tended to be based on pragmatic necessity, in that neither side could emphatically defeat the other. Neither Catholicism nor Protestantism was intrinsically tolerant of any teaching that was different to its own.

IV

Religion and Power in England

1. INTRODUCTION

THIS CHAPTER IS primarily about the influence of religion upon the English monarchs Henry VIII, Edward IV, Mary Tudor, Elizabeth I and James I. It is the first part of the context leading up to the English civil war. Although the conventional interests of all these monarchs overlapped in terms of gaining power and territory, and Parliament played a supplementary role for each of them (albeit becoming progressively stronger), overall the period 1520 to 1610 is about religion and the changes that saw England evolve from a Catholic to a Protestant country. In the course of this, religion as a cause of war went from being a relatively minor consideration at the beginning of the sixteenth century, to the dominant paradigm at the end of that century. Within this timeline, and especially in the reign of Elizabeth I, considerations of religion and the autonomy of England dominated the context.

2. HENRY VIII

A. Henry's Marriage to Catherine of Aragon and His 'Cleansing' of the Church in England

The papacy initially enjoyed very good relations with the English king, Henry VIII. Pope Leo X recognised Henry as 'Defender of the Faith' (*Fidei Defensor*—a subsidiary title still used by British monarchs to this day) in 1521 due to Henry's writings, particularly his *Defence of the Seven Sacraments* which was written in response to some of Martin Luther's attacks on the papacy. Pope Leo was also impressed by the zeal of influential men in Henry's court, such as Thomas More, the Lord Chancellor, who persecuted and burnt all heretics who questioned Catholicism, arguing that they should 'be kept for the fire, first here and then in hell'.[1]

---

[1] More, as noted in Mackie, J (1985) *The Early Tudors* (Oxford Clarendon) 196–201, 346–47, 355–58. Also Henry, A (2008) 'Thomas More on Inquisitorial Due Process', *The English Historical Review* 123 (503), 847–94.

The seed for the Reformation in England was planted in 1525, when Henry VIII became enamoured with Anne Boleyn, a lady-in-waiting to his queen, Catherine of Aragon. Within two years, Henry had decided that he wanted to divorce his wife and marry Anne. In addition to his desire for Anne, he also professed to believe that God had denied him a male heir from his marriage to Catherine (Although Catherine had had seven pregnancies, Catherine would give birth to only one child who survived past infancy—Mary Tudor. Henry believed he was denied a male heir because the union of a man and the wife of his brother was contrary to God's law (as stated in the Bible), and that therefore the papal dispensation granted by Pope Julius II in 1503, which allowed the then Prince Henry to marry his brother Arthur's widow, Catherine, was invalid. As he had been a good servant of the papacy, Henry expected that Rome would grant him his wish and allow him to marry whomever he wanted. There seemed no reason to expect difficulty as, quite apart from the good relations between the papacy and England, annulments of royal marriages were far from unheard of.[2]

The difficulties for the current pontiff, Pope Clement VII, were fourfold. First, Queen Catherine did not want to be divorced from Henry. Secondly, there were conflicting texts in the Bible that allowed such marriages between brothers, and to suggest that the dispensation from Julius II was wrong, was to suggest that the Pope had erred. This in itself was a direct challenge to the idea of papal authority. Thirdly, Henry had declared war on the Emperor Charles V. Henry's declaration of war followed the sack of Rome, due to Charles's attack on the Pope, his failure to resolve the Ottoman threat and his failure to pay money owed to Henry.[3] As Charles had forced that debt on to the French king Francis I, in the *Treaty of Madrid*,[4] the declaration of war came to nothing, although any good faith between the two monarchs dissipated at the very time it was needed. That is, the greatest problem for Henry was not theological but political, in that Rome was held by Charles V and the Pope was at the Emperor's mercy. It was not that Henry VIII was not a friend of Rome, but more that Rome needed to appease Charles V rather than Henry VIII. The fourth and last difficulty was that Charles V was Catherine of Aragon's nephew. Henry offered to return Catherine's dowry to Charles (worth some 300,000 crowns), but Charles replied that he was not a tradesman and his aunt's honour was not for sale. Pope Clement, desperately trying to secure his own pontificate and interests, did not want to provoke Charles. Accordingly, he tried to steer a middle course, arranging for a papal commission to examine the English king's request. This commission found against Henry, and thus Pope Clement VII refused to allow the King of England to annul his marriage to Catherine.[5]

---

[2] The biblical passages in question are Leviticus, xviii, 16; xx, 21, and Deuteronomy, xxv, 5. See 'Catherine of Aragon Defends Herself Before the Papal Legate, 1529', as in Millward, J (1961) *Sixteenth Century: Portraits and Documents* (Hutchinson, London) 51; Scarisbrick, J (1997) *Henry VIII* (London, Yale UP) 46–47, 150–67, 180, 185.

[3] See page 53.

[4] See pages 52–53.

[5] Zimmermann, P (1967) 'A Note on Clement VII and the Divorce of Henry VIII', *The English Historical Review* 82 (324), 548–56; Sharkey, J (2011) 'Between King and Pope: Thomas Wolsey', *Historical Research* 84 (224), 236–48.

Upon hearing the news in 1529 that his request to end his marriage had been refused, Henry summoned the greatest tool at his disposal, the English Parliament. This body was fully subservient to Henry, and allowed the king to spread a canopy of legal propriety over the radical initiatives he wanted to employ to curb the power of the Church in Rome in England. It was supplemented by the Star Chamber, which had by now evolved into a body that operated without the standard protections of the common courts, and which could be used against the enemies of the king.[6]

Henry wanted to undertake reform of apparent abuses in the English Catholic Church. Henry's process here began with a list of charges, based on abuses, that was drawn up against the bishops and many of the monasteries in England. After further requests for the annulment of his marriage to Catherine were refused in 1530 and 1532, Henry made the clergy promise they would never again make any new church law without first obtaining royal permission. In the same year (1532), he passed the *First Act of Annates*, which stopped payments from clergy in England to the Church in Rome. Henry then enacted the *Act in Restraint of Appeals*, which asserted that all English citizens were 'bounded and owe to bear, next to God, a natural and humble obedience' to the king, after which he decreed that no English person could be summoned to a Roman court, thus preventing Catherine of Aragon from appealing to the Pope against the annulment.

In 1533, Henry's marriage to Catherine of Aragon was annulled without the permission of the Pope, and Henry married Anne Boleyn, after his Parliament had found his first marriage 'definitely, clearly, and absolutely invalid'.[7] The *Act of Succession* was passed, under which Henry's daughter by Catherine, Mary, was declared illegitimate, Henry's marriage to Anne was declared legitimate and any children from the marriage with Anne was declared Henry's heir. Later that year, Anne bore Henry a daughter, Elizabeth.[8]

Pope Clement VII excommunicated Henry VIII (although this was a deferred sentence) and declared the annulment and Henry's remarriage void. Henry's Parliament replied with the *Second Act of Annates* of 1534, which made all ecclesiastical appointments dependent on the Crown (and not on the Pope) and stopped the flow of all taxes going to Rome, diverting them to the Crown. All dispensations and doctrine were to be determined by the king. The *Act of Supremacy* 1534 was then passed. This provided 'that the King our Sovereign Lord, his heirs and successors kings of this realm, shall be taken, accepted, and reputed the only Supreme Head in earth of the Church of

---

[6] Roberts, P (2007) 'Henry VIII, Francis I and the Reformation Parliament', *Parliament, Estates and Representation* 27 (1), 129–44; Pollard, A (1922) 'Council, Star Chamber and Privy Council Under the Tudors', *The English Historical Review* 37 (148), 516–39; Meyer, G (2011) *The Tudors* (NYC, Bantam) 47–55, 65–69, 71, 103, 140–42, 145–47.

[7] The Bill from 1533, in Scarisbrick, J (1997) *Henry VIII* (London, Yale University Press) 311, 331, 362–65, 400–01.

[8] The 1533 Act against Appeals to Rome, as in Elton, G (ed) (1968) *Renaissance and Reformation* (London, Macmillan) 198–99. The 1534 'Ecclesiastic Appointments Act' in Adams, M (ed) (1947) *Select Documents on English Constitutional Law* (London, Macmillan) 232–35; Bernard, G (2011) 'The Dissolution of the Monasteries', *History* 96 (324), 390–419.

England, called *Anglicana Ecclesia*.[9] As Supreme Head of the Church, Henry had 'full power and authority ... to visit, repress, redress, reform, order, correct, restrain and amend such all errors, heresies ... [and] abuses' as he saw fit, within all of the churches of England.[10]

Henry was not taking control of religion from the Pope and giving religious freedom to the Protestants but appropriating supremacy in religious matters in England to himself. This was a step too far for many of Henry's ministers: some 45 of Henry's senior advisers and ministers were executed for supporting the papacy and not accepting Henry's wishes in this matter. The most well-known of Henry's opponents was Sir Thomas More. Although More could accept some of Henry's actions, when required to take the *Oath of Supremacy* under the 1534 Act (above), acknowledging the king as the Supreme Head of the Church, More could not. This refusal was deemed treasonous. The specific charges for which Sir Thomas More was sentenced to death were (i) refusing to accept the king's supremacy; and (ii) stating that the *Act of Supremacy* was not legitimate, describing it as a double-edged sword that killed either the body or the soul. More considered his own death the price for 'the just necessity of his cause for the discharge of his conscience'.[11] The king then informed More that, as a special favour, he would allow him to be beheaded, rather than hanged, drawn and quartered, which was the usual punishment for treason. More's Catholic head was accompanied by a number of Protestant heads, as the crimes for which all these men and women were executed by Henry tended to involve denial of the absolute authority of the king and trifling offences such as opposing Henry's divorce from Catherine of Aragon (a traitorous act intended to 'disturb the peace and tranquility of the realm'), not which theological interpretation was correct.[12]

B. The Dissolution of the Monasteries

In 1536, Henry began the 'voluntary' dissolution of the English monasteries and the acquisition of their wealth. At that time there were some 600 monasteries across England, and 200 other houses, holding nearly 10,000 monks and 1,600 nuns. Having rooted out apparent abuses as part of his 'crusade' against Rome starting in 1529 (see above),

[9] The 1534 'Act of Supremacy', as in Cowie, L (ed) (1970) *The Reformation of the Sixteenth Century* (London, Wayland) 88–89; Skinner, Q (1978) *The Foundations of Modern Political Thought*, Vol II (Cambridge, Cambridge University Press) 67, 74.

[10] Rex, R (2014) 'The Religion of Henry VIII', *The Historical Journal* 57 (1), 1–23.

[11] More, T (1535) 'The Speech on Trial for His Life' in Barker, E (ed) (1955) *International University Reading Course* (London, International University Society) 6, 291–95. Also More, T 'True Faith and False Heresy' as reproduced in Elton, ibid. 71-72. The 1534 Treasons Act, in Adams, M (ed) (1947) *Select Documents on English Constitutional Law* (London, Macmillan) 240.

[12] Foley, M (2009) 'A Saint on Trial: Analysing the Condemnation of Sir Thomas More', *Moreana* 46 (176), 25–29; Watt, D (1997) 'The Political Prophecies of Elizabeth Barton, 1506–1534', *Renaissance Quarterly* 50 (1), 136–63.

the remaining 250 small monasteries were sequestrated after Henry found them full of 'manifest sin, viscous, carnal and abominable living … [which was causing] … high displeasure to Almighty God, slander of good religion, and to great infamy of the king's highness and the realm'.[13] As most of the senior clergy resettled into similar positions in the emerging new Church of England regime, initially there was not a lot of opposition in England to Henry's actions. However, in 1536—the year in which Henry executed his second wife, Anne Boleyn, for high treason, on charges including adultery, incest and plotting to kill the king—the Pilgrimage of Grace began, a pro-Catholic, anti-tyranny uprising against the English king's break with Rome, dissolution of the monasteries and other grievances. Although this rebellion was crushed and its leaders executed for treason, in Ireland, the implementation of Henry's policies was less contested. There, although there was some disquiet and debate over Henry's actions (the Earl of Desmond having signed a treaty with Charles V in 1534, declaring himself the vassal of the Emperor), in 1537 the Irish Parliament agreed to follow Henry, and suppressed 13 monasteries and 42 monastic communities. A tax was imposed on the clergy, and an oath, acknowledging the king's supremacy over the Church and abrogating papal jurisdiction in Ireland, was agreed.[14]

Pope Paul III had come to power in 1534. He implemented the excommunication of Henry VIII without reservation, and all of England was placed under interdict. As a result, all Catholic Church services in England were stopped and Henry's subjects were absolved by the Pope from obedience to their king. Any English who supported Henry and deserted the Catholic Church were threatened with slavery. These threats did not have the hoped effect. The people of England did not rise up against Henry, and the Continental powers did not apply sanctions nor threaten military intervention into England. Consequently, Henry continued on his course. The last of the monasteries were persuaded to surrender to the king, with the few remaining forcibly dissolved by an Act of Parliament in 1539, by which they were 'suppressed, renounced, relinquished, forfeited, given up, or by any other means to come to his highness'.[15] Those who opposed Henry's agents were often found dead. Henry then finished his work in this matter with the *Act of Six Articles* of 1539, which showed him to be occupying a theological middle ground, somewhere between Catholicism and Protestantism. Accordingly, the Protestant Reformation did not advance further under Henry VIII, but neither was it strangled. Henry went on to pass his *Act for the Advancement of True Religion*, in which all versions of the Bible that were not authorised were prohibited; and regarding those that were authorised, they could only be read by either the clergy

---

[13] The 1536 'Act for the Dissolution of the Lesser Monasteries', in Adams, *ibid*, 243.

[14] Bush, M (2007) 'The Tudor Polity and the Pilgrimage of Grace', *Historical Research* 80 (207), 42–72; Bernard, G (1991) 'The Fall of Anne Boleyn', *The English Historical Review* 106 (420), 584–94; Mackie, J (1985) *The Early Tudors* (Oxford, Clarendon) 428–34.

[15] The 1539 'Act for the Dissolution of the Greater Monasteries', as reproduced in Adams, M (ed) (1947) *Select Documents on English Constitutional Law* (London, Macmillan) 251. Also 'Commissioners Report on the Dissolution of the Monasteries', as reproduced in Millward, J (1961) *Sixteenth Century: Portraits and Documents* (London, Hutchinson) 58.

or nobles—they were not for public consumption. Standardised prayers and psalms, glorifying the actions and goals of Henry, who was compared to King David in the Bible, that is, as a king directly anointed by God, were then said and sung every Sunday throughout the kingdom.[16]

C. The Last Wars of Henry VIII

The last five years of the life of Henry VIII were spent engaged in war with France and her allies. Notably, although Henry's anger with the papacy had led to his breaking away from the Church in Rome, and although his violence inside England was often about religion, his more conventional wars were not. Rather, they were waged for the traditional reasons associated with monarchs of this period, namely, the acquisition of further power and/or the territory of others.

At this point, the forces of Ireland were not arrayed against him. In 1541, Henry VIII had himself crowned King of Ireland, and statutes to this effect were passed in the Irish Parliament. The proclamation stated that the (Anglo-Irish) realm 'should be united and annexed to our imperial crown of the realm of England' and that 'the King and his Successors be Kings of Ireland'.[17] To buttress his rule, Henry sent a new governor to Ireland to try to establish a measure of control over the whole country, through a policy known as 'surrender and re-grant', under which Gaelic chiefs agreed to recognise the authority of the English Crown in exchange for feudal titles such as earldoms, passed on by primogeniture, from England, and assurances that the monarch would abandon any unrealistic claims to their land. Henry also recruited Irish troops for his armed forces with relative ease, both from the Anglo-Irish areas and from the Irish-controlled areas, to support his military efforts elsewhere.[18]

Henry's relationship with Scotland was not as uneventful. As King James V came of age, the border skirmishes stopped and the Scottish king concentrated on consolidating his power in his own realm, following which Henry VIII concluded a truce with Scotland in 1533, which became a peace in 1534. Despite this, James remained close to France, declining Henry's offer of a marriage to Henry's daughter, Mary Tudor.

---

[16] The 1539 'Six Article Act', as reproduced in Adams, *ibid*, 253; Bernard, G (2016) 'Henry VIII: Catholicism Without the Pope?', *History* 101 (345), 202–23; White, M (2015) 'The Psalms, War and Royal Iconography: Katherine Parr's Psalms and Prayers and Henry VIII as David' *Renaissance Studies* 29 (4), 554–75; Smith, P (1910) 'Luther and Henry VIII', *The English Historical Review* 25 (100), 656–72.

[17] The 1541 Act, 'King of England and His Successors Be Kings of Ireland', as reproduced in Curtis, E (ed) (1943) *Irish Historical Documents 1172–1922* (London, Methuen) 77–79. Note also the 1541 'Conditions of Submission Offered to Bacach O'Neil', ibid, at 107–09. See also 'the Proclamation of Henry VIII' in Lenman, B (2001) *England's Colonial Wars, 1550–1688* (London, Longman) 37; Mackie, J (1985) *The Early Tudors* (Oxford, Clarendon) 364–67; Connolly, S (2012) *Contested Island: Ireland 1460–1630* (Oxford, OUP) 87–90, 92–94.

[18] Maginn, C (2007) 'Surrender and Regrant in the Historiography of Sixteenth Century Ireland', *The Sixteenth Century Journal* 38 (4), 955–69; McGurk, J (2009) *The Elizabethan Conquest of Ireland* (Manchester, Manchester University Press) 3–10.

James preferred, in succession, two French brides, the second being the strongly Catholic Mary of Guise. He also refused to dissolve the monasteries as Henry had done in England, preferring to tax them. The unwillingness of James and his wife to oppose the Pope overlapped with a planned rebellion in the north of England against the 'tyrant Henry', who was disliked for his high taxes and economic depression in that part of the country.[19]

When Henry heard that James was linked to the possible rebellion, he demanded to meet his nephew in person. When James, fearing the risk of being kidnapped, failed to turn up, war was declared and Henry crossed the border, with a haughty declaration that asserted the traditional claim of English suzerainty over Scotland. James responded with a counterattack involving some 20,000 men at Solway Moss, but was hopelessly defeated, with minimal loss of English lives but hundreds of Scottish dead and over 1,200 prisoners taken. Although James V escaped the disaster at Solway Moss, he died a natural death a few weeks later, leaving behind his wife, Mary of Guise, and new-born daughter, Mary, the infant Queen of Scots. Henry saw this as the opportunity he had been waiting for: In 1543, the *Treaties of Greenwich* were signed by Henry and Mary's then regent, the Earl of Arran; these tresties promised peace, on the one hand, and a marriage, on the other, the young Mary Stuart being intended as wife to Henry's son, Edward, following which the two Crowns—England and Scotland— would be fully united.[20]

With Scotland seemingly in hand, Henry turned his attention to France. In an alliance with the Emperor Charles V, he agreed in 1544 to send 42,000 Englishmen to invade France, an equal number of imperial troops also being deployed. Henry then declared war on France, advanced his forces from Calais and seized Boulogne. However, before he could go further, Charles and Francis concluded the *Peace of Crépy*,[21] without the involvement of the King of England. Henry's anger at having been excluded came on the heels of his having been told that the French were preparing for an invasion of England (which was not true) and had renewed their *Auld Alliance* (which was true) with the Scots after the Scottish Parliament, under the influence of Mary of Guise, had annulled the *Treaties of Greenwich*. Henry reiterated his claims to suzerainty of Scotland in uncompromising terms, and in the spring of 1544 launched a further army north of the border with instructions to

[p]ut all to fire and sword, burn Edinburgh town, so razed and defaced when you have sacked and gotten what you can of it as there may remain forever a perpetual memory of the vengence of God lightened upon them for their falsehood and disobedience.[22]

[19] Sansom, C (2008) 'The Wakefield Conspiracy of 1541 and Henry VIII's Progress to the North Reconsidered', *Northern History* 45 (2), 217–38; Reid, S (1948) 'Clerical Taxation: The Scottish Alternative to Dissolution of the Monasteries, 1530–1560', *The Catholic Historical Review* 34 (2), 129–53.

[20] The 1533 'Treaties of Greenwich' are reproduced in Dickinson, W (ed) (1958) *A Sourcebook of Scottish History*, Vol II (London, Nelson) 129; Scarisbrick, J (1997) *Henry VIII* (London, Yale University Press) 437; Grant, R (2011) *1001 Battles* (London, Penguin) 265, 267.

[21] See pages 55–56.

[22] Henry VIII, 'Instructions to the Privy Council', as reproduced in Dickinson, W (ed) (1958) *A Sourcebook of Scottish History*, Vol II (London, Nelson) 132.

The English forces followed their orders to the letter, torching Edinburgh, the Palace of Holyroodhouse and Leith. For the next three years, until Henry VIII's death, his forces remained in occupation of large parts of Scotland, burning crops and destroying (Catholic) religious establishments. At least 16 castles, seven major abbeys, five towns and 243 villages were destroyed.

Simultaneously, there was a real fear of an invasion of England, in support of the Scots, after French forces landed on the Isle of Wight, but the French withdrew within 24 hours. The bulk of the two naval forces then met in the Solent the following year, in 1545, when an English fleet of 80 vessels opposed 175 French ships. Although this was a tentative encounter, the most noteworthy incident being the accidental sinking of the king's flagship *The Mary Rose*, with the loss of 400 men, the show of English force deterred the French invasion. Peace was reached between the English and French the following year with the *Treaty of Ardres*. The core terms of this treaty provided that neither side would construct further fortifications in France, and King Francis promised to pay 95,000 golden crowns each year during Henry's life (just as in the payments that were promised earlier)[23] and 50,000 crowns in perpetuity, for the return of Boulogne in 1554. The French also insisted that Scotland be made party to the treaty and benefit from its peace. Accordingly, Henry pledged not to attack the Scots again, without just cause.[24]

The problem for Scotland was not the threat from England but the fact that it was on the brink of civil war once the English left. Radical Protestants seized strategic assets, such as the castle at St Andrews, which the future theologian, John Knox, was helping to defend. The Scottish Parliament requested help from France. The new King of France, Henri II, unlike his father, Francis I, responded favourably. Henri II explained that although the castle at St Andrews was held by Scotsmen, these men were 'rebels against the sovereign lady the young Queen of the Scots, towards whom, and whose country, he was bound by a close and ancient friendship'.[25] The French king then sent a fleet, along with engineers, to effect a bombardment of the castle, to dislodge the Scottish rebels. Henri argued that his action was only in support of the Queen of Scotland, and did not undermine the *Treaty of Ardres* between England and France.

3. Edward VI

Edward VI was the son of Henry VIII and his third wife, Jane Seymour. He was crowned King of England in early 1547, at the age of nine. He (through a Council of

---

[23] See pages 54–55.

[24] Phillips, G (1999) 'Strategy and Its Limitations: The Anglo-Scots Wars, 1480–1550', *War in History* 6 (4), 396–416. Mackie, J (1985) *The Early Tudors* (Oxford, Clarendon) 363–64, 404–11, 486.

[25] Henri II, as noted in Bonner, E (1996) 'The Recovery of St Andrew's Castle in 1547: French Naval Policy and Diplomacy in the British Isles', *The English Historical Review* 111 (442), 578, 594.

Regency) ruled for only six years before his premature death. During his short reign, the Protestant Reformation in England saw radical progress. Edward, publicly set out his personal views in *A Small Treastise Against the Primacy of the Pope* in which it was written that 'many papists curse us and name us heretics, because we have forsaken the antichrist [ie the Pope]'.[26] With the help of Parliament, Edward further ensured that Protestantism gained ground in England by, first, introducing the *Book of Common Prayer* through the *Act of Uniformity 1549* and then, secondly, replacing it with the more Protestant *Book of Common Prayer* under the *Act of Uniformity* 1552. Failure by the clergy to use the 1552 *Book* was punishable by up to life imprisonment. Amongst the other measures adopted in 10 different Acts of Parliament were the dissolution of chantries/small chapels established to offer prayers for the dead (along with sequestration of their wealth), the removal of religious images in churches, abolition of clerical celibacy, and the seizing of any remaining superfluous church wealth by the Crown. Edward also repealed his father's *Act for the Advancement of True Religion*, allowing all (not just priests and nobles) to read the Bible.[27]

Edward's actions caused discontent in some parts of his kingdom. Tensions began to rise in Ireland as Edward's officers took a much more direct approach in dictating how the churches in the Anglo-Irish realm should be run. In England, there was a rebellion on the church service in Devon and Cornwall in 1549, which was brutally crushed. At the Battle of Clyst Heath near Exeter in 1549, 900 bound and gagged prisoners had their throats slit in 10 minutes. There was also the so-called Ket's rebellion in the same year. The 'Articles of the Rebels' for Ket's Rebellion underlined their religious purpose, stating that 'we will have the mass in Latin ... we Cornishmen ... utterly refuse the New English'.[28] These concerns were accompanied by disquiet about price controls, the enclosure of the commons and the traditional view of all peasants against serfdom, that 'all bond men shall be made free, for God made all free'.[29] The rebellion was suppressed with brutality. Edward celebrated his victory by passing a *Second Act of Uniformity*, under which attendance at the Church of England, 'diligently and faithfully', was made obligatory, as a 'great number of people' were not attending the new church services, as demanded by the king.[30]

[26] Edward IV, as noted in Cohen, M (ed) (2004) *History in Quotations* (London, Cassell) 348.

[27] The 1549 'First Act of Uniformity', in Adams, M (ed) (1947) *Select Documents on English Constitutional Law* (London, Macmillan) 272; the 1547 'Dissolution of Chantries Act' can be found ibid, at 269; also MacCulloch, D (2015) 'Parliament and the Reformation of Edward VI', *Parliamentary History* 34(3), 383–400.

[28] Kamen, H (1994) *European Society: 1500–1700* (London, Routledge) 262.

[29] 'The Demands of the Rebels', as reproduced in Millward, J (1961) *Sixteenth Century: Portraits and Documents* (London, Hutchinson) 62; Meyer, G (2011) *The Tudors* (NYC, Bantam) 164, 218–22, 227–31, 300–03, 308, 349–53.

[30] The 1552 'Second Act of Uniformity', as reproduced in Adams, M (ed) (1947) *Select Documents on English Constitutional Law* (London, Macmillan) 278. On the Western Rebellion of 1549, see Millward, J (1961) *Sixteenth Century: Portraits and Documents* (London, Hutchinson) 63–64; Sandall, S (2012) 'Representing Rebellion: Memory and Social Conflict in Sixteenth Century England', *Integrative Psychological and Behavioral Science* 46 (4), 559–88; Shagan, E (2000) 'Popularity and the 1549 Rebellions Revisited', *The English Historical Review* 115 (460), 121–33.

Edward also decided that the actions of Henri II in Scotland against the rebels at St Andrews castle did constitute a breach of the *Treaty of Ardres*, and in an alliance Spain again declared war on France. English forces then advanced over the border with Scotland, with the intention of exporting the Reformation and securing the young Scottish Queen Mary as Edward's bride, thus smashing the *Auld Alliance* once and for all. The goal of securing a marriage with the Scottish queen led to this war's becoming known as the Rough Wooing. At Pinkie Cleugh in 1547, although the English forces were almost outnumbered two-to-one, they destroyed the Scottish army, causing over 16,000 casualties and taking a few thousand prisoners, all for the price of a few hundred English soldiers. Fearing a full English conquest of Scotland, Mary's regents entered into the 1548 *Treaty of Haddington* with France, promising, in exchange for French assistance, that Mary would marry the future French king, the Dauphin Francis. The French duly obliged, and in 1548, 6,000 French troops were landed at Leith, and the infant Mary was spirited away to France, where she was betrothed to the four-year-old Dauphin. Mary lived at the royal court for the next 10 years, and was married to Francis in 1558, when they were both of age. Under the marriage contract, it was promised that Scotland would remain independent, but Francis would become King of Scotland alongside his queen. If they were to have a son, he would inherit both realms. If there were no heirs, then Scotland, and also Mary's claim to the English throne, would be inherited by the successors of Francis II. Mary also promised that any subsequent acts to nullify these promises would be invalid.[31]

The risk of Scotland's becoming a French province was now large. To be able to prepare for this risk, a truce was agreed with France by which Edward decided to abandon Boulogne, which his father had taken with great effort. This handing over of a strategic port, for a total of 400,000 golden crowns, was deemed necessary, as it was proving impossible to defend on both economic and military grounds. The English troops remaining in France were then ordered back to the last English stronghold in Calais, in anticipation of the next stage of the wars with France.[32]

4. Mary Tudor

The use of violence in England in the name of religion became much more pronounced in the reign of Mary Tudor/I. Mary I, who succeeded her half-brother Edward VI, ruled from 1553. Mary was the only child of Henry VIII and his first wife, Catherine of Aragon, to survive infancy. Edward had attempted to remove Mary from the line

---

[31] The 1547, 'Treaty of Haddington', as reproduced in Dickinson, W (ed) (1958) *A Sourcebook of Scottish History*, Vol II (London, Nelson) 142–43; Bonney, R (2012) *The European Dynastic States* (Oxford, Oxford University Press) 125; Bryce, M (1907) 'Mary Stuart's Voyage to France in 1548', *The English Historical Review* 22 (85), 43–50; Dunn, J (2003) *Elizabeth and Mary, Cousins, Rivals, Queens* (NYC, Harpers) 12–16, 25, 70–71, 97–100, 130–40.

[32] Mackie, J (1985) *The Early Tudors* (Oxford, Clarendon) 486, 522–39.

of succession because of religious differences between them, Mary being a staunch Catholic. On Edward's death, their first cousin, the young Protestant, Lady Jane Grey, was proclaimed queen, in accordance with Edward's wishes, excluding both Mary and his other half-sister, Elizabeth. Jane held power for only nine days, during which Mary assembled an armed force and the Privy Council agreed that Jane should not sit on the throne, as she was not in a direct line of descent from King Henry VIII and there-fore did not come within the *Third Act of Succession* of 1544. The *Third Act of Succession* was critical, as this had returned both Mary and Elizabeth to the line of succession behind their half-brother, Edward. Specifically, Henry VIII had directed that his son Edward should take the throne first (and then Edward's children) followed by Henry's daughters, Mary (and then any children of Mary) and Elizabeth. One of the last laws of Henry VIII, the *Treason Act* of 1547, made it high treason to interrupt the line of succession to the throne established by the *Act of Succession*, which was exactly what Edward had tried to do through the person of Jane. Even though Jane had occupied the throne for only a few days, this was in direction contravention of the Act, for which she was sentenced for high treason and imprisoned in the Tower of London, although she was not, at this point, executed. Mary then went on to be crowned as the first anointed Queen Regnant of England, and to rule as an independent, resolute and determined Catholic monarch, who for the previous five years had lived the life of a religious pariah for her faith, in an increasingly Protestant England.[33]

Once in power, Mary attempted to bring the Counter Reformation to England and repeal many of the acts of her father, Henry VIII, and half-brother, Edward VI. Her Parliament, which increased its own powers governing England in exchange for supporting the Queen's goals, agreed to a reconciliation with the papacy. It addressed all of the laws passed by Edward that related to furthering the Protestant Reformation, which were 'utterly repealed, void, annihilated and of none effect'. The *First Statute of Repeal* in 1553 noted the importance of re-establishing the 'authority of the Catholic Church' as a necessary counterweight to the 'numbers of diverse and strange opinions and diversities of sects, and thereby ... great unquietness and much discord, to the great disturbance of the commonwealth of this realm'.[34] The *Second Statute of Repeal* in 1555 had the English Parliament repeal Henry VIII's laws against the supremacy of the papacy, and then record that it was 'very sorry and repentant of the schism and disobedience committed in this realm' against the Catholic Church.[35]

Mary's subsequent injunctions to restore the old religion, and to repeal all laws and statutes to the contrary, reclassified as heresies all other Christian interpretations,

[33] The 1544 'Act Fixing Succession' as reproduced in Adams, M (ed) (1947) *Select Documents of English Constitutional History* (London, Macmillan) 266–70; Whitelock, A (2007) 'A Woman in a Man's World: Mary I and Political Intimacy: 1553–1558', *Women's History Review* 16 (3), 323–34; Whitelock, A (2007) 'Princes Mary's Household and the Succession Crisis, July 1553', *The Historical Journal* 50 (2), 265–87.

[34] The 'Act of 1553', as in Cowie, L (ed) (1970) *The Reformation of the Sixteenth Century* (London, Wayland) 105.

[35] The 1555 'Second Act of Repeal of Mary', as reproduced in Adams, M (ed) (1947) *Select Documents on English Constitutional Law* (London, Macmillan) 290–91; Hunt, A (2009) 'The Monarchical Republic of Mary I', *The Historical Journal* 52 (3), 557–72.

following her revival of the earlier *Heresy Acts* in 1554. Subsequently, over 2,000 beneficed clergy (of the Church in England) were dispossessed, and over 300 were arrested and burned at the stake, many others fleeing the country. The most prominent victim of Mary's purge was Thomas Cranmer, the Archbishop of Canterbury whom Henry VIII had placed in office, who was burned at the stake after having spent two years in prison, being stripped of his offices and publicly humiliated. He had been forced to stand down and sign six documents admitting his heresy. When brought out to admit his heresy in public, he refused to do so, for which he was burned alive and made into a martyr for the Protestant cause. Although the Queen of England became known as 'Bloody Mary' for such acts, she had little doubt that the execution of some of her erring subjects was necessary to bring the majority back on to the path of salvation.[36]

Mary's accession was welcomed in Ireland, where the Irish Parliament quickly recognised Mary's legitimate birth and repealed all statutes of the previous 30 years directed against papal authority. However, unlike in England, there was no retribution against Protestants, although when Mary introduced the first 'plantation' into Ireland of English settlers on formerly Irish lands, some eyebrows were raised. Mary's accession was not welcomed in Scotland, with the radical preacher John Knox printing his *Admonition to the Professors of God's Truth* in 1554, in which he accused the English queen of being an 'incestuous bastard' and compared her actions in restoring the Catholic Mass to those of Queen Jezebel, before fleeing to safety in Geneva. The Scottish Parliament, anxious to protect its own interests by defending Mary of Scots, responded against Knox by passing an *Act Against Those Speaking Evil of the Queen*.[37]

A. Philip II of Spain

In 1554, with the approval of the English Parliament, Mary married Prince Philip (later Philip II) of Spain. Philip held a deeply entrenched view of monarchial authority, and was the foremost Catholic ruler of his age. Philip was the son of the Emperor Charles V and Isabella of Portugal. He succeeded to the Crowns of Spain, Portugal, Naples and Sicily, as well as to the Duchy of Milan. His empire stretched around the New World, a major addition being the islands named after him, the Philippines. From 1555, when his father abdicated, he was also in charge of the Seventeen Provinces of the Netherlands. For four years, Philip was also King of England, in a personal capacity by right of his marriage to Mary I, the English Queen. The marriage treaty, promising

---

[36] Harrison, C (2008) 'The Oxford Martyrs and the English Protestant Movement, 1553–1558', *The Historian* 70 (1), 146–54; Black, J (1985) *The Reign of Elizabeth* (Oxford, Oxford University Press) 188.

[37] The 'Act Against Speaking Evil of the Queen' in Dickinson, W (ed) (1958) *A Sourcebook of Scottish History*, Vol II (London, Nelson) 158; Connolly, S (2012) *Contested Island: Ireland 1460–1630* (Oxford, Oxford University Press) 184–87.

to keep the realms separate, with Philip having no claim to the English throne if Mary died and nothing to be done by Philip to alter the customs of England, was better than could have been expected from the English point of view.[38]

Despite the legal niceties, this marriage may have been Queen Mary's greatest mistake, as the English had long hated the meddling of foreigners in their affairs and feared that the marriage was the gateway to a loss of English sovereignty. The anger at the proposed marriage was such that Thomas Wyatt led a rebellion of some 4,000 men, which nearly succeeded in toppling the queen but failed when Mary refused to flee from London. Unlike many of the ring-leaders, the Princess Elizabeth survived the aftermath of the rebellion by keeping a low-profile during the uprising, and convincing her half-sister Mary that she, Elizabeth, despite being a popular focus for every kind of dissent and discontent, was not in league against her with the rebels. Lady Jane Grey, who was still in the Tower of London at this point, did not have the same luck, as some of her family members were involved in the rebellion, for which she lost her head, and the villainous reputation of Mary was enhanced.[39]

Following her marriage to Philip (now King Philip II of Spain), Mary supported her husband in his wars against France, although this was more due to the Wyatt rebellion in England having been supported by France than to Mary's direct relationship with her Philip. Nonetheless, she committed 7,000 English soldiers to a combined assault on France. These men were a small part of the largest engagement of the war at the Battle of Saint Quentin in northern France in 1557, where the French lost half of their force of 24,000 men, while the Spanish lost only a few of their 47,000-strong army. The French then made a surprise attack, managing to seize the last long-standing English toehold on the Continent—Calais. A further battle, at Gravelines, near Calais, in July 1558 saw King Henri II lose another 12,000 men (killed, wounded or taken prisoner) while retaining Calais, despite the best efforts of the English to take back what they had held for 220 years. Henri II had ended, once and for all, the medieval anomaly of an English settlement in the midst of a homogeneously French community.[40] A forlorn Mary then pleaded for her husband, Philip, to return to London (he had returned to England only once since leaving to prosecute the war with France), to which he replied that he would only do so if he was formally crowned King of England with full powers. This was something the English Parliament could not agree to. Mary died later that

---

[38] Samson, A (2005) 'The Marriage and Royal Entry of Philip, Prince of Austria and Mary Tudor, 1554', *The Sixteenth Century Journal* 36 (3), 761–84.

[39] The 1554 'Act for the Marriage of Queen Mary to Philip of Spain', as reproduced in Adams, M (ed) (1947) *Select Documents on English Constitutional Law* (London, Macmillan) 283–89; and the 'Revival of the Heresy Acts' of the same year, ibid, at 289. Wyatt's Rebellion of 1554 is to be found in Millward, J (1961) *Sixteenth Century: Portraits and Documents* (London Hutchinson) 67, 69; Vannan, A (2013) 'The Death of Queen Jane: Ballad, History and Propaganda', *Folk Music Journal* 10 (3), 76–89; Thorp, M (1978) 'Religion and the Wyatt Rebellion of 1554', *Church History* 47 (4), 363–80.

[40] Greengrass, M (2015) *Christendom Destroyed: Europe 1517–1648* (NYC, Penguin) 145, 294–96, 347; Armstrong, E (1915) 'The Italian Wars of Henry II', *The English Historical Review* 30 (120), 602–12; Spencer, D (2016) 'A Precious Jewel: English Calais, 1347–1558', *Historian* 128, 6–10.

year, in November 1558, possibly of uterine cancer, having mistakenly believed that she was pregnant with Philip's child following his visit to England in 1557.[41]

5. ELIZABETH I

Elizabeth succeeded her half-sister, Mary I, in 1558. She instantly found herself in the midst of a religious conflagration. This was being actively stoked by Pope Paul IV. Pope Paul was responsible for the creation of the Jewish ghetto in Rome, as part of a campaign against the Jewish communities, designed to make the Jews convert to Christianity or leave. The tools that were used were demands that the Jews live in ghettos, that they were forbidden to trade in any commodity except food and second-hand clothes, and they were allowed only one synagogue (the other six were destroyed in Rome). Accompanying this intolerance was the *Index Librorum Prohibitorium* (the Index of Prohibited Books). Although censorship had been practised for centuries, it was under Pope Paul IV that the Church attempted to make it more pervasive and institutionalised. His demands ranged from ordering the nude figures in Michelangelo's *The Last Judgment* to be painted draped in veils, through to compiling the original list, in 1559, of 550 books to be banned. The list covered works by authors ranging from Erasmus to Machiavelli, through to unauthorised editions of the Bible. Vernacular bibles, which allowed the scriptures to be read by the common person, without Latin and the need for the clergy to interpret them, were a particular target. Correspondingly, the authorised version of the Bible was upheld as being of such repute that no one should 'dare or presume under any pretext whatsoever to reject it'.[42]

With regard to England, Pope Paul had issued a papal bull in 1555, *Ilius, per quem Reges regnant*, which recognised Mary I and Philip II of Spain as King and Queen of England and its dominions, including Ireland. Needless to say, when the Protestant Elizabeth came to the throne, he was not happy. The Pope insisted on the restitution of confiscated Church lands and required Elizabeth to submit her claim to him. When she refused to do so, Pope Paul rejected her claim to the throne of England. Although he did not mention Elizabeth by name, he added in his bull *Cum ex apostalatus* that all sovereigns who supported heresy in their dominions lost their right to be ruler.[43]

Elizabeth worked through her Parliament, which, as during her father's reign, was kept on a very short leash, enjoying a restricted sphere of activity. Sessions were short, and Parliament was only called on an irregular basis when Elizabeth wanted it; as Elizabeth explained, 'it is in me and my power to call Parliaments; it is in my power to

---

[41] Elton, G (1968) *The New Cambridge Modern History: The Reformation*, Vol II (Cambridge, Cambridge University Press) 254, 273; Dickens, A (1965). *Reformation and Society* (London, Thames) 50–51.

[42] 'The Index', as in Reddaway, F (ed) (1930) *Select Documents in European History*, Vol II (London, Methuen) 77; Murphy, C (2011) *God's Jury: The Inquisition and the Making of the Modern World* (London, Penguin) 105, 125; Green, T (2007) *Inquisition: The Reign of Fear* (London, Macmillan) 272–78.

[43] Maitland, R (1900) 'Elizabethan Gleanings: Queen Elizabeth and Paul IV', *English Historical Review* 15, 100–14.

assent or dissent to anything done in Parliament'.[44] Her preference was for her work to be done through her Council, from which she could issue proclamations modifying the law, provided they did not introduce new penalties or new resource requirements (which required Parliament to be involved). Regarding significant issues, Elizabeth realised the legitimacy that Parliament's involvement gave her, from which two key pieces of legislation quickly emerged.

First, the *Act of Uniformity* reinstated all of Edward VI's laws on religion, whilst also slowing more radical (Protestant) types of worship. Commonly recognised groups of heretics, such as the Anabaptists, were deported, or occasionally burned at the stake, 'in great horror with roaring and crying'.[45] Of greater concern was a new species of religious enthusiast—Puritans. This group, infused with radical, and evolving, Protestant teachings from the Continent, were beginning to express disquiet about the Crown's interference in multiple areas, reading the Bible as a manifesto against tyranny in both religious and secular matters. They also suggested that the Reformation in England did not go far enough, due its retention of many Catholic practices.[46]

Secondly, the *Act of Supremacy* of 1558 replaced Henry VIII's original *Act of Supremacy* of 1534, which had been repealed in Mary's reign, confirming Elizabeth as Supreme Governor of the Church of England. All senior religious and civil authority figures were obliged to take an oath of allegiance to Elizabeth, affirming that she was 'the only supreme governor of this realm … in all spiritual and ecclesiastical things or causes'.[47] The small minority who failed to swear the oath lost their political or religious offices and/or were deprived of their economic incomes.

The churches were emptied of all forms of 'papist gear', in terms of roods, crucifixes, images of the Virgin Mary and altar cloths, and anyone who failed to attend the Church of England on a regular basis, as required, risked being fined, as attendance moved from being an ecclesiastical to a state matter. In theory, this should have made one type of church obligatory for all people, but in practice, as Elizabeth did not wish to risk an uprising of Catholics in England, in the 1560s she repeatedly vetoed legislation designed to make life more difficult for Catholics, whilst continuing to create loopholes that allowed them to function, more or less normally, as members of the English nation (although they were excluded from Parliament in 1563). In this period, no more than 300 priests were removed from their positions for failing to conform with

[44] Elizabeth, as noted in Black, J (1985) The Reign of Elizabeth (Oxford, Oxford University Press) 217, also at 35–38.

[45] As noted in Black, J (1985) *The Reign of Elizabeth* (Oxford, Oxford University Press) 204–05. The 1559 Act of Uniformity can be found in Millward, J (1961) *Sixteenth Century: Portraits and Documents* (London, Hutchinson) 75.

[46] For an early Puritan position, see John Field, 1572, 'An Admonition to the Parliament', as reproduced in Hillerbrand, H (ed) (2009) *The Protestant Reformation* (NYC, Harper) 257. In 1593, Elizabeth forbade Puritans from holding their own services. The Act is in Cowie, L (ed) (1970) *The Reformation of the Sixteenth Century* (London, Wayland) 115. Also Tyacke, N (2010) 'The Puritan Paradigm of English Politics', *The History Journal* 53 (3), 527–50.

[47] The 1559 'Act of Supremacy', as in Adams, M (ed) (1947) *Select Documents of English Constitutional History* (London, Macmillan) 297; Black, J (1985) *The Reign of Elizabeth* (Oxford, Oxford University Press) 14–16, 20–21, 33.

the *Act of Uniformity*, whilst at the same time 'compounding' was developed, to allow Catholics to elude the statutory penalties by purchasing what amounted to a licence to practise their faith. This allowed, in practice, all English Catholics a non-intrusive tolerance into their private lives, without 'inquisition or examination of their consciences in causes of religion'.[48]

These laws were then carried over into Ireland. Although far from the militant confrontations that were bubbling up on the Continent, tension between Protestants and Catholics was increasing in Ireland. This overlapped with the continual, yet often confused and alienating, policy of Elizabeth's ministers of identifying and rewarding her favourites, under which land was taken from one and given to another. It was made worse by the downgraded use of the Irish Parliament and the promotion of ideals of English colonisation, with the benefits that could be delivered to the Irish, if the English Crown were to assume complete control over the entire country.[49]

The counterweight to Elizabeth's approach to religion came in 1563, when the Council of Trent finally concluded its work. The Council's conclusions formed the foundation for a revitalised and centralised Europe-wide Catholic Church. Although it sought to put discipline and structure back into Catholicism and its leaders, it was no congress of peace with the Protestants. It upheld many of the sources of contention, such as the veneration of images, penance, indulgences, the Mass, purgatory and transubstantiation, and threatened anathema to anyone who denied them.[50] All of the conclusions of Council of Trent were subsequently ratified by Pope Pius IV in his bull, *Benedictus Deus*, of 1564. This led to the codification of the *Tridentine Profession of Faith* (the Tridentine Creed), which remained the primary form of the Profession of Faith for the next 400 years, by which the clergy had to swear publicly that they 'recognise the Holy Catholic and Apostolic Roman Church as the mother and mistress of all churches' and 'vow and swear true obedience to the Roman Pontiff, the successor of blessed Peter, the chief of the Apostles and the representative of Jesus Christ'.[51]

Elizabeth I responded with the *Thirty Nine Articles*, the defining statements of doctrines and practices of the Church of England. They cemented the Church of England in place. In doing so, the *Thirty Nine Articles*, adopted by convocation and then

---

[48] Elizabeth, as noted in Dunn, J (2003) *Elizabeth and Mary, Cousins, Rivals, Queens* (NYC. Harpers) 451; Field, C (2008) 'A Shilling for Queen Elizabeth: The Era of State Regulation of Church Attendance in England', *Journal of Church and State* 50 (2), 213–52; Kirby, T (2006) 'Law Supremacy: Reform of the Canon Law of England from Henry VIII to Elizabeth I', *Reformation and Renaissance Review* 8 (3), 349–70; Meyer, G (2011) *The Tudors* (NYC, Bantam) 375–78, 386, 450, 482, 513.

[49] The 1560 Acts of Uniformity and Supremacy, as reproduced in Curtis, E (ed) (1943) *Irish Historical Documents 1172–1922* (London, Methuen) 120–30; McGurk, J (2009) *The Elizabethan Conquest of Ireland* (Manchester, Manchester University Press) 3–10, 13.

[50] Decrees of the Council of Trent, as reproduced in Webster, D (ed) (1969) *Documents in Renaissance and Reformation History* (Sydney, Cassell) 199–203.

[51] The Tridentine Profession of Faith, as reproduced in Cowie, L (ed) (1970) *The Reformation of the Sixteenth Century* (London, Wayland) 67; Elton, G (ed) (1968) *Renaissance and Reformation* (London, Macmillan) 228–30, 232.

ratified by royal ordinance, not only showed how the English Church was different, but also added:

> The Church of Rome hath erred, not only in their living and manners of ceremonies, but also matters of faith ... the[ir] doctrines of purgatory, pardons, worshipping and adoration, as well of images ... and invocation of saints, is a fond thing vainly invented, ... repugnant to the Word of God ...[52]

A. Mary Queen of Scots

Elizabeth I of England did not like Henri II of France, who had seized the last English holding on the Continent, Calais. Any hope that Elizabeth had that the relationship with France would improve upon the death of Henri II was dashed following the accession of Henri's son, Francis II, to the throne in the middle of 1559. Francis II was married to Mary, Queen of Scots. The French argued that Mary and her French husband had a better claim to the English throne than Elizabeth. Mary was the daughter of the late Scottish king, James V, and grand-daughter of Margaret Tudor, Henry VIII's sister. The nub of the problem was whilst both Elizabeth and Mary could claim descent from King Henry VII, Elizabeth was the daughter of Henry VIII's second wife, which meant that most Catholics viewed Mary as next in line to the English throne, especially in light of Pope Clement VII's declaration that Henry's marriage to Anne Boleyn was void. Elizabeth dismissed these claims as 'unjust, unreasonable and perilous'.[53] Her Parliament then passed the *Act of Recognition of the Queen's Title*, under which Elizabeth was recognised as 'our most rightful and lawful sovereign'.[54]

The situation in Scotland in 1559 was tense. It had been made worse by publication in 1558 of John Knox's *A First Blast of the Trumpet Against the Monstrous Regiment of Women*.[55] This was a polemic in which Knox railed against female rulers, in particular the Catholic Mary of Guise (mother of Mary, Queen of Scots, and her regent) and Mary Tudor, claiming that rule by females was contrary to the Bible. With such rhetoric firing them, a number of Scottish nobles with Protestant inclinations forced Mary of Guise and her French counsel from Edinburgh, declaring her deposed. Having taken refuge in the fortress of Dunbar, she urged her daughter, now Queen Consort of France, to send troops to help her. Thousands of French were then landed in Scotland in support of Mary of Guise, prompting the Protestant rebels to appeal to Elizabeth for

---

[52] The 'Thirty Nine Articles of the Church of England', as reproduced in Webster, D (ed) (1969) *Documents in Renaissance and Reformation History* (Sydney, Cassell) 156–57.

[53] Elizabeth, as noted in Dunn, J (2003) *Elizabeth and Mary, Cousins, Rivals, Queens* (NYC, Harpers) 26.

[54] The 1559 'Act of Recognition of the Queen's Title', as reproduced in Adams, M (ed) (1947) *Select Documents of English Constitutional History* (London, Macmillan) 306.

[55] Panofre, C (2015) 'Radical Geneva: The Publication of Knox's First Blast of the Trumpet', *Historical Research* 88 (239), 48–66; Abreu, M (2003) 'John Knox: Gynaecocracy: The Monstrous Empire of Women', *Reformation and Renaissance Review* 5 (2), 166–87; Healey, R (1994) 'Waiting for Deborah: John Knox and Four Ruling Queens', *The Sixteenth Century Journal* 25 (2), 370–86.

help. Elizabeth, who was less than impressed with Knox and his misogynistic claims, was concerned that Mary, Queen of Scots might be about to press her claims to the English throne. She therefore agreed to the request for help from the Scottish Protestant lords, concluding the 1560 *Treaty of Berwick*. An English army of 8,000 soldiers then crossed the border to oppose the French troops who were defending Mary of Guise and thus, allegedly, seeking to overthrow Scottish independence and 'conquer the realm of Scotland, suppress the liberty thereof, and unite the same to the Crown of France perpetually'.[56]

After a short military engagement, the French, now encountering their own difficulties at home, decided that they were not keen to get bogged down in Scotland. Through the 1560 *Treaty of Edinburgh* with Elizabeth I, with the agreement of the Protestant Scottish lords, the French agreed to quit Scotland if the English did the same. Both sides promised no further interference in Scotland. Within her realm, Queen Mary had to accept a council made up of both 'rebel' and 'loyalist' factions, and the formation of a more tolerant regime towards Protestant practices of Christianity, with the outlawing of papal authority and practices in Scotland, although she was allowed to continue practising Catholicism for her own private benefit. Mary was guaranteed her Scottish throne, but had to stop using the heraldic arms of England. It was added that 'the realms of England and Ireland belong by right to the serene land and princess Elizabeth and no other is therefore allowed to call, write, name or entitle themselves … King or Queen of England or Ireland'.[57] This point appealed greatly to Elizabeth, who had held deep-seated insecurities about her own legitimacy in claiming the English throne. Of even greater satisfaction to the English, the young French king and husband to Mary of Scots, Francis II, died at the end of 1560, leaving the Queen of Scots bereft. Although Mary would delay ratifying the treaty, Elizabeth was aware that the paradigm had shifted. For the first time in centuries, the English soldiers who had entered Scotland as allies left as friends, as now a mutual dislike of France and Rome formed the basis for a new relationship. The *Auld Alliance*, which had dominated Scottish foreign policy and represented a continual threat to England for hundreds of years, disappeared from view, as the religious affinities of Scotland and England became greater than their traditional sovereign animosities.[58]

Mary left France after her husband's death and returned to Scotland, to be met by the Scottish (Protestant) Lords of the Congregation. Mary ruled Scotland for the following seven years until 1567. True to her word, Mary persecuted a number of Catholics and supported the Protestant churches. It appeared that the relationship between Elizabeth

---

[56] The 'Treaty of Berwick', as quoted in Dunn, J (2003) *Elizabeth and Mary, Cousins, Rivals, Queens* (NYC, Harpers) 188. The text of the agreement is fully reproduced in Dickinson, W (ed) (1958) *A Sourcebook of Scottish History*, Vol II (London, Nelson) 169; Black, J (1985) *The Reign of Elizabeth* (Oxford, Oxford University Press) 42–44, 68–71.

[57] The 1260 'Treaty of Edinburgh', as reproduced in Dickinson, W (ed) (1958) *A Sourcebook of Scottish History*, Vol II (London, Nelson) 180; Wernham, R (1968). *The New Cambridge Modern History: The Counter Reformation* (Cambridge, Cambridge University Press) 209–11.

[58] Goodare, J (1965) 'The First Parliament of Mary, Queen of Scots', *The Sixteenth Century Journal* 36 (1), 55–75.

and Mary was going to be positive. However, a sequence of events, which began with Mary's marriage to her cousin, Henry Stuart, Lord Darnley, in 1565 and culminated with the death of Darnley two years later, turned everything on its head. Darnley was also a descendant of Margaret Tudor, Henry VII's daughter, and thus had a claim to the throne of England. When mixed with his leanings towards Catholicism, this led to great concern in London that this marriage could present a direct threat to Elizabeth I. However, the marriage was short-lived, and it was rumoured that Mary may have been involved in Darnley's death in an explosion in 1567 at Kirk o' Field, a house in Edinburgh where he had been staying. This escalated into a scandal after Mary took as her third husband James, Earl of Bothwell, who was thought to be behind the murder of Lord Darnley. Due to the scandal and civil disorder that followed, rebel lords eventually took charge of the infant Prince James (the future James I of England and James VI of Scotland), who had been born in 1566, and captured both Mary and Bothwell after a stand-off at the Carberry Hill, involving a number of Scottish lords who objected to the rule of Mary after her marriage to Bothwell, and who were intent on avenging Darnley's death. To avoid the threat of a public trial, exposure, defamation of character and possible death, and for the price of allowing Scotland to be ruled by a regent until her son should come of age, Mary agreed to abdicate and to suffer confinement.[59]

In early 1568 Mary escaped her prison and raised an army of perhaps 6,000 men, which was defeated at the Battle of Langside. After seeing her army destroyed, she fled to England, seeking refuge with her Protestant cousin, Elizabeth. Although Elizabeth was sympathetic to the plight of her cousin, who had lost her throne, she would not help Mary until the question of her involvement in the murder of her husband had been settled, to which end an enquiry was undertaken while Mary was kept in captivity. This enquiry did not give a definitive ruling, holding only that nothing could be proved to the dishonour of Mary or the nobles who had deposed her. The difficulty for Elizabeth was although Mary may not have been guilty of Darnley's murder, she remained a magnet for Catholic discontent in both England and Scotland. The risks became even more pronounced when a rebellion of Catholic nobles broke out in the North of England in 1569. This followed an uprising in Ireland, in which Shane O'Neil, the self-styled King of Ulster, had begun to put himself forward as a defender of the faith against the heretic Elizabeth, offering the throne of Ireland to the French king, Charles IX. For his actions, Elizabeth waged war against O'Neil, paying a price for taking Ulster with the loss of 3,500 of her own men. In Northern England, although the rebellion was defeated with relative ease, and was followed by the execution of some 800 rebels and the large-scale loss of property for those deemed traitors, the problem of what to do with Mary remained. The answer presented itself in an age when political

---

[59] The 'Abdication of Queen Mary', as in Dickinson, W (ed) (1958) *A Sourcebook of Scottish History*, Vol II (London, Nelson) 200–02; Mary's 'Alteration of the State of Religion' and 'Mary's Concessions to the Reformed Church', ibid, at 194–95. Also Dawson, J (1986) 'Mary Queen of Scots, Lord Darnley and Anglo-Scottish Relations in 1565', *International History Review* 8 (1), 1–24.

assassinations were becoming common, when Mary, still in captivity, became linked to a plot to assassinate Elizabeth when she allegedly sent a letter to Philip II of Spain, saying '[if you] help me, I shall be queen of England in three months, and Mass shall be said all over the country'.[60]

B. War with Spain and the Death of a Queen

Elizabeth I was now setting herself directly in opposition to the goals of the Catholic Church at home and abroad. At home, her refusal to accept the authority of the Pope whilst entrenching her own authority over the Church of England angered the authorities in Rome. Abroad, she had supported Protestants in France and The Netherlands. She also authorised privateering missions by John Hawkins and Francis Drake in the 1560s, to sell or take valuable commodities, slaves and/or gold, from areas the Spanish believed were their sole preserve. Throughout the 1560s, over 1,000 prizes were taken. Drake's freedom of action became harder to defend when a fleet of seven well-armed ships, under the authority of Hawkins and Drake, came into direct contact with the Spanish fleet, with only only three vessels returning to England and more than 120 men missing, dead or seized as prisoners.[61]

In 1570, Elizabeth was excommunicated by Pope Pius V in his bull, *Regnans in Excelsis*. This charged her with being 'the servant of crime' by failing to support the old religion. She was then declared to be a heretic, and all of her subjects were released from any allegiance to her. The edict added that 'all who disobey our command we involve in the same sentence of anathema'.[62] Elizabeth responded by ending her tolerance of Catholics in England. She became more determined to establish a fully national Church within England that was absolutely independent from the papacy. She put in place institutional machinery, not dissimilar to the Inquisition, to ensure compliance with her theological and political dictates. In 1571 she made the bringing of any papal decrees into England a treasonable offence, as was the conversion of any Anglicans to the Catholic faith. The next Pope, Gregory XIII, responded to Elizabeth's actions by reissuing the bull for her excommunication and creating a special seminary for Jesuit missionaries who were to go and do service in the realm of Elizabeth, 'for

---

[60] Mary, as noted in Dunn, J (2003) *Elizabeth and Mary, Cousins, Rivals, Queens* (NYC, Harpers) 404; Connolly, S (2012) *Contested Island: Ireland 1460–1630* (Oxford, Oxford University Press) 142–50, 156–64, 199; Kesselring, K (2013) 'Assassination and the Politics of Murder in Elizabethan and Early Stuart England', *Canadian Journal of History* 48 (3), 421–40.

[61] Conybeare, J (1993) 'State Sponsored Violence as a Tragedy of the Commons: England's Privateering Wars with France and Spain', *Public Choice* 77 (4), 879–99; Roger, N (2004) 'Queen Elizabeth and the Myth of Sea Power in English History', *Transactions of the Royal Historical Society* 14, 153–74; Lenman, B (2001) *England's Colonial Wars, 1550–1688* (London, Longman) 84–85, 89–90.

[62] The bull 'Excommunicating Elizabeth' is in Cowie, L (ed) (1970) *The Reformation of the Sixteenth Century* (London, Wayland) 113; Petriburg, M (1892) 'The Excommunication of Elizabeth', *The English Historical Review* 7 (25), 81–88.

the preservation and augmentation of the faith of Catholics in England'.[63] Elizabeth subsequently ordered all Jesuits and priests trained on the Continent to be expelled from her country. Of those who refused to go, or those who continued to defy her rulings on this matter, some 130 Catholic priests, together with some 60 members of prominent Catholic families (over the next two decades), were executed. Senior Church officials would advise loyal Catholics that if they wished to assassinate Elizabeth, 'there is no doubt that whosoever sends her out of the world with the pious intention of doing God service, not only does not sin but gains merit'.[64]

Elizabeth I and Philip II teetered close to war in the early part of the 1570s, after England became a refuge for those fleeing from Spanish rule in the Netherlands, whilst also being a supplier of English volunteers and weaponry to the Protestants fighting in the Low Countries. When Elizabeth went one step further and intercepted money being carried by the bankers of Genoa, who had sailed into English ports to avoid storms in the Channel, persuading the bankers to lend it to her instead of to the Spanish, Spain and England were on the brink of war. However, outright conflict was avoided when both sides agreed to the *Treaty of Bristol* of 1574, in which, much to the anger of Protestants in Parliament who wanted to deepen religious solidarity with the Protestants in The Netherlands, Elizabeth promised that she would no longer help the Prince of Orange in The Netherlands. In exchange, English traders could once more safely frequent Spanish-controlled ports and commerce between the two nations flourished. Goodwill was furthered by a visit from the Spanish fleet to Portsmouth.[65]

Three years later, in 1578, King Sebastian of Portugal died fighting the Moors in North Africa, leaving no sons to inherit his throne. An elderly relative succeeded him, who also had no children. Several candidates then also put their names forward to occupy the Portuguese throne, including Philip II of Spain, who had dynastic connections to Portugal. Despite his promises to protect local customs and institutions, and the benefits that would come from union with Spain, his proposal was not accepted, as a number of other contenders, already within Portugal, attempted to seize control. The result was that in 1580, a Spanish army of 23,000 men marched into Portugal, whilst a Spanish fleet of 157 ships was dispatched from Cadiz to prevent the escape of any other claimants. The main pretender (Antonio) who was occupying the Portuguese

---

[63] This quote is from Black, J (1985) *The Reign of Elizabeth* (Oxford, Oxford University Press) 174; also see ibid, at 92, 98–102, 123–25, 130,140–45, 184–86, 240–41.

[64] The letter of 1580 from the Cardinal Secretary in Madrid, Como, as quoted in Black, J (1985) *The Reign of Elizabeth* (Oxford, Oxford University Press) 178–79; the 1585 'Act Against Jesuits and Seminary Priests', as reproduced in Millward, J (1961) *Sixteenth Century: Portraits and Documents* (London, Hutchinson) 78–79; the 1571 'Act Against Bringing Decrees of the Pope into England' is reproduced in Adams, M (ed) (1947) *Select Documents on English Constitutional Law* (London, Macmillan) 316.

[65] Parry, G (2015) 'Foreign Policy and the Parliament of 1576', *Parliamentary History* 62–89; Jason, E (2010) 'English Merchants, the Trade with Spain, and Elizabethan Foreign Policy, 1563–1585', *Journal for Early Modern Cultural Studies* 10 (1), 5–28; Weis, M (2009) 'International Protestantism: The Fears and Hopes of a Dutch Refugee in the 1570s', *Reformation and Renaissance Review* 11 (2), 203–20; Black, J B (1931) 'Queen Elizabeth, the Sea Beggars and the Capture of Brill', *The English Historical Review* 46 (181), 30–47.

throne was killed, along with 1,000 of his men, and a further 3,000 were captured by the superior Spanish forces outside of Lisbon. A final battle at Ponta Delgada off the Azores saw 11 Portuguese vessels and 1,500 men, but no Spanish vessels, lost. Although France intervened and Catherine de' Medici launched an armada to (from which France lost 60 ships) to secure the Azores and make a claim for the throne of Portugal, Philip II of Spain won the day. The *Cortes* of Portugal accepted Philip II as their monarch, as a result of which Philip gained a million new subjects and a second overseas empire. Although the union with Portugal was to last for only 60 years, Philip II, believing that he was being directly rewarded by God, started to pursue a more aggressive overseas policy.[66]

Although Spain and England remained, in theory, at peace, religious tensions continued to simmer elsewhere around Elizabeth. In 1579, in Ireland, James Fitzmaurice FitzGerald, in launching the Munster Revolt, proclaimed:

> This war is undertaken for the defense of the Catholic religion against the heretics ... Pope Pius V has deprived Elizabeth, the patroness of the aforesaid heresies, of all royal power and dominion, as it is plainly declared ... we fight not against a lawful sceptre and honorable throne of England, but against a tyrant which refuses to hear Christ speaking by his vicar.[67]

The Munster Revolt of 1579 to 1584 was supported by outside forces, including some 600 papal troops and a few dozen Spanish officers. These soldiers and the associated uprisings were defeated, and the local communities, which may, or may not, have been sympathetic to them, suffered terribly, with one-third of the population of Munster perishing through fighting, famine or disease. The pacified area of Munster was then 'planted' with up to 4,000 new English settlers, with land being taken from the defeated and gifted to others in return for their loyalty to the English Crown.[68]

As Elizabeth suspected Spanish and papal involvement in the uprisings in Ireland, she responded by reversing her earlier position regarding Spain. Perhaps in recognition of the fact that the Spanish were going to have to be fought sooner or later, she decided that if this were so, the Low Countries would make a better battleground than England. As well as trying to make alliances with the Ottomans, whose shared enemy was Spain (just as France had done decades earlier, although Elizabeth could not replicate the depth of their relationship),[69] Elizabeth directly supported the rebellion

[66] Philip II, 'The Portuguese Succession', as reproduced in Cowans, J (ed) (2003) *Early Modern Spain: A Documentary History* (Philadelphia, PA, Penn State University Press) 112–16; James, A (2012) 'A French Armada: The Azores Campaigns, 1580–1583', *The Historical Journal* 55 (1), 1–20; Curtis, B (2013) *The Habsburgs: The History of a Dynasty* (London, Bloomsbury) 91, 93; Grant, R (2011) *1001 Battles* (London, Penguin) 289.

[67] The Fitzmaurice Declaration, as reproduced in Morton, G (ed) (1971) *Elizabethan Ireland* (London, Longman) 126.

[68] Connolly, S (2012) *Contested Island: Ireland 1460–1630* (Oxford, Oxford University Press) 176, 179.

[69] For the earlier French-Ottoman relations, see pages 245–246. In terms of formal relationships, see 'The Grant of Trading Privileges' and 'Treaty of Commerce', both reproduced in Hurewitz, J (ed) (1956) *Diplomacy in the Near and Middle East: A Documentary History* (Ottawa, Nostrand) 5–10; Burton, J (2000) 'Anglo-Ottoman Relations', *Journal of Medieval and Early Modern Studies* 30 (1), 125–56; Barton, E (1893) 'The Spanish Armada and the Ottoman Porte', *The English Historical Review* 8 (31), 439–66.

against Spanish rule in the Low Countries by signing the 1585 *Treaty of Nonsuch* with the Dutch rebels. Elizabeth, explicitly recognising the ancient liberties of the Low Countries and implicitly recognising their abjuration of Philip's authority, agreed to supply 7,400 soldiers and an annual subsidy worth about one-quarter of the annual cost of revolt. In exchange, the Dutch were to hand over Brill and Flushing to England, and would accept two English councillors on the council of state of the United Provinces.[70]

King Philip II of Spain took the English signing of the *Treaty of Nonsuch* as a declaration of war. The new Pope, Sixtus V, was of the same opinion and reissued the bull of excommunication against Elizabeth. He then sent Philip a golden sword, as a symbol of the Crusade in the name of God, and made a promise (on which he would later renege) of one million ducats to Philip II for his projected invasion of England. Philip described the planned invasion as being 'for the sake of God's service'.[71] This service required him to assist Mary, Queen of Scots, to seize the throne of England and to restore Catholicism in that country, especially since 'God has already granted that by my intervention and my hand that kingdom has previously been restored to the Catholic church once before'. He added:

> Although human prudence suggests many inconveniences and difficulties, and places before us worldly fears ... the confidence that we can justly place in the cause of God will remove them, and will inspire and strengthen us to overcome them. Certainly, we could not avoid remaining with great guilt in our soul, and great regret, if because of some failure on my part that queen [Mary] and those Catholics—indeed the [entire Catholic] faith—should suffer.[72]

Philip then ordered the confiscation of any shipping lying in Spanish ports that belonged to England, Holland and Zeeland, 'that are in rebellion against me'.[73] Elizabeth responded in kind, issuing letters of marque to Francis Drake, to undertake more privateering raids to make good the resulting losses. Drake, a 'terrible monster' in the eyes of the Spanish, went on to attack and burn Spanish possessions in the Canaries and Cape Verde Islands. He then took San Domingo, holding the city to ransom, before sailing back to England at the end of 1586.[74]

Elizabeth was now keenly aware of the need to fortify her frontiers and control any internal threats to her crown. Her principal concern at this point was Scotland and the former Queen, Mary Stuart. In the early part of the reign of the young Scottish king, James VI, in the 1570s, Elizabeth had declined to get too involved in Scotland's

---

[70] Adams, S (2004) 'Elizabeth I and the Sovereignty of the Netherlands, 1576–1585', *Transactions of the Royal Historical Society* 14, 309–19.

[71] Philip II, as quoted in Hanson, N (2003) *The Confident Hope of a Miracle. The True Story of the Spanish Armada* (London, Corgi) 76, 245; Fosi, I (1993) 'Justice and Image: the Pontificate of Sixtus V', *The Sixteenth Century Journal* 24 (1), 75.

[72] Philip II, as quoted in Parker, G (2002) 'The Place of Tudor England in the Messianic Vision of Philip II of Spain', *Transactions of the Royal Historical Society* 12, 167, 191.

[73] Philip II, as noted in Black, J (1985) *The Reign of Elizabeth* (Oxford, Oxford University Press) 368; also ibid, at 160–65, 171–74.

[74] Jenner, G (1901) 'A Spanish Account of Drake's Voyages', *The English Historical Review* 16 (61), 46–66; McCloskey, J (2013) 'Crossing the Line in the Sand: Francis Drake', *Hispanic Review* 81 (4), 393–403.

internal affairs, preferring to remain neutral, despite pleas from James's regent for help for the 'maintenance and protection of the true religion' and in 'pacifying the troubling estate of our realm'.[75] However, by the 1580s, matters were much more dangerous, and a much closer alliance was needed to nullify the threat from Spain. The 1586 *Treaty of Berwick*, establishing a Protestant League between James and Elizabeth, agreed

> [t]hat both their majesties, finding by the course of the present proceedings in foreign parts, that princes terming themselves Catholics and acknowledging the pope's authority were joined in confederacy for extirpating true religion, not only within their own states and dominions but also in other kingdoms ... [agree] that they should labour and procure by their best endeavours to draw the princes professing the same religion to join and concur with them in the like defence ... [T]his league should be offensive and defensive against all that should attempt to disturb the exercise of true religion within their kingdoms ... That in the case of invasion they should aid each other in matter and form ...[76]

James was also promised a large pension from the English state, leading some to believe that Elizabeth meant to name him the heir to the English throne. Although no articles were added to this agreement guaranteeing James's succession to the throne of England, Elizabeth did inform James that she would not prejudice whatever 'right, title or interest' he might have for such a claim.[77]

The trust between James and Elizabeth was so strong that, soon after the conclusion of the 1586 agreement, the English Council proceeded against his mother, Mary. Mary by this point had become implicated in even more plots to overthrow Elizabeth, seize the English throne and restore the country to Catholicism. For these alleged attempts, Elizabeth ordered Mary to be tried for treason, of which, despite her having no defence attorneys and denying all knowledge of the plots, she was found guilty, Parliament recommending that 'a just sentence might be followed by a just execution'.[78] James VI made a strong plea for his mother's life, 'as the dictates of honour and shame and of filial piety demanded',[79] but also realised that it was impossible to save the life of his mother and still obtain Elizabeth's support for his claim to the English throne. Mary, despite the Scottish and French ambassadors pleading for mercy from Elizabeth, was led to the scaffold on 8 February 1587 at the age of 44, where she was beheaded in a unique act of regicide, one queen killing a fellow queen, in which considerations of power and religion trumped claims based on family and status. Despite James's pleading and protestations, he did no more. After a year of chilly relations, James

---

[75] The 1570 'Request', as in Dickinson, W (ed) (1958) *A Sourcebook of Scottish History*, Vol III (London, Nelson) 430.

[76] The 1586, 'Protestant League Between James VI and Elizabeth', as reproduced in Dickinson, W (ed) (1958) *A Sourcebook of Scottish History*, Vol III (London, Nelson) 551.

[77] Elizabeth, as noted in Dickinson, W (ed) (1958) *A Sourcebook of Scottish History*, Vol III (London, Nelson) 444.

[78] Parliament, as noted in Black, J (1985) *The Reign of Elizabeth* (Oxford, Oxford University Press) 384; also ibid, at 108–18, 372.

[79] James, as noted in Dickinson, W (ed) (1958) *A Sourcebook of Scottish History*, Vol III (London, Nelson) 444.

acknowledged himself to be content with Elizabeth's explanation that his mother was trying, wrongfully, to usurp the Crown of England and bring back Catholicism to the realm.[80]

C. The Spanish Armada

In 1585, an Armada of Spanish and Portuguese vessels, comprising some 56 warships and 271 armed merchant vessels began to be assembled with a view to toppling Elizabeth from her throne. The aim was to destroy the English navy and transport Spanish troops from the Low Countries to England. The hope was that once the troops had landed, they would be supported by an estimated 25,000 strong army of disgruntled English Catholics. Over the following months, Elizabeth's navy engaged in skirmishes with the Spanish; and in the spring of 1587, Francis Drake attacked the Spanish fleet assembled in the Bay of Cadiz, 'singeing the king of Spain's beard' when 33 Spanish ships were lost at the cost of one English vessel. However, such acts could not stop the deployment of the Armada, which finally set sail for the English Channel in May 1588. Pedro de Ribadeneyra gave the sermon as they set off:

> This journey, gentlemen, has in its favor all of the reasons of a just and holy war that there can possibly be in the world. And though it may at first seem an offensive rather than a defensive war, in that we are attacking another kingdom instead of defending our own, if we look more closely we will see that it is indeed a defensive war in that we are defending our sacred religion and our most holy Roman Catholic faith; we are also defending the extremely important reputation of our king and lord, and that of our nation; we are also defending all of the property and wealth of all the kingdoms of Spain ... [In England] ... Henry VIII ... [and] ... Elizabeth ... [ruled that] ... thousands of monasteries of great servants of God [should be] laid waste, and ten thousand churches profaned and destroyed, the temples robbed, the sanctuaries sacked ... Elizabeth has persecuted, mistreated, deposed, jailed, imprisoned and finally murdered all the Catholic bishops in England ... she is the one supporting the long, costly, and bloody war of the states of Flanders ... She is the one who has taken over Holland ... against our king, our holy religion and God ... Along with us go faith, truth, and the blessing of the pope ... for the glory of God, will not be absent, but will go with us ... [W]e have nothing to fear, for victory is ours.[81]

[80]   Beemer, C (2015) 'The Mercy Letters of Elizabeth I and Mary, Queen of Scots', *Rhetoric Review* 35 (2), 75–90; McKaren, A (2002) 'Gender, Religion and Early Modern Nationalism: Elizabeth I and Mary Queen of Scots', *The American Historical Review* 107 (3), 739–67; Dickinson, W (1928) 'Negotiations Between Elizabeth and James VI Relating to the Execution of Mary Queen of Scots', *Economica* 22, 121–43; Dunn, J (2003) *Elizabeth and Mary, Cousins, Rivals, Queens.* (NYC, Harpers) 280–93, 303, 309–11, 320, 329, 352, 362–66, 382, 396–98, 410–17, 426–31, 447, 450–55, 480–83.

[81]   Ribadeneyra, 'Exhortation for the Soldiers', as in Cowans, J (ed) (2003) *Early Modern Spain: A Documentary History* (Philadelphia, PA, Penn State University Press) 127, 130; Loomie, A (1973) 'The Armadas and the Catholics of England' *The Catholic Historical Review* 59 (3), 385–403; Black, J (1985) *The Reign of Elizabeth* (Oxford, Oxford University Press) 394–97.

Despite these stirring words, victory was not for the Spanish. Outraged that 'Spain, or any prince of Europe should dare to invade the borders of my realm',[82] Elizabeth found that English technology, tactics, bravery and, ultimately, the weather were on her side. The decisive battle was conducted off the small port of Gravelines in July 1588, then part of Flanders in the Spanish Netherlands, the closest Spanish-controlled territory to England. In the ensuing Battle of Gravelines, the smaller, more nimble English ships provoked Spanish fire whilst staying out of range. The English ships then closed with the larger, less manoeuvrable Spanish vessels, firing broadsides into them and shooting the gunners. Over the course of the day, several Spanish ships ran aground. Soon after, the English attacked the Spanish fleet, anchored at Calais, with fire-ships, as a result of which five Spanish ships were disabled. It was these actions that, in conjunction with the Spanish admirals' inability to communicate with the Spanish army, resulted in the decision's being made to return to Spain. Unfortunately, southwest winds forced the Spanish ships to sail north into the North Sea and around the rocky coasts of Scotland and Ireland. As a result, over one-third of the Spanish and Portuguese fleet and their crews failed to return to home, being destroyed by the weather rather than by the English.[83]

In addition to her ongoing general support to those engaged in wars against Philip II, in 1596 Elizabeth joined forces with France and the Republic of the Seven United Netherlands, to form the *Triple Alliance*.[84] Soon after, a joint Anglo-Dutch attack, with 47 English and 18 Dutch warships, together with 8,000 troops, captured the Spanish port of Cadiz, as a result of which Philip II would lose some 12 million ducats. In reply, despite having incurred massive national debt, Philip II assembled a second (in late 1596) and then a third (in 1597) Armada, with the intention of again attempting to invade England, in the hope of starting a Catholic uprising. However, as before, the weather made the Spanish objectives impossible to achieve.[85]

When the Spaniards finally made a successful landing, it was in Ireland, under the leadership of the new King of Spain, Philip III, the son of Philip II (who had died in 1598). Philip III landed troops to support Hugh O'Neill of the clan Tyrone, who was at the forefront of a revolt against English rule in Ireland. O'Neill had asked for military assistance, requesting money and men 'to restore the faith of the Church and to secure you a kingdom'.[86] Pope Clement VIII recognised O'Neill as 'Captain general of the

---

[82] Elizabeth's 'Speech to Her Troops', as reproduced in Millward, J (1961) *Sixteenth Century: Portraits and Documents* (London, Hutchinson) 100.

[83] Younger, N (2008) 'If the Armada Had Landed: A Reappraisal of England's Defences in 1588', *History* 93, 355; Grant, R (2011) *1001 Battles* (London. Penguin) 292, 293, 294, 296.

[84] The 1596 'League of France, England and the Republic of the Seven United Netherlands Against Spain' in Davenport, F (ed) (1917) *European Treaties Bearing on the History of the United States and its Dependencies to 1648* (NYC, Carnegie Institute) 229–35.

[85] Tenace, E (2003) 'A Strategy of Reaction: The Armadas of 1596 and 1597 and the Spanish Struggle for European Hegemony', *The English Historical Review* 118 (478), 855–82; Borman, T (1997) 'Untying the Knot? The Survival of the Anglo-Dutch Alliance, 1587–97', *European History Quarterly* 27 (3), 307–37; Cheyney, E (1905) 'International Law under Queen Elizabeth', *The English Historical Review* 20 (80), 659–72.

[86] O'Neill, as in McGurk, J (2009) *The Elizabethan Conquest of Ireland* (Manchester, Manchester University Press) 21.

Catholic army in Ireland', and granted him and his followers a plenary indulgence, that is the removal of all the temporal punishment due for their sins, whether to be served in this world or in purgatory. O'Neill repeatedly played the religion card against Elizabeth, although in Ulster, where freedom of conscience was relatively secure, this did not gain him much additional leverage. This was especially so since Elizabeth was keen to ensure that religious persecution was not to be an excuse for rebellion in Ireland. Nonetheless, conflict did occur, after local disputes over the power of English sheriffs around the territory of Ulster quickly escalated throughout much of Ireland, turning into a general rebellion against both settlers and soldiers. Regarding the former, the ruthless destruction of some 4,000 or so of the planted English settlements in Munster was notable. By this stage, the original goal of preserving the autonomy of Ulster had expanded into something much larger. O'Neill's War Aims of 1599 stipulated:

1. That the catholic, apostolic and Roman religion be openly preached and taught throughout Ireland ...
2. That the Church of Ireland be wholly governed by the pope.
3. That all cathedrals and parish churches, abbeys, and all other religious houses ... now in the hands of the English, be restored to the Catholic Churchmen.
4. That all Irish priests and religious men, now prisoners in England, be set at liberty, with all temporal Irishmen that are troubled for their conscience, to go where they will, without further trouble.
5. That no Englishman may be a churchman in Ireland.
6. That the Governor ... Chancellor ... and all principal men of Government ... shall be Irish ...[87]

When the decisive battle finally came at Yellow Ford in 1598, out of some 8,000 men, roughly equally divided between the two sides, the largest ever loss of English soldiers on a battlefield in Ireland occurred, with about 1,000 deaths. This loss resulted in an escalation of the English effort in Ireland, to which Philip III responded, sending 23 Spanish ships with 4,500 men to Ireland in 1601. Elizabeth saw this Spanish effort in Ireland as an attempt to 'restore the superstitions of Rome and to reduce that Realm under Spanish tyranny'.[88] However, the Spanish assistance was two years too late, landed in the wrong place and could not secure victory. The forces of Hugh O'Neill and others were eventually overwhelmed by the weight of the English military response, their final defeat being at the siege of Kinsale in 1602, which left 1,200 Irish dead.

The subsequent subjugation of Ulster was particularly vicious, with scorched earth policies once more being utilised to subdue the local population, killing tens of

[87] The 1599 'War Aims of O'Neill', as reproduced in in Curtis, E (ed) (1943) *Irish Historical Documents 1172–1922* (London, Methuen) 119–20; Connolly, S (2012) *Contested Island: Ireland 1460–1630* (Oxford, Oxford University Press) 234–40; Bonney, R (2012) *The European Dynastic States* (Oxford, Oxford University Press) 140, 142–43.

[88] Elizabeth, as noted in McGurk, J (2009) *The Elizabethan Conquest of Ireland.* (Manchester, Manchester University Press) 14, 240–46; Connolly, S (2012) *Contested Island: Ireland 1460–1630* (Oxford, Oxford University Press) 239–41, 249.

thousands by starvation. Peace was only reached in 1603, when O'Neill agreed to the *Treaty of Mellifont,* ending the Nine Years' War in the Kingdom of Ireland. This oversaw the expulsion of all of the remaining Spanish and a pardon for all of the Irish involved in the conflict. New grants of land created some independent lordships on the local borders around O'Neill and his former allies, whilst the Crown also retained military outposts. Private armies had to be abandoned, and the rebels had to swear allegiance to the Crown of England. In return, O'Neill was guaranteed his life, his lands and his earldom.[89] However, when the conditions of the peace proved undesirable, especially as the English began to encroach upon the remaining lands held by the earls and condemned traditional Irish land tenure systems, O'Neill (and others) left Ireland. Their exit helped pave the way for the authorisation of the confiscation of nearly half a million acres from those earls who, with O'Neill, had fled to mainland Europe, as the Plantation of Ulster. This was in addition to the figure of somewhere between 50,000 and 100,000 soldiers and civilians who had been killed in Ireland during the reign of Elizabeth I, as violence became commonplace.[90]

6. James I/VI

The first decade of the seventeenth century in England saw the arrival of a new monarch. James VI of Scotland was the son of Mary, Queen of Scots, and great-great grandson of the English king, Henry VII. James succeeded Elizabeth I, the last Tudor monarch of England, as King James I of England, the first English monarch of the Stuart dynasty. He had been King of Scotland since 1567, and came to the throne of England and Ireland in 1603. His path to the throne of England was relatively smooth, especially given the potential for foreign, Catholic intervention over who was a legitimate ruler, given the papal interdicts and bulls of excommunication issued against Henry VIII and Elizabeth I. However, Pope Clement VIII did not intervene, fearing a greater rift within Christendom if he did, as the French king, Henri IV, supported James.[91]

Although the *Act of Recognition of the King's Title* of 1604 referred to the 'famous and greater union, or rather reuniting, of two mighty and famous kingdoms of England and Scotland, under one imperial crown',[92] Scotland and England were (despite the

---

[89] McGurk, (2009) *The Elizabethan Conquest of Ireland* (Manchester, Manchester University Press) 7–9, 21–24, 58–61, 63, 244; Connolly S (2012) *Contested Island 1460–1630* (Oxford, Oxford University Press) 243–55, 270; Martines, L (2013) *Furies: War in Europe: 1450–1700* (London, Bloomsbury) 28.

[90] Gajda, A (2009) 'Debating War and Peace in Late Elizabethan England', *The Historical Journal* 52 (4), 851–78; Morgan, H (2004) 'Never Any Realm Worse Governed: Queen Elizabeth and Ireland', *Transactions of the Royal Historical Society* 14, 295–308; Kane, B (2014) 'Ordinary Violence: Ireland as Emergency in the Tudor State', *History* 99 (336), 444–67; Grant, R (2011) *1001 Battles* (London, Penguin) 279, 303, 307, 312.

[91] Schneider, C (2015) 'A Kingdom for a Catholic: Pope Clement VIII, King James VI/I and the English Succession in International Diplomacy', *The International History Review* 37 (1), 119–41.

[92] 'The Act of Recognition of the King's Title, 1604', as reproduced in Adams, M (ed) (1947) *Select Documents on English Constitutional Law* (London, Macmillan) 326–27.

attempts of James towards true union)[93] individual sovereign states, with Scotland retaining full independence over questions of law, religion and civil administration, akin to that in England. Both were ruled over by James through a personal (not constitutional) union, for which he styled himself the King of Great Britain and Ireland.[94]

James had a patchy relationship with his Parliaments in both England and Scotland, repeatedly clashing with them over the origin and extent of Parliamentary powers and privileges, such as the freedom of election, freedom of speech and freedom from arrest whilst in Parliament. He took it for granted that the king alone was to make all final decisions on foreign and domestic policy, and laid particular emphasis upon his supremacy in ecclesiastical matters. Although he knew how to tone down his greater claims when he needed something from Parliament, he was prone to anger when it did not grant him the subsidies he wanted. His anger was such that in 1614 he dissolved the English Parliament when the Commons hesitated to give him the money he desired, ruling without Parliament until 1621, finding his income from alternative sources.

The basis of James's thinking, akin to the theories of the absolute power of the monarch developing in France, and aware of the practices of Henry VIII in England, was that although a good king would frame 'all his actions according to the law',[95] he was not, ultimately, bound by the law if necessity required him to act in a contrary way. Kings, he believed, were appointed by God alone, and they were therefore ultimately responsible to God alone. James explained:

> The state of monarchy is the supremest thing upon Earth: for Kings are not only God's lieutenants upon Earth and sit upon God's throne, but even by God himself they are called gods ... [I]t is sedition to dispute what a King may do in the height of his power ... I shall rule my actions according to my laws.[96]

It followed that kings should not be resisted or disobeyed by any of their subjects, in any circumstances, 'For a king cannot be imagined to be so unruly and tyrannous that the commonwealth will be in better order ... by his taking away.'[97]

On the question of religion, although his mother had been a Catholic, James was brought up within the Protestant Church of Scotland and was married to Anne of Denmark, the daughter of the strongly Protestant Danish king, Frederick II. In his coronation speech, he pledged, inter alia, to maintain the religion, 'presently professed' in England.[98] This pledge to support the status quo meant that a number of notable

---

[93] See the 'Commission for Negotiating a Union with Scotland', as reproduced in Adams, M (ed) (1947) *Select Documents on English Constitutional Law* (London, Macmillan) 327–28.

[94] Croft, P (2003) 'The Reign of James VI and I: The Birth of Britain', *History Compass* 1, 1–13; Griffiths, H (2003) 'Britain in Ruins: the Union of Two Crowns', *Rethinking History* 7 (1), 89–105; Richards, J (2002) 'The English Accession of James VI'. *The English Historical Review* 117 (472), 512–25.

[95] James I, as noted in Davies, G (1987) *The Early Stuarts* (Oxford, Oxford University Press) 32.

[96] James I, 'Divine Right', as in Millward, J (ed) (1961) *The Seventeenth Century: Portraits and Documents* (London, Hutchinson) 61; Friedrich, C (1952) *The Age of the Baroque* (NYC, Harper) 133.

[97] James I, 'The True Law of Free Monarchies', as reproduced in Elton, G (ed) (1968) *Renaissance and Reformation* (London, Macmillan) 237–39.

[98] Carlyle, AJ (1910) *A History of Medieval Political Theory in the West*, Vol VI (London, Blackwood) 437–40.

scholars, such as Robert Filmer in his work *Patriarcha*, came to support James's argument regarding the divine right of kings, stating that since monarchs had been instituted by God, they inherited their power by descent from Noah, and that therefore they were responsible to God alone.[99]

Such views ran directly counter to the views of Catholics, who believed that the Pope was superior to the king. James also had difficulties with the Puritans, who disagreed that James was equal to a living God, to be exalted above his subjects, disagreed with his allowance of certain sports and recreations on Sundays, and who also wanted to continue the persecution of Catholics in Scotland and England. Although James gave way to some of the Puritans' demands, he nevertheless expected that they would conform, and for those who did not wish to do so, emigration to the nascent colonies in the New World was an option. Perhaps James's best known contribution to posterity was the *King James Bible*, an English translation of the Bible for the Church of England, begun in 1604 and completed in 1611, which addressed some of the difficulties with earlier translations identified by the Puritans.[100]

The Catholic question was much more difficult for James. In the case of Ireland, although he carried on supporting the plantations, he inherited a land where the killing had stopped, at least for a time.[101] This calm made it possible for James (despite Puritan objections) to seek peace with Spain and Philip III. Both James and Philip were able to reach an accord, painting earlier wars between Spain and England as personal quarrels between monarchs now past. With the 1604 *Treaty of London*, Spain renounced its intention to restore Catholicism in England, whilst James (contradicting a 1603 agreement he had reached with France, agreeing a defensive alliance between England, Spain and the Seven Provinces)[102] promised to stop intervening in and supporting the Dutch rebellion against Spanish rule. James would have included the Dutch in the treaty, but they refused all terms. For Spain and England, the deal meant freedom of trade and the first English colonies in America.[103]

The success of this treaty was such that when it was discovered that there was a plot by a group of provincial English Catholics to assassinate James I, blow up Parliament

[99] Cuttica, C (2011) 'Anti-Jesuit Patriotic Absolutism: Robert Filmer', *Renaissance Studies* 25 (4), 559–79.

[100] Winship, M (2009) 'Freeborn (Puritan) Englishmen and Slavish Subjection: Popish Tyranny and Puritan Constitutionalism', *The English Historical Review* 124 (510), 1050–74; Ellison, J (2003) 'Measure for Measure and the Executions of Catholics in 1604', *English Literary Renaissance* 45–87; Questier, M (1998) 'The Politics of Religious Conformity and the Accession of James I', *Historical Research* 71 (174), 14–27; Croft, P (2011) 'The Emergence of the King James Version of the Bible', *Theology* 114 (4), 243–50.

[101] The 'Condemnation of Irish Law of 1606' and the 'Plantation of Ulster' in Curtis, E (ed) (1943) *Irish Historical Documents 1172–1922* (London, Methuen) 126–27, 128–33; Maxwell, C (1923) 'The Plantation of Ulster at the Beginning of James I's Reign', *The Sewanee Review* 32 (2), 164–77.

[102] The 1603 Agreement between the King of France and the King of England, in Davenport, F (ed) (1917) *European Treaties Bearing on the History of the United States and its Dependencies to 1648* (NYC, Carnegie Institute) 243.

[103] The 1604 Treaty Between Spain and Britain, in Davenport, F (ed) (1917) *European Treaties Bearing on the History of the United States and its Dependencies to 1648* (NYC, Carnegie Institute) 246; Ungerer, G (1998) 'The Spanish and English Chronicles on the Anglo-Peace Negotiations', *Huntington Library Quarterly* 61 (3), 309–24; Cooper, J (ed) (1970) *The New Cambridge Modern History: The Decline of Spain and the Thirty Years War*, Vol IV (Cambridge, Cambridge University Press) 107, 129, 264–65.

and spark a rebellion (the so-called 'Gunpowder Plot'), there was little government reaction beyond the capture, torture and execution of those involved, although at the social level Protestantism became indelibly associated with patriotism. James himself was remarkably measured in his response. His most forthright action was demanding that his Catholic subjects take an *Oath of Allegiance* to him in 1606, recognising him as the lawful and rightful king, and repudiating the papal claim to depose heretical princes, which claim Pope Paul V forbade English Catholics to repudiate. Although the execution of those who refused to take the oath, typically priests, continued (accounting for the deaths of some 60 individuals between 1606 and 1660), James controlled his response in order to preserve domestic stability and maintain peace with Spain. This desire for peace went so far as to allow the execution of Sir Walter Raleigh, hero of the Elizabethan age, later to be deemed traitor and disobedient servant in the Stuart age, for attacking Spanish interests without the authority of the king.[104]

7. CONCLUSION

This chapter has primarily examined the influence of religion upon the English monarchs Henry VIII, Edward IV, Mary Tudor, Elizabeth I and James I. Although the conventional interests of all these monarchs overlapped in terms of gaining power and territory, and Parliament played a supplementary role for each of them (albeit becoming progressively stronger), overall, for my purposes, this period is about religion and the change of England from a Catholic to a Protestant country. Religion as a cause for war went from a relatively minor consideration at the beginning of the sixteenth century, to the dominant paradigm at the end of the century.

This process began with Henry VIII. Henry started off as a favourite of the Catholic Church. He ended up its enemy. Driven by his anger when the Pope refused to give him the divorce he desired, he severed most of the theological and political ties between England and Rome. Henry cleaved the Catholic Church in England away from Rome, taking supreme control and making loyalty to him in this area absolute. Failure to take the Oath of Supremacy was a treasonable offence that ensnared thousands. Over the course of Henry's actions, he began to turn the Catholic Church in England into the Church of England. Despite their radical nature, though, the violence of his actions was relatively slight.

When he did wage war with France and/or Scotland, it was over traditional matters, with Henry trying very hard to bring Scotland directly under his control, a move that the Scots and their French allies resisted. Similarly, Henry was quite happy

[104] Nicholls, M (2007) 'Strategy and Motivation in the Gunpowder Plot', *The Historical Journal* 50 (4) 787–807; Okines, A (2004) 'Why Was There So Little Government Reaction to the Gunpowder Plot?', *Journal of Ecclesiastical History* 55 (4), 275–87; Dodd, A (1938) 'The Spanish Treason, The Gunpowder Plot and the Catholic Refugees', *The English Historical Review* 53 (212), 627–50; Beer, A (1996) 'The Execution of Sir Walter Raleigh', *Modern Philology* 94 (1), 19–38.

to join Catholic Spain in its war against Catholic France, as long as he thought he could benefit from it. When religious tension did start to boil over in Scotland, it was because of the Scots' own radical theologians, not Henry's influence. Henry's son, Edward VI, continued religious reform, deepening the Protestant roots in England, before his half-sister, Mary Tudor, came to the throne. Her reversal of the religious policies of her father and brother, coupled with her marriage to Philip of Spain, brought about an escalation of violence in both England and Scotland. However, as regards the external wars in Mary's reign, religion was not a factor that drove the alliances she pursued.

External war over the religious question broke out with the next English monarch, Elizabeth I. Elizabeth reverted back to the patterns laid down by her father, Henry VIII, and brother, Edward VI, entrenching the Anglican faith. The resulting excommunication of Elizabeth by the papacy, seeking to encourage Catholic rebellion against her reign, only intensified the anger of Elizabeth and her loyal subjects. Although her conflicts were multifaceted, her short-lived intervention in Scotland, to repel the French force that had landed to aid Mary of Guise against the Protestant lords, and the subsequent execution of Mary, Queen of Scots, in 1587, were coloured by religious considerations. Her eventual war with Spain was triggered by her support for the Protestants in the Low Countries, which led her to believe that she could no longer sit quietly on the sidelines. The response from Spain came not only in the form of various Armadas launched against England, but also direct support for the rebellion against Elizabeth and her Protestant rule in Ireland. Peace was achieved between Spain and England only with the accession of two new monarchs, namely, James I of England and Philip III of Spain, both of whom promised not to support religious factions to the detriment of the other.

V

The Wars of Religion in France

1. Introduction

IN THE FEW decades leading up to the middle of the sixteenth century, Germany split over questions of religion, but then managed to find peace with a compromise allowing opposing Christian faiths to coexist within one, still united realm. Conversely, England remained relatively at peace with itself over religious questions during the sixteenth century. In France, on the other hand, in the last four decades of the sixteenth century, some 3 million people would lose their lives, as two opposing interpretations of Christianity, and their followers' associated quests for dominance or autonomy, led to war.[1]

2. The Huguenots

A. Introduction

The Protestant group in France known as the Huguenots, possibly named after the French adapted the word used for an oath (*Eugenos*) for members of the reformed faith, as inspired by John Calvin—a French theologian and pastor who, like Martin Luther before him, had a significant influence on the Protestant Reformation. By 1560, there were probably a million Huguenots in France (at about one fifteenth of the total population). Calvin's teachings not only emphasised certain theological differences from Catholicism, but also political differences, in that he (and the Huguenots) favoured a type of mixed government combining democracy and aristocracy. Calvin also came to the conclusion that if rulers were to rise up against God, they would lose their divine right to govern and might be put down.[2]

Such views ran directly contrary to the thoughts of the French kings, who believed in the absolute power of the monarch and aspired to rule a realm held together by

---

[1] White, M (2011) *Atrocitology: Humanities 100 Deadliest Achievements* (Melbourne, Text Publishing) 198–205.

[2] Calvin, 'The Authority of Civil Government', as reproduced in Elton, G (ed) (1968) *Renaissance and Reformation* (London, Macmillan) 173–79; Pellerin, D (2003) 'Calvin: Militant or Man of Peace', *The Review of Politics* 65 (1), 35–39; Armstrong, E (1889) 'The Political Theory of the Huguenots', *The English Historical Review* 4 (13), 13–40.

a single religious faith. This meant that Francis I, despite originally supporting the Protestants (in Germany) for his wars against the Emperor Charles V, had no wish to show tolerance towards them in France. He issued the *Edict of Fontainebleau*, ordering his authorities to 'proceed against them [Protestants], sparing no one, by arresting them in whatever place they may be found'.[3] Similar edicts followed in 1540, 1542, 1543 and 1545, as a result of which over 3,000 Protestants were either executed or deported as slaves.[4] Francis' son, Henri II, followed the same path, passing his *Edict of Compiègne*, which proclaimed that the sole punishment for heresy would be death. The *Edict of Chateaubriant* followed in 1551, which brought in strict censorship of Protestant material, and promised one-third of the property of any Protestants to whoever informed against and denounced them. In 1559 he issued the *Edict of Écouen*, in which he would proclaim, 'I swear that if I can settle my disputes abroad I will make the streets run with the blood and heads of the vile Lutheran dogs'.[5]

B. Catherine de' Medici

After the death of Henri II in 1559, Francis II succeeded to the French throne. Francis, who was married to the young Mary, Queen of Scots, ruled for little more than a year before his premature death at the age of 16.[6] He was succeeded by his brother, who came to the throne as King Charles IX at the age of 10. The Queen Regent during this period was Catherine de' Medici. She had been the wife of Henri II, who bore him 10 children (including three future kings of France—Francis II, Charles IX and Henri III—and one Queen Consort of Spain, Elizabeth of Valois, who was the third wife of the Spanish king, Philip II). This process of quick succession precipitated a crisis in which many problems became intertwined, as a number of ambitious noble families within France jockeyed for position, whilst at the same time the Government turned back to a model of periodic meetings in some regions, made up of representatives of the clergy, nobility and the Third Estate.

Catherine initially believed that the 'good of the kingdom' would be secured by promising the Huguenots that if they lived quietly without scandal (that is, did not profess publicly), they would be tolerated and not hunted and/or arrested for 'the crime of heresy'.[7] Despite this offer, some Huguenot adventurers tried to seize certain areas,

---

[3] 'Speech of Francis I', as reproduced in Reddaway, F (ed) (1930) *Select Documents in European History 1492–1715*, Vol II (London, Methuen) 89. Also Knecht, R (2007) *The Valois* (London, Hambledon) 149.

[4] Elton, G (1968) *The New Cambridge Modern History: The Reformation*, Vol II (Cambridge, Cambridge University Press) 165-68, 221, 355; MacKinnon, J (1906) *A History of Modern Liberty*, Vol II (London, Longmans) 160, 221.

[5] Henri II, as noted in Cohen, M (ed) (2004) *History in Quotations* (London, Cassell) 374.

[6] See page 92.

[7] See the 1560 'Edict of Romorantin', as reproduced in Potter, D (ed) (1997) *The French Wars of Religion: Selected Documents* (London, St Martins) 24–25; Crouzet, D (2008) 'A Strong Desire to be a Mother to All of Your Subjects: A Rhetorical Experiment by Catherine de Medici', *Journal of Medieval and Early Modern*

arguing that the peace could not be guaranteed whilst the royal family was under the control of powerful Catholic advisers. The Catholic leaders claimed that the Huguenot claims of religious freedom were just a cover for individual ambition, treason and heresy. In the second half of 1561 they issued the so-called *Treaty of the Triumvirate*. This sought to 'restore the old and pristine state' and 'spare the lives of none who have made profession of this [Protestant] sect'.[8] Catherine replied to such calls with the *Edict of Saint-Germain / Edict of Toleration* of 1562, which recognised the Huguenots' right to 'freedom of conscience', via a freedom of worship in their private places. Such people could not be injured, reproached or provoked 'for the sake of religion'.[9]

Catholic forces responded to Catherine's calls for freedom of conscience by seizing control of various areas to the exclusion of Huguenots, and the Huguenots acted likewise. The Huguenots, who did not see themselves as either heretics or traitors, justified their actions as self-defence against unjust persecution, resisting the aggression of the overt Catholic influences over the royal family, while seeking to rescue the precarious throne of France. When a French Duke then tried to stop a Huguenot congregation at Vassy from worshipping in a barn, killing dozens of the congregants in the process, reprisals escalated. The two sides met in their first major battle at Dreux in 1562. The Catholics narrowly won the day, losing 5,800 of their 19,000 men but killing 4,500 of the Huguenot force of 12,000. Undeterred, the Huguenots tried (but failed) to seize the royal family, justifying their action by claiming that they were protecting them so that they could uphold the *Edict of Saint-Germain*.[10]

Appeals for assistance were sent by the Huguenots to Protestants in England and Germany, in an effort to secure help for what they portrayed as a defence of the Reformation in France. Queen Elizabeth I of England agreed to send 3,000 troops to help garrison Protestant Le Havre, after she realised that Philip II was unlikely to intervene in France due to pressures on Spain in the Low Countries. The deal was that Elizabeth would occupy Le Havre until Calais was returned to her at the end of the conflict. Elizabeth justified this act as being against those in France 'who have advanced themselves in force beyond the authority of the king'.[11] That is, Elizabeth dressed up her intervention into France as being against Catherine's regency, not the young King

---

Studies 38 (1), 103–18; Crawford, K (2000) 'Catherine de Medici and the Performance of Political Motherhood', *Sixteenth Century Journal* 31 (3), 643–70; Knecht, R (1999) 'Catherine de Medici and the French Wars of Religion', *Historian* 62, 18–27.

[8] 'The Treaty of the Triumvirate', in Potter, D (ed) (1997) *The French Wars of Religion: Selected Documents* (London, St Martins) 29; ibid, at 10–11, 31–32.

[9] The 'Edict of 1562', as reproduced in Reddaway, F (ed) (1930) *Select Documents in European History*, Vol II (London, Methuen) 103; Parrow, K (1993) 'Neither Treason nor Heresy: Use of Defence Argument to Avoid Forfeiture During the French Wars of Religion', *The Sixteenth Century Journal* 22 (4), 705–16.

[10] Parrow, K (1993) 'From Defence to Resistance: Justification of Violence During the French Wars of Religion', *Transactions of the American Philosophical Society* 83 (6), 1, 39–40; Greengrass, M (2015) *Christendom Destroyed: Europe 1517–1648* (NYC, Penguin) 404–07.

[11] Elizabeth, as noted in Black, J (1985) *The Reign of Elizabeth* (Oxford, Oxford University Press) 58–59; Wernham, R (1968) *The New Cambridge Modern History: The Counter Reformation* (Cambridge, Cambridge University Press) 136–39, 220–21.

Charles IX. The action was a failure, as the English defenders were attacked by a force four times that number and were forced out of Le Havre in the middle of 1563. Elizabeth then agreed to the *Peace of Troyes* (in 1564), under which she received 120,000 gold crowns, which the French understood as compensation for England's earlier losses in Le Havre and of Calais.[12]

As soon as the English had departed from France, Catherine reverted to trying to steer a middle course between the two sides, to bring peace to France, by issuing the *Edict of Amboise* in 1563. This reiterated Catherine's view that all citizens 'can have liberty of conscience in the houses where they live and the practice of the religion they called Reformed, along with their family and subjects who wish to attend, freely and without constraint'. In their own homes, these people could not be 'pursued or molested, forced or constrained in matters of conscience'.[13] This satisfied neither side, meaning that the divided communities could not be knitted back together. A number of Catholic-controlled institutions resisted registering the *Edict* in full, or even in part. The killings that followed were brought to a stop by the *Peace of Longjumeau* in 1568, on the basis of the acceptance by both sides of the *Edict of Amboise*. Peace did not last, though, and the third and most destructive phase of the French wars of religion began within a few months, as many Catholic communities refused to recognise the limited freedoms promised to the Huguenots, and Catherine turned against the Huguenots after they had tried to kidnap her and her son. She abandoned peace-making attempts. Major battles were fought at Jarnac and Moncontour in 1569, with the Huguenots, supplemented by English volunteers whom Queen Elizabeth would not prevent joining the conflict, losing at least 10,000 men in the second battle. The peace that concluded this phase, which remained unwinnable by either side, was the 'perpetual and irrevocable'[14] 1570 *Edict of Pacification/Saint Germain*. This reiterated freedom of conscience, recognised four 'fortified towns' under Huguenot control (La Rochelle, Montauban, Cognac and La Charite) and spelled out the places where public (and not just private) Protestant worship was to be allowed. When the French king, Charles IX, attempted to strengthen the peace by arranging for his sister, Margaret of Valois, to marry the Protestant leader, King Henri III of Navarre (later King Henri IV of France), the Huguenots became optimistic that their rights might be protected and that they would not become second-class citizens, as the two Christian faiths would exist side by side within the realm of France.[15]

---

[12] Black, J (1985) *The Reign of Elizabeth* (Oxford, Oxford University Press) 54–56, 57–62,131–32, 419, 427–29; Grant, R (2011) *1001 Battles* (London, Penguin) 272.

[13] The 'Edict of Amboise, 1563', as reproduced in Potter, D (ed) (1997) *The French Wars of Religion: Selected Documents* (London, St Martins) 82–83; Roberts, P (2007) 'The Languages of Peace During the French Religious Wars', *Cultural and Social History* 4 (3), 297–315.

[14] The 'Edict of Saint Germain', as in Potter, D (ed) (1997) *The French Wars of Religion: Selected Documents* (London, St Martins) 118–19; the 'Peace of Longjumeau, 1568', ibid, at 105.

[15] Diefendorf, B. (2012). 'Rites of Repair: Restoring Community in the French Religious Wars'. *Past and Present* 214: 31-50; Knecht, R. (2007). *The Valois*. (Hambledon, London). 168-169, 190-199.

C. Henri of Navarre/Henri IV of France

(i) The St Bartholomew's Day Massacre

The marriage of Margaret of Valois to Henri of Navarre was meant to bring peace to the realm. Leaders from all over France made their way to Paris to attend the wedding on 18 August 1572. For some Catholic factions, it was an unprecedented chance to assassinate some of the Huguenot elite, who would be assembled in one location. On 24 August 1572, St Bartholomew's Day, the assassins made their move. Although the attempt failed, a large-scale riot quickly ensued, at which point, probably with the support of Catherine de' Medici, King Charles IX allegedly screamed, 'Kill them all!'[16] In the resulting frenzy, some 3,000 unarmed Huguenot citizens were killed in Paris, and perhaps 10,000 in other areas of France, as the alleged order was carried out into the provinces. 'Huguenot hunting' became something of a sport, the Huguenots being labelled as treasonous heretics who could be pursued without mercy and their property confiscated. Henri of Navarre only survived because, after he was captured, he agreed to live at the French court and convert to Catholicism.[17]

Reactions across Europe varied. In England, Elizabeth rescinded her commitment to the 1572 *Treaty of Blois*, which she had signed with Catherine de' Medici earlier that year and under which England and France established an alliance against Spain, and despite publicly professing neutrality, began to commit men and munitions and allow the free transit of Protestant volunteers to fight in France. In Spain, Philip II, upon hearing the news of the massacre, described his reaction as being 'to laugh, with signs of extreme satisfaction'.[18] In Rome, Pope Gregory XIII celebrated, thanking 'God for granting so great a favour to the Christian people … [as] to cleanse and purge completely the Kingdom of France from the plague of Huguenots'.[19]

In France, although the primary authorship of the massacre was a matter of dispute, the Protestants believed that the royal family was behind it, as Catherine de' Medici went on to defend what happened as being necessary because of 'the evils caused by the diversity of religions'.[20] The Huguenots now found themselves in a direct revolutionary confrontation with the French monarchy, which they believed was tyrannising them. They retreated into the areas they still held, where they were besieged. When

---

[16] Charles IX, as quoted in Seward, D (2013), *The Bourbon Kings of France* (London, Jones) 5; Bonney, R (2012) *The European Dynastic States* (Oxford, Oxford University Press) 169–71.

[17] Parrow, K (1993) 'From Defence to Resistance: Justification of Violence During the French Wars of Religion', *Transactions of the American Philosophical Society*, 83 (6), 141–42; Knecht, R (1999), 'Catherine de Medici and the French Wars of Religion', *Historian* 62, 18, 26–27.

[18] Philip II, as in Parker, G (2002) 'The Place of Tudor England in the Messianic Vision of Philip II of Spain', *Transactions of the Royal Historical Society* 12, 167.

[19] 'Pope Gregory XIII and the News', as reproduced in Reddaway, F (ed) (1930) *Select Documents in European History*, Vol II (London, Methuen) 95. Also Cowie, L (ed) (1970) *The Reformation of the Sixteenth Century* (London, Wayland) 51.

[20] Catherine, as noted in Cowie, L (ed) (1970) *The Reformation of the Sixteenth Century* (London, Wayland) 53.

the siege of the Protestant seaport of La Rochelle was lifted following a five-month blockade, more than 50 per cent of the Huguenot army of 18,000 men lay dead, dying or had deserted. Nevertheless, they held out against the forces of Charles IX and were rewarded with a further peace in the 1573 *Edict of Boulogne*. This Edict was a retreat from earlier recognitions of the rights of Huguenots. Now, they were only permitted freedom of conscience in terms of private worship, and only in the three areas which remained under Huguenot control.[21]

(ii) Henri III and the Catholic League

The French king, Charles IX, died in1574. His successor was his brother, Henri, who had for a few months been the King of Poland and Grand Duke of Lithuania. Upon accession to the French throne, following more conflict in 1575 and the risk of intervention by German and/or English Protestants increasing, Henri III attempted to calm relations with England and reaffirmed the 1572 *Treaty of Blois*. Furthermore, following what he had learnt in his short time in Poland and Lithuania,[22] he disavowed the approach adopted by his brother, Charles IX, and undertook an experiment in toleration with the 1576 *Edict of Beaulieu*. This Edict expanded the areas for freedom of conscience, giving the Huguenots the right of public worship throughout France, except in Paris and at the royal court. They were also to be allowed to build their own churches, and admission to all public professions was granted. In addition, the senior administrations were to be remodelled to allow an equal number of Huguenots and Catholics. A disclaimer of the Massacre of St Bartholomew was also included, and those who had been excluded from power were to be reinstated. The problem was that the terms of the Edict were not implemented by the king, and within the realm Catholic opposition to the Edict resulted in the formation of the *Catholic League*, which aimed to 'restore and maintain the exercise of our catholic, apostolic, and Roman religion …　in which we resolve to live and die'.[23] In the face of the determination of the Catholic League, the *Edict of Beaulieu* and all attempts to promote toleration were withdrawn.[24]

　　The difficulty for Henri III was that as he was the last Valois, his youngest brother and heir presumptive, Francis, Duke of Anjou, having died and Henri being without children, according to Salic law,[25] Henri of Navarre was next in line to the French throne (as the next senior agnatic descendent of Louis IX). However, Henri of Navarre had escaped the French court, abjured his commitment to Catholicism and rejoined

[21]　Skinner, Q (1978) *The Foundations of Modern Political Thought*, Vol II (Cambridge, Cambridge University Press) 215–16, 242, 285, 320; Martines, L (2013) *Furies: War in Europe: 1450–1700* (London, Bloomsbury) 12–14.

[22]　See page 192.

[23]　The 1577 'Catholic League' in Reddaway, F (ed) (1930) *Select Documents in European History*, Vol II (London, Methuen) 98.

[24]　The 'Edict of Beaulieu, 1576' in Potter, D (ed) (1997) *The French Wars of Religion: Selected Documents* (London, St Martins) 163–68; Braghi, G (2014) 'The Death of Charles IX Valois: An Assassin's or a Martyr's Blood?', *French History* 28 (3), 303–21.

[25]　See page 28.

the ranks of the Protestants who now had significant holdings in south-western France. The prospect of a Protestant King of Navarre as ruler of a Catholic France, led to the reforming of the *Catholic League* in 1584. This body, which included strong urban groupings with clear Catholic leanings, started to challenge the idea of monarchy and its responsibilities in France. The League's rebellion was in accordance with the bull issued by Pope Sixtus V that attempted to deprive Henri of Navarre of the right to the French throne by declaring him excommunicate. Subsequently, the secret 1584 *Treaty of Joinville* was concluded between France's Catholic nobles, notably the House of Guise, and Spain. This was aimed at preventing Henri of Navarre from succeeding to the French throne and, working jointly, at achieving 'a perpetual offensive and defensive union for the defence and conservation of the Catholic religion and the entire extirpation of all heresies of France and the Low Countries'.[26] King Henri III then agreed the 1585 *Treaty of Nemours* with the Catholic League. This not only excluded Henri of Navarre from succession to the throne, it also abolished all attempts to include Protestants in government, withdrew the right for Huguenots to hold any fortified towns and repealed all previous edicts establishing peace with the Huguenots. Thus, 'in this our kingdom ... there will be no practice of [Protestantism] but only that of the Catholic religion'.[27] The Council of Trent was to be upheld in all parts of France, and the Inquisition was to be established.[28]

Henri of Navarre responded by denouncing the 'tyranny and usurpation' of the Pope and the Catholic League, and declared a 'perpetual and irreconcilable war'[29] to secure his rights as the next King of France and religious toleration. Supplementary political arguments, in which religion and politics now clearly overlapped, appeared to support Henri of Navarre, whose idea of kingship was clearly linked to the sovereignty and consent of the community. Philippe du Plessis Mornay argued this in 1579 in his *Defence of Liberty Against Tyranny*:

> We say that the people make their kings, confer the right to rule, approve their election by their voices. God wanted this to be done in this manner in order that kings should acknowledge that they all owe all their authority and power, next to Himself, to the people. Therefore they are to concentrate all their care, thought and diligence on the needs of the people ... Since kings are made by the people, it is entirely manifest that the whole people is above the king ... Innumerable peoples manage to survive without kings, but one cannot even conceive of a king without a people.[30]

---

[26] The 'Treaty of Joinville, 1585' in Potter, *The French Wars of Religion: ibid*, 188–89. Also Tingle, E (2002) 'Nantes and the Origins of the Catholic League', *The Sixteenth Century Journal* 33 (1), 109–28.
[27] 'Royal Edict Revoking Religious Toleration' in Potter, *The French Wars of Religion ibid*, 194–95; Knecht, R (2007) *The Valois* (London, Hambledon) 220–30.
[28] For the Council of Trent in this volume, see page 92 commentary, see Luc, R (2009) 'Reasons of State, Religious Passions and the French Wars of Religion', *The Historical Journal* 52 (4), 1075–83; Parrow, K (1993) 'From Defence to Resistance: Justification of Violence During the French Wars of Religion', *Transactions of the American Philosophical Society* 83 (6), 1, 50–54.
[29] Navarre, in Bonney, R (2012) *The European Dynastic States* (Oxford, Oxford University Press) 174; ibid, at 47, 52–54, 64–66, 172–75.
[30] Philippe Duplessis-Mornay, 'An Attack on Tyrants' in Elton G (ed) (1968) *Renaissance and Reformation* (London, Macmillan) 234–36.

The two sides clashed again at the Battle of Coutras in 1587, where the Catholics lost 2,000 men (of a force numbering 20,000) to a much smaller number of Huguenots, who won the day under the leadership of Henri of Navarre. Undeterred by such a loss, the Royal *Edict of Union* in 1588 reflected a hardened position, with Henri III promising 'to live and die in the Catholic religion, to promote its advance and preservation, ... to extirpate from our kingdom, lands and territories in our obedience all schism and heresies condemned by the holy Councils'.[31] However, by the end of that year it was apparent that Henri III could not beat Henri of Navarre militarily, although the latter was definitely on the defensive. As Henri III wavered in his commitment to completely destroy non-Catholic communities in France, attempts were made to take his power from him by the Committee of Sixteen a junta of fanatical Catholic nobles and bourgeoisie, who took control of Paris and established a more militant, pro-Catholic government. Henri III recognised that there was now not only a risk of France's being split apart in the war with Henri of Navarre, there was also a substantial risk that he might lose his crown to more dogmatic Catholics, with their evolving views of kingship (which would enhance their traditional status and diminish his) and their preferences as to who should succeed him.[32]

It was in this atmosphere that Jean Bodin, the French jurist and member of the Paris *Parlement*, penned his most influential works, rejecting all theories of resistance and/ or shared political power, and advocating the acceptance of a strong monarchy as the only means of restoring political unity and peace in France. For Bodin, the fundamental aim of government was to secure order, not liberty. He doubted any other political options, other than absolute authority of the king, could achieve this goal. Accordingly, 'the sovereign cannot in any way be subject to the commands of another'.[33]

(iii) Reconciliation and Assassination

How much the views of Bodin influenced either Henri of Navarre or Henri III is a matter of conjecture, although it is notable that in these turbulent times, Henri III took a sudden change of course that was designed to secure the absolute authority of the Crown. Specifically, he had some of the most provocative Catholic leaders executed or imprisoned, and then came to terms with Henri of Navarre, recognising him as his successor. Henri III and Henri of Navarre then joined forces after the public reconciliation, and soon controlled the entire area between the Loire and the Seine. Together,

---

[31] The 'Royal Edict of Union, 1588' in Potter, D (ed) (1997) *The French Wars of Religion: Selected Documents* (London, St Martins) 201; Skinner, Q (1978) *The Foundations of Modern Political Thought*, Vol II (Cambridge, Cambridge University Press) 248–50.

[32] Love, R (1999) 'A Game of Cat and Mouse: Henri De Navarre and the Huguenot Campaigns of 1584–89', *Canadian Journal of History* 34 (1), 1–22.

[33] Bodin, *On Sovereignty*, trans Franklin, T (1992) (Cambridge, Cambridge University Press) 28; ibid, at 18 and 120; Salmon, J (1996) 'The Legacy of Jean Bodin: Populism or Constitutionalism?', *History of Political Thought* 17 (4), 500–22; Carlyle, AJ (1910) *A History of Medieval Political Theory in the West*, Vol VI (London, Blackwood) 284–85, 415–18.

they assembled an army of 40,000 to besiege Paris. These acts allowed the Sorbonne to declare Henri III guilty of murder and tyranny, and to absolve all Frenchmen from their allegiance to him. The *Catholic League* then became an openly revolutionary party, a member of which, the Dominican friar, Jacques Clément, decided to kill the king, on the understanding that such an act was 'not from any motive of private or public vengeance' and that the assassin's act was 'solely from his zeal for God's honour and for his religion, for his country's welfare and general peace'. For such a killing, the assassin would 'earn great merit and God will take pleasure in the deed'.[34] On 1 August 1589, Clément gained access to Henri III's presence and stabbed him to death.

(iv) Henri IV's Conversion to Catholicism

Whether God took pleasure from Henri III's assassination cannot be known. What is certain is that it did not stop Henri of Navarre's accession to the French throne, as Henri IV, the first Bourbon monarch of France. The difficulty for Henri IV was that, although he held the throne, as a Protestant, many of his Catholic subjects wanted to wage war against him. Accordingly, he had to find friends to come to his aid. Elizabeth I, hoping to regain a port on the Atlantic seaboard of France, lent Henri both money and 4,000 men. With this support, Henri IV went to war against the extremist Catholic elements in his kingdom, who in turn, were openly supported by Spanish forces. Despite winning a series of military victories, with the Battle of Ivry (1590) being most significant, where the Catholic League lost 10,000 of its army of 17,000, Henri lacked the heavy artillery necessary to take well-fortified areas. When he besieged Paris with 15,000 men, preferring not to bombard the city, he tried to force the Parisians to bend to his will by starving them into submission, as a result of which between 13,000 and 30,000 died. However, they would not surrender, though they were only saved when Spanish troops entered France, under the leadership of King Philip II. Realising that France was now an international battleground, Henri concluded, 'it is high time that all of us, drunk with war, sobered up'.[35] To this end, Henri IV publicly converted to Catholicism in 1593 at which point he is rumoured to have said, 'Paris is worth a mass'.[36] Along with his own personal commitment to Catholicism, he rescinded all of the divisive acts of his predecessor, mandating the realm of religious tolerance that Catherine de' Medici originally attempted, but also, amongst other things, allowed Protestants to hold public office. These acts, especially his conversion to Catholicism, took the wind of out of the sails of many of the Catholics who had previously opposed him.[37]

---

[34] As in Wernham, R (1968) *The New Cambridge Modern History: The Counter Reformation* (Cambridge, Cambridge University Press) 303; Dickerman, E (2000) 'Mission Impossible: The Policies of Henri III', *Canadian Journal of History* 35 (3), 421–39; Potter, D (1995) 'Kingship in the Wars of Religion: The Reputation of Henri III of France', *European History Quarterly* 25 (4), 485–525.

[35] Henri IV, as noted in Cohen, M (ed) (2004) *History in Quotations* (London, Cassell) 380.

[36] Henri IV, in Cohen, *ibid*, 379; cf Greengrass, M (2015) *Christendom Destroyed: Europe 1517–1648* (NYC, Penguin) 430.

[37] Seward, D (2013) *The Bourbon Kings of France* (London, Jones) 8–10, 11–12.

The new Pope, Clement VIII, was dogmatic on a number of issues. He expelled all Jews from the papal territories and tried to ban their sacred books. He also, initially, did not believe in the sincerity of Henri IV's conversion to Catholicism. Philip II of Spain responded to this by sending further Spanish troops into France to help the *Catholic League*, as did the papacy, sending a contingent of troops to France in support of the more extreme Catholics. This time, Philip II added that his help was contingent on recognition of the claim of Isabella, Philip's daughter, to the throne of France, through a right of descent from her mother, Elizabeth of Valois.[38] Very simply, Philip II was determined to bypass the Salic law and exclude the house of Bourbon from the throne of France. However, the French were becoming exhausted with fighting. This discontent was such that a third group, the peasantry, the *Croquants*, briefly arose in both central and southern France between 1593 and 1595, advocating social justice and religious tolerance, focusing more on the bourgeoisie as their enemy than on differences of religion. Henri IV did not need to fight the *Croquants*, and their rebellion eventually dissolved. Similarly, when Henri IV marched on Paris for a third time in 1594, he entered the capital almost unopposed, with most Parisians preferring to accept the sincerity of Henri IV's conversion over the military support of Philip II of Spain.[39]

(v) The Edict of Nantes

Henri IV joined forces with England and the Seven United Netherlands, in their *Triple Alliance* of 1596 against Spain as Philip II also advanced and captured the cities of Amiens and Calais. However, realising that the momentum could not be maintained and that the war was too financially draining, Philip agreed to peace after Pope Clement VIII accepted the sincerity of Henri IV's conversion to Catholicism (Henri having obtained permission to reform the Catholic Church in France, it being feared that if he did not, the French Church could try to break free from Rome) and solemnly absolved Henri from earlier papal condemnations. With this reconciliation Henri IV was able to bring peace to France. He did this in two steps. First, he agreed to the 1598 *Treaty of Vervins* with Spain, quitting the *Triple Alliance*, after Philip II (reluctantly) recognised Henri IV as King of France and withdrew his forces from French territory, thus starving the remaining anti-Bourbon forces of oxygen, whilst also averting the chance of France's becoming a European battleground. Second, Henri IV also passed the *Edict of Nantes* in 1598, despite the objections of the papacy. This was largely based upon the principles of toleration found in the earlier edicts, allowing for the practising of the Protestant religion in private dwellings, but it could not be publicly preached,

---

[38] See page 124.

[39] Bonney, R (2012) *The European Dynastic States* (Oxford, Oxford University Press) 177; Norwich, J (2011) *Absolute Monarchs: A History of the Papacy* (London, Random) 216, 316; Murphy, C (2011) *God's Jury: The Inquisition and the Making of the Modern World* (London, Penguin) 79; Rogerson, B (2010) *The Last Crusaders* (London, Abacus) 61, 134, 282–85; Elliot, J (2002) *Imperial Spain* (London, Penguin) 109; Carr, M (2009) *Blood and Faith: The Purging of Muslim Spain* (NYC, New Press) 32–36; Green, T (2007) *Inquisition: The Reign of Fear* (London, Macmillan) 103.

nor Protestant books sold, except in cities or on estates where the Huguenot religion was upheld.[40] In a masterpiece of statecraft that brought peace to France, the Edict explained:

> And in order to leave no occasion for troubles or differences between our subjects we have permitted and herewith permit those of the said religion called Reformed to live and abide in all the cities and places of this our kingdom ... without being annoyed, molested or compelled to do anything in the matter of religion contrary to their consciences ...[41]

Despite this peace, Henri IV realised that many of his former Huguenot comrades could be just as dangerous as his traditional Catholic enemies. His goal was to maintain a balance between the two sides, whilst encouraging tolerance and public disputations between theologians of the two Churches. At the same time, buoyed by the earlier philosophy of the need for the absolute power of the monarchy, as articulated by Bodin,[42] a new generation of scholars, such as Charles Loyseau, advanced the argument that '[t]he Kings of France are Kings, elected and chosen by God, ... Kings are the living images of God ...',[43] who did not need the consent of the Estates to govern.[44]

In terms of external threats, Henri IV was concerned about France being encircled by the Habsburgs, whose lands stretched from The Vosges to the Carpathians. The Spanish branch of the family, as led by the King of Spain, had been the principal foreign power trying to stop Henri from gaining the throne of France. Thankfully, after peace was made with Philip II in 1598 under the *Treaty of Vervins*, although Philip II died soon after, his son, Philip III, respected it, allowing Henri IV to turn his attention to the Duchy of Savoy (historically, lying below Switzerland, between France and the Duchy of Milan), which Henri had also been fighting, as its leader had not agreed to the *Peace of Vervins*. Henri achieved peace with the Duke Savoy, with a territory exchange between the two powers in 1601, under the *Treaty of Lyon*.

Although Henri may have been preparing for war against Spain in the last years of the decade, before he could proceed, he was assassinated in 1610 by a lone Catholic zealot, François Ravaillac, who was angry that Henri was contemplating alliances with Protestant groups in Germany.[45]

---

[40] Wolfe, M (1999) 'La Paix de Vervins, 1598', *The Sixteenth Century Journal* 30 (3), 839–49; Betten, F (1935) 'The Pontificate of Pope Clement VIII', *The Catholic Historical Review* 20 (4), 420–26; Martines, L (2013) *Furies: War in Europe: 1450–1700* (London, Bloomsbury) 125–35.

[41] Arts III and VI of the 1598 *Edict of Nantes*, reproduced in Reddaway, F (ed) (1930) *Select Documents in European History*, Vol II (London, Methuen) 103. Note, Paris was the exception to the rule. Also Tulchin, A (2015) 'Ending the French Wars of Religion', *The American Historical Review* 120 (5), 1696–1708; Roberts, P (2007) 'The Languages of Peace During the French Religious Wars', *Cultural and Social History* 4 (3), 297–315.

[42] See page 122.

[43] Howell, A (ed and trans) (1994) *Loyseau: A Treatise of Orders and Plain Dignities* (Cambridge, Cambridge University Press) 9. Also Cooper, J (ed) (1970) *The New Cambridge Modern History: The Decline of Spain and the Thirty Years War*, Vol IV (Cambridge, Cambridge University Press) 118–19.

[44] Hodson, S (2005) 'The Politics of the Frontier: Henri IV', *French History* 19 (4), 413–39.

[45] Walker, A (1995) 'Mind of an Assassin: Ravaillac and the Murder of Henri IV', *Canadian Journal of History*, 30 (2), 201–29; Seward, D (2013) *The Bourbon Kings of France* (London, Jones) 24–27.

3. Conclusion

Unlike Germany, which dealt with division and the reconciliation of the religious question in the first half of the sixteenth century, France had to deal with essentially the same question in the second half of the century. This question had to be answered, as the Huguenots—Protestants in France inspired by the theologian Jean Calvin—had come to represent over 1 million people by the year 1560. This group made clear that although they were fundamentally loyal to the French Crown, to deny them the ability to practise their religion and/or persecute them for it, would be tantamount to tyranny, which they would oppose, by force if necessary.

The first French monarchs to deal with this problem, Francis I and Henri II, were uncompromising. Conversely, the Queen Regent, Catherine de' Medici, learning from the example of Germany, initially proposed a type of tolerance, allowing Huguenots freedom of religion in some specific areas, in private. For decades thereafter, wars were waged over the adequacy of such measures, over whether they should be tolerated at all, or whether such toleration should be extended. Neither side was able to gain the upper hand, and the conflict sucked in other interested countries, such as England to a degree, but especially Spain. The solution only came when the French king, Henri III, realised that the biggest threat to France was not the existence of different religious views but the fact that some of the supporters of those views were willing to usurp the throne and use Spanish help to achieve it. In the face of such threats, he reconciled with his foremost Protestant opponent, Henri of Navarre. In turn, when Henri of Navarre came to the throne of France as Henri IV, he brought peace by converting to Catholicism but passing the *Edict of Nantes*, allowing religious freedom for the Huguenots—in private in Catholic areas, but in public in the few areas the Huguenots controlled.

VI

The Rise of the Dutch Republic

1. INTRODUCTION

BEFORE PROGRESSING WITH this chapter, it is necessary to understand some of the nomenclature, as the area covered has been known by many names. The general area is often known as the Low Countries, which is a low-lying coastal region in Western Europe. In modern-day terms, it primarily consists of the Netherlands, Belgium and the French-speaking parts of Flanders and Hainaut. The Seventeen Provinces arose from the Burgundian Netherlands, which sought but failed to achieve independence under Charles the Bold. Through negotiation of marriage contracts, they became the Imperial Habsburg Netherlands. In the war that followed in this region, seven areas broke free of their Habsburg overlords to become known as either the United Provinces or the Seven Provinces. In 1581, this group of provinces started to describe themselves as the Dutch Republic. This breakaway was monumental, as for the first time in the wars of religion that were convulsing Europe, a new nation emerged.

2. A LEGACY OF AUTONOMY

The Dutch Revolt was a conflict that lasted 80 years (1568–1648), consuming tens, if not hundreds, of thousands of people in their bid for independence from Spanish rule. To many minds, this was the blueprint for many later great revolutions. The roots of the bid for independence lay in the fact that the communities of the Burgundian Netherlands had a long history of greatly valuing their independence, as recognised by Mary of Burgundy in the 1477 *Great Privilege*. The Holy Roman Emperor Charles V subsequently promised that he would uphold these privileges, and not allow them and other rights and liberties 'to be injured or diminished … in any way'.[1] However, an uprising occurred in 1539, when the citizens of Ghent attempted to reject the centralising tendencies of the Spanish and the imposition of a tax upon the city to which they had not consented. Charles V personally directed the military actions to retake this city,

---

[1] Note, this particular quotation is taken from the promise of Charles V to the city of Leuven. See 'Privileges of Subjects Confirmed' as reproduced in Rowen, H (ed) (1972) *The Low Modern Countries in Early Modern Times* (London, Macmillan) 12–13.

and in doing so, noted that although not a driving factor in the rebellion, the teachings of John Calvin were taking root in the area.

Charles V's successor, King Philip II of Spain, adopted the same pattern, promising to respect traditional liberties, but then reacted strongly when the citizens of the Netherlands objected to having new taxes imposed upon them without their consent, for which they found themselves punished for 'the sin of insolence'.[2] Concerns escalated in 1559 when Pope Paul IV issued the papal bull *Super universas*, which called for a thorough reorganisation of the traditional ecclesiastical structures in the Seventeen Provinces (removing the right of local election). This was seen as necessary because Protestant dissent was beginning to appear in a number of areas. Philip II responded by sending in the Inquisition to root out heresy, without compromise. As a result, many were executed and thousands fled towards the safety of England. As Philip's grip tightened, at the end of 1565 a league was formed, of about 400 lesser nobles, including some Catholics, who, due to the shabby dress of some of the members, were known as the 'Beggarly Nobles'. This group supported the liberties granted in the 1477 *Great Privilege*, regional autonomy and religious freedom, and rejected the imposition of the Inquisition in the Netherlands. Thus:

> Not only is this Inquisition iniquitous and contrary to all laws of God and man, in its barbarity exceeding the worst practices of tyrants; it cannot but result in great dishonor to God's name and in the utter ruin and desolation of all these Low Countries … [I]t would destroy all public law and order and all equity, completely weaken the sanction and respect for the ancient laws, customs and ordinances … and deprive the States of the country of any freedom to express their opinions … and thereby make the burghers and common people of this country wretched and everlasting slaves of the Inquisitors.[3]

Philip was unimpressed by these assertions. He made clear that there would be no permissive edict, expressing tolerance of the practice of Protestantism in the Seventeen Provinces, such as would later be found in the 1598 *Edict of Nantes* in France, and ordered that all of his edicts against heretics must be enforced. Local authorities were also banned from meeting. The following year, 1566, was marked by famine throughout the land and further attempts to suppress Protestant worship. This was especially so since the Protestant prayer meetings sometimes ended up with crowds rioting and engaging in iconoclasm, destroying any religious images they could find. These riots came to be led by ad hoc rebels known as the 'Beggarly Poor', who were committed to destroying the vestiges of Catholicism and regaining control over their own communities. The result was general anarchy against many forms of authority, with widespread attacks on the established churches being common. Philip II promised the Pope that he

---

[2] Cardinal Granville, as reproduced in Rowen, H (ed) (1972) *The Low Modern Countries in Early Modern Times* (London, Macmillan) 27.

[3] 'The Declaration of the Beggarly Nobles' in Cowie, L (ed) (1970) *The Reformation of the Sixteenth Century* (London, Wayland) 29, 30; Cruz, L (2007) 'The Dutch Revolt in Historical Perspective', *History Compass* 5 (3), 914–34; Wernham, R (1968) *The New Cambridge Modern History: The Counter Reformation* (Cambridge, Cambridge University Press) 266, 286, 311–13.

would regain full control of the Seventeen Provinces, as he had no intention of being 'a ruler of heretics'.[4]

Philip followed up on his promise in 1567, by sending an army of 9,000 men (which quickly multiplied eightfold), under the command of Fernando Alvarez de Toledo, Duke of Alba, to put down the disturbances. This was done under the auspices of what Alba called the 'Council of Troubles'. This tribunal, with its unrestrained definitions of treason, convicted approximately 12,000 people of crimes and executed or exiled over 1,000, including a number of prominent nobles, after Philip said that 'the hardness, wickedness and obstinacy of the said rebels has reached the point that no one can doubt that they deserve rigorous and exemplary punishment'.[5] The scholar Balthasar de Ayala would justify these actions because, 'no matter how grievous are the burdens which a king imposes on his subjects, they may not rebel'.[6] Thus, killing them and taking everything they owned without restriction was justified.

3. WILLIAM OF ORANGE

It was the Council of Troubles that prompted Prince William of Orange, the most powerful nobleman of the Seventeen Provinces, who had until this point been relatively neutral though in exile in Germany, to mount an invasion of the northern provinces, 'to drive the Spanish vermin from the land'.[7] William argued for rebellion and the use of force against the tyranny of the Spanish on the grounds of breach of feudal obligation to protect their own citizens, local autonomy and freedom of religion. He explained:

> In order to prevent the ruin and desolation of these lands, which are being assaulted by the Spaniards, whose ... purpose is to bring them and hold them in intolerable slavery, sorrow and misery under their government ... the Low Countries face the danger not only of being robbed of their contracts, leagues and privileges ... because the Spaniards further endeavor by promulgation and renewal of edicts to extirpate the word of God ... Therefore, having been earnestly beseeched by the inhabitants of the county of both Protestant and Roman faiths to take action ... to protect the freedom and liberty of everyone in his religion and conscience, we ...[shall fight].[8]

[4] 'Philip II to his Ambassador in Rome', as reproduced in Cohen, M (ed) (2004) *History in Quotations* (London, Cassell) 338; Constance, M (1928) 'Spanish Rule in the Netherlands', *The Catholic Historical Review* 14 (3), 365–422.

[5] Philip II, in Waxman, M (1997) 'Philip II and Sixteenth Century Warfare', *War in History* 4 (3), 339–47.

[6] Ayala, B (1574) in Westlake, J (ed) (1917) *The Offices of Military Discipline*, Vol I (Oxford, Oxford University Press) 2.23.

[7] William, Prince of Orange, as quoted in Cowie, L (ed) (1970) *The Reformation of the Sixteenth Century* (London, Wayland) 58. Also Geevers, L (2010) 'Family Matters: William of Orange and the Habsburgs after the Abdication of Charles V', *Renaissance Quarterly* 63 (2), 459–90; Bonney, R (2012) *The European Dynastic States* (Oxford, Oxford University Press) 135, 149.

[8] William, Prince of Orange, 'Against Spain' in Cowie, L (ed) (1970) *The Reformation of the Sixteenth Century* (London, Wayland) 38–39; Stipriaan, R. (2007) 'Words at War: The Early Years of William of Orange's Propaganda', *Journal of Early Modern History* 11 (4), 331–49.

Battle was engaged at Jemmingen in 1568. In this conflict, at least 6,000 Dutch out of a force of perhaps 12,000 were slaughtered by the more professional Spanish forces. The Duke of Alba then continued his campaign of pacification of the provinces. Things only began to turn around when a band of semi-piratical 'Sea Beggars', in command of about 30 vessels, under the commission of the Prince of Orange and working out of English ports, took one town after another in Holland and Zeeland, after Alba had left the two provinces largely undefended. The Sea Beggars trumped the Spanish navy in the Zuiderzee, taking six Spanish vessels (out of 30) for the loss of only one of their own. In a wish to drive this momentum, William of Orange called upon all of the inhabitants of the Low Countries to rise up against the Duke of Alba and the King of Spain, who was 'in violation of his oath, and contrary to the liberties and privileges of the country'. He iterated the importance of fighting the excessive taxes and 'the present enslavement by cruel, foreign and bloodthirsty oppressors'. He promised 'freedom of conscience' and being able to escape the 'fears, anxieties, persecutions, slayings, robberies and harassments by tyrants, the Spanish foreigners, the inquisitors, bishops and the edicts'.[9] The Prince of Orange's rallying call was supplemented by a continual stream of political pamphlets, like *Defence and True Declaration*, which argued the people were above the king, and that the king had no authority to undertake any action that affected the liberty of the people or pass laws without 'the will and assent of the estates of the whole country'.[10]

A revolutionary assembly met at the end of 1572 in Dordrecht, with the purpose of coordinating resistance against the Duke of Alba. It proclaimed that it represented the 'lawful States of Holland', and although many issues went unresolved, such as how much autonomy each province and city might expect, the fight against the 'tyranny of Alba' was a clear priority. Philip II of Spain recognised that to restore some form of calm to the region, he would have to recall Alba, who was clearly the source of a great deal of hatred. The opportunity for him to do this came with the 1573 *Convention of Nymegen* between England and Spain. In this agreement, compensation for previous losses caused by privateers was agreed as a principle, as was non-assistance to rebels. Furthermore, it was agreed that the Duke of Alba would leave the Seventeen Provinces, to undertake other matters pertaining to the Spanish court elsewhere. Before the ink on the 1573 agreement was dry, privateers under the authority of the Prince of Orange captured Brill from the Spaniards and proceeded to fortify it. This was taken as a signal for widespread revolt, with the inhabitants of Flushing, Rotterdam, Schiedam and Gouda expelling their Spanish garrisons.[11]

---

[9] William, Prince of Orange, 'A Call to Rise Up' in Cowie, L (ed) (1970) *The Reformation of the Sixteenth Century* (London, Wayland) 40–41; Wernham, R (1968) *The New Cambridge Modern History: The Counter Reformation* (Cambridge, Cambridge University Press) 232, 292; Grant, R (2011) *1001 Battles* (London, Penguin) 279, 286.

[10] 'A Defence and True Declaration' in van Gelderen, M (ed) (2001) *The Dutch Revolt* (Cambridge, Cambridge University Press) 1, 7; Swart, E (2006) 'The Low German Foot Soldiers in the Second Half of the Sixteenth Century', *International Institute for Social Geschiedenis* 51, 75–92; Grant, R (2005) *Battle: 5000 Years of Combat* (London, DK) 146.

[11] Martines, L (2013) *Furies: War in Europe: 1450–1700* (London, Bloomsbury) 64–69.

In the areas where the Spanish were not expelled, large numbers of troops rioted. Towns and villages were plundered or held to ransom by a licentious soldiery who treated the civilian population with extreme cruelty. In Antwerp in 1576, over 8,000 locals were killed by Spanish soldiers who rioted because of their lack of pay. This was what the Prince of Orange had been waiting for. Repugnance at what happened in Antwerp was so great that for the first time in nine years, all Seventeen Provinces came together and agreed the 1576 *Pacification of Ghent*, for 'firm and unbreakable friendship and peace' amongst all of the Dutch provinces. The first article of the treaty affirmed their shared desire to 'restore the citizens to their rights, privileges and liberties and to their former prosperity'.[12] Further articles sought to suspend all edicts against heresy and strike a truce in matters of religion. Philip, realising that some form of concessions were required if peace was to be achieved in the Seventeen Provinces, directed a new governor general, Alexander Farnese, to be sent to the region as governor general. In 1578, he was joined by the nephew of Philip, Matthias who was invited to the Netherlands by the States-General of the rebellious provinces. Despite the position of Matthias not being accepted by Philip II, Matthias quickly made peace with William of Orange, after it appeared that either France and/or England might intervene directly in the conflict. Matthias promised to try to secure the removal of Spanish troops from the northern provinces and end many of the practices that were causing resentment (such as religious intolerance) in the occupied zones. He was then at the forefront of the conclusion of the 1578 *Peace of Religion*, which was a reaffirmation of the *Pacification of Ghent*, with additional provision for avoidance of religious conflict, such as preventing the slander of either faith.[13]

The promises of the 1578 agreement went unfulfilled, and a new campaign was planned against the Dutch rebels, after Philip baulked at the idea of tolerance and the attempts of his nephew Matthias to find a middle ground. Thus, 'there is to be no flaw, no change, no concession or otherwise of liberty of conscience or religious peace or anything of that sort. They are all to embrace the Catholic religion, and the exercise of that alone is to be permitted'.[14] As the fighting restarted, the Dutch began to look for help from the Queen of England, but she initially stood by her commitments to the Spanish in the *Treaty of Bristol* of 1574.[15] The result was that when the next large-scale battle did occur at Gembloux in 1578, the Spanish forces easily won the day, killing at least 10,000 rebels, with the Spanish suffering few losses.

In light of the defeat at Gemloux, the southern states of the Seventeen Provinces (today in northern France and Belgium) distanced themselves from the rebels in the

---

[12] The 'Events in Antwerp', as reproduced in Cowans, J (ed) (2003) *Early Modern Spain: A Documentary History* (Philadelphia, PA, Penn State University Press) 110–11; 'The Pacification of Ghent' in Rowen, H (ed) (1972) *The Low Modern Countries in Early Modern Times* (London, Macmillan) 58–62.

[13] 'The 1578 Peace of Religion' in Rowen, *The Low Modern Countries ibid*, 64–66; Soen, V (2012) 'Reconquista and Reconciliation in the Dutch Revolt', *Journal of Early Modern History* 16, 1–22.

[14] Philip II, in Hanson, N (2003) *The Confident Hope of a Miracle. The True Story of the Spanish Armada* (London, Corgi) 138.

[15] See page 103.

north with the 1579 *Union of Arras*, which expressed their loyalty to Philip II. In return, Spain agreed not to station troops in the territories that had signed the treaty, and even to pay the nobles' previous military expenses. Opposing them, the Seven Provinces in the north, with Holland and Zeeland at their core, confirmed their commitment to keep fighting with their *Union of Utrecht* (also of 1579). This drew 'the narrow union' of the strongly Calvinist regions, under the leadership of William of Orange, into a military alliance to 'drive out of these lands the Spaniards and other nations … [and for the Seven Provinces] … to withdraw themselves from the Holy Roman Empire'. It was added, on the point of religion, that 'each individual shall remain free in his religion, and that no-one shall suffer any tribulation on account of his religion'.[16]

For these words, from which the nucleus of what might be called the Dutch state emerged, Philip II declared William of Orange an outlaw, 'a traitor and miscreant, an enemy of ourselves and our country … an enemy of the human race'.[17] He then offered a reward of 25,000 golden crowns for whoever caught or killed 'the plague of the Christian community'.[18] Before he was assassinated on 10 July 1584 by the Burgundian Catholic, Balthasar Gérard, William defied Philip in his *Apologia*, an open letter addressed to all of the Seventeen Provinces, thus:

> I am no foreigner, no rebel, no traitor … I was bred up a Catholic … but the horrible persecution that I witnessed by fire, sword and water, and the plot to introduce a worst form of Spanish Inquisition … made me resolve in my soul not to rest till I have chased from the land these locusts of Spain … And of the resistance to the tyranny of Spain, I take responsibility, for I view with indignation the bloodthirsty cruelties, worse than any tyrant of Antiquity, which they have inflicted upon the people of this land.[19]

4. The Act of Abjuration

The *Act of Abjuration*—the Dutch declaration of independence, and the formal point from which the Dutch Republic emerged—was signed in 1581. Those provinces that were signatories declared that they were becoming independent because

> [a]ll mankind know that a prince is appointed by God to cherish his subjects, even as a shepherd to guard his sheep. When, therefore, the prince does not fulfil his duty as protector, when he oppresses his subjects, destroys their ancient liberties, and treats them as slaves, he is to be

[16] Preamble to and Art 13 of the 1579 Union of Utrecht, as reproduced in Reddaway, F (ed) (1930) *Select Documents in European History*, Vol II (London, Methuen) 105; Grant, R (2011) *1001 Battles* (London, Penguin) 288.
[17] Philip II, as quoted in Cowie, L (ed) (1970) *The Reformation of the Sixteenth Century* (London, Wayland) 59.
[18] The Order of 1580, as reproduced in Rowen, H (ed) (1972) *The Low Modern Countries in Early Modern Times* (London, Macmillan) 78–79.
[19] Philip II, as quoted Cowie, *The Reformation. Ibid*, 60. William of Orange's *Apologia* is reproduced in Rowen, H (ed) (1972) *The Low Modern Countries in Early Modern Times* (London, Macmillan) 80–85.

considered not a prince, but a tyrant. As such, the Estates of the land may lawfully and reasonably depose him and elect another in his room.[20]

By this point there was, as the author of a 'Brief Discourse' pointed out, no chance of reconciliation with King Philip of Spain, as he was 'full of injustice' and could not be trusted since his overriding goal was, always, to deprive the Low Countries of their liberty and bring them into eternal servitude. By doing so, the author argued, Philip had forfeited his sovereignty and been replaced by the states of the *Union of Utrecht*, which had 'reserved the power to decide on all matters concerning the sovereignty to themselves'.[21] Despite such a vision based upon their ancient liberties, and eventual English support in 1585 with the signing of the *Treaty of Nonsuch*,[22] the Dutch found that the Spanish continued to tighten their control. The last city to fall in this region was Antwerp in 1585, with the Dutch losing several thousand men and the English failing to prevent Spanish relief columns from reaching their goal.[23]

The Seven Provinces managed to survive because Philip became distracted by the attempt of his armada to invade England, and then in 1590 he found himself at war with Aragon. The war with Aragon occurred after Philip's secretary, Antonio Perez, armed with potentially damaging information, was given refuge at the Aragonese court. Perez had fled following the assassination of the secretary of Don John of Austria, one of the illegitimate children of Charles V. When Philip's agents went to get Perez back, they were killed in a riot that broke out, in what the Aragonese saw as the defence of their ancient privileges (to give sanctuary). Philip replied by sending 12,000 men into Aragon, quickly subduing the uprising and executing all of the leaders. He then made the men on the governing body removable at his pleasure, and majority voting was substituted for the principle of unanimity in the Aragonese *Cortes*.[24]

These events gave the Seven Provinces the space they needed to regroup. In 1590, Breda was captured from the Spanish, and this was largely achieved without the assistance of the English. A few months later, the States General of the Netherlands declared themselves 'the sovereign institution of the country', with 'no overlord except the deputies of the provincial states themselves'.[25] The Dutch progress continued, taking all Spanish outposts north of the river Meuse, as Philip II started to pull troops out of the region to fight in France. They went on the offensive in 1596 with the

[20] The 1581 'Abjuration of Philip's Sovereignty', reproduced in Reddaway, F (ed) (1930) *Select Documents in European History*, Vol II (London, Methuen) 109; also Gerritsen, J (2003) 'The Text of the Edict of Abjuration', *Quaerendo* 33 (3), 285.
[21] 'Brief Discourse' in van Gelderen, M (ed) (2001) *The Dutch Revolt* (Cambridge, Cambridge University Press) 165, 189.
[22] See page 105.
[23] Black, J (1985) *The Reign of Elizabeth.* (Oxford, Oxford University Press) 168–370; Grant, R (2011) *1001 Battles* (London, Penguin) 308; MacKinnon, J (1906) *A History of Modern Liberty*, Vol II (London, Longmans) 297.
[24] Wernham, R (1968) *The New Cambridge Modern History: The Counter Reformation* (Cambridge, Cambridge University Press) 232, 250–52.
[25] Bonney, R (2012) *The European Dynastic States* (Oxford, Oxford University Press) 162.

Triple Alliance,[26] with both France and England attacking Cadiz, and although France dropped out of the trilateral relationship in 1598, the bilateral alliance with England continued. At the Battle of Nieuwpoort, which followed in 1600, the Dutch and their English allies won their first significant land battle against the Spanish, even though both sides lost about 2,500 men.[27]

5. PHILIP III AND THE TWELVE YEARS' TRUCE

Although Spain had been bankrupted three times during the reign of Philip II due to his wars, the last wish of the King of Spain was that his son, Philip III, should carry on fighting both the Seven Provinces and England. The latter was especially important, as the question of succession to the English throne would only get more pressing upon the death of Elizabeth. However, as noted above, when the Queen of England did die, in 1603, Philip III opted to make peace with King James, the new monarch of England and Scotland. This peace then allowed him to direct all his efforts against the Seven Provinces. Despite his determination in this regard, victory was elusive. The three-year battle for Ostend concluded in 1604, and although the Spanish took the last Protestant settlement in Flanders, the cost, of at least 60,000 Spanish dead (as opposed to 30,000 Dutch), was very high and the momentum could not be maintained. Even worse, in 1607 a bold raid by the Seven Provinces on the Spanish fleet in Gibraltar, without any loss to the Dutch, succeeded in destroying all 21 ships, killing some 3,000 Spanish sailors. In addition, Dutch vessels harassed Portuguese and Spanish shipping and stations throughout the New World and the East Indies. By this point, Philip III was financially exhausted, and was willing to consider a pause in the fight against the Seven Provinces. They, however, would not agree to anything but full independence from Spain.[28]

Although a permanent peace could not be reached, in 1608 a temporary peace was achieved and the *Twelve Years' Truce* was agreed.[29] This was a compromise. The protection of Catholic persons and their right to practise their faith freely in the Seven Provinces (which Philip III dearly wanted) was not agreed, nor was the right of the Seven Provinces to trade in any of the colonies of either Spain or Portugal (a primary aim of the Seven Provinces). Despite agreement on these two matters not being reached, the truce was a victory for the Dutch, as not only did they not have to give up land, but Philip III also effectively recognised their independence when he recorded that he

---

[26] See page 108.

[27] The 1598 'Treaty Between the Netherlands and England', reproduced in Davenport, F (ed) (1917) *European Treaties Bearing on the History of the United States and its Dependencies to 1648* (NYC, Carnegie Institute) 240–50; see also the 'Triple Alliance', ibid, at 229–35.

[28] See 'Terms of Peace, if Only for a Time' in Rowen, H (ed) (1972) *The Low Countries in Early Modern Times: Select Documents* (London, Macmillan) 109–11; Greengrass, M (2015) *Christendom Destroyed: Europe 1517–1648* (NYC, Penguin) 571–74; Grant, R (2011) *1001 Battles* (London, Penguin) 312, 314.

[29] 'Truce Between Spain and the United Netherlands' in Davenport, F (ed) (1917) *European Treaties Bearing on the History of the United States and its Dependencies to 1648* (NYC, Carnegie Institute) 258.

considered the Seven Provinces as 'free lands, provinces and States, against whom [he] makes no claims'.[30] Both France and England supported the Seven Provinces in this, promising to come to their aid if Spain broke the truce.[31]

6. CONCLUSION

The rise of what became the Dutch Republic was one of the most significant events in international history emerging from the middle of the sixteenth century. The Seventeen Provinces began to break free, arguing that they were fighting against the tyranny of their Spanish and Habsburg overlord. This overlord, who was heavy-handed in his attempts to control the Dutch, would not allow them to practise the considerable degrees of autonomy they had long possessed and which had been guaranteed to them. Within this ambit, the right to practise their own Protestant faith came to the fore. Accordingly, they abjured the right to be ruled by others on both political and religious matters. With external support, primarily from England, they managed to force the Spanish to a truce, at which point both sides took advantage of a breathing space before the Dutch made their final push for full independence.

---

[30] 'The Twelve Year Truce' in Rowen, H (ed) (1972) *The Low Countries in Early Modern Times: Select Documents* (London, Macmillan) 113; also Vermeir, R (2010) 'Implementing the Truce: Negotiations Between the Republic and the Archducal Netherlands', *European Review of History* 17 (6), 817–33.

[31] The 1609 'Treaty of Guaranty Between the United Netherlands, France and Great Britain' in Davenport, F (ed) (1917) *European Treaties Bearing on the History of the United States and its Dependencies to 1648* (NYC, Carnegie Institute) 270–75.

VII

The Culmination: The Thirty Years' War

1. INTRODUCTION

URING MUCH OF the sixteenth century in Europe, the question of war waged for reasons of religion and political balance had caused mass conflicts in Germany, France, England, Scotland, Ireland and parts of what is today the Netherlands. These conflicts over questions of religious and political autonomy culminated in the Thirty Years' War. This war, which was fought primarily in Germany, resulted in the deaths of between seven to eight million people.[1] The lack of precision regarding the numbers results from the fact that it depends on when the counting began and what theatres of war are included. Lower estimates focus on the conflict within Germany between 1618 and 1648. Higher estimates prefer not to see the Thirty Years' War as an isolated and coherent conflict, looking beyond the wars in Germany to include interrelated conflicts, such as those in the Netherlands and northern Europe, and even the distant, but related, fighting ranging from the New World to Africa, as belligerents killed each other over questions of—initially—religion and autonomy before the wars evolved into a conflict between two Catholic superpowers—Bourbon France and the Habsburgs—extending between Spain and Austria.[2]

2. THE IRONY

The irony of this situation, where religion was one of the key catalysts for mass killing, was that by this time, the influence of the papacy had sunk to its lowest point. In theory, famous Catholic scholars, such as Francesco Suarez, would argue that the Pope, as the supposed promoter of peace within Europe and with binding authority over all Christians

> may correct and reform, or may evenly fittingly punish, a rebellious prince ... [A] Christian king may be deprived of his power and dominion over his vassals; and therefore, [this] is

---

[1] White, M (2011) *Atrocitology* (NYC, Norton) 215–16.
[2] Wilson, P (2008) 'The Causes of the Thirty Years' War', *The English Historical Review* 123 (502), 554–86; Thornton, J (2016) 'The Kingdom of Kongo and the Thirty Years' War', *Journal of World History* 27 (2), 189–213; Mortimer, G (2001) 'Did Contemporaries Recognise a Thirty Years' War?', *The English Historical Review* 116 (465), 124–36.

in itself sufficient to endow the Pope with power to punish the Christian princes, lawfully depriving them of their kingdoms and employing for this purpose, the sword of other princes … for the sake of mutual aid in defending and protecting the Church.[3]

In reality, Suarez was dreaming of centuries past. In the seventeenth century, the influence of the papacy was in rapid decline. The foremost example of this was the conflict between Pope Paul V and Venice. Venice had allowed foreign diplomats to practise their own religious beliefs, had been inconsistent in enforcing the Index of Prohibited Books and had given sanctuary to two clerics fleeing Rome, the Senate of Venice informing Pope Paul V that the matters at hand were temporal and not spiritual, and therefore that he had no right to make demands. The Pope claimed that such assertions 'reeked of heresy' and placed Venice under interdict. The interdict read that the Pope

> pronounce[s] excommunicate the Doge and members of the Senate and their supporters and accomplices … [W]e are moved only by zeal for the honour of the Holy See, the defence of ecclesiastical liberty and jurisdiction, and the salvation of the souls of those who are in the greatest danger on this account.[4]

The Senate then replied:

> You must know that we are, every one of us, resolute and ardent to the last degree, not merely the Government but the whole nobility and people of our State. We ignore your excommunication: It is nothing to us. Think of where this resolution would lead, if our example were to be followed by others.[5]

Pope Paul V had to face the terrible truth that the interdict had no impact. The most powerful weapon in the papal armoury—which had brought down kings and emperors centuries earlier—was useless. Thankfully, for the papacy, the French intervened and helped mediate a face-saving outcome over the specifics of the issue, but the overall reality of the situation was lost on no one. The Catholic Church never again issued an interdict against temporal rulers. Thereafter, the Church concentrated on matters over which it had greater control, such as convicting Galileo on vehement suspicion of heresy and sentencing him to 'formal imprisonment at the pleasure of the Inquisition'.[6]

---

[3] For Suarez, see Scott, J (ed) (1944) *Selections from Three Works of Francisco Suarez*, Vol II (Oxford, Clarendon Press) 697, 701–02; Wright, H (1933) *Francisco Suarez: Addresses in Commemoration of his Contribution to International Law and Politics* (Washington, Catholic University of America) 22; Medina, V (2013) 'Just War Thinking of Vitoria and Suarez', *Ratio Juris* 26 (1), 47–64; Skinner, Q (1978) *The Foundations of Modern Political Thought*, Vol II (Cambridge, Cambridge University Press) 182–84.

[4] The 'Interdict of Pope Paul V, 1606' in Chambers, D (ed) (2001) *Venice: A Documentary History* (London, University of Toronto Press) 224.

[5] The Reply from the Senate, as in Norwich, J (2011) *Absolute Monarchs* (London, Random House) 331.

[6] As quoted in Miller, D (2008) 'The Thirty Years' War and the Galileo Affair', *History of Science* 46 (1), 49–74; Ord, M (2007) 'Venice and Rome in the First English Embassy to Venice, 1604–1610', *The Seventeenth Century* 1–23; Bury, J (2007) *Freedom of Thought: A History* (NYC, Prometheus) 70–75.

3. Rudolf II

Rudolf II, the son of the Holy Roman Emperor Maximilian II, was the King of Hungary, Croatia and Bohemia, and succeeded as Holy Roman Emperor from 1576. His mother was Maria of Spain, a daughter of Charles V and Isabella of Portugal. This made King Philip II of Spain his uncle, and King Philip III his cousin. Philip III was married to Margaret of Austria, the granddaughter of the former Emperor Ferdinand I. This meant that the two parts of the House of Habsburg, in Spain and Austria, were very close.

Rudolf inherited a legacy of decades of peace in Germany, provided by the 1555 *Peace of Augsburg.*[7] However, by the seventeenth century, the 1555 agreement was beset with three problems. First, it only covered the legal rights of the original adherents to the Augsburg Confession, that is, Lutherans, and not those of equally prominent groups that had evolved subsequently, such as Calvinists. Secondly, the *Ecclesiastical Reservation*, which stipulated that ecclesiastical rulers (such as prince-bishops) must give up their offices and rights (including to real property) should they change religions, was never accepted as binding by most Protestants, and it had never been fully enforced by Emperors after 1555, meaning that thousands of ecclesiastical properties had long been secularised and claimed by Protestant princes, most of whom feared that these lands would be reclaimed. The third, and largest, problem was that the Counter-Reformation was gathering steam. While Germany had been at peace since 1555, the Wars of Religion had swept through France, the Netherlands, England, Scotland and Ireland, before turning full circle.

Rudolf II's support for the Counter-Reformation was all too evident. This Emperor, who had not attended the Reichstag since 1594, and only called it together when he needed money (in 1594, 1597, 1603 and 1608), was interested in seeing how far he could push the Counter-Reformation in Germany. By the turn of the seventeenth century, in cities such as Graz and Vienna, Lutheran establishments were closed down, books were burned and people were ordered to leave. In 1607, Rudolf re-established Roman Catholicism in Donauworth, and then in 1608 a majority of the Imperial Diet decided that the *Peace of Augsburg* should be conditional upon the restoration of all Catholic Church land appropriated since 1552. It response, Frederick IV, the Elector Palatine of the Rhine, orchestrated the formation of a Protestant Union of German states, to defend the rights, lands and persons of each member of the Union. Although the Protestant Union was weak (due to discord between the Lutherans and Calvinists, and the failure of the Protestant Elector of Saxony to participate), the Catholic League was created by the Duke of Bavaria the following year, in 1609.[8]

Rudolf II was not predisposed to conflict and was familiar with the need for compromise. This first occurred in Hungary, where he, through his brother Matthias

---

[7] See pages 80–81.
[8] Daniel, D (1980) 'The Dilemma of the Protestants in the Lands of the Austrian Habsburgs', *Church History* 49 (4), 387–400; Parker, G (1998) *The Thirty Years' War* (London, Routledge) 6–7.

(who had earlier been active in the Netherlands)[9] made peace with Hungarian Protestant rebels in the *Peace of Vienna* of 1606. In exchange for the rebels accepting Matthias as their king, the religious rights and privileges of the Lutherans and Calvinists in both Hungary and Transylvania were recognised. Rights of the election for independent princes were also recognised in Transylvania.[10]

Rudolf II then directed a similar peace in Bohemia, after it appeared that conflict was looming with the Protestants in this region. The Protestants, with their strong (Hussite) traditions of dissent[11] and their belief in their 'traditional liberties' and an independent Diet (in which only about 20,000 out of 2 million citizens had political rights, with the majority of the peasants existing in semi-serfdom), had clear differences of opinion with Rudolf over both religion and his desire for more autocratic rule. The specific spark for rebellion was Rudolf's granting of Crown lands to Catholic prelates in Bohemia. Rudolf initially refused to back down, until the Bohemian Diet authorised a levy of 4,500 troops and defeated a force of Rudolf's soldiers who were sent to enforce the Emperor's will. At this point, rather than make matters worse, Rudolf backed down and issued his *Letter of Majesty*. In one of the most liberal charters of the age ever granted to a country of many creeds, Rudolf gave Bohemia limited self-government and confirmed all existing rights. In addition to committing magistrates to ensuring observance of the guarantees, and promising that lords were forbidden to force their subjects to change religion, Rudolf vowed:

> That they may be granted all that has been laid down in the Confession, commonly called Bohemian, but by some the Augsburg Confession ... They shall not oppress one another, but remain good friends, not shall one party revile the other ... all citizens shall be allowed to practice their Christian religion ... in all places, and to keep their priests and church regime ... they may freely build their churches and schools and nobody has a right to interfere with them ... We ordain that no existent law, nor any law to be passed in the future, can deprive the present Letter of Majesty of its force.[12]

Rudolf II was succeeded as Holy Roman Emperor by his brother Matthias in 1612. Matthias was also King of Hungary and Bohemia, after his brother ceded the crowns to him. Matthias, who had earlier been so influential in the Netherlands and Hungary, finding a middle ground between the opposing religious sides in the Empire, began to become more conservative. He forbade Protestants the rights of assembly, freedom of speech and to build their churches in certain areas. The Reichstag he called in 1613 broke down following a series of escalating political tensions (such as over the rights of the Emperor; rights of primogeniture; the rights of princes; rights of

---

[9] See page 131.

[10] Greengrass, M (2015) *Christendom Destroyed: Europe 1517–1648* (NYC. Penguin) 443–46, 584–85.

[11] See pages 63–65.

[12] 'The Letter of Majesty of Rudolf II', reproduced in Reddaway, F (ed) (1930) *Select Documents in European History*, Vol II (London, Methuen) 121; also Zdenk, D (1999) 'Utraquists, Lutherans and the Bohemian Confession of 1575', *Church History* 68 (2), 294–336.

communities), all multiplied through the prisms of different Christian faiths that were becoming endemic throughout an increasingly divided Germany and associated territories.[13]

4. THE REBELLION IN BOHEMIA

Ferdinand II became Holy Roman Emperor in 1619, following the death of his childless cousin, Matthias. Before becoming Emperor, he had been elected King of Bohemia by the Bohemian Diet in 1617 (after promising to uphold the *Letter of Majesty*) and the following year King of Hungary, elected by the Hungarian estates. Ferdinand was a devout Catholic, who believed, despite his promises of tolerance, that it was his mission to restore Catholicism as the only Christian religion. In the areas he controlled he had Protestant books burned, Protestants expelled, appointed Catholic clerics to rule and gave the Church a near monopoly on education. Such goals were not possible to pursue in countries such as Bohemia, as by 1618, the majority of residents of Bohemia had embraced Protestant beliefs in one form or another, and doctrinaire Catholicism had become a distinctly minority religion both in Bohemia and in the surrounding territories of Silesia, Lusatia and Moravia. Ferdinand did not like this and began to interfere directly with Bohemian liberties by the promotion and planting of Jesuits. This interference caused the Bohemians to hold a Diet in the middle of 1618. The meeting, which the Emperor had forbidden to take place, saw the Emperor's regents thrown out of a window (in conscious imitation of an act that had taken place during the Hussite Wars), which act they survived, but their defenestration triggered the start of a war. The Diet then unequivocally asserted the principle of election to the throne and reversed Ferdinand's attempted re-Catholicisation of Bohemia by expelling all Jesuits and seizing Catholic Church property. The members of the Diet explained that they themselves were seeking nothing more than was promised in the *Letter of Majesty*. They told Ferdinand's regents:

> [Y]ou are enemies of us and of our religion, [you] have desired to deprive us of our *Letter of Majesty*, [and] have horribly plagued your Protestant subjects … [If] we lose the *Letter of Majesty* and our religion, all of us would be stripped and deprived of our lives, honour and property, for there can be no justice.[14]

The Bohemian rebels then justified their rebellion in 1618 by having their *Apologia* printed throughout Europe. The basis of their claim was that that they had

> suffered and endured many and various kinds of terrible hardships and tribulations in both political and ecclesiastic affairs. These were instigated and provoked by evil and turbulent

---

[13] Curtis, B (2013) *The Habsburgs: The History of a Dynasty* (London, Bloomsbury) 113.
[14] 'The Defenestration of Prague, 1618' in Helfferich, T (2009) *The Thirty Years' War: A Documentary History* (Cambridge, Hackett) 14; also Buzek, V (2004) 'From Compromise to Rebellion: Religion and Political Power of the Nobility in the First Century of the Habsburgs' Reign in Bohemia', *Journal of Early Modern History* 8 (1), 1–45.

people, both clergy and laymen, but especially by members of the Jesuit sect … fraudulently subjugating the *Letter of Majesty* … [The King's ministers were proceeding] … without gaining the proper legal authority from the Diet [of Bohemia].[15]

The rebels in Bohemia were now joined by the estates of Austria and Moravia, as well as by rogue elements from Ottoman-controlled Transylvania who wanted to fight the Habsburgs. The rebels were supported by the head of the Protestant Union, the Protestant Elector Palatine, Frederick V, the successor to Frederick IV. In an act of clear revolution, after refusing to accept Ferdinand as their hereditary king, the Bohemians created an army of 4,000 men to defend and enforce their claims. They also declared Ferdinand deposed and offered the throne (with restricted rights, and much greater deference to local rights and privileges) to Frederick V. At the same time Ferdinand II began to muster his forces. Although Sigismund III Vasa, King of Poland and Grand Duke of Lithuania, wanted to join the fight and help his Habsburg in-laws, the Polish *sjem* would not allow him to engage. Conversely, Ferdinand's Habsburg cousin in Spain, who sent an army over from Flanders (in exchange for a promise of Alsatian fiefs), was willing to help. So too the Catholic Elector of Bavaria, Maximilian, to whom rewards were offered, to be taken from the conquered Bohemia, along with the promise of his own title's being made hereditary. As these forces were being assembled, those of Bohemia took full control of their area, and twice advanced into Austria, and even bombarded Ferdinand's residence in Vienna, before retreating.[16]

5. Frederick V

Frederick was the leader of the Protestant Union. In 1613, he had married Elizabeth Stuart, the daughter of King James I of England, at a wedding many saw as a foundation for international Protestant relations. Frederick took this vision seriously, believing that he was God's instrument to further the cause of Protestantism. He accepted the offer from Bohemia to be their king, and was crowned in Prague in late 1619, seeing his decision as a 'divine calling that I must not disobey. My only end is to serve God and his Church'.[17] He added that his decision to accept the crown of Bohemia was also

> for the comfort and protection of those who are so greatly distressed, for the maintenance of the common liberty and welfare, for other even more urgent motives and reasons, and in response to the diverse deferential and humble written appeals sent to us by the estates of Bohemia … [N]o one shall be molested or oppressed on account of religion, nor

---

[15] 'Apologia of the Bohemian Estates, 1618' in Helfferich, T (2009) *The Thirty Years' War: A Documentary History* (Cambridge, Hackett) 20; Macartney, C (ed) (1970) *The Habsburg and Hohenzollern Dynasties* (NYC, Harper) 33.

[16] Cooper, J (ed) (1970) *The New Cambridge Modern History: The Decline of Spain and the Thirty Years' War*, Vol IV (Cambridge, Cambridge University Press) 260, 286, 307–09.

[17] Frederick, as noted in Parker, G (2013) *Global Crisis: War, Climate and Catastrophe in the Seventeenth Century* (New Haven, CT, Yale University Press) 40.

hindered in his traditional religious practice, not even those who still confess to the Roman Church.[18]

Such justification for taking the crown, and his promises of religious toleration, did little to convince many of Frederick's cause, as his actions transformed a rebellion in Bohemia into a German, and ultimately international, war. Catholic princes in particular were greatly concerned with how all this might affect their delicate political and religious balance with Protestants in the Holy Roman Empire. That is, with Frederick now having two votes in the electoral college, combined with those of the Calvinist Elector of Brandenburg and the Lutheran Elector of Saxony, the Protestants would in theory now have a majority of the votes, and therefore the next Emperor would likely be Protestant. The Catholic Duke Maximilian I of Bavaria, who went on to lead the Emperor Ferdinand's armies, suggested:

> The Bohemian disorders obviously aim at the extermination of the Catholic religion ... [T]he heretical electors and princes in the empire now work to remove the Bohemian crown completely from the House of Austria in order to turn it over to a heretic and thereby gain the majority in the electoral college, so they can then choose a heretical emperor.[19]

Emperor Ferdinand II published his version of the struggle in early 1620. He argued that Frederick's acts caused a dangerous precedent, and that the matter should not be seen as one of religion but rather as about private property rights, laws and just punishment. His core argument was that this was an 'odious rebellion under the mantle of religion', as the real issue was that if local estates could elect and depose their own leaders, none of the princes in the Empire would be safe in their possessions. The rebels would face justifiable violence because they had

> seized and took up arms, and without the least respect for their absent but duly reigning king and lord, deposed the ... regents and officers from their offices. They then took possession of the regalia of the kingdom and established a completely new form of government ... to their own ends. They far exceeded both the goal and means of the ... *Letter of Majesty* ... They upset all of the fundamental statutes of our kingdom ... and the traditional observances of eight hundred years ... and instead created an entirely new constitution for the kingdom ... We object to all that has been done against us and our house ... but especially the invalid election and coronation undertaken to our detriment ... [W]e hereby, by our imperial and royal authority, abrogate and annul it, proclaiming that all of this is, in itself, illegal, null and void.[20]

Frederick faced an enemy of 30,000 troops (which included many notable volunteers, such as the philosopher Descartes), who marched into Upper Austria under the

---

[18] 'Declaration of Elector Frederick V' in Helfferich, T (2009) *The Thirty Years' War: A Documentary History* (Cambridge, Hackett) 78; also, Chovanec, K (2015) 'The British Pharaoh? James I and VI and Internationalist Religious Writings at the Wedding of Frederick V and Elizabeth Stuart', *The Seventeenth Century* 30 (4), 391–409.

[19] Maximilian I, in Helfferich, T (2009) *The Thirty Years' War: A Documentary History* (Cambridge, Hackett) 7.

[20] 'Edict of Ferdinand II Annulling the Bohemian Election, 1620' in Helfferich, T (2009) *The Thirty Years' War: A Documentary History* (Cambridge, Hackett) 39.

leadership of General Tilly. This force crushed the rebels in Austria. John George of Saxony seized Lusatia and Silesia; and the Spanish army in Flanders advanced and overwhelmed most of Frederick's lands in the Rhine Palatinate. At the Battle of White Mountain towards the end of 1620, the imperial army of over 24,000 men advanced towards Prague. The army of 16,000 Protestant rebels stood in their way for a short time before it was destroyed, leaving at least 4,000 dead on the battlefield. The imperialists reclaimed Prague. Ferdinand II refused to engage in peace talks, stating that there was 'nothing more to be gained from treaties ... complete obedience from his subjects could only be assured by the sword'.[21]

Frederick gained almost nothing from his pleas for assistance from the outside Protestant world. Within Germany, even the Lutheran ruler of Saxony, John George, horrified at Frederick's blatant disregard for the maintenance of peace in the Empire, decided to join the Emperor Ferdinand's side. In exchange for his help, the Emperor promised that Lutheranism would be protected in Saxony and Bohemia, secularised lands would not be reclaimed as Catholic and the province of Lusatia would be granted to John George. The other Protestant rulers were equally unwilling to join the fight. Their collective response was the *Treaty of Ulm*, in which they (as the Protestant League) agreed with the Catholic League, to try to keep the conflict isolated. Both sides would uphold the *Peace of Augsburg* everywhere else, and in exchange for Protestant neutrality, other Protestant lands would not be invaded in the conflict and Frederick would not be deprived of his hereditary lands in the Palatinate if he lost (in other words, although Frederick might be defeated, his punishment would not involve the loss of his heritage). Neither of these terms was kept.[22]

The following year, in 1621, the Spanish arm of the Habsburgs struck quickly as the *Twelve Years' Truce*[23] between the Dutch and the Spanish came to an end. The new King of Spain, Philip IV, carried on the war of his father and grandfather, acting without restraint as he viewed the Dutch as aggressors who had kept up their attacks on the overseas empires of Spain and Portugal during the Truce, and who had kept tight their stranglehold on the Spanish Netherlands. Hence, Spain went back to war not to reconquer its lost Dutch provinces but to defend its economic and temporal interests. Spanish forces captured Breda in 1625. This last great Spanish victory in the Dutch Revolt cost the defenders at least 13,000 civilians and soldiers, with Spanish losses amounting to some 5,000 out of 23,000.

As the Spanish Habsburgs made advances, the Austrian Habsburgs pursued Frederick's remaining Protestant forces. The rebels suffered further massive defeats at Fleurus in 1622 (a further 5,000 dead) and Stadtlohn in 1623 (6,000 dead and 4,000 made prisoner). Although Frederick escaped with his life, fleeing to the Dutch Republic, those remaining in Bohemia and responsible for the defenestration of the

---

[21] Ferdinand, in Parker, G (1998) *The Thirty Years' War* (London, Routledge) 54–55; also Reiss, T (1991) 'Descartes and the Thirty Years' War: Political Theory and Political Practice', *Yale French Studies* 80, 108–45.

[22] 'The 1620 Treaty of Ulm' in Helfferich, T (2009) *The Thirty Years' War: A Documentary History* (Cambridge, Hackett) 46; Friedrich, C (1952) *The Age of the Baroque* (NYC, Harper) 152, 165–66.

[23] See pages 134–135.

Emperor's regents were publicly executed. A further 1,500 were brought to trial, and at least half had their property confiscated. Elective monarchy was abolished in Bohemia, the *Letter of Majesty* was torn up, and in accordance with the principle *Cuius region, eius religio* ('whose realm, his religion') set out in the 1555 *Peace of Augsburg*,[24] Catholicism was reintroduced throughout those lands as Protestantism was suppressed. Protestants could either convert or leave (with the exception of nobles, who had 50 years in which to change their faith). Frederick's capital of Heidelberg succumbed to General Tilly in the middle of 1521. The town was brutally sacked, with its famous library being given to the papacy as a gift. Such heavy-handed actions troubled Catholics and Protestants alike. They feared that Frederick's removal was a vast transgression of the Emperor's power. In the words of the Elector of Saxony, they saw their status 'afflicted by a not inconsiderable assault' from the Emperor, and they began to reconsider their loyalty.[25] Such fears were deepened even more when, in 1627, Ferdinand II gave Bohemia a new constitution that made the Habsburgs hereditary, rather than elective, monarchs; making the king the sole authority over all civil servants; and moving the main governmental office to Vienna. Catholicism was the only permitted religion and the *Letter of Majesty* was formally abolished.[26]

6. CONTAINING THE WAR

A. England

Outside of Germany, Frederick V found limited support. Only Denmark, Sweden, Venice and the Dutch Republic recognised his election as King of Bohemia. Others were much more cautious, not wanting the war to spread. With regard to England, Frederick's wife Elizabeth wrote to her father, King James I, pleading, 'I most humbly entreat your Majesty to take care of the King [Frederick] and myself by sending us help. Otherwise we shall be entirely ruined.'[27] James refused the pleas from his daughter and son-in-law, only going so far as to provide a loan to Elizabeth and Frederick, and turn a blind eye as 2,000 English volunteers made their way to Bohemia to fight for the Protestant cause.

Although the people of England and their Parliament were very concerned with the interests of the Protestants in Germany, James I refused to allow his realm to become more deeply involved in the conflict for two reasons. First, he was concerned with questions of dynasty, regarding which he asked his son-in-law, 'can you show me a good ground for the Palatine's invasion of the property of another? ... So you are of

---

[24] See page 80.

[25] 'Letter of Elector John George of Saxony, 1623' in Helfferich, T (2009) *The Thirty Years' War: A Documentary History* (Cambridge, Hackett) 63; Grant, R (2011) *1001 Battles* (London, Penguin) 318.

[26] Curtis, B (2013). *The Habsburgs* (London, Bloomsbury) 134; Greengrass, M (2015) *Christendom Destroyed: Europe 1517–1648* (NYC, Penguin) 590–93.

[27] Elizabeth, as noted in Royle, T (2005) *Civil War: The Wars of the Three Kingdoms* (London, Abacus) 15.

the opinion that subjects can dispossess their kings?'[28] Secondly, James, who saw himself as an international peacemaker, thought that peace could more easily be achieved in Europe through diplomacy than war. James preferred to pursue a rapprochement with Spain with his proposed 'Spanish Match' (that is, a royal marriage between his son Charles and the Spanish, Catholic Habsburgs). He hoped this match would give him leverage over the King of Spain. When Parliament (representing the majority of the English, many of whom had clear memories of Elizabeth I and her strong sense of England's Protestant mission) expressed its concern at this warming of relations with Spain, the king warned them not to interfere in matters of what he saw as the royal prerogative, threatening Members of Parliament with imprisonment. Parliament responded with the Protestation of 1621, in which the members denied, by implication, the king's claim to have the right to imprison members at his will, asserting that their rights were ancient privileges. They added that they were very much within their rights to discuss foreign relations, the defence of the realm and religious matters. James responded by dissolving Parliament, imprisoning some members and placing others under house arrest.

When the negotiations for the Spanish Match failed to bear fruit (after the Spanish refused to entertain any idea that James's son-in-law, Frederick V, would have his rights or territories in the Palatinate restored to him, and insisted that Prince Charles later King Charles I would have to convert to Catholicism and live in Spain for a year), James changed tack. At this point, it was decided that Prince Charles would instead marry the Catholic Princess Henrietta Maria, the youngest daughter of King Henri IV of France and sister to the future French King, Louis XIII. Accompanying this shift from a pro-Spain to a pro-France policy, James summoned Parliament and restored the topic of foreign relations as being within its prerogative. Subsequently, the likelihood of war with the Catholic Habsburgs became very real, as Parliament voted to give the king an unprecedented amount of money:

> [f]or the maintenance of that war that may hereupon ensue, and more particularly for the defence of this realm of England, the securing of your kingdom of Ireland, the assistance of your neighbours the states of the United Provinces ... [W]e have resolved to give ... the greatest aid which ever was granted in Parliament.[29]

B. France

In the decade following the assassination of Henri IV of France in 1610, there was little likelihood that the French would go to war against the Habsburgs. The foreign

---

[28] James I, as noted in Davies, G (1985) *The Early Stuarts* (Oxford, Clarendon Press) 56.

[29] The 'Subsidy of 1624' in Cohen, M (ed) (2004) *History in Quotations* (London, Cassell) 420; also Pursell, B (2002) 'The End of the Spanish Match', *The Historical Journal* 45 (4), 699–726; Pursell, B (2000) 'James I and the Dissolution of the Parliament of 1621', *History* 85 (279), 428–45; Davies, G (1987) *The Early Stuarts* (Oxford, Oxford University Press) 3–4, 27, 49.

policy of Henri IV had been reversed by the regent and advisers of the young King Louis XIII. Louis, who was crowned when he was nine years old, was married in 1615 to Anne, the daughter of Philip III of Spain and his wife Margaret of Austria (and sister of Philip IV). At the same time, Elizabeth, the oldest daughter of Henri IV (and sister of Louis XIII), became the first wife of Philip IV of Spain. These marriages were designed to cement military and political alliances between Spain and France, and to promote cooperation, not conflict, between the two superpowers.[30]

The initial years of Louis XIII's reign were tense within France. The last meeting of the Estates General to be held before the French Revolution in 1789 took place before the 12-year old King of France in 1614. His father, Henri IV, had carefully controlled the Estates General as part of the process of building a united France. Upon the death of Henri, rebellions started to break out within the realm, as a result of which the regency government of Marie de' Medici agreed to the calling of the Estates General, as a way to keep the peace. However, at the gathering, when the first article of debate proposed that royal authority was above all other human authority in France, the First Estate (the clerics) vigorously objected, due to their belief in the primacy of the Pope. The Second (nobles) and Third (the representatives of the remainder of the population) Estates then entered into acrimonious argument over whether the Third Estate could call the Second Estate 'brothers' or not. When it was clear that agreement was not possible, the meeting was dissolved. The following year, when the *Parlement* of Paris decided to try to assemble on its own initiative, it was decreed that anyone who tried to assemble without authority would be guilty of lese-majesty.[31]

In terms of conflict based around religious differences, Louis XIII initially faced great difficulties, as rebellion broke out following his promotion of Catholicism in a number of Protestant areas. Louis' forces went on to defeat the Huguenot uprising, after which, although the *Edict of Nantes* was upheld, most of the fortified Huguenot areas (except La Rochelle and Montauban) were reduced as a consequence of the 1622 *Treaty of Montpellier*. Although Louis was not going persecute his Huguenot subjects for their religion, due to fears centred on what he had seen happen with the United Provinces, he was not going to tolerate separatism in France, as this was incompatible with royal power. When the Huguenots in La Rochelle rebelled again, Louis entered into an agreement with the British for military assistance, although English ships would not attack La Rochelle, which contained 'innocent Protestants ... on behalf of a popish king'.[32]

[30] Seward, D (2013) *The Bourbon Kings of France* (London, Jones) 32–33; Cooper, J (ed) (1970) *The New Cambridge Modern History: The Decline of Spain and the Thirty Years' War*, Vol VI (Cambridge, Cambridge University Press) 313–15, 481, 518–25.

[31] Sager, J (2012) 'The Development of Royal Authority in Early Bourbon France', *The Catholic Historical Review* 98 (3), 456–75; Nelson, E (2000) 'Defining the Fundamental Laws of France: The Proposed First Article of the French Estates General of 1614', *The English Historical Review* 115 (464), 1216–30; Rothroc, G (1960) 'The French Crown and the Estates General of 1614', *French Historical Studies* 1 (3), 295–318.

[32] Davies, G (1985) *The Early Stuarts* (Oxford, Clarendon Press) 64.

The English failure to help led to the French king's turning to the Dutch for assistance. This was agreed in the Franco-Dutch *Treaty of Compiègne* of 1624. With this, in the wake of the *Twelve Years' Truce*,[33] France agreed to subsidise the Dutch war effort against Spain as part of their general efforts to undermine the Habsburgs, and in exchange the Dutch provided ships to be used by the French against the Huguenots rebelling at La Rochelle. In addition, Dutch actions regarding French enterprises in the New World were to be more cooperative, and not competitive or hostile.[34]

With Dutch assistance, Louis was finally able to defeat the Huguenots, despite the latters' assistance from England, concerning which King Charles I had authorised some 8,000 men (of which only 3,000 ever returned) to participate in their defence. In so doing, Charles ended up fighting against his brother-in-law, Louis XIII, after the relationship between the French and English thrones became tense over the treatment of Henrietta Maria and the expulsion of most of her Catholic household. Charles I's military help came to nothing and the Huguenot surrender was unconditional. In the *Peace of Alais* that followed, the Huguenots lost all of their territorial, political and military rights, and their existence as an independent Protestant state within France ceased. Although they were allowed to retain their religious freedom, granted by the *Edict of Nantes*, they were now at the mercy of the monarchy—a king with absolute authority who could govern without restraint over a fully united land. As Cardinal Richelieu, the Chief Minister to Louis XIII, suggested:

> The roots of heresy, rebellion, disorder and civil war, which have exhausted France for so long, are dried up ... It is certain that the end of La Rochelle is the end of the miseries of France and the beginnings of her happiness.[35]

7. THE EXPANDING WAR: DENMARK

Despite the reluctance of his father, James I, to get drawn into the war in Europe, the new King of England, Charles I, who came to the throne in 1625, saw things differently. He feared what an all-powerful Habsburg dynasty could achieve. His first step to confront this threat was taken in September 1625, when he agreed the *Treaty of Southampton* between the United Netherlands and Britain, 'for the purpose of attacking the King of Spain in open war in all his realms ... in all places, on this side and beyond the line, by land and sea'.[36] This alliance was to last as long as the King of Spain attacked

---

[33] See page 134.

[34] 'The 1624 Treaty of Compiegne' in Davenport, F (ed) (1917) *European Treaties Bearing on the History of the United States and its Dependencies to 1648* (NYC, Carnegie Institute) 285–90.

[35] Cardinal Richelieu, as reproduced in Cohen, M (ed) (2004) *History in Quotations* (London, Cassell) 412; Cooper, J (ed) (1970) *The New Cambridge Modern History. The Decline of Spain and the Thirty Years' War*, Vol VI (Cambridge, Cambridge University Press) 322, 487–88.

[36] 'The 1625 Treaty of Southampton Between the United Netherlands and Britain' in Davenport, F (ed) (1917) *European Treaties Bearing on the History of the United States and its Dependencies to 1648* (NYC, Carnegie Institute) 290.

the Netherlands, or occupied the estates of Frederick's Palatinate. Like the *Treaty of Compiègne* before it, the *Treaty of Southampton* also tried to calm the increasingly tense rivalry between the Dutch, English and French colonies on the east coast of North America. The second step was taken in December 1625, when the *Treaty of The Hague* was agreed. Although this treaty was limited by the fact that France was not a signatory (as France was currently angry about the English support for the Huguenots and was working on a building a peaceful relationship with Spain through the 1626 *Treaty of Monzon*), the English, Dutch and Transylvanians, and even the Sultan of the Ottoman Empire (the last by proxy), agreed to come together against a common enemy.[37]

What this meant in practice was that the Dutch and the English paid King Christian IV of Denmark-Norway, who was the dominant power in northern Europe, having recently defeated the forces of his main rival, Gustavus Adolphus, the King of Sweden, to fight in Germany. Specifically, the Dutch and the English (although the English Parliament later blocked the commitments of Charles I to help his uncle, the Danish king) promised Christian IV the sum of 144,000 *thalers* per month, to invade and retake the Rhineland Palatinate and Bohemia for Frederick V. This suited Christian IV, as his son had been elected to certain positions of power in some of the secularised bishoprics, as a result of which Christian IV sought to bring these territories under the permanent hereditary control of his family. Although the Danish aristocracy was not keen on the war, the Protestant clergy supported it, arguing that the conflict was the manifestation of divine wrath brought upon the people of Denmark for their collective sins, and only by killing the enemy could they be saved from their own iniquity. Christian IV avoided such colourful language, preferring to focus on the conflict as a political or confessional necessity. Thus:

> In order to save [Bohemia] which, though completely innocent, had been attacked contrary to the imperial constitution and the sworn capitulations, and to save German liberty, we joined with [the Dutch and the English] in a confederation so that, with the grace of God, liberty and the Religious and Secular Peace [of 1555] might not be lost ... [W]e will not rest until it comes to pass that the princes and estates of the Roman Empire—of both one and the other religion—shall all live together in binding peace.[38]

Christian IV then crossed the River Elbe and marched south with 20,000 mercenaries. Johann Tserclaes, the Count of Tilly, with 30,000 men of the Catholic League at his disposal, first stopped Christian IV in 1626 at Dessau, and then completely destroyed the Danish forces at Lutter. This victory was monumental for the Catholics and, following further small mopping-up operations, the wider Protestant alliance fragmented. Rather than being pursued further, Denmark agreed to the *Treaty of Lubeck* with the

---

[37] Davies, G (1985) *The Early Stuarts* (Oxford, Clarendon Press) 52–53; Childs, J (2001) *Warfare in the Seventeenth Century* (London, Cassel) 39.

[38] 'Letter of King Christian IV of Denmark, 1626' in Helfferich, T (2009) *The Thirty Years' War: A Documentary History* (Cambridge, Hackett) 77; also Lockhart, P (2001) 'Political Language and Wartime Propaganda in Denmark, 1625–1629', *European History Quarterly* 31 (1), 542; Beller, E (1928) 'The Military Expedition of Sir Charles Morgan to Germany, 1627–29', *The English Historical Review* 43 (172), 528–39.

Holy Roman Emperor Ferdinand II. This restored Christian IV to most of his pre-war possessions and allowed him not to be crippled with paying compensation for the war. In exchange, Christian IV was obliged to cede his claims to the Lower Saxon bishoprics and discontinue his alliances with the North German states. He also had to promise not to interfere in imperial affairs in the future. At the same time, King Philip IV of Spain offered the United Provinces peace, with large degrees of autonomy, but they had to guarantee the protection of the Catholic religion and recognise the Spanish king as their eternal protector.[39]

By 1629, The Emperor Ferdinand II was feeling so confident in his military victories, and in his theological drive to 'placate God by obeying His laws and by making sure others obey them, without exception',[40] he decided to roll back 75 years of Protestant advances with his *Edict of Restitution*. The 1629 *Edict* was an attempt to enforce the 1555 *Peace of Augsburg* and its predecessor, the 1552 *Peace of Passau*, which had allowed Protestant princes to keep all ecclesiastical properties they had seized before 1552, but had stipulated that no further ecclesiastical properties should be reformed or secularised. The 1629 *Edict* sought to enforce the Ecclesiastical Reservation of 1555, which had stipulated that ecclesiastical rulers (such as prince-bishops) must give up their offices and rights should they change religions. Over time, many princes had failed to abide by this stipulation, meaning that large amounts of Catholic Church land had fallen into the hands of the Protestants. The *Edict of Restitution* demanded the return of this property. This demand changed the map of northern Germany, implicating five bishoprics, about 30 cities, nearly 100 convents and an incalculable number of parishes. In addition, the *Edict* sought to ensure that only those named in the 1555 Peace, namely Lutherans, were entitled to any tolerance. Thus:

> We hereby ... declare and recognise that the Religious Peace concerns and includes only those of the ancient Catholic religion and the adherents of the unaltered Augsburg Confession ... All other contrary doctrines and sects, of whatever name and whether they have already arisen or are still to arise shall be impermissible, excluded from the peace, forbidden, and neither tolerated nor suffered.[41]

As Denmark reached for peace with Emperor Ferdinand II, England also bowed out of the arena. King Charles I, who was soon to be engulfed in his own civil war,[42] agreed to peace with France (following his earlier failed intervention to help the Huguenots) with the 1629 *Treaty of Susa*, and then in 1632 with the *Treaty of Saint-Germain-en-Laye*, through which France recovered the territories the English and Scottish had occupied in New France, including, inter alia, Quebec and Nova Scotia, which had been taken

---

[39] Friedrich, C (1952) *The Age of the Baroque* (NYC, Harper) 161, 174.

[40] Ferdinand II, as in Parker, G (2013) *Global Crisis: War, Climate and Catastrophe in the Seventeenth Century* (New Haven, CT, Yale University Press) 42.

[41] 'The Edict of Restitution, 1629', as reproduced in Reddaway, F (ed) (1930) *Select Documents in European History*, Vol II (London, Methuen) 123.

[42] See chapter VIII.

in their recent conflict.[43] Charles also made peace with Spain in the 1630 *Treaty of Madrid*, and withdrew from his alliance with the Dutch, in large part due to the ongoing difficulties caused by Dutch commercial activities at the expense of the English.[44]

8. THE EXPANDING WAR: SWEDEN

As the English bowed out, the French re-entered the conflict. Despite initially reconciling over a few issues with Spain in the *Treaty of Moncon* of 1526, Louis XIII and his principal adviser, Cardinal Richelieu, realised that the biggest threat to the French monarchy was no longer wars caused by religious division, but rather encirclement by their fellow Catholics, the Habsburgs. Specifically, 'with regard to foreign policy, a constant scheme for putting a stop to the progress of Spain should be adopted ... whenever an opportunity should present itself.'[45] The significance of this recognition was monumental, as at this point the Thirty Years' War could no longer easily be disguised as a war about religion since both the Habsburgs and the Bourbons were Catholic. Now it was a war between dynasties. The plan that Louis XIII then created to oppose the Habsburgs was multi-layered. First, in 1631, peace was made with Savoy under the *Treaty of Cherasco*, which allowed France, inter alia, control of a pass over the Alps that guaranteed the French access to Italy. In the same year, the French agreed (but did not keep) the secret *Treaty of Fontainebleau*, whereby they promised they would not attack Catholic Bavaria. Secondly, and most significantly, they repeated the trick the Dutch and English had tried with the Danish, paying someone else to fight in Germany. The difference was that the French paid Gustavus Adolphus, the very Lutheran King of Sweden, to enter the war.

Gustavus Adolphus was already engaged in a conflict with the Catholic forces of Europe, in particular against Sigismund III Vasa, the King of Poland and Grand Duke of Lithuania. The two rulers hated each other. Sigismund was firmly of the belief that Gustavus Adolphus was wrongfully in possession of the Crown of Sweden, which he believed belonged to him. Conversely, Gustavus Adolphus was of the view that Sigismund was wrongfully oppressing his non-Catholic subjects. War had broken out earlier, as Gustavus Adolphus, after concluding a peace with Russia in 1617 with the *Treaty of Stolbovo*,[46] decided to seize Livonia (which was part of Sigismund's territory).

---

[43] 'The 1629 Treaty of Susa Between Britain and France' in Davenport, F (ed) (1917) *European Treaties Bearing on the History of the United States and its Dependencies to 1648* (NYC, Carnegie Institute) 300–04; the 1632 'Treaty of Saint Germaine', ibid, 315–32.

[44] 'The 1630 Treaty of Peace and Commerce Between Spain and Britain' in Davenport, F (ed) (1917) *European Treaties Bearing on the History of the United States and its Dependencies to 1648* (NYC, Carnegie Institute) 305–14.

[45] See generally, Cardinal Richelieu, 'Advice to Louis XIII: Foreign Policy' in Reddaway, F (ed) (1930) *Select Documents in European History*, Vol II (London, Methuen) 117. See also Richelieu, 'Political Testament', as reproduced in Elton, G (ed) (1968) *Renaissance and Reformation* (London, Macmillan) 141–42.

[46] See page 197.

His military successes between 1621 and 1625 gave him and his 50,000 soldiers the confidence to go on and attack Sigismund in his heartland of western Prussia in 1626. His military successes over the following three years saw the whole coastline, except Danzig, under his control, with a Swedish drive into central Poland a real possibility. The six-year armistice agreed at Altmark in the middle of 1629 suited both sides. The Swedes gained all of Livonia, except a few districts in the south-east. In western Prussia, they won possession of all of the ports, apart from Danzig and Puck, and in the Duchy of Prussia, almost the entire coastline, except for Koenigsberg. The Polish Diet ratified the armistice without blinking, not wanting to get drawn into the even larger conflict that was exploding around them. They were suspicious of the intentions of their king, Sigismund III Vasa. They were particularly angry at him for the high taxes he demanded to pay for his war, and for his refusing to compromise over the Swedish throne, after Gustavus Aldophus hinted that he was willing to surrender Livonia if Sigismund resigned his dynastic claim to Sweden.[47]

As the Polish Diet was trying to keep Poland out of the conflict that was engulfing Europe, Gustavus Adolphus was trying to involve Sweden in it. The pathway to his entry was the *Treaty of Barwalde*, which he agreed with France. Under the terms of the treaty, there would be 'an alliance for the defence of the friends of both of them [France and Sweden] for the safeguarding of the Baltic and Oceanic Seas, the liberty of commerce and the restitution of the oppressed States of the [Holy] Roman Empire'.[48] France was required to give 400,000 *reichstalers* in exchange for Sweden's maintaining an army of 36,000 troops in Germany. Sweden also had to promise religious tolerance towards Catholics in any territories it captured. Gustavus Aldophus expressed himself as content to sign the treaty and involve Sweden in the conflict, since he saw the dangers that an overly strong Emperor posed to Sweden, wished to aid his fellow Protestants, and did not want the Habsburgs to control the Baltic and its trade. He proclaimed he was protecting 'German Liberties', seeking to rescue the imperial constitution and end the illegal suppression of Protestants. He added, 'I am seeking no profit for myself accept the safety of my realm ... I will not hear of neutrality ... God is fighting with the devil'.[49]

Gustavus Aldophus' rhetoric was not successful in all areas. The Lutheran ruler of Saxony, John George, remained loyal to the Emperor, and George William of Brandenburg, even though he was the brother-in-law of Gustavus Aldophus, remained neutral. The 1631 *Leipzig Manifesto* recorded this neutrality, the Protestant estates attempting to create a Protestant defensive association to occupy the middle

---

[47] Frost, R (2000) *The Northern Wars 1558–1721* (London, Longman) 102–10, 115–20.

[48] The 'Treaty of Barwalde', as reproduced in Cohen, M (ed) (2004) *History in Quotations* (London, Cassell) 455.

[49] 'Gustavus Adolphus address to the Brandenburgers, 1630', as reproduced in Reddaway, F (ed) (1930) *Select Documents in European History*, Vol II (London, Methuen) 125; also 'Gustavus Adolphus Invasion of the Empire, 1630' in Helfferich, T (2009) *The Thirty Years' War: A Documentary History* (Cambridge, Hackett) 98; Piirimae, P (2002) 'Just War in Theory and Practice: The Legitimation of Swedish Intervention in the Thirty Years' War', *The Historical Journal* 45 (3), 499–523.

ground between Ferdinand II and Gustavus Adolphus, whereby they promised to uphold 'the basic laws, the Imperial constitution and the German liberties of the Protestant states'.[50] Where Gustavus Aldophus was successful was in the city of Magdeburg, which decided to ally itself with the King of Sweden. However, before Magdeburg could put its support into action, the city was besieged by imperial forces, with as many as 20,000 defenders and 25,000 civilians dying in the course of the siege. The ferocity of the action shocked Europe and inspired both Saxony and Brandenburg to change their views on neutrality. John George joined the Swedes when he felt the threat of the imperial troops surrounding Saxony was becoming too much to bear. The combined Swedish and Saxon army then met the imperial forces in battle at Breitenfeld near Leipzig soon afterwards. General Tilly's imperial army, which numbered over 24,000, was comprehensively defeated, with more than 7,000 soldiers killed by Swedish gunfire and a further 9,000 captured. Gustavus Adolphus then marched his armies west towards the Rhineland, with General Tilly being one of the further 2,000 dead, as the General's force of 22,000 men failed to stop the 37,000-strong army of Gustavus Adolphus from entering Bavaria. With Tilly dead, General Wallenstein took charge of the imperial troops. Ferdinand II enticed him with the promise of 'an Austrian hereditary territory as recompense for his regular expenses', as well as his being able to 'exercise the highest jurisdiction over the territories he occupies'.[51] General Wallenstein attacked the Swedish forces in November 1632. Although the Swedes were victorious at the Battle of Lutzen, Gustavus Aldolphus (along with an estimated 12,000 men dead on the battlefield, divided equally between the two sides) was killed. Nevertheless, his forces were now in occupation of about half of Germany.[52]

As both sides took stock after the Battle of Lutzen, the *Heilbronn League* was formed. This 1633 agreement brought together France and Sweden with princes from the courts of Swabia, Franconia and the Lower Rhine. They agreed to pay for a new, united League army and to keep fighting until the Empire's constitutional and religious problems were resolved, and Sweden was compensated for its troubles.[53] In the meantime, the Emperor Ferdinand II, fearing that General Wallenstein was becoming too powerful (after Wallenstein, believing that the Emperor wanted to kill him, made his colonels swear an oath of allegiance to him), had him denounced as a traitor and assassinated.[54]

---

[50] The 1631 'Leipzig Manifesto' in Parker, G (1998) *The Thirty Years' War* (London, Routledge) 106; also Bodo, N (1979) 'Brandenburg's Reformed Rate and the Leipzig Manifesto', *Journal of Religious History* 10 (4), 365–83.

[51] The 'Contract Between Wallenstein and Ferdinand II' in Cohen, M (ed) (2004) *History in Quotations* (London, Cassell) 455.

[52] Cooper, J (ed) (1970) *The New Cambridge Modern History. The Decline of Spain and the Thirty Years' War*, Vol IV (Cambridge, Cambridge University Press) 398–99, 470–72; Grant, R (2011) *1001 Battles* (London, Penguin) 328–29.

[53] 'Memorandum of Hoe von Hoenegg' in Helfferich, T (2009) *The Thirty Years' War: A Documentary History* (Cambridge, Hackett) 137.

[54] Greengrass, M (2015) *Christendom Destroyed: Europe 1517–1648* (NYC, Penguin) 614–15.

Ferdinand II and his armies then vanquished the Swedish-German Protestant force in 1634 at the Battle of Nördlingen, the Protestants losing some 8,000 men on the battlefield, with a further 4,000 being captured. The imperial and Spanish armies, who had lost only 1,500 men out of a combined force of over 30,000, advanced easily through Franconia, Swabia and Württemberg. The entire populations of towns fled as the armies advanced and the Swedish forces withdrew from central Germany to the coast. Realising that they could not afford to fight on two fronts—against the Emperor and against Sigismund III Vasa—in 1635 the Swedes agreed the *Treaty of Stuhmsdorf* with Poland-Lithuania. This provided for a 26-year armistice between the two sides. In exchange, although Sweden kept Livonia, Poland regained what she had lost in Prussia, and the Swedes had to give up all their 'licences' in Prussian ports. Although nothing was said on the long-standing dynastic questions between the two realms, this treaty kept Sweden in the war, and kept one potential enemy, Poland-Lithuania, out of it.[55]

As the Heilbronn League dissolved, the Protestant Elector of Saxony, soon to be followed by other German estates and princes, made peace with Ferdinand II in the *Peace of Prague* in May 1635. This treaty sought to put an end to the 'wretchedness, want and destruction' caused by the dissension between warring parties and by the armies of foreign peoples 'on the soil of the beloved fatherland of the noble German nation'.[56] The political essence of this Peace was that Ferdinand II was willing to compromise, relinquishing some of the militancy that had accompanied his earlier positions. The technical essence of this peace was that the *Edict of Restitution* that Ferdinand wanted to enforce would not be applied for 40 years, and the date from which the *Edict of Restitution* would be applied would not be 1555 but rather 1627. Thus, any ecclesiastical lands seized before 1627 would not have to be repatriated. The people of Saxony were also granted an amnesty. In exchange, they had to cede their right to independent military forces and direction, and support the Emperor in his wars against any foreign forces, especially the Swedish.[57]

9. THE EXPANDING WAR: FRANCE

The last stage of the Thirty Years' War saw the French getting directly involved in the fighting. Louis XIII was becoming increasingly concerned about the war-weariness of the Dutch and the retreats by Swedish forces in Germany. When Spain arrested

[55] Cooper, J (ed) (1970) *The New Cambridge Modern History. The Decline of Spain and the Thirty Years' War*, Vol IV (Cambridge, Cambridge University Press) 398, 600.

[56] As noted in Mowat, R (1888) *A History of European Diplomacy: 1451–1769* (London, Butler) 102–05.

[57] 'The Peace of Prague, 1635' in Helfferich, T (2009) *The Thirty Years' War: A Documentary History* (Cambridge, Hackett) 170; Bireley, R (1976) 'The Peace of Prague and the Counter-Reformation in Germany', *The Journal of Modern History* 48 (1), 31–70; Moutoux, E (1982) 'Wallenstein: Guilty and Innocent', *The Germanic Review* 57 (1), 23–40.

the Bishop of Triers, who was under French protection, Louis XIII had the excuse he needed to declare war on Spain, mobilising 150,000 men in 1635. To bolster the anti-Habsburg effort, the French renewed their alliances with the Dutch and then increased their subsidies to the Swedes (first under the *Treaty of Wismar* of 1636 and later under the *Treaty of Hamburg* of 1641), promising 1,000,000 *livres*, about one-third of Sweden's domestic income, if the Swedes remained engaged in the fight and followed French direction, continuing to fight in Silesia and Bohemia.[58]

The Habsburgs retaliated swiftly. In the middle of 1636, imperial troops invaded Burgundy, while a Spanish army attacked Picardy. It advanced across the Somme, only to find its advance blocked by some 40,000 French troops commanded by Louis XIII, standing between the Spanish and Paris. Thereafter, the tide turned. Victory after victory followed for the French and Dutch, with them retaking Breda in 1637. In 1638, an imperial army was destroyed at Rheinfelden, thus allowing most of Alsace to be conquered. In the same year, the fortress town of Breisach was lost, which cut the vital 'Spanish Road' linking Habsburg possessions from Milan to Brussels, thus meaning that reinforcements now had to come by sea. When this was next attempted, at the Battle of the Downs in the English Channel in 1639, the Spanish lost 54 ships (with more than 7,000 dead and 1,800 captured), while the Dutch lost only one vessel. To make matters even worse for King Philip IV of Spain, in 1640 there was an uprising in Catalonia, in which a disgruntled peasantry, angry over persistent demands for men and money to support Philip's wars, turned on the aristocracy. When the President of Catalonia pledged allegiance to the French king, Louis XIII, Philip IV ended up having to find another army to defeat the rebels. His first major battle in this conflict, at Montjuric, was a disaster, with over 1,500 of Philip's men killed as the rebels established control over Barcelona.[59]

Although the revolt in Catalonia was eventually brought under control, a coup in Portugal (in part due to the costs of Philip's wars and foreigners making decisions for the Portuguese) in 1640 saw the Duke of Braganza named as the new King John IV of Portugal. Although Philip IV would repeatedly try to reclaim Portugal by force, the determination of the Portuguese, supplemented by money and support from England, the Seven Provinces and France, made it impossible for Philip IV to reclaim this part of the Habsburg Empire.[60]

As both branches of the Habsburgs began to search for peace, the advances of the Dutch, Swedes and French continued. By 1641, the French and the Swedes had

[58] Lesaffer, R (2006) 'Defensive Warfare, Prevention and Hegemony: The Justifications for the Franco-Spanish War of 1635', *Journal of the History of International Law* 8, 91–123, 141–79; Parker, G (2013) *Global Crisis: War, Climate and Catastrophe in the Seventeenth Century* (New Haven, CT, Yale University Press) 32.

[59] Grant, R (2011) *1001 Battles* (London, Penguin) 320, 334, 335, 336, 337, 340, 341, 344.

[60] 'The 1641 Treaty of Alliance Between Portugal and France' and the '1641 Treaty of Truce and Commerce Between the United Netherlands and Portugal' in Davenport, F (ed) (1917) *European Treaties Bearing on the History of the United States and its Dependencies to 1648* (NYC, Carnegie Institute) 324–46; Curtis, B (2013) *The Habsburgs* (London, Bloomsbury) 125–29; Seward, D (2013) *The Bourbon Kings of France* (London, Jones) 60–63.

actually joined forces. At the second Battle of Breitenfeld in 1642, the Swedes defeated the imperial army (which suffered losses of 5,000 dead and 5,000 captured), allowing them to occupy Saxony. The Habsburg hope was that when Denmark was persuaded to attack a distracted Sweden in 1643, some relief could be found. However, the Danish forces were quickly pushed back and subsequently punished with the *Peace of Bromesbro* in 1645, in which the Swedes acquired a number of Danish provinces and islands, and the Danish heir to the throne had to resign.

Once the Danes were in hand, the collective push into the Habsburg areas continued. At Rocroi, on the border of the Spanish Netherlands, in May 1643, despite their own loss of 2,000 men, the French killed 6,000 Spanish veterans in one evening (and captured a further 5,000) as they tried to withstand a French artillery bombardment. The following year, in 1644, following a Swedish alliance with the Transylvanian Prince, Gyorgy Rakoczi I, Habsburg Hungary was invaded. At Freiburg in 1644, although the French suffered heavier casualties (7,000 out of 25,000), they again defeated the imperial forces (2,500 out of 16,500), forcing them to retreat, allowing the French to gain mastery over the central Rhine region. Despite the fact that the French were defeated at Tuttlingen in 1644, the Spanish Netherlands lost Gravelines, Hulst in 1645 and Dunkirk in 1646. By the time of the Battle of Jankov in Bohemia, in 1645, the imperial cause was desperate. The Swedish victory not only left 4,000 imperial troops dead on the field, with another 4,500 captured (at a cost of 2,000 dead to the Swedes), it also opened the way for threatening Habsburg Vienna. Realising that they had to reduce the number of enemies against them, in the same year, 1645, the Emperor Ferdinand III broke the Transylvanian Prince, Gyorgy Rakoczi off from the French-Swedish alliance with the *Treaty of Linz*. In exchange for the ending of their alliance, the seven provinces Gyorgy had control over were granted religious freedom, Protestants who had fled were allowed to return and land that had been confiscated by the Catholics was restored. However, this remained insufficient for the Habsburg's to regain their military composure. A comprehensive peace was essential for both parts of the Habsburg Empire if they were going to survive as a dynasty. If there was any doubt over this possibility, at Zusmarshausen, in May 1648, the retreating imperial army narrowly avoided being completely annihilated (but still losing 2,200 men) by a French-Swedish army that continued to pursue it.[61]

10. The Peace of Westphalia

The so-called 'Peace of Westphalia', which brought an end to the Thirty Years' War, was made up of three separate treaties, negotiated between January and October 1648. Delegations from all of Europe, bar England, Poland, Russia and Turkey, were

---

[61] Mowat, R (1910) 'The Mission of Sir Thomas Roe to Vienna, 1641', *The English Historical Review* 25 (98), 264–75.

present at the negotiations. Peace was brought to most (but not all) of the Continent with, first, the *Peace of Munster*, signed in January 1648, between the Dutch Republic and the Kingdom of Spain. Two complementary treaties signed in October 1648 were the *Treaty of Munster*, between the Holy Roman Emperor and France and their respective allies; and the *Treaty of Osnabruck*, involving the Holy Roman Empire, Sweden and their respective allies.

The *Peace of Munster* of 1648 was made against the will of the national leader of the Seven Provinces, the stadtholder, William II, Prince of Orange, and a number of Calvinists, who wanted to keep fighting the Catholics and recover the southern provinces to establish a truly united Netherlands. The majority, however, wanted to establish peace so that the Netherlands could trade, make money, pay war debts and become recognised as a sovereign country. Accordingly, the States General agreed, by a thin majority, to ratify the *Peace of Munster*, to which Philip IV of Spain agreed to put his signature. Article 1 of the *Peace of Munster* stated:

> The Lord King [Philip IV] recognises that the United Netherlands and the respected provinces thereof … are free and sovereign states, and he … does not now make any claim, … his successors and descendants will in the future never make any claim … and is therefore satisfied to negotiate a perpetual peace, on the conditions hereinafter.[62]

In addition to the standard promises to engage in normal commerce, cooperate against pirates, not build new forts, offer amnesty for crimes committed and the exchange of prisoners, the Seven Provinces kept those parts of Flanders, Brabant and Limburg they had conquered following the 1608 Truce.[63] Spanish efforts to obtain religious liberty for these homogeneously Roman Catholic areas failed. These became, in effect, conquered territories. No special protection was given to the citizens on grounds of religion, although it was added that when the subjects of either signatory were in the lands of the other, they should 'conduct themselves in the matter of public exercise of religion with all piety, giving no scandal by word or deed and speaking no slander'.[64]

The *Treaty of Munster* of 1648 brought a 'universal, perpetual, Christian peace' between the Holy Roman Emperor Ferdinand III and France (and their allies).[65] Aside from the standard promises regarding amnesty and the exchange of prisoners, although Louis XIV, through his regent, his mother Queen Anne, and chief minister Cardinal Mazarin, had to restore much of what his father's troops had conquered, the Bishoprics of Metz, Toul and Verdun were all ceded to France. Part of the provinces of Alsace and Lorraine were also to go to France, but the terms of cession were extremely vague. The *Treaty of Munster* also recorded that the princes had 'territorial

[62] Art 1 of the 'Peace of Munster' in Rowen, H (ed) (1972) *The Low Countries in Early Modern Times: Select Documents* (London, Macmillan) 181; also Manzano, B (2007) 'Negotiating Sovereignty: The Peace Treaty of Munster, 1648', *History of Political Thought* 28 (4), 617–41.

[63] See page 134.

[64] See Article 19.

[65] The 'Treaty of Munster' in Reddaway, F (ed) (1930) *Select Documents in European History*, Vol II (London, Methuen) 134.

superiority in all matters ecclesiastical as well as political'. They thus had the right to conclude treaties between themselves and with other sovereign powers. The 'old liberties' of the prince were thus transformed into sovereignty, even though this word was not used.[66]

The final agreement in the trilogy, the *Treaty of Osnabruck*, established 'a Christian, universal, perpetual, true and sincere peace and friendship' between Ferdinand III and Sweden (and their allies).[67] In addition to the standard rules on amnesty for crimes committed and a return of prisoners, Sweden negotiated handsome rewards, which also made it a power in the affairs of Germany. These included the cession of Pomerania, Rugen, Stettin, the mouth of the great northern river, Oder Wismar, the Archbishopric of Bremen and Verden. In addition, 600,000 gold crowns and 5 million *rixdollars* were agreed as the amount needed to get Swedish mercenaries demobbed and out of German territories. Calvinism was recognised as being equal to the Catholic and Lutheran faiths, and the *Convention of Passau* of 1552 and the *Peace of Augsburg* of 1555 were again underlined. The year 1624 was set as the date for the coming into force of the *Edict of Restitution*, not the original 1555.[68]

Although religious toleration only extended to three Christian groupings, and its limits were still apparent, it was nonetheless agreed that 'subjects whose religion differs from that of their prince are to have equal rights with his other subjects.'[69] The independence of the Swiss was acknowledged, and the Rhine Palatinate was split into two parts. The Upper Palatinate and the district of Cham were handed over to Bavaria, whilst an eighth electorate was created and given to the deprived Elector Palatinate and his heirs. The Lower Palatinate was restored to the Elector Palatinate. Article VIII of the Treaty recognised the sovereignty of the members of the Holy Roman Empire, and provided for their free assembly to conduct all imperial affairs, to make laws, to make war or peace or alliances, and to raise taxes and/or soldiers. Lastly, both France and Sweden succeeded in inserting a clause into the peace treaties, providing that the election of the King of the Romans would not be permissible during the Emperor's lifetime, except in case of necessity. This was an attempt to stop the practice of monopolising the Imperial Crown, the Emperor's overseeing the election of his eldest son during the father's lifetime, thus keeping power in the family.[70]

[66] See Arts 62, 63, 69–70 and 85; also Croxton, D (1999) 'The Peace of Westphalia of 1648 and the Origins of Sovereignty', *The International History Review* 21 (3), 569–83; Cooper, J (ed) (1970) *The New Cambridge Modern History. The Decline of Spain and the Thirty Year War* (Cambridge, Cambridge University Press) 354–55.

[67] As reproduced in Reddaway, F (ed) (1930) *Select Documents in European History*, Vol II (London, Methuen) 132.

[68] See pages 80–81.

[69] See Art V(34); also Asch, R (2000) 'Religious Toleration, the Peace of Westphalia and the German Territorial Estates', *Parliaments, Estates and Representation* 20 (1), 79–89.

[70] See Arts X and XVI; also Straumann, B (2008) 'The Peace of Westphalia as a Secular Constitution', *Constellations* 15 (1) 98–134.

11. Rethinking War: Crucé, Sully and Grotius

Out of all the carnage of the Thirty Years' War three scholars emerged who planted ideas that took root and went on to have impacts that would resonate throughout the centuries ahead.

The first was the French writer, Émeric Crucé, who in 1623 wrote the masterpiece, *The New Cyneas: Or Discourse on the Occasions and Means for Establishing General Peace and Free Trade Throughout the World*. His core proposition was, simply, that humanity would better spend its time pursuing commerce and communication rather than conflict. He recognised the importance of free trade, free travel and a universal currency. On the question of religion, he stressed tolerance not only between the different Christian faiths, but also of non-Christians such as the Muslims and Jews. He reasoned that since the ultimate answers about religion were unknowable, it was pointless to fight over differences in ceremonies. Waging war and killing others simply on the basis of their being different in terms of religion or nationality was the antithesis of humanity. As Crucé explained:

> Why should I, a Frenchman, wish to harm an Englishman, a Spaniard, or a Hindu? I cannot when I consider that they are men like me, that I am subject like them to error and sin and that all nations are bound together by a natural and consequently indestructible tie, which ensures that a man cannot consider another to be a stranger.[71]

Crucé also suggested the founding of an international assembly in Venice, as it was neutral and well situated between all of the different nations. He recommended inviting the territories of the Pope, the Ottomans, the Habsburgs, as well as the Kings of Spain, Moscow, Poland, England and Denmark, as well as the republics of Venice and Switzerland. Persia, China, Japan, Ethiopia and the lands of the New World should also be included. The system he proposed involved committees, rotating chairpersons, and binding decisions based upon majority votes after hearing the cases put forward by opposing countries, as a result of which a country could be expelled from the assembly. Rules of conduct would involve recognition of the territorial status quo and non-intervention in the internal matters of member countries. Quite simply, Crucé envisaged an idealised League of Nations (then United Nations) 400 years before its foundation.[72]

The second of these scholars was the adviser to the French king, Henri IV, Maximilien de Béthune, the first Duke of Sully, who published his *Grand Dessein de Henri IV* in 1638. This aimed to defuse the religious problems in Europe. Sully's foundation was religious tolerance in Europe between Lutherans, Catholics and Calvinists. This would be followed by the principle of equilibrium, under which all nations in Europe needed to be, more or less, the same size and with similar wealth. The Habsburg Empire

---

[71] Crucé, E (1623) *The New Cyneas* (reprinted (1972) New York, Garland Publishing) 35; also Villaverde, M (2016) 'The Long Road to Religions Toleration: Emeric Crucé, Predecessor of the Enlightenment', *History of European Ideas* 1–14.

[72] Heerikhuizen, A (2008) 'How God Disappeared from Europe: Visions of a United Europe from Erasmus to Kant', *The European Legacy* 13 (4), 401, 404–05.

was obviously too large and too dominant, and therefore gave rise to a lack of balance and was the cause of revolutions and conflict. What Sully proposed was a type of European confederation (of 66 representatives) representing (as they were as Sully saw them) the six hereditary monarchs, together with six elective powers and three federated republics.[73] Together the members of the confederation would come together to decide on matters collectively, through a permanent forum. He argued that a general council could levy troops and direct military operations against groups such as Orthodox Russia, or the Muslim Ottomans, and then preside over the division of the spoils. This approach was clearly more limited than what Crucé proposed, looking only to maintaining peace within Europe and establishing similarly sized countries. It did not encompass ideas of free trade, the status quo as regards territory or a much wider, more cosmopolitan view of the world.[74]

The third great thinker of this epoch was Hugo Grotius. Grotius also sought answers to end conflict, based on reason and practice (not theology), that were ahead of his time. He recognised the wrongfulness of fighting over things that should be owned by all, not monopolised by any one nation, of which the high seas were most obvious. This argument was presented in his first famous book, *Mare Liberum* ('The Free Sea'), which linked freedom of trade to freedom of the seas, open to all nations to utilise freely. This argument was the antithesis of the idea that the Pope could divide up the Earth and award either land or seas to favoured sovereigns.[75] Grotius also argued that war based on plunder was not justifiable. He added, 'neither can the desire of emigrating to a more favourable soil and climate justify an attack on a neighbouring power.'[76] Moreover, it was unjust to base war on the 'discovery of things belonging to others'. Of the latter, and clearly with the conquests of Spain in the New World in mind, Grotius wrote:

> Neither can wickedness, and impiety, nor any other incapacity of the original owner justify such a claim. Neither moral nor religious virtue, not any intellectual excellence is requisite to form a good title to property. Title and right by discovery can apply only to countries and places that have no owner … [T]here is equal injustice in the desire of reducing, by force of arms, any people to a state of servitude, under the pretext of it being the condition for which they are best qualified by nature. It does not follow that, because any one is fitted for a particular condition, another has a right to impose it upon him. For every reasonable creature ought to be left free in the choice of what may be deemed useful or prejudicial to him.[77]

[73] Hereditary monarchies: France, Spain, Britain, Denmark, Sweden and Lombardy; elective powers: the Papacy, Venice, the Holy Roman Empire, Poland, Hungary and Bohemia; federated republics: those in Italy, Belgium and what became the Netherlands.

[74] Heerikhuizen, A (2008), 'How God Disappeared from Europe: Visions of a United Europe from Erasmus to Kant', *The European Legacy* 13 (4), 401, 405–06.

[75] Thomson, E (2009) 'The Dutch Miracle, Modified: Hugo Grotius's Mare Liberum, Commercial Governance and Imperial War', *Grotiana* 30, 107–30; Ittersum, J (2012) 'Hugo Grotius' Justification of Dutch Expansion Overseas', *History of European Ideas* 36 (4), 386–411.

[76] Grotius, H (1625) *The Rights of War and Peace* (reprinted (1901) London, Dunne) 269; ibid, at 77–84. Also Rupp, M (1924) 'Hugo Grotius and His Place in the History of International Peace', *The Catholic Historical Review* 19 (3), 358–66.

[77] Grotius, H (1625) *The Rights of War and Peace* (reprinted (1901) London, Dunne) 269–70.

Despite these reservations, in his most famous work, *De jure belli ac pacis libri tres* ('On the Law of War and Peace'), Grotius argued that killing and warfare could be lawful and just, although the methods by which war could be waged should always be limited. If peaceful arbitration could not resolve matters, war could be waged (for self-defence, recovery of property or debt, or the punishment of offences committed) if there was a formal decision to do so, originating from the correct sovereign authority. For Grotius, that authority was not restricted to monarchs, suggesting that sovereignty that could authorise war could also be held through 'government by nobles'.[78]

Grotius also went on to write about and advocate religious tolerance, for which he was imprisoned. This occurred because he fell foul of the increasingly intolerant Dutch in the Seven Provinces (not those in America, who went on to become exemplarily tolerant), after becoming engaged in debates between Calvinists of a dogmatic persuasion and groups espousing a more Erasmian tolerance. Despite being imprisoned by his own government, he warned about entering into foreign conflicts to protect individuals who were being abused by other governments. This was especially so if the risk to the protecting country was great. Thus, 'under some circumstances it is impossible successfully to oppose cruelty and oppression, the punishment of which must be left to the eternal judge of mankind'.[79]

12. Conclusion

The Thirty Years' War was the culmination of the violence, wrapped around considerations of religion and autonomy, which had spilled over from the sixteenth century. The irony of this situation was that by the seventeenth century, the driving force behind much of the religious dissent, the papacy, was itself a spent force. However, both kings and emperors decided to advance the Counter-Reformation and undo much of the peace which worked in Germany, by adopting interpretations that were both very strict, and missing the spirit of what the earlier peace agreements were about. These approaches became problematic in Bohemia, where promises which were made became the epicentre of the ensuing dispute, that the Protestants could retain their traditional rights and religious autonomy. It was when these traditional rights and autonomy were threatened by the Emperor Ferdinand II that the Bohemians attempted to

---

[78] Grotius, H (1625) *The Rights of War and Peace* (reprinted (1901) London, Dunne) 65, 314–15, 321; also, Pena, E (2014) 'Hugo Grotius: War Through Law', *Araucaria* 16 (32), 69–92; Lee, D (2011) 'Popular Liberty, Princely Government and the Roman Law in Hugo Grotius', *Journal in the History of Ideas* 72 (3), 371–92; Blois, M (2011) 'Grotius on Just War and Christian Pacifism', *Grotiana* 32, 20–39; Dunthorne, H (2013) 'History, Theology and Tolerance: Grotius and his Contemporaries', *Grotiana* 34, 107–19; Bangs, J (2010) 'Dutch Contributions to Religious Tolerance', *Church History* 79 (3), 585–613; Parker, C (2015) 'Hugo Grotius's Vision of Global Citizenship and Christian Unity', *Journal of Policy History* 27 (2), 364–81; Bull, H (1991) *Hugo Grotius and International Relations* (Oxford, Clarendon) 242–46; Forde, S (1998) 'Hugo Grotius on Ethics and War' *The American Political Science Review* 92 (3), 639–48.

[79] Grotius, H (1625) *The Rights of War and Peace* (reprinted (1901) London, Dunne) 288.

break free from the Holy Roman Empire, electing their own king, the Protestant leader, Frederick V. Although religion provided the initial gloss for the conflict, the Emperor and his allies justified it as being about illegal electoral processes, which threatened the integrity of the entire political apparatus.

Initially, both France and England tried to stay out of the war. However, as the power and success of the Habsburgs grew, Catholic France decided to throw her weight behind the Protestant cause. This was not because France had come to accept the principle of religious tolerance within its own possessions, but because it feared the growing encroachment of the Habsburgs on French territories. The French made alliances with the Protestant countries of the Dutch Republic, Denmark and, most importantly, Sweden. Support for this alliance grew, as the religious element, and intolerance for the defeated, became increasingly prominent after 1629. The war that destroyed much of Germany over the next 19 years only came to an end in Westphalia in 1648. Peace was agreed, and the Habsburgs survived, bruised, after agreeing several principles. First, territory changed hands, with France and Sweden benefiting, and the Dutch Republic became a sovereign state and independent. Money was handed over to demobilise the armies and pay reparations. Finally, the sovereign autonomy of all members of the Holy Roman Empire was increased, including on the issue of religious tolerance, via a somewhat extended understanding of the *Peace of Augsburg*, as agreed nearly a century earlier.

Progress beckoned in the form of the three great thinkers of this period—Crucé, Sully and Grotius. These three men helped draft the blueprints for what ultimately became the League of Nations, the European Union and the United Nations, urging international cooperation and competition via commerce, not weapons. Grotius, the father of international law, would further condemn many of the traditional causes of war, going on to sketch a much more rational international order based on principles of tolerance, commerce and sovereignty, which could be found in peoples and not just monarchs.

VIII

The English Civil War

1. Introduction

FROM 1570 TO 1639, Britain, that is England and Scotland, enjoyed its longest period of domestic peace since 1066. This was a remarkable achievement, as much of Western Europe was being ripped apart by causes of war related to religion and political autonomy. In Britain, in a conflict that was given the gloss of religion but that was ultimately about the division of power between the king, Parliament and the army, the slide towards war began soon after Charles I succeeded to the throne of England, Scotland and Ireland upon the death of his father, King James I (King James VI of Scotland). Like his father before him, Charles I was a firm believer in the divine right to rule of anointed kings. The difficulty he faced was that the peoples he governed doubted this right, and the power he alleged it gave him to rule on both theological and constitutional matters. Failure to resolve this disagreement led to Charles later paying the ultimate price—regicide—and for a short period England would become a republic, albeit only for those who enjoyed privilege and property.

2. Charles I

A. The Divine Right of Kings

Charles I shared the same beliefs as his father about the divine nature of his absolute monarchy.[1] However, unlike his father, he did not initially know when to trim his beliefs when in public so as to obtain his political goals. Even before he was king, whilst he was serving his political apprenticeship in the Parliaments of 1621 and 1624, when his father was still on the throne, Charles believed that he could manipulate Parliament to his own ends. The relationship soured further with Charles's marriage to the French Catholic, Henrietta Maria, daughter of the French king, Henri IV, and sister of the future Louis XIII. This was just one of many grievances held by Parliament, which was also concerned about the ongoing influence of papists in England, Scotland and Ireland, the ill-guarding of the seas, the misuse of subsidies and the state of British

---

[1] See pages 111–112.

involvement, or non-involvement, in the wars of religion on the Continent. Charles's initial response to these accusations was simply that Parliament should trust him and the power 'which God hath put in my hands'.[2]

The year after Charles succeeded to the throne, in 1626, he dissolved Parliament, which continued to express its ongoing concerns, noted above, in order to prevent it from impeaching his favourite, the Duke of Buckingham (who had been trying to engineer Britain's involvement in the war against Spain, and dealt with many of the king's matters in Parliament), over mismanagement of maritime affairs.[3] Thereafter, being in need of money to prosecute a war with Spain, Charles resorted to levying taxes ('tonnage and poundage', relating to tax on imported and exported wine and merchandise) unauthorised by Parliament (which had made 'tonnage and poundage' a duty that required consent each year, rather than a lifetime grant, as it had been under previous monarchs) in order to raise the necessary funds. Charles imprisoned without charge five high-profile knights who refused to pay this 'forced loan'. This prompted those imprisoned to stand firm against the king's demands, lest the English monarchy should go the way of those on the Continent (ie espousing absolutism). However, as Charles required more funds than he could acquire by these means, he resummoned Parliament in March 1628, releasing those already imprisoned but asking for more money. Parliament, which was now also angry over Charles's intervention in the Huguenot rebellion in France,[4] responded to his demands with the *Petition of Right* in the middle of 1628. This was, and remains, a major English constitutional document that sets specific liberties that the king is prohibited from infringing. This read:

> No person shall be compelled to many any loans to the King against his will, because such loans are against reason and the franchise of the land ... no freeman may be taken or imprisoned or be disseised of his freehold or liberties, or outlawed or exiled, ... but by the lawful judgement of his peers, or by the law of the land; ... no man should be put out of his lands, nor taken, not imprisoned, nor disinherited, nor put to death without being brought to answer by due process of law.[5]

The king accepted this Petition, as he saw its demands as consistent with what he already did, but added that 'his subjects have no cause to complain of any wrong or oppressions, contrary to their rights and liberties, to the preservation whereof he holds himself as well obliged as of his prerogative'.[6] Although this should have calmed

[2] Charles, as noted in Cooper, J (ed) (1970) *The New Cambridge Modern History: The Decline of Spain and the Thirty Years War*, Vol IV (Cambridge, Cambridge University Press) 556; also Kyle, C (1998) 'Prince Charles in the Parliaments of 1621 and 1624', *The Historical Journal* 4 (3), 603–24; Kiryanova, E (2015) 'Images of Kingship: Charles I, Accession Sermons and the Theory of Divine Right', *History* 100 (339), 21–39; Havran, M (1983) 'The Character and Principles of an English King: The Case of Charles I', *The Catholic Historical Review* 69 (2), 169–208.

[3] Cogswell, T (2011) 'The Warre of the Commons for the Honour of King Charles: The Parliament Men and Reformation of the Lord Admiral in 1626', *Historical Research* 84 (226), 618–35.

[4] See pages 146–147.

[5] 'The Petition of Right, 1628', as in Millward, J (ed) (1961) *The Seventeenth Century: Portraits and Documents* (London, Hutchinson) 73.

[6] 'The Kings Reply, 1628' in Adams, M (ed) (1947) *Select Documents on English Constitutional Law* (London, Macmillan) 342.

matters, the assassination of the Duke of Buckingham reinvigorated debate, as Charles tried to fill the void left by Buckingham's death and manage Parliament directly himself. Tensions came to a head when some in the Commons wanted to challenge violations of the *Petition of Right* (especially on the continued collection of tonnage and poundage) and the emergence of Arminianism (a variation on Calvin's theology). In this tense atmosphere, the *Three Resolutions of 1629* were presented to the king. These stated, inter alia:

1. Whoever shall bring in innovation of religion … or seek to extend or introduce Popery or Arminianism disagreeing from the true and orthodox church [of England] shall be reputed a capital enemy to this kingdom.
2. Whoever shall counsel or advise the taking of levying of the subsidies of tonnage and poundage … shall be a capital enemy to this kingdom.
3. If any merchant or person shall voluntarily yield, or pay the said subsidies of tonnage and poundage, not being granted by Parliament, he shall be reputed a betrayer of the liberties of England.[7]

Charles rejected the Resolutions and dissolved Parliament. He explained that as Parliament was trying to take away the profit from 'my' tonnage, 'I am forced to end this Session … For none of the Houses of Parliament, either joint or separate, have any power either to make or declare a law without my consent'.[8] He asserted that he was not beholden to Parliament, thus 'I owe the account of my actions to God alone'.[9]

B. Personal Rule

For the next 11 years, Charles governed without Parliament. In this period the autocratic nature of the king became increasingly apparent, as peace was largely secured by the silence of the governed, although with each new step he took, dissent began to grow. First, he levied additional taxes ('ship money', originally for coastal areas in times of war) over much of England (that is, coastal and non-coastal areas in times of peace), without Parliamentary consent. Secondly, he increased the power of Star Chamber to control the press and books available in his realm, and to persecute arch Puritans[10] who opposed his theological directives. Thirdly, Charles got involved in ecclesiastical debates: he was determined to defend the Anglican Church, by trying to stop the spread of Calvinism and Puritan doctrines in his realm, as well as those of outspoken

---

[7] 'The Three Resolutions, 1629' in Millward, J (ed) (1961) *The Seventeenth Century: Portraits and Documents* (London, Hutchinson) 74–75.

[8] 'The King's Speech Proroguing Parliament' in Adams, M (ed) (1947) *Select Documents on English Constitutional Law* (London, Macmillan) 345.

[9] Charles, as noted in Davies, G (1987) *The Early Stuarts* (Oxford, Oxford University Press) 33. Also, Cust, R (2005) 'Was There an Alternative to the Personal Rule? Charles I, the Privy Council and the Parliament of 1629', *History* 90 (299), 330–52.

[10] See page 97.

Catholics. To achieve this goal, he reissued King James's *Declaration of Sport*, which specified which recreational activities could be pursued on Sundays (much to the anger of the Puritans). He also insisted upon new canons for the Church of England in 1640 (despite the objections of the Puritans), the first of which read:

> The most high and sacred order of kings is of divine right, being the ordinance of God himself, founded in the prime laws of nature, and clearly established by express texts both of the Old and New Testaments … For subjects to bear arms against their kings, offensive or defensive, upon any pretence whatsoever, is at least to resist the powers which are ordained of God … and they receive to themselves damnation.[11]

Of greater significance in the slide towards conflict, Charles also became directly involved in religious affairs, sanctioning a process of ecclesiastical reform that embraced controversial ceremonial practices. Further, despite causing riots, Charles forced the *Book of Common Prayer* of the Anglican Church of England upon the Church of Scotland, rather than allowing the latter to use its own version. Charles's actions also gave rise to grievances from many of the most powerful nobles in Scotland, when he tried to increase finances for the established clergy by transferring ownership of lands on which churches were built away from some of the Scottish nobility and to the bishops.[12]

By 1638, the opposition of the Scottish clergy to Charles's attempt to reform their religious practices first became apparent. A *National Covenant*, a formal document of protest, was drafted, which Church leaders signed. It was created 'for the maintenance of religion and the King's Majesty's authority, and for the preservation of the laws and liberties of the kingdom'.[13] The significance of this Covenant lay not in its widespread agreement amongst the Scots that the king could not force his religious reforms on Scotland, but its insistence that Charles I had to respect the established laws and practices of the Scots to self-govern on such issues. Although Charles replied that he would 'rather die than yield to those impertinent and damnable demands',[14] he indicated that he might be able to agree to the abolition of some of the practices that were causing offence. To help with this, Charles agreed to the holding of the Glasgow Assembly. However, as this became constituted (stacked) in a way with which Charles did not agree, he ordered it to be dissolved, a ruling that the Scots ignored. The Assembly then upheld all of its earlier theological concerns, excommunicated a number of Charles's bishops in Scotland, and called upon the king to maintain 'the liberties of Christ's [Scotland] and Kingdom [and] the King's honour in maintaining

---

[11] The new canons proposed for Charles I, in Davies, G (1987) *The Early Stuarts* (Oxford, Oxford University Press) 94. For the period, see Duinen, J (2011) 'Revealing Dissent under Charles I's Personal Rule', *Parergon* 28 (1), 177–96.

[12] See the 'Act of Revocation and the Settlement of the Teinds' in Dickinson, W (ed) (1958) *A Sourcebook of Scottish History*, Vol III (London, Nelson) 66–71; 'The Grievances of the Nobles', ibid, at 77–83. Also Prior, C (2013) 'Religion, Political Thought and the English Civil War', *History Compass* 11 (1), 24, 25–28.

[13] The 1638 'National Covenant' in Dickinson, W (ed) (1958) *A Sourcebook of Scottish History*, Vol III (London, Nelson) 93.

[14] Charles, as noted in Royle, T (2005) *Civil War: The Wars of the Three Kingdoms* (London, Abacus) 73.

the established laws and judicatories of [Scotland]'.[15] In essence, the Scots called for a restoration of the status quo, as it was in the time of Elizabeth I, before the Stuarts acceded to the throne.

Charles refused to ratify the acts of the Glasgow Assembly and continued to play for time. The Covenanters, for their part, began assembling men and munitions, and then in early 1639 they seized a number of fortresses, after Alexander Henderson, a Scottish Presbyterian clergyman, issued his *Instructions for Defensive Arms*, in which he argued for the Christian necessity of resisting tyranny and taking up arms for the defence of a free Scotland. Unless its religious liberties were defended, he warned, Scotland and its people could 'look for nothing but miserable and perpetual slavery'.[16] With Scotland now effectively in the hands of the Covenanters, the so-called 'Bishops' War' began.

C. The Short Parliament

In 1640, when an army of 12,000 Covenanters marched to the border between Scotland and England, Charles I indicated that he was willing to let the Scottish Parliament and a further General Assembly meet. When these bodies came together and the Scottish Parliament began to discuss constitutional matters, Charles had this body annulled. At this point, Charles reassembled the English Parliament (the 'Short Parliament'). This Parliament, which sat for three weeks only before Charles annulled it, had a greater interest in pursuing the list of concerns it had from 1629, rather than voting the king funds to pursue his war against the Scottish Covenanters.

Charles subsequently faced more Scottish forces, which this time, after receiving direction from the Scottish Estates, had assembled without Charles's consent, crossed the border and occupied Newcastle upon Tyne. When Charles's army retreated, it allowed the Scots to occupy the whole of Northumberland and the neighbouring county of Durham. Only by agreeing to the *Treaty of Ripon* in 1640 did Charles stop their advance, finally making peace with the *Treaty of London* of 1641, the drafting of which made it necessary for Charles to recall the English Parliament.

D. The Long Parliament

Under the *Treaty of London*, Charles, who was anxious to be rid of his Scottish problem, agreed to pay the Scots' expenses in recompense for the war, and promised not to persecute the Covenanters and to allow them the full autonomy they desired on religious

---

[15] The 1638 'Glasgow Assembly' in Dickinson, W (ed) (1958) *A Sourcebook of Scottish History*, Vol III (London, Nelson) 106–09.

[16] Henderson, in Royle, T (2005) *Civil War: The Wars of the Three Kingdoms* (London, Abacus) 82.

matters.[17] In order to meet his financial obligations to the Scots, he had to recall Parliament (the 'Long Parliament'), one which would sit for 20 years as Charles was later made to agree that only Parliament, and not the king, could call for its dissolution.[18]

It was this body that brought civil war to England. It exercised a type of power—in the name of the people—that Charles could only imagine. One of its first demands (as a price for allowing peace with the Scots), was the *Clerical Disabilities Act*, by which all bishops and other people in Holy Orders were removed from Parliament. Next, Parliament went after Thomas Wentworth, Lord Strafford and the Lord Deputy of Ireland. Strafford was a favourite of the king, who was impeached for a politicised interpretation of treason, on the assumption that, amongst other charges, he had assembled an army in Ireland that was intended to be used to invade England. Strafford was found guilty of these charges (which Charles had signed off, despite promising that he would protect the Lord Deputy) and executed.[19] Another strong supporter of the king, William Laud, the Archbishop of Canterbury and member of the House of Lords, was also arrested and charged with treason at the instigation of the Puritans in Parliament, although he was not executed until 1645.[20]

The Long Parliament of 1641 passed a flow of legislation that quickly eroded the powers of King Charles I. Although some of it, such as the *Protestation*, which every Church or state official had to sign if they wished to continue to hold office, swearing an oath of allegiance to King Charles and the Church of England,[21] was broadly supportive of the king, most of the legislation from 1641 was not. First, the *Triennial Act* created machinery for summoning Parliaments when needed (at least every three years), especially since the king had failed to do this in the past, regarding which the Act noted, 'it is by experience found that the not holding of Parliaments accordingly hath produced sundry and great mischiefs and inconveniences to the King'.[22] The *Act for the Abolition of the Court of Star Chamber*[23] followed, as did the *Act for the Abolition of Court of High Commission*.[24] The *Act Declaring the Illegality of Ship-Money* (ie a tax originally levied on coastal areas in time of war) prohibited this source of cash for the king, 'contrary

[17] Royle, T (2005) *Civil War: The Wars of the Three Kingdoms* (London, Abacus) 118–20.

[18] 'The Act Against Dissolving the Long Parliament Without its Own Consent', as reproduced in Adams, M (ed) (1947) *Select Documents on English Constitutional Law* (London, Macmillan) 362.

[19] 'Act for the Attainder of Strafford, 1641', as reproduced in Adams, M (ed) (1947) *Select Documents on English Constitutional Law* (London, Macmillan) 361; also 'The Trial and Execution of the Earl of Strafford' in Millward, J (ed) (1961) *The Seventeenth Century: Portraits and Documents* (London, Hutchinson) 81. For comment, Koabel, G (2016) 'Interpreting Gesture in the Treason Trial of the Earl of Strafford', *Canadian Journal of History* 51 (2), 243–68; Russel, C (1965) 'The Theory of Treason in the Trial of Strafford', *The English Historical Review* 80 (4) 30–50.

[20] Parry, M (2015) 'Bishop William Laud', *Historical Research* 88 (240), 230–48.

[21] 'The Protestation, 1641' in Adams, M (ed) (1947) *Select Documents on English Constitutional Law* (London, Macmillan) 359–60.

[22] 'The Triennial Act, 1641' in Millward, J (ed) (1961) *The Seventeenth Century: Portraits and Documents* (London, Hutchinson) 82–83.

[23] 'The Act for the Abolition of the Court of Star Chamber' in Adams, M (ed) (1947) *Select Documents on English Constitutional Law* (London, Macmillan) 363.

[24] 'Act for the Abolition of the Court of High Commission, 1641' in Adams, M (ed) (1947) *Select Documents on English Constitutional Law* (London, Macmillan) 366.

to and against the laws and statutes of this realm, the right of property, the liberty of subjects, and the *Petition of Right*.[25] The *Act Prohibiting the Extraction of Knighthood Fines* (another source of indirect income for Charles) followed, along with the *Habeas Corpus Act*, clearly stating that anyone imprisoned by the King or his Privy Council could apply for a writ of *habeas corpus*, so that the cause of their imprisonment might be tested in court.[26]

As Charles acquiesced to all of these Acts and failed to react with violence, as many expected, to the formation of a type of mixed constitutional government, and as Parliament began to seek unprecedented increases in taxation, public opinion began to shift away from the triumphant Parliament and towards the beleaguered king. The Commons, primarily lead by John Pym, tried to reorientate the public perception. Pym's basic philosophy was that liberty was based on the collective consciousness of the people, as represented by Parliament not by a privileged elite, suggesting that 'the parliament is that to the commonwealth which the soul is to the body'.[27] Pym wanted to move power away from the monarchy towards Parliament, as liberty, he believed, came not from God to the Crown and to the people, but from God to the people and to their representatives.[28]

The Commons presented King Charles with the *Grand Remonstrance*. This document, which was, in essence, the principal foundation for Parliament in the ensuing war, listed over 150 perceived misdeeds during the reign of Charles I. It claimed that all mischiefs were due to a 'pernicious design of subverting the fundamental laws and principles of government upon which the religion and justice of this kingdom are firmly established'.[29] Based on a general conspiracy theory that the Catholics were about to try to seize power, the *Grand Remonstrance* sought improvements that would create real constitutional governance and remove the absolute power of the monarch. Specifically, the *Remonstrance* required, inter alia, that the king's children should be educated by and married to those in whom Parliament had confidence; that the laws against the Catholics should be strictly enforced (a matter on which Charles had slowed down); that popish peers be excluded from the House of Lords; that the king should accept such a reformation of the Church as Parliament advised; and that peers should not be admitted to the House of Lords without the consent of both Houses of Parliament. The demand that privy councillors and great officers of the state should be appointed only with the approval of Parliament was followed by the warning that 'without which

[25] 'Act Declaring the Illegality of Ship Money, 1641' in Adams, M (ed) (1947) *Select Documents on English Constitutional Law* (London, Macmillan) 370–71.

[26] Bowen, L (2007) 'The Long Parliament', *The English Historical Review* 122 (499), 1258–86.

[27] Pym, as in Davies, G (1987) *The Early Stuarts* (Oxford, Oxford University Press) 93.

[28] Kuypers, J (2009) 'John Pym, Ideographs and the Rhetoric of Opposition to the English Crown', *Rhetoric Review* 28 (3), 225–45; Zagorin, P (1994) 'The Political Beliefs of John Pym', *The English Historical Review* 109 (433), 867–90.

[29] 'The Grand Remonstrance, 1641' in Adams, M (ed) (1947) *Select Documents on English Constitutional Law* (London, Macmillan) 380; also in Millward, J (ed) (1961) *The Seventeenth Century: Portraits and Documents* (London, Hutchinson) 87–88.

we cannot give his Majesty such supplies for support of his own estate, or such assistance to the protestant party beyond the sea [in Ireland] as is desired'.[30]

Charles answered the *Grand Remonstrance* by promising to defend the Anglican Church against both Puritans and Papists. However, he could not agree with excluding people from power on the basis of their class, preferring that it should be done on a case-by-case basis. He added that it was 'for the King to decide which councillors and ministers he wants',[31] not Parliament, and if he accepted the *Remonstrance* in full, it would destroy royal power, leaving nothing but an empty form of majesty.[32]

Events moved quickly after Charles signalled that he could not accept the *Grand Remonstrance*. Parliament asserted control over the appointment of army and navy commanders, to which Charles refused to give the royal assent. The following month, when rumours reached Charles that Parliament was planning to impeach the Queen for alleged involvement in Catholic plots, Charles decided to arrest five of Members of Parliament (who he already suspected had been stirring up trouble in the Bishops' Wars), including Pym, for treason. The charges were that the accused were attempting to subvert the fundamental laws of England, to deprive the monarch of his rightful power, to alienate the affections of his people, and inviting and encouraging a foreign (Scottish) army to invade England. The five men had been warned in advance and fled, before Charles transgressed the parliamentary privilege and entered the Commons, to start preparing for the civil war that awaited them all. Given that over 30,000 English, Scots and Irish had been fighting as volunteers or mercenaries in the Thirty Years' War in Europe, Britain was flush with men with the skill required to resolve the debate, which was, as Edward Hyde, the Earl of Clarendon, suggested, 'whether the King was above Parliament, or Parliament, above the King'.[33]

E. Ireland

The execution of Lord Strafford by the Long Parliament was problematic not just for the king, but also because Strafford had kept the peace in Ireland, and Ireland did not figure very high in Charles's thinking. Although Charles allowed some concessions to the Catholic nobles in Ireland, and allowed its Parliament to be called twice, he failed to grasp the context of the evolving situation. Specifically, although the Catholic Church in Ireland had been crippled by encroachments, and Strafford had maintained

---

[30] Clauses 184 and 185. Also Weston, C (1960) 'The Theory of Mixed Monarchy Under Charles I', *The English Historical Review* 75 (196), 426–43.

[31] 'The King's Answer to the Petition Accompanying the Grand Remonstrance' in Adams, M (ed) (1947) *Select Documents on English Constitutional Law* (London, Macmillan) 380–82.

[32] See Knight, O (1960) 'The Grand Remonstrance', *The Public Opinion Quarterly* 24 (1), 77–84; Coates, W (1932) 'Some Observations on the Grand Remonstrance', *The Journal of Modern History* 4 (1), 1–17.

[33] Clarendon, in Royle, T (2005) *Civil War: The Wars of the Three Kingdoms* (London, Abacus) 164; Davies, G (1987) *The Early Stuarts* (Oxford, Oxford University Press) 122–23 and ibid, at 6–7, 32–33.

a blatant prejudice against the Catholics, the Catholic hierarchy had not died. Rather, it effectively reorganised itself and linked this revitalisation to overlapping calls for independence from England. At the same point, there was a growing Presbyterianism amongst the Ulster Scots, who were seeking to expand the lands and controls they held over the areas under their possession in Ireland. By 1638, the Ulster Plantation, as started by James I, had at least 20,000 Scottish settlers. Charles, who was confident in the advice he was receiving that 'plantations must be the only means under God and your majesty to reform this subject as well in religion as in manners',[34] extended the plantation process into, inter alia, Wexford, Longford and Leitrim. Despite the growing alienation of the Irish on the ground from Charles's monarchy, when Charles called for help in 1640 in his war with the Scots, the Irish Parliament enthusiastically supported the king.[35]

When Strafford was executed in 1641, the controls that had been maintaining the peace failed, and the Irish Catholic gentry tried to seize control of the country, as they feared that the Long Parliament was about to vote to invade Ireland. The coup failed, and despite pleas for restraint, the rebellion developed into a conflict between Irish Catholics on one side and English and Protestant settlers on the other, as a result of which several thousand settlers were massacred. The scale and the brutality of the massacres was magnified, if not exaggerated, in England and Scotland, whilst the context for what had happened was lost.[36] Soon after, the *Confederation of Kilkenny*, as made up of Catholic prelates, nobles, gentry and clergy, declared that in addition to an end to plantations and a partial reversal of the existing ones, they would commit to 'faith and true allegiance unto our sovereign lord, King Charles' if, amongst other concerns:

1. The Roman Catholic Church in Ireland shall have and enjoy the privileges and immunities [as they were in the time of Henry III] ... the common laws of England, which are not against the Roman Catholic Church, ... shall be observed.
2. ... A supreme council of the confederate Catholics of Ireland ... shall be established ... [This] ... council shall have power to order advance the Catholic cause, and good of this kingdom ...[37]

For the next seven years, two-thirds of Ireland was governed by the Irish Catholic Confederation, the political representation of the *Confederation of Kilkenny*. Although there was a cessation of violence in some parts and local truces, Ulster, Munster and Leinster held out, loyal to royalists, parliamentarians or Scottish Covenanters.[38]

---

[34] The Lord Deputy of Ireland, as in Royle, T (2005) *Civil War: The Wars of the Three Kingdoms* (London, Abacus) 36.

[35] The 'Parliament of 1640' in Curtis, E (ed) (1943) *Irish Historical Documents 1172–1922* (London, Methuen) 142; Downing, T (1991) *Civil War* (London, Gardner) 91.

[36] Gibney, J (2010) 'Protestant Interests: The 1641 Rebellion and State Formation in Early Modern Ireland', *Historical Research* 84 (223), 67–86; Noonan, K (1998) 'The Cruel Pressure of an Enraged, Barbarous People: Irish and English Identity in Seventeenth Century Policy and Propaganda', *The Historical Journal* 41 (1), 151–77.

[37] 'The 1642 Confederation of Kilkenny' in Curtis, E (ed) (1943) *Irish Historical Documents 1172–1922* (London, Methuen) 148–52.

[38] Davies, G (1987) *The Early Stuarts* (Oxford, Oxford University Press) 160–62.

3. The First Civil War

Following Charles's attempt to arrest the five Members of the Commons, and his unprecedented entry into the chamber of the Lower House, Parliament seized London and the king was forced to flee the capital. Both sides (the king and Parliament, and their supporters) then started to raise armies, with Charles setting up his court in Oxford and Oliver Cromwell, the Member of Parliament for Cambridge, taking command of the Parliamentarian force. In the third week of August 1642, Charles I ended any further hope of peace, after riding to Nottingham with just under 4,000 armed supporters and raising his standard, stating that he was going to use force to defend with his Cavaliers (a derogatory terms, linked to Catholics on the Continent) against the Roundheads (so named for their short hair) of Parliament. This war, which began with the Battle of Edgehill in late October 1642, when Charles made it clear that he was fighting for his honour and dignity as the monarch of England, Scotland and Ireland against a group of men who were traitors, would go on to consume some 80,000 fighting men. The toll began at Edgehill when, although Charles's forces had the upper hand, the battle ended in what was essentially a draw, with costs to both sides of perhaps 2,000 dead or dying on the field. At the Battle of Newbury the following September, similar numbers of dead littered the battlefield, but the risk of Charles proceeding to take London, and thus crush the rebellion, was removed.[39]

As the two sides were considering their next steps, evidence was adduced that Charles was trying to secure military assistance from pro-royal but predominantly Catholic Ireland. The response to this discovery helped lead to the passing of the 1643 *Solemn League and Covenant*. By this document, the signatories—the English Parliamentarians and the Scottish Covenanters (through the Scottish Parliament)—made an alliance 'against the enemies of their religion and their liberties'.[40] Together they pledged (the Scots delivering an army of 20,000 men) to defend the Protestant faith, as manifested in the reformed Churches of Scotland and England and Ireland, promising that 'we shall bring the Churches of God in the three kingdoms to the nearest conjunction and uniformity in religion', as part of their campaign seeking 'the extirpation of Popery'. They added that whilst they had no intention to 'diminish his Majesty's just power and greatness', they would 'preserve the rights and privileges of the Parliaments, and the liberties of the kingdoms'.[41] At the same time, the English Parliament established

---

[39] Graham, A (2010) 'The Earl of Essex and Parliament's Army at the Battle of Edgehill: A Reassessment', *War in History* 17 (3), 276–93; Burne, A (1998) *The Great Civil War* (Witney, Windrush Press) 17–36, 97–108, 190–91; Grant, R (2011) *1001 Battles* (London, Penguin) 336, 337; Parker, G (2013) *Global Crisis: War, Climate and Catastrophe in the Seventeenth Century* (New Haven, CT, Yale University Press) 28.

[40] This language is from the 'The Ordinance Appointing the First Committee of Both Kingdoms', as reproduced in Adams, M (ed) (1947) *Select Documents on English Constitutional Law* (London, Macmillan) 386–88.

[41] 'The Solemn League and Covenant, 1643' in Millward, J (ed) (1961) *The Seventeenth Century: Portraits and Documents* (London, Hutchinson) 94–95; also Vallance, E (2001) 'The Solemn League and Covenant in England', *The English Historical Review* 116 (465), 50–75.

the Westminster Assembly, consisting of churchmen, lawyers and lay observers from Scotland and England, to clear the Church of 'all false aspersions and misconstructions' of liturgy and governance.[42]

Another example of the English Parliament's desire to conform to the new religious orthodoxy, in the wake of the abolition of the Star Chamber, was its decision to retain strict censorship under the Licensing Order of 1643, under which Parliament required authors to submit their works for approval by the government before they could be published. It was this Order that made John Milton pen his *Areopagitica* in defence of a free press (which failed in his time, but was of huge significance subsequently), as 'books are not absolutely dead things, but do contain a potency of life in them'. He added, 'he who destroys a good book, kills reason itself, kills the image of God, as it were in the eye'.[43] On the topic of free speech, Milton famously said, 'Give me the liberty to know, to utter, and to argue freely according to conscience, above all other liberties.'[44]

As these debates were raging in London, although King Charles could make some progress in the south and west of England, as well as obtaining possession of cities such as Bradford and Leeds, he had little success further north. The decisive battle fought outside York, at Marston Moor in July 1644, gave Parliament and its Scottish allies full control of the north, as the Royalists lost 4,150 men, as opposed to only 2,000 from the Parliamentarian side. This victory was, in the words of the Parliamentarian commander, Oliver Cromwell, 'an absolute victory obtained by God's blessing'.[45] Amongst the significant battles that followed, in a conflict which became increasingly bitter and unrestrained, Cromwell's reformulated New Model Army was given the aim 'to advance Christ's kingdom' and the mission to scourge the land of papists, bishops and superstitious clergy, and to 'bring to justice the enemies of our church and State'.[46] This army went on to achieve significant victories over the Royalist forces at both Longport and Naseby in the summer of 1645, as a result of which, in the latter instance, 1,000 Royalist soldiers were killed and a further 5,000 captured (whilst the Roundheads lost fewer than 500 men). Despite his defeat, Charles refused to consider surrender, explaining that he would not, 'in conscience or honour, abandon God's cause, injure my [royal] successors, or forsake my friends'.[47]

Although the Royalists continued to fight in Scotland, and achieved a significant victory at Kilsyth in August 1645 (where over 5,000 Presbyterian Covenanters were

[42] 'The Westminster Assembly' in Dickinson, W (ed) (1958) *A Sourcebook of Scottish History*, Vol III (London, Nelson) 125–31; Prior, C (2013) 'Religion, Political Thought and the English Civil War', *History Compass* 11 (1), 24, 26.

[43] See Morehouse, I (2009) 'Areopagitica: Milton's Influence on Classical and Modern Political Thought', *Libertarian Papers* 1 (38), 1–23.

[44] Milton, in Dzelzainis, M (ed) (2003) *Milton: Political Writings* (Cambridge, Cambridge University Press) 194.

[45] Cromwell, as noted in Royle, T (2005) *Civil War: The Wars of the Three Kingdoms* (London, Abacus) 300; also Wanklyn, M (2010) 'Oliver Cromwell and the Performance of Parliament's Armies', *History* 96 (321), 3–25.

[46] As noted in Robertson, J (2006) *The Tyrannicide Brief* (London, Vintage) 66.

[47] Charles, as noted in Parker, G (2013), *Global Crisis: War, Climate and Catastrophe in the Seventeenth Century* (New Haven, CT, Yale University Press) 41; also Cust, R (2005) 'Why Did Charles I Fight At Naseby?', *History Today*, 10 October, 12.

killed), in England they were largely spent. After remaining strongholds started to be overrun or to surrender, the king realised that he had to negotiate a peace. Having taken shelter with a Presbyterian Scottish army in Nottinghamshire in May 1646 (believing he was safer surrendering to them than to a Parliamentary force), Charles I was handed over to the English Parliament by the Scots (in exchange for £100,000 and the promise of more money) in early 1647.[48] After being moved around the country under house arrest over the next few months, in November Charles made an attempt to escape abroad. He was captured on the Isle of Wight and subsequently confined in Carisbrooke Castle.

A. The Levellers

The Leveller movement came together in London in 1645. It was a third force, which emerged from within disillusioned sections of the army in the debate between those fighting for the supremacy of either the king or Parliament. The Levellers, acting as the voice of the emerging artisans, local merchants and small landholders, all of whom had been excluded from the political paradigms of either king or Parliament, sought to influence political matters, arguing for expanded understandings of tyranny, liberty, tolerance, enfranchisement and constitutional law.[49]

At the micro level the Levellers sought a simplified legal system that would stop imprisonment for debt; introduce a more humane prison system; allow an affordable justice system; and impose penalties that were proportionate to the crimes committed. They wanted the removal of legal privileges based upon membership of a group, such as birth or possession of assets. At the macro level, where they were most radical, they argued two unique principles. First, they produced arguments for religious non-conformity (for Protestants, not Catholics) against the emerging powers of the new Presbyterian Church.[50] Secondly, working on the principle that all free men were equal,[51] most (but not all) of the Levellers claimed that every adult male should have a vote in electing 'the Representative' and be eligible for membership of the Commons, with no House of Lords or king (or only a figurehead) above them. This call for universal male suffrage and government by consent at a time when only perhaps 2.5 per cent of England's five million people were represented in Parliament was truly radical.[52]

---

[48] Burne, A (1998) *The Great Civil War* (Witney, Windrush Press) 191–209; Grant, R (2011) *1001 Battles* (London, Penguin) 338, 342, 344; Royle, T (2005) *Civil War: The Wars of the Three Kingdoms* (London, Abacus) 298–300, 333–36, 349–51.

[49] Peacey, J (2000) 'John Lilburne and the Long Parliament', *The Historical Journal* 43 (3), 625–45; Kishlansky, M (1979) 'The Army and the Levellers: The Road to Putney', *The Historical Journal* 22 (4), 795–824.

[50] Walwyn, W (1646) 'Toleration Justified' in Sharp, A (ed) (1998) *The English Levellers* (Cambridge, Cambridge University Press) 9–31, 168–79.

[51] See Overton, R (1647) 'An Arrow Against All Tyrants' in Sharp, A (ed) (1998) *The English Levellers* (Cambridge, Cambridge University Press) ibid, 55-72.

[52] Foxley, R (2007) 'Problems of Sovereignty in Leveller Writings', *History of Political Thought* 28 (4), 642–51; Loughlin, M (2007) 'The Constitutional Thought of the Levellers', *Current Legal Problems* 60 (1), 1–22.

The proposal was best articulated by Thomas Rainsborough, who suggested that 'every man that is to live under a government ought first by his own consent put himself under that government; and I do not think that the poorest man in England is not at all bound in a strict sense to that government that he has not had a voice to put himself under'.[53] John Wildman added that the right to vote should not be equated with a property qualification, 'every person in England has as clear a right to elect his representative as the greatest person in England'.[54] This idea, that all 'free born Englishman'[55] (excluding servants and beggars) would be entitled to vote, subsequently crystallised in the 1649 *Agreement of the Free People of England*. The first principle read:

> That the supreme authority of England ... shall be ... a Representative of the People, consisting of four hundred persons ... all men of the age of 21 and upwards ... shall have their voices, and be capable of being elected to that supreme trust.[56]

The advocacy of the Levellers and their calls for religious tolerance and a widespread constitutional democracy based upon a popular, as opposed to an elitist, republicanism were short-lived. Although there had been debate at Putney and Whitehall on their proposals, involving Oliver Cromwell, the conclusions of the debate were overshadowed by the escape of the king and the resumption of the civil war. Afterwards, although the Levellers fought with the Parliamentarians against the Royalist forces in the second civil war, Oliver Cromwell was of the view that this radical group could not be tolerated. In 1649, the key Leveller leaders were arrested and charged with treason, after the Levellers questioned what the difference was between being ruled by a King without restraint and ruled by a purged Commons (the Rump Parliament) backed by the military. Moreover, it was simply intolerable to the powerful Members of Parliament that the traditional distinctions within society, of nobleman, gentleman and yeoman, should be dissolved. After the leaders of the Levellers were targeted, the rebellious sections in the army were quarantined and the risk of mutiny faded. Thereafter, the Levellers and their political questioning quickly dissolved.[57] The same fate awaited the Diggers, a radical splinter group that argued for the additional consideration of the communal ownership of land, thereby undermining the entire edifice of the right to own private property. They too were crushed.[58]

---

[53] Rainsborough, in Sharp, A (ed) (1998) *The English Levellers* (Cambridge, Cambridge University Press) xv.

[54] Wildman, as noted in Royle, T (2005) *Civil War: The Wars of the Three Kingdoms* (London, Abacus) 407.

[55] Foxley, R (2004) 'John Lilburne and the Citizenship of Free-Born Englishmen', *The Historical Journal* 47 (4), 849–74.

[56] Lilburne, J et al (1649) 'An Agreement of the Free People of England' in Sharp, A (ed) (1998) *The English Levellers* (Cambridge, Cambridge University Press) 168, 169; also Vernon, E (2010) 'What Was the First Agreement of the People?', *The Historical Journal* 53 (1), 39–59.

[57] Polizzotto, C (2014) 'What Really Happened at the Whitehall Debates', *The Historical Journal* 57 (1), 33–51; Glover, S (1999) 'The Putney Debates: Popular Versus Elitist Republicanism', *Past and Present* 164 (10) 47–80; Bass, J (1991) 'Levellers: The Economic Reduction of Political Equality in the Putney Debates', *Quarterly Journal of Speech* 77, 427–45; Gleissner, R (1980) 'The Putney Debates of 1647', *Journal of British Studies* 20 (1), 74–89.

[58] Hessayson, A (2009) 'Early Modern Communism: The Diggers and the Community of Goods', *Journal for the Study of Radicalism* 3 (3), 134–50; Hardcare, P (1958) 'Gerrard Winstanley in 1650', *The Huntington Library Quarterly* 22 (1), 345.

4. THE SECOND CIVIL WAR

The Parliamentarians' suspicions of Charles's lack of good faith increased as he attempted to flee their custody at the end of 1647, but the place where he sought sanctuary, the Isle of Wight, was not as sympathetic to his cause as he had hoped, given that Colonel Robert Hammond was Parliamentary Governor of the island. Hammond informed Parliament that the king was in his custody.

At the same time, Charles secretly negotiated an agreement with the Scots known as the *Engagement*, whereby:

> An army shall be sent from Scotland into England, for preservation and establishment of religion, for defence of his Majesty's person and authority, and restoring him to his government ... for defence of the privileges of Parliament and liberties of the subject ...[59]

The Scottish Estates (but not the Assembly) agreed to the *Engagement* because they feared that the English army was becoming too powerful under the English Parliament, and that their goals, as laid down in the *Solemn League and Covenant*—inter alia, to advance questions of religion whilst at the same time respecting the king—were about to be thwarted. Accordingly, the Scots invaded England with a view to restoring Charles I to the throne, on condition, amongst other things, that he agreed to the establishment of Presbyterianism for three years. The Scottish intervention was supplemented by pro-royal uprisings in Kent, Essex, Cumberland and Wales. Over the next two years, the various factions in Parliament remained united and worked effectively together, putting down each uprising, blunting the Scottish invasion, and then largely destroying the Scottish forces at the Battle of Preston in Lancashire in August 1648, where General Cromwell won the day, killing 2,000 of the opposition and taking a further 9,000 prisoner. This put an end to any chance of a Royalist victory. A number of the Royalist leaders who had broken their word and resumed the fight, in violation of their promises when they surrendered at the end of the first civil war, were executed.[60]

Whilst in captivity, King Charles I was meant to be negotiating a peace with Parliament in the proposed *Treaty of Newport*. He was hoping to play off the different factions against one another, but this proved hard, with most of them being unwilling to compromise on questions of religion, requiring the abolition of the *Book of Common Prayer* and episcopacy, and the introduction of Presbyterianism in their place. There were moderates within Parliament, who looked for limited political, constitutional and religious reforms, and who had no quarrel with the king himself, but there was also a minority comprising Independents, for whom the war had been fought for very different reasons. They sought the radical reconstruction of Church and state, and the beginning of a new era of godliness. For them, Charles stood in the way of introducing wider-ranging social and religious reforms.

---

[59] 'The Engagement, 1647' in Dickinson, W (ed) (1958) *A Sourcebook of Scottish History*, Vol III (London, Nelson) 133–38.

[60] Royle, T (2005) *Civil War: The Wars of the Three Kingdoms* (London, Abacus) 425; Grant, R (2011) *1001 Battles* (London, Penguin) 345.

By the end of 1648, the unity of Parliament in the war against the king began to splinter. On 5 December 1648, Parliament voted to continue negotiating with King Charles I, with the majority wishing to honour the *Solemn League and Covenant*, under which the king would be respected. However, Oliver Cromwell and the army opposed any further talks with someone they viewed as the root cause of all of the difficulties in England, Scotland and Ireland, and on 6 December 1648, the English Parliament suffered its first military coup. Members of Parliament who were not sympathetic to the views of the leaders of the army, who wanted to bring Charles to justice (as opposed to a settlement in which he would have been restored with curtailed powers), were purged, being either arrested or exiled from Parliament, by Colonel Thomas Pride. The result was that Parliament went from a membership of just over 500 seats, in which there was active debate, to just over 200. This body, known as the Rump Parliament, had a clear view of the future it wanted, crushing all dissent.[61]

A. The Execution of the King

The Rump Parliament voted to put King Charles I on trial. As the House of Lords refused to allow this to be done by an act of law, the Rump of the House of Commons proceeded, by Ordinance, to legislate alone, establishing a High Court of Justice for the Trial of Charles I in early January 1649. This stipulated:

> Whereas it is notorious that Charles Stuart, the now King of England, not content with many encroachments which his predecessors had made upon the people in their rights and freedoms, hath had a wicked design totally to subvert the ancient and fundamental laws and liberties of this nation, and in their place introduce an arbitrary and tyrannical government, and that besides all other evil ways and means to bring this design to pass, he hath prosecuted it with fire and sword, levied and maintained a civil war in the land, against the Parliament, and kingdom ... but Parliament ... did forbear to proceed judicially against him, but found that such remissness served only to encourage him ... raising new commotions, rebellions and invasions ... to try to enslave or destroy the English nation and expecting impunity for so doing ... It is hereby enacted [that 135 Commissioners ...] shall take order for the charging of him, Charles Stuart, with the crimes and treasons mentioned above.[62]

The intellectual aristocratic architects of the English Republic, Puritans like John Cooke and John Milton, then proceeded to gather the public support needed to execute the king. Milton, already known for his defence of free speech and freedom of the press in his celebrated *Areopagitica*, now penned his works, *The Tenure of Kings and*

---

[61] See Peacey, J (2013) 'Parties, Parliaments and Pride's Purge', *History Compass* 11 (5), 352–62; Kishlansky, M (2010) 'Mission Impossible: Charles I, Oliver Cromwell and the Regicide', *The English Historical Review* 125 (515), 844–74; Carlson, L (1942) 'A History of the Presbyterian Party from Pride's Purge to the Dissolution of the Long Parliament', *Church History* 11 (2), 83–122.

[62] 'The Act Erecting a High Court of Justice for the Trial of Charles I', as reproduced in Adams, M (ed) (1947) *Select Documents on English Constitutional Law* (London, Macmillan) 389–90; also Kelsey, S (2003) 'The Ordinance for the Trial of Charles I', *Historical Research* 76 (193), 310–31.

Magistrates and *Eikonoklastes*. Together, they sought to justify the execution of a tyrant king by the people (even bypassing the Parliament, if necessary).[63]

At trial, Charles refused to accept the legality of the court and enter a plea, asking 'by what authority I would brought from thence and carried place to place ... when I know by what lawful authority, I shall answer'. His question was answered by the judge, John Bradshaw, to the effect that the authority was 'the name of the people of England, of which you are elected [as in approved by Parliament] King, to answer'. Charles responded, 'England was never an elective kingship, but a hereditary kingship'. He added, 'Let me see a legal authority warranted by the word of God, the scriptures or warranted by the Constitution of the Kingdom, and I will answer.' Bradshaw replied, 'that is in your apprehension—and we are your judges'.[64] The judges then proceeded to find against Charles on counts both of levying war against his own people and committing what amounted to crimes of war in the process. The sentence, as read out at the end of January 1649, stated:

> Charles Stuart, ... trusted with a limited power to govern by, and according to the law of the land, and not otherwise ... for the good and benefit of the people, and for the preservation of their rights and liberties; yet nevertheless, out of a wicked design to erect and uphold in himself an unlimited and tyrannical power to rule according to his will, and to overthrow the rights and liberties of the people, and to take away and make void ... the fundamental constitutions of this kingdom ... traitorously and maliciously levied war against the present Parliament and the people represented ... [H]e hath caused and procured many thousands of the free people of this nation to be slain ... Charles Stuart is guilty of levying war against the said Parliament and people ... as a tyrant, traitor, murderer and public enemy to the good people of this nation, shall be put to death by the severing of his head from his body.[65]

After Charles I was executed on 30 January 1649, the Rump Parliament completely reorganised the constitutional make-up of England. In the middle of May 1649, Parliament declared England to be a Commonwealth, which would be governed 'by the supreme authority of this nation, the representatives of the people in parliament'.[66] To ensure that the Commons was the only body that could make law, the 'useless and dangerous' House of Lords was abolished, and so too the office of the king. Thus:

> And whereas it is and hath been found by experience that the office of a King in this nation and Ireland, and to have the power thereof in any single person, is unnecessary, burdensome and dangerous to the liberty, safety and public interest of the people, and for the most part, use hath been made of the regal power and prerogative to oppress and impoverish and enslave

[63] Dzelzainis, M (ed) (2003) *Milton: Political Writings* (Cambridge, Cambridge University Press) 13, 16, 83, 90, 108, 130, 184, 190.

[64] Robertson, J (2006) *The Tyrannicide Brief* (London, Vintage) 124–29, 156–58; also Davies, G (1987) *The Early Stuarts* (Oxford, Oxford University Press) 33–34.

[65] 'Sentence of the High Court of Justice upon Charles I', as reproduced in Adams, M (ed) (1947) *Select Documents on English Constitutional Law* (London, Macmillan) 391; also Holmes, C (2010) 'The Trial and Execution of Charles I', *The Historical Journal* 53 (2), 289–316; Kelsey, S (2003) 'The Trial of Charles I', *The English Historical Review* 118 (477), 583–616.

[66] 'Act Declaring England to be a Commonwealth, 1649', as reproduced in Adams, M (ed) (1947) *Select Documents on English Constitutional Law* (London, Macmillan) 400.

the subject ... that the Office of King shall not henceforth reside in any single person ... a most happy way is made for this nation to return to its just and ancient right, of being governed by its own representatives or national meetings in council ... chosen by the Commons assembled in Parliament.[67]

B. Cromwell in Ireland

Once the king was dead, Cromwell and the Rump Parliament turned their attention to Ireland. Throughout the 1640s, Ireland had been split, the majority of the territory being held by the Irish Catholic Confederation and the (divided) rest by Protestants. Both sides had, in the midst of the first civil war in England, petitioned Charles, with both promising allegiance in exchange for either religious toleration of Catholicism in Ireland, or religious intolerance of Catholicism of Ireland, respectively.[68]

As Charles became embroiled within the first civil war in England and Scotland, despite objections from both England and France, Pope Innocent X became a strong supporter of a Confederate Ireland, and provided money and arms to the more radical Catholic factions. When word of this papal support broke, combined with news that Charles was trying to negotiate military support from both pro-Catholic and pro-royal forces in Ireland, the reaction against Charles was one of anger. As this was bubbling up, the Irish Protestants and Catholics, nominally engaged in a truce, then tried to negotiate a common position to present to Charles. Debating points, over two different rounds of the *Ormond Peace*, focused on questions of religious tolerance of Catholicism in Ireland, retention of some of the lands taken in the 1641 uprising, an end to much of the Plantation of Ulster and allowing greater self-government in Ireland. As the Parliamentarian armies began to gain the upper hand, it appeared that Charles, in exchange for Confederation troops joining his Royalist forces, would agree to many of the terms under debate. Despite agreement being close, the Confederation split over whether to accept the *Ormond Peace*, or not, just as the second civil war in England was starting. Whilst the landed gentry were generally supportive of the deal, the more Gaelic, staunchly pro-Catholic Irish wanted to completely overturn all English influence in Ireland, desiring a completely independent and fully Catholic state, away from the heretical tyrants (and their descendants) of the English monarchy.[69]

---

[67] 'Act Abolishing the Office of the King, 1648', as reproduced in Adams, M (ed) (1947) *Select Documents on English Constitutional Law* (London, Macmillan) 397.

[68] See the 'Catholic Demands' and 'Protestant Demands', both of 1644, in Curtis, E (ed) (1943) *Irish Historical Documents 1172–1922* (London, Methuen) 152–55, 156–58.

[69] O'hannrachain, T (2004) 'Conflicting Loyalties, Conflicted Rebels: Political and Religious Allegiance Among the Confederates of Ireland', *The English Historical Review* 119 (483), 851–72; Forkan, K (2008) 'Ormond's Alternative: The Lord Lieutenant's Secret Contacts with Protestant Ulster', *Historical Research* 81 (214), 303–25.

The one thing the rebels had in common was that their multiple reasons for resistance, namely religious tolerance for Catholicism, self-government or pro-royalty, were all anathema to Oliver Cromwell, the Rump Parliament and its defenders, like John Milton, who all used increasingly extreme rhetoric to justify the forthcoming conflict. When the Irish Confederates then began negotiating with the Catholic Duke of Lorraine, a cousin of Maximilian I, the Elector of Bavaria, for him potentially to be their new leader, the English had every excuse they could ever want to invade.[70]

Some 12,000 soldiers under the direction of Oliver Cromwell landed in Ireland, to prosecute a conflict that would see the deaths of some 400,000 people through war, starvation and pestilence over the next few years. The promise was that the country would be 'replanted with many noble families [of England] and of the Protestant religion'.[71] The first decisive battle between the Parliamentarians and the Royalist coalition occurred at Rathmines, just outside Dublin, on 2 August 1649. The Parliamentarians won, killing 3,000 Irish Royalists and taking a further 2,500 prisoner (out of a total of 11,000). At Drogheda the following month, after refusing to surrender, the Irish lost 2,800 men out of a force of 3,100, with another 200 being captured. He next marched to Wexford, where a further garrison, which refused to surrender, was slaughtered. Cromwell explained his harsh actions: 'I am persuaded that this is a righteous judgement of God upon these barbarous wretches, who have imbrued their hands in so much innocent blood; and that it [extreme action] will tend to prevent the effusion of blood in the future.'[72] As Catholic forces began to try to negotiate with him before his army arrived, although he promised that the people would be allowed to live peaceably, free from violence, he made clear that public manifestations of Catholic worship, as in England, would not be tolerated.[73]

5. CONCLUSION

Charles I inherited a realm that had enjoyed its longest period of domestic peace since 1066. This was a remarkable achievement, as much of Western Europe was being ripped apart by war related to religion and political autonomy. Charles's father, James I, had gone to great lengths not to involve his realm in these wars. Charles would continue to keep the country out of external wars, but would see everything he owned,

[70] O'Siochru, M (2005) 'The Duke of Lorraine and the International Struggle for Ireland, 1649–1653', *The Historical Journal* 48 (4), 905–32; Raymond, J (2004) 'Complications of Interest: Milton, Scotland, Ireland and National Identity in 1649', *The Review of English Studies* 55 (220), 315–45.

[71] Cromwell, in Royle, T (2005) *Civil War: The Wars of the Three Kingdoms* (London, Abacus) 524. The figure 400,000 is from White, M (2011) *Atrocitology: Humanities 100 Deadliest Achievements* (Melbourne, Text Publishing) 231.

[72] Cromwell, in Davies, G (1987) *The Early Stuarts* (Oxford, Oxford University Press) 163; Larson, M (2006) 'The Holy War Trajectory Among the Reformed', *Renaissance and Reformation Review* 8 (1), 7–27.

[73] Grant, R (2011) *1001 Battles* (London, Penguin) 347, 348; Royle, T (2005) *Civil War: The Wars of the Three Kingdoms* (London, Abacus) 533–37.

including his life, lost in the civil war that raged throughout England, Scotland and Ireland.

Charles believed that he had absolute authority in his lands, and that Parliament was there to serve him. He dissolved Parliament for 11 years when it failed to give him what he wanted, while trying to steer a middle ground theologically, upholding the Anglican faith against the increasingly vocal Puritans. When these efforts saw him attempting to manipulate theological questions in Scotland, he sparked a rebellion. Charles reassembled the English Parliament to obtain the resources he needed to fight the Scots, but when it failed to deliver them, preferring to focus on the previous failures of the administration of the country and the king's rule, he dissolved it again, only to reassemble it when he realised he could not act without its authorisation of additional resources.

The Long Parliament that followed targeted a number of the favourites of the king, both personally and as regards their resources. It then went further, implementing constitutional changes that fundamentally would have removed some of the king's power and independence. When Charles began to fear that Parliament meant to impeach his wife for her possible links to Catholic plots, his action in trying to arrest five leaders of the Parliamentarians sparked the first civil war. Although in Ireland this became a war in which violence was meted out around the rights to be and practise as Catholics (and Charles was willing to utilise such force if it would secure his throne), in England and Scotland it was principally about preserving the rights and privileges of Parliament and the liberties of the kingdom.

Charles I lost the first civil war, and then the second, after he attempted to flee abroad after escaping from the Parliamentarians' custody. The English Parliament could not agree how to deal with to the king, at which point it was purged by elements linked to Oliver Cromwell's military forces. The Rump Parliament that followed the purge ordered the king to be tried on charges of tyranny and treason against his own people. King Charles I was found guilty of all charges and was sentenced to be executed for his crimes. Parliament then turned its attention to effecting a revolution, though it was determined that it would not be too radical. That is, Parliament's goal was to establish a republic for the propertied elite, not to enfranchise all and sundry. In one of the most remarkable acts of the age, the king lost his head and all of the powers of the sovereign moved to the English Parliament, albeit one that was very vulnerable to the manipulation of the leaders of the military.

IX

Eastern Europe

1. INTRODUCTION

THIS CHAPTER COVERS the countries that are today known as Russia, Poland, Lithuania and the Ukraine, as well as some historical regions, such as Livonia, which together created the vortex within which they all, plus Sweden, battled. Out of this group, Poland-Lithuania developed to possess not only full political independence, but also the most advanced constitutional structures of the day. This was not the case for what became Russia, with Moscow utilising elective processes only rarely, and preferring to snuff them out where they existed in other Rus lands whenever they acquired those territories. Their justifications for war were that the lands they desired once belonged to them, and that they needed to intervene to protect members of the Orthodox Christian faith. For the others, their interventions in the core Rus lands were based either on invitations to take hold of the reins of power, and/or on the desire to possess the title of *Tsar* in Moscow without being invited to do so.

2. POLAND AND LITHUANIA

A. Independence

The union of Poland and Lithuania began the fifteenth century, when both provinces started to rid themselves of the Teutonic Order and reclaim the lands that the Order possessed.[1] The Battle of Grunwald/Tannenburg (in modern-day north Poland) in 1410 was one of the largest battles of medieval Europe, in which some 39,000 soldiers of the Polish-Lithuanian union vanquished an opposing force of 27,000, killing over 8,000, including the Grand Master of the Teutonic Order, and capturing a further 14,000. Although help for the Teutonic Knights came from Sigismund, the King of Germany (and future Holy Roman Emperor), in terms of money and more men, and Prussia was saved for the moment, the Order realised that it had to sue for peace, as it lacked the numbers it once had.

The treaty of 1411 that followed this battle involved the repatriation of some land to Poland and promised 'eternal peace'. However, further conflict broke out as many

---

[1] Gillespie, A (2017) *The Causes of War*, Vol 2: *1000 CE to 1400 CE* (Oxford, Hart Publishing) 72–74.

locals in the areas the Order still controlled were not sympathetic to their Teutonic overlords, and the topic became a matter for debate at the Council of Constance,[2] that is, whether it was lawful to wage war against those who the Order asserted were pagans. The opposing view, put by Pawel Wlodkowic on behalf of the Polish and Lithuanian authorities, was that all nations, including pagan ones, had a right to exist peacefully and not be warred against purely on account of their being non-Christian, unless they committed clear and significant breaches of natural law, such as cannibalism. Moreover, if peaceful conversion was working and there were no historical injustices at hand (such as the land's having originally been Christian), they should be left in peace. This was also the conclusion reached by the special commission set up by the Council of Constance. Accordingly, as the Polish king and the Lithuanian Grand Duke had both been appointed vicars in recognition of their Catholicism, the 1422 *Treaty of Melno* was concluded, under which the Teutonic Knights and Pope Martin V renounced all of their territorial, political or missionary claims against Lithuania, and further territory was ceded to the (now Christian) Lithuania and Poland.[3]

Peace did not last. Further battles occurred in the 1460s, with the Order's being forced out of Danzig and then losing over 1,000 men at the Battle of Swiecino in 1462. The *Peace of Thorn* of 1466 that followed partitioned the Teutonic State into two halves. The western half became part of Poland as the autonomous province of Royal Prussia, with its own Diet. The eastern half, now called East Prussia, was to remain in the control of the Order, but as a Polish fief, for which they would have to perform homage to the Polish Crown. In essence, peace was only achieved when the Order promised to abandon all of its ties to the Holy Roman Empire.[4]

B. Social Context

As the sovereign independence of Poland and Lithuania grew, so too did their empowering social context. This was most obvious from around the middle of the fifteenth century, when Casimir IV Jagiellon, the Grand Duke of Lithuania and the King of Poland, began to put in place concrete arrangements that would take them to the forefront of constitutional government in the period, thus creating both stable peace in the realm and strong support for his projects. The *Charter of Casimir IV* was issued in 1447, in which the union between Poland and Lithuania was strengthened with the promise

---

[2] See pages 60–61.

[3] Sweda, A (2014) 'The Teutonic Order's Attitude Towards Poland and Lithuania in 1411–1414', *Prace Historczne* 141 (2), 531–53; Johnson, L (1996). *Central Europe: Enemies, Neighbours, Friends* (Oxford, Oxford University Press) 42–45; Grant, R (2011) *1001 Battles* (London, Penguin) 214; Graff, T (2014) 'The Council of Constance and its Attitude Towards the Polish-Lithuanian Monarchy', *Prace Historyczne* 141 (2), 511–99; Ozog, K (2014) 'The Catholic Church in the Kingdom of Poland at the Time of Jagiello's Rule', *Prace Historyczne* 141 (2), 289–313; Belch, S (1965), *Paulus Vladimiri and His Doctrine Concerning International Law and Politics*, Vol II (The Hague Mouten) 43–114.

[4] Urban, W (2003) *The Teutonic Knights* (London, Greenhill) 176, 210–20; Grant, R (2011) *1001 Battles* (London, Penguin) 230; Christiansen, E (1997) *The Northern Crusades* (London, Penguin) 241–50.

that 'in perpetuity, [the nobles of Lithuania would have] all the same rights, liberties and immunities that the prelates, lords, princes, nobles and towns of the Kingdom of Poland enjoy'.[5] Casimir then went on settle his grievances with his Polish nobles by the *Charter of Cerekwice* of 1454. This entrenched the importance of the Polish representative system and its input into matters of national importance, such as summoning the army or raising new taxes, via a representative system operating at local, regional and national levels. From that point on, the nobles of each province met together at frequent intervals to conduct their political and legislative business, and to consider royal policy. In Poland, supplementary 'little diets' (*sejmiki*), of which there were 37 in total, complemented the largest diet, the *Sejm*. In Lithuania there were a dozen of these little diets, and they, like their Polish counterparts, had a strong role in influencing the direction of Lithuanian policy in cooperation with Casimir. These policies were continued by successive rulers over the following decades.[6]

The grandson of Casimir IV, Sigismund Augustus, continued down the constitutional path his grandfather had mapped out. He (like his father Sigismund the Old) too governed via an elective monarchy for Poland and Lithuania, with a common Senate and Diet/Parliament (the *Sejm*), those bodies having a defining voice in matters for which the king needed to get consent, that is, considerations of dynasty (as in, who could marry who), war and taxes. Equally unique was Sigismund Augustus's support for religious tolerance in his realms, where not only were the rights of Lithuanian and Russian nobles of the Orthodox faith guaranteed, but so were those of the Protestants. The type of liberty of conscience and tolerance found in Poland-Lithuania in the last decades of the sixteenth century was not found elsewhere, as both France and what became the Netherlands were steeped in religious violence.[7]

Despite these achievements, it is useful to note that, for peasants, the situation was dire. In 1496, Polish peasants were formally tied to the soil, wages were set and freedom of movement was prohibited without the consent of the landowner. Attempts at representation at the village level were repressed, whilst common lands were continually taken into private ownership. Very similar approaches occurred in Hungary and Russia at the turn of the sixteenth century, resulting in a resurgence of slavery in some areas, as people sold themselves to landowners, if only to get food, shelter and some small level of security. Armed revolt under the leadership of Gyorgy Szekely-Dózsa broke out in Hungary in 1514, when peasants abandoned their lords' estates and flocked to

---

[5] The 'Charter of Casimir IV' in Vernadsky, G (ed) (1972) *A Sourcebook for Russian History*, Vol I (London, Yale University Press) 96–97.

[6] The 1506 'Charter of Sigismund' in Vernadsky, G (ed) (1972) *A Sourcebook for Russian History*, Vol I (London, Yale University Press) 98; the 1492 'Charter of Alexander', ibid, at 97. Also Bonney, R (2012) *The European Dynastic States* (Oxford, Oxford University Press) 260; Gorki, K (1996) 'The Origins of the Polish Sejm', *The Slavonic and East European Review* 44 (102), 122–38.

[7] Lenaghan, J (2015) 'The Sweetness of Polish Liberty', *Reformation* 15 (1), 133–50; Louthan, H (2014) 'A Model for Christendom? Erasmus, Poland and the Reformation', *Church History* 83 (1), 18–37; Davies, N (2005) *God's Playground: A History of Poland*, Vol I (Oxford, Oxford University Press) 117, 130–32, 136, 144–45, 148, 153, 254–56, 312, 322–26; Podemska, M (2015) 'Elections vs Political Competition: The Case of the Polish-Lithuanian Commonwealth' *The Review of Austrian Economics* 28, 167–78.

join Dózsa's forces. He had been trying to generate support for a crusade against the Ottomans, but many nobles were not willing to fight. Dózsa's peasants were willing to join a crusade, but primarily against the nobles, who they felt were both betraying and exploiting them. The forces of the King of Hungary, John Zapolya, then had to turn their attention away from the Ottoman threat to deal with the uprising in their own country. Their response resulted in the deaths of, reportedly, more than 50,000 people. All of the captured peasant commanders were then starved for 14 days, and the rebellion's leader, Dózsa, was executed by being placed on a red-hot iron throne, a heated crown hammered into his skull and a red-hot sceptre pushed into his lap. His starving comrades were then released from their cells and forced to eat his flesh. The following year the Diet of Nobles declared that the Hungarian peasants had 'forfeited their liberty and become subject to their landlords in unconditional and perpetual servitude'.[8]

3. RUSSIA

Vasili I, the Grand Prince of Moscow, was in power from 1389 until 1425. He was married to Sophia, the only daughter of Vytautas, the Grand Duke of Lithuania. His biggest achievement was surviving total destruction by Timur, as did the Golden Horde, of whom Vasili was a vassal.[9] When the Golden Horde returned to restake their claim as masters of the land, after watching them torch Novgorod, Gorodets and Rostov, Vasili decided to reinstate tribute to the Horde, and recommended his fellow Rus to do the same, or else 'meet their final doom'.[10]

When Vasili I died in 1425, civil war broke out between his son (Vasili II) and his brother (Yuri) and Yuri's sons. The essence of the dispute was whether the throne to Moscow was meant to have been passed laterally, which was common in *Rus* practice, to the brother (Yuri) of the deceased king (Vasili I) or, more uniquely, down (as was the tradition in Western Europe) to his only surviving son (Vasili II). Yuri responded by approaching the Golden Horde, receiving their blessing for him to take the throne of Moscow. However, as the Golden Horde was occupied with its own matters, splitting into the khanates of Kazan, Crimea and Sarai (later Astrakhan), it offered Yuri little help in waging war against Prince Vasili. As such, although Yuri was successful in capturing Moscow in 1433, fearing that he could not hold on to what he had taken, he returned to his northern homeland.[11]

---

[8] As in Hay, D (1996) *Europe in the Fourteenth and Fifteenth Centuries* (London, Longman) 43–44, 87, 157, 260–61; Norman, H (1998) 'Crusading as Social Revolt: The Hungarian Peasant Uprising of 1514', *The Journal of Ecclesiastical History* 49 (1), 1–28; Kamen, H (1994). *European Society: 1500–1700* (London, Routledge) 150–62, 259, 262–67; Davies, N (2005) *God's Playground: A History of Poland*, Vol I (Oxford, Oxford University Press) 98, 105, 111–15, 160, 121, 249–51.

[9] See Gillespie, A (2017) *The Causes of War*, Vol 2: *1000 CE to 1400 CE* (Oxford, Hart Publishing) 224–27.

[10] The 1409 'Moscow Chronicle' in Vernadsky, G (ed) (1972) *A Sourcebook for Russian History*, Vol I (London, Yale University Press) 113.

[11] Stevens, C (2007) *Russia's Wars of Emergence* (London, Pearson) 16–19; Gilmore, M (1952) *The World of Humanism* (NYC, Harper) 96–98.

Although Vasili II had to continue to fight against his cousins (Yuri's sons), given that the latter lacked any effective support from the Golden Horde, Vasili tightened his grip on power, backed by the Orthodox Church. His masterstroke in achieving this backing lay in his supporting the independence of the Orthodox Church in Moscow, having had his representative—who had been involved in the attempts in Florence in 1437 to relink the Orthodox and Catholic Church—arrested, on charges that 'the living light, and the faith of piety was surrendered to the Latins; the Orthodox tsar and patriarch fell into the deceit of Latin heresies'.[12] Vasili II proclaimed a new bishop in 1448 without recourse to the views of the Orthodox hierarchy in Constantinople; and when the Byzantine Empire fell in 1453, it was seen as God's punishment for their apostasy in Constantinople. Although the Orthodox Church survived in Istanbul, the fact that it was subject to the ruling power of the Sultan meant that, in 1461, the Russian Orthodox Church was proclaimed independent.[13]

Although theological independence in support of his power was one thing, political independence in defiance of his power was another. Accordingly, Vasili II also focused on regions that were seeking independence, such as Novgorod. To reclaim this jewel, in 1449 Vasili signed a treaty with Casimir IV of Poland-Lithuania, which recognised Moscow's predominance as regards Novgorod and Pskov.[14] In 1456 he attacked and defeated Novgorod on the grounds it had earlier supported Yuri, and then, through the *Treaty of Iazhelbitsy*, brought the government of the defeated republic further under the control of Moscow. Finally, in an attempt to ensure that the civil war that plagued the beginning of his reign did not happen again, Vasili made his own son, Ivan, co-ruler, without asking the approval of the khan, patriarch or any type of constitutional bodies. This not only showed the autocratic nature of Vasili, it also put paid to the principle of collateral succession, which had been a major cause of internecine struggles in this part of the world.[15]

A. Ivan the Great

Ivan III ('Ivan the Great'), was the son of Vasili II. He was the Grand Prince of Moscow and also Grand Prince of all *Rus*. This man, who followed in the autocratic ways of his father, taking advice from his *Duma* only when he wished to do so, is regarded as the founder of modern Russia. The foundation from which he built his empire was laid

---

[12] The 1441 'Voskresensk Chronicle', as reproduced in Vernadsky, G (ed) (1972) *A Sourcebook for Russian History*, Vol I (London, Yale University Press) 126.

[13] Zernov, N (1949) 'Vladimir and the Origin of the Russian Church', *The Slavonic and East European Review* 28 (70), 123–38; Moss, W (2005) *A History of Russia*, Vol I (London, Anthem) 85–87, 90–91, 140; Norwich, J (2011) *Absolute Monarchs: A History of the Papacy* (London, Random) 240–44.

[14] See page 183.

[15] Woodworth, C (2009) 'The Birth of the Captive Autocracy: Moscow, 1432', *Journal of Early Modern History* 13 (1), 49–69; Woodworth, C (2009) 'Sophia and the Golden Belt: What Caused Moscow's Civil Wars of 1425–1450', *The Russian Review* 68 (2), 187–98; the *Treaty of Iazhelbitsy* is reproduced in Vernadsky, G (ed) (1972) *A Sourcebook for Russian History*, Vol I (London, Yale University Press) 76.

by enhancing his own dynastic legitimacy through marriage to Sophia Palaiologina, the niece of the last Byzantine Emperor, thus establishing a degree of continuity with Constantinople, Byzantium and (depending on how the schism between the Orthodox and Catholic Churches was viewed) even Rome. Philotheus of Pskov explained the concept thus:

> [The tsar] is on earth the sole emperor of the Christians, the leader of the Apostolic church which stands no longer in Rome or Constantinople, but in the blessed city of Moscow. She alone shines in the whole world brighter than the sun ... Two Romes have fallen, but the third stands and a fourth there will not be.[16]

Ivan began to call himself *Tsar*, an allusion to the title 'Caesar' borne by the Roman emperors. He also cast Moscow as the 'Third Rome', and rebuilt the city is a way designed to suit its imperial status, as the spiritual heir to Byzantium. The Orthodox Church, lavishly supported by Ivan, also embraced this idea. In addition to creating its own inquisitions, to ensure purity of thought in its followers, the Orthodox Church also gave its full support to the Tsar: as Joseph of Volokolamsk explained, 'the Tsar by nature is like unto all men, but in authority he is like unto God Almighty'.[17]

Ivan III went on to expand the realm under his control from 15,000 to 600,000 square kilometres, by fighting three interrelated enemies, namely, independent communities in *Rus*; the fragmented tribes of the former Golden Horde; and the countries to the west of him, that is Poland, Lithuania and Livonia. He was, without doubt, a fully independent sovereign, beholden to no one else. His insular nature was made even more clear when an emissary of the Holy Roman Emperor, Frederick III, offered Ivan a king's crown in 1489. Ivan replied:

> By God's grace we have been sovereigns in our own land since the beginning, since our earliest ancestors: our appointment comes from God, as did that of our ancestors, and we beg God to grant us and our children to aide for ever in the same state, namely as sovereigns in our own land; and as beforehand we did not desire to be appointed [sovereign] by any one, so now too do we not desire it.[18]

Of the independent communities of the same culture, when Ivan III became the Grand Prince of Moscow in 1462, four other great principalities (Yaroslavl, Riazan, Rostov and Tver) plus three independent city states (Novgorod, Pskov and Viatka) existed in tandem. Ivan III annexed Yaroslavl and Rostov. He married his sister to the Riazan prince, and repeatedly fought Novgorod between 1471 and 1478 before it was finally annexed. Ivan's justification for attacking Novgorod was primarily that it was abusing its independence, becoming too close to Poland after the 1470 treaty between

---

[16] Philotheus, as noted in Cohen, M (ed) (2004) *History in Quotations* (London, Cassell) 171. Also Bogatyrev, S (2007) 'Reinventing the Russian Monarchy in the 1550s: Ivan the Terrible, The Dynasty and the Church', *The Slavonic and East European Review* 85 (2), 271–92; Gustave, A (1967) 'Reflections on the Boya Duma in the Reign of Ivan III', *The Slavonic and East European Review* 45 (104), 76–123.

[17] Volokolamsk, as noted in Elton, G (1968) *The New Cambridge Modern History: The Reformation*, Vol II (Cambridge, Cambridge University Press) 546; Pavlov, A (2003) *Ivan the Terrible* (London, Pearson) 16–18; Runciman, S (1965) *The Fall of Constantinople 1453* (Cambridge, Cambridge University Press) 7–10.

[18] Ivan, as noted in Hay, D (1996) *Europe in the Fourteenth and Fifteenth Centuries* (London, Longman) 287.

Novgorod and Casimir IV of Poland had been agreed, under which Casimir was agreed to be the 'illustrious king for all of Novgorod'. This agreement was conditional on the commitment that 'he protected the Orthodox faith' and would 'not erect Roman Catholic Churches in Novgorod ... nor anywhere in the land'.[19] Ivan mistrusted this commitment, fearing it was a ruse by Casimir to obtain full control over Novgorod. Accordingly, when a Lithuanian prince arrived in Novgorod soon afterwards, Ivan had the reasons he needed to go to war against Novgorod: not only were the people of Novgorod guilty of impiety, abandoning Orthodoxy and bowing to Rome, they now about to give up their sovereignty to Casimir. Before Casimir could respond, Novgorod was defeated. Although allowed to retain all of the republic's 'ancient rights', the people of Novgorod had to accept that they 'would not by any deceit renounce [Ivan] or place ourselves under the rule of the king and the grand duke of Lithuania, and we shall not leave you [Ivan] for anyone'.[20]

Ivan had no faith in the new rulers of Novgorod, and when some of Ivan's supporters were executed, he entered the city again in 1477. This time Novgorod was forced to abolish the post of mayor and give complete sovereignty to Ivan. He then had the assembly's famous *veche* bell, which called the citizens together, removed, thus curtailing the ability to call representative assemblies. A further campaign was undertaken in 1479 when Ivan believed that the citizens of Novgorod were preparing to commit treason. Thousands were executed as the territory was annexed to Moscow, and 3 million acres of land were confiscated for Ivan's soldiers. Over 8,000 wealthy citizens were forcibly moved to Moscow and replaced by those who were more compliant. All defensive fortifications were removed. Tver faced a similar fate in 1485, after it too made overtures to Poland-Lithuania. Even Ivan's own family members had to sign oaths, promising that they would abstain from foreign relations.[21]

The second remarkable feat of Ivan the Great's reign was his ending of the so-called 'Tatar yoke'. Ivan was fortuitous in this area, as the Golden Horde as a whole had begun to split in the 1430s. By the time of Ivan, three sub-khanates existed—Crimea, Kazan and Astrakhan—while the fourth part, the remaining core of the Golden Horde, was now known as the Great Horde, as led by Khan Akhmad. It was Akhmad who invaded Muscovite territory in 1472 and threatened to crush Ivan unless he reinstated payment of tribute. Ivan responded by working with the khanates of Crimea and Astrakhan, concluding treaties of support in 1473 and 1483. Akhmad replied by making an alliance with Casimir IV. However, when Akhmad drew up his forces to fight Ivan, Casimir failed to arrive, and since he was outnumbered, Akhmad withdrew.

---

[19] The 1470 'Treaty Between Novgorod and Casimir IV of Poland', as reproduced in Vernadsky, G (ed) (1972) *A Sourcebook for Russian History*, Vol I (London, Yale University Press) 77.

[20] The 1471 'Peace Treaty with Ivan III', as reproduced in Vernadsky, G (ed) (1972) *A Sourcebook for Russian History*, Vol I (London, Yale University Press) 80; Morfell, W (2014) 'Establishment of the Autocracy and Consolidation of the Empire', *Russia, China and Eurasia* 30 (5), 511–38.

[21] Elton, G (1968) *The New Cambridge Modern History: The Reformation*, Vol II (Cambridge, Cambridge University Press) 368, 535, 537, 542; Kaiser, D (ed) (1994) *Reinterpreting Russian History* (Oxford, Oxford University Press, 1994) 83.

This withdrawal was an important moral victory for the Muscovites. After this, regular payment of tribute stopped, although irregular 'gifts' continued to be made to some khans. This was especially the case for the Khan of Kazan, which khanate, over the following three decades, Ivan went on to manipulate, control, and eventually fully subdue and sequestrate.[22]

B. Clashes Between Poland-Lithuania and Russia

When the Polish King Casimir IV died in 1492, a large army from Moscow was dispatched to Lithuania. Tsar Ivan III justified the attacks because he was trying to recover land, such as Kiev and Smolensk, which was 'the patrimony of Saint Vladimir'.[23] He added he was also defending Orthodox subjects, who were being subjected to the Catholic faith. After two years of fighting, a peace treaty was signed with Lithuania in 1494. By the terms of the treaty, Ivan, who insisted on the title 'Sovereign of all Russia', made considerable territorial gains, taking control over a large band of territory both east and west of the upper River Oka. That same year, Ivan agreed to the marriage of his daughter Helena, provided she could retain her Orthodox faith, to the new Grand Duke of Lithuania, Alexander Jagiellon, son of Casimir IV.[24]

Despite this peace treaty and marriage, Ivan attacked Lithuania again in 1500. His pretext this time was Lithuanian mistreatment of Orthodox believers (through forcing a union of the Catholic and Orthodox Churches), including his daughter. His daughter denied this, and Alexander refuted the persecution, but his attempts to prevent war were of no avail as Ivan's forces, supplemented by his Crimean allies, raided deep into Poland and crossed the River Vistula. In 1501, a Lithuanian force was annihilated near Mstislav, as was a Teutonic force at Helmed. By 1502, although Kiev remained out of Ivan's grasp, one-third of Lithuanian territory, primarily in north-east Ukraine, had been acquired by Moscow. The six-year truce that followed in 1503 recognised these conquests of Ivan III. In the same year, Ivan compelled the Livonian Knights to make a humiliating peace, under the terms of which their possession of Dorpat was confirmed only on payment of an annual tribute.[25]

The 1503 truce was made into the *Treaty of Perpetual Peace* in 1508 with Vasili III, who had taken up the reins of power (by excluding or imprisoning his brothers) upon the death of his father, Ivan III, in 1505. Sigismund the Old, the King of Poland and

[22] The 1473 and 1483 'Treaties of Ivan III' as reproduced in Vernadsky, G (ed) (1972) *A Sourcebook for Russian History*, Vol I (London, Yale University Press) 114–15; Morfell, W (2014) 'Russia Under the Mongols', *Russia, China and Eurasia* 30 (5), 503–10; Moss, W (2005) *A History of Russia*, Vol I (London, Anthem) 93–95; Grousset, R (2010) *The Empire of the Steppes* (New Brunswick, NJ, Rutgers University Press) 471; Stevens, C (2007) *Russia's Wars of Emergence* (London, Pearson) 29, 51.
[23] Ivan III, as noted in Hay, D (1967) *The New Cambridge Modern History: The Renaissance*, Vol I (Cambridge, Cambridge University Press) 369; also ibid, at 196–97, 222, 373, 376–77, 380.
[24] Hay, D (1996) *Europe in the Fourteenth and Fifteenth Centuries* (London, Longman) 260–61, 287, 369.
[25] Vernadsky, G (ed) (1972) *A Sourcebook for Russian History*, Vol I (London, Yale University Press) 84–85, 120.

Grand Duke of Lithuania, who had come to power in 1506 was the counter-signatory. The 1508 *Peace* recognised all the territorial acquisitions of Ivan III, with the exception of Lyubech, as possessions of Moscow. Vasili III then turned his attention to annexing all of the last surviving autonomous provinces around him. The first to go was Pskov in 1510 (following a quarrel between two sides within the city), which Vasili occupied after arbitration failed. The *veche* bell was then removed, 300 leading families were deported and Vasili controlled the choice of mayor. The annexation of Ryazan followed, and the remaining autonomy of Novgorod disappeared.[26]

Sigismund the Old, for his part, in spite of the 1508 *Peace*, hoped to create a grand coalition of Poland-Lithuania, Livonia, and the Tatars of Crimea and Kazan against Moscow. Hungary was added to the alliance through the marriage of Sigismund's sister, Isabella, to the King of Hungary, John Zapolya. Vasili III viewed the link between Sigismund and Zapolya as beneficial, as Emperor Maximilian I had a grudge against Zapolya, believing that all of Hungary was meant to be a Habsburg possession. Accordingly, with the knowledge that Maximilian was not on Sigismund's side, Vasili struck as Sigismund was complaining that Moscow was giving asylum to enemies of his court in Moscow. The forces of Vasili III advanced westwards into Lithuania, following which Smolensk fell in 1514 before the Russian forces were halted at Orsha, where the Muscovite dead numbered over 30,000. The following year, 1515, Maximilian reconciled with Sigismund the Old at the First Congress of Vienna, at which the Polish house of Jagiellon was linked by marriage to the House of Habsburg via a double wedding. Although this did not work out in practice,[27] in theory the Empire and Poland-Lithuania were once more friends. At the same time, Vasili found his own allies from the Kazan and Crimean khanates turning against him, joining Poland and Lithuania after Vasili decided to stop paying tribute and/or tried to exploit their internal problems. The allies reacted quickly, plundering southern Russia, right up to the walls of Moscow. This was too much for Vasili. A five-year truce was reached in 1522, and later extended until 1534. Although the killing stopped, very little else improved. There was no prisoner exchange, and Poland-Lithuania had to accept that control of Smolensk was now a matter for Moscow.[28]

C. Ivan the Terrible

Ivan IV ('Ivan the Terrible') came to power in Russia upon the death of his father Vasili III in 1533, when he was three years old. Ivan controlled over 2.8 million square

[26] Moss, W (2005) *A History of Russia*, Vol I (London, Anthem) 93, 99, 103, 109.

[27] On the Hungarian side, the groom, the son of Vladislaus II, Louis II, would end up dying at Mohacs in 1526 fighting the Ottomans, without an heir, leaving Hungary as a three-cornered battlefield.

[28] Stevens, C (2007) *Russia's Wars of Emergence* (London, Pearson) 28–30, 54–59; Johnson, L (1996) *Central Europe: Enemies, Neighbours, Friends*, (Oxford, Oxford University Press) 54, 61, 75; Davies, N (2005) *God's Playground: A History of Poland*, Vol I (Oxford, Oxford University Press) 99, 113–14; Grant, R (2011) *1001 Battles* (London, Penguin) 247.

kilometres of territory, an area five times the size of modern France. By the end of his reign in 1584, he would hold just over 4 million square kilometres, after conquering the khanates of Kazan, Astrakhan and Siberia. Although the young Ivan's regents could bring stability on some of his borders (such as with the 60-year truce agreed in 1537 between Moscow and Sweden in the *Treaty of Novgorod*), Ivan had to survive a period of threats within his own realm, as many *boyars* tried to gain power via conspiracies, coups and treason. Ivan survived but was continually haunted by the idea of disloyalty and the need to use force and fear to maintain authority. He evolved into a leader who manage to weave monarchy, dynasty and religion into a new political culture after being crowned as the first 'Tsar of All the Russias' in 1547, governing 'by God's will, and not by the turbulent desires of humanity'.[29]

(i) Internal Conflict

The conflict for which Ivan is most well-known was that instigated against his own citizens. This began in 1565, when Ivan announced that he was going to relinquish the throne. He blamed the *boyars* for forcing him to make this decision, who had attempted to deny him the right to bequeath his realm to his son as he pleased, and whom he accused of being disloyal and treasonous. Panic gripped Moscow: Church leaders, *boyars* and common people all implored Ivan not to abdicate. He agreed, but only on condition that he was given the right to deal with 'traitors' as he saw fit. When this was agreed, a separate royal court and administration were established, in addition to the *Oprichnina*, a force of about 6,000 men answerable only to the Tsar. They dressed completely in black and rode black horses, fitted out with black harness. This force, which lasted until 1572 (when Ivan disbanded them), was at the forefront of punishing those whom Ivan disliked, including through the widespread use of torture, exile, confiscation of estates and even death. This process was often facilitated by political trials. In Moscow, at least 3,000 were executed with the explicit sanction of the Tsar, including some members of his own family, who were killed with poison.[30]

(ii) External Conflicts

The first war that Ivan undertook against external enemies was that against Kazan in 1547. During Ivan's regency, his court had been involved in the coups affecting the throne of Kazan, with the leader of this khanate changing seven times between 1535

---

[29] As noted in Pavlov, A (2003) *Ivan the Terrible* (London, Pearson) 86–87, also at 28 and 35. See also Shaposhnik, V (2014) 'Ivan the Terrible: The First Russian Tsar', *Russian Studies in History* 53 (1), 74–80; Bogatyrev, S (2007) 'Reinventing the Russian Monarchy in the 1550s: Ivan the Terrible, the Dynasty and the Church', *The Slavonic and Eastern European Review* 85 (2), 271–93.

[30] Pavlov, A (2003) *Ivan the Terrible* (London, Pearson) 100–05, 118–20, 127–28, 133, 138, 150–55, 157–60; Dunning, C (2003) 'Terror in the Time of Troubles', *Kritika: Explorations in Russian and Eurasian History* 4 (3), 491–513; Elton, G (1968) *The New Cambridge Modern History: The Reformation*, Vol II (Cambridge, Cambridge University Press) 195, 113–14, 465, 474, 551, 555, 591–92.

and 1552. This meant that the Kazan leader was the favourite either of Moscow, or of the khanate of the Crimea. Ivan's forces attacked in 1549 and then in 1551, to get the Kazan crown on the head of his favourites. In 1552, Ivan's forces captured Kazan. The Russian troops, fighting beneath large Christian banners, were portrayed as 'soldiers of Christ' and the Kazan Tatars as 'infidels and enemies of Christ ... who had always spilled Christian blood and destroyed holy churches'.[31] When the city was secure, the mosque was made into a new cathedral. Ivan also ordered the destruction of other mosques, had Kazan's streets blessed with holy water, and granted monasteries and churches land within the city and beyond. A program of forced conversion was then encouraged, to achieve religious uniformity in all of the regions Ivan controlled. Ivan then captured the city of Astrakhan, near the mouth of the River Volga, thus giving him dominance in the region and access to English merchants who were seeking to establish trade links, as a result of which trading privileges (but not treaty relations) were concluded. This left only the Crimean khanate, the last khanate of the Golden Horde, which would retain its independence and go on to attack Moscow in the coming decades, killing tens of thousands in at least two attacks which nearly overcame the city in 1571 and 1572.[32]

The second war of Ivan IV against external enemies, which occupied decades of his reign, involved Livonia. Livonia, a region on the shores of The Baltic, included the important commercial ports of Riga, Revel and Narva. Although the German Teutonic Knights had ruled over these lands and Livonia's Estonian and Latvian peasants since the thirteenth century, the Knights were no longer formidable, being split between the opposing theologies of the Reformation, exploding into their own civil war between 1555 and 1557. In Ivan's estimation, the conflict between the Protestants and Catholics in Livonia was putting the Orthodox subjects of that country at risk. However, the spark that ignited the conflict between Livonia and Moscow was the failure to pay nearly 50 years of tribute in accordance with the 1503 treaty between the Livonian Knights and Moscow. Although the Livonians agreed to pay, and also to allow Russian merchants greater access to their ports, they failed to deliver on their promises immediately; and when Ivan demanded that Livonia declare itself a Russian protectorate, the Livonians appealed for help to neighbouring countries. Ivan added that he was recovering 'the patrimony of his forebear, St Vladimir',[33] and then invaded with a new generation of weapons and military organisation, taking Narva, Dorpat and the whole of eastern Estonia except Reval.[34]

[31] As in Moss, W (2005) *A History of Russia*, Vol I (London, Anthem) 133; also ibid, at 135, 137, 139. See futher Stevens, C (2007) *Russia's Wars of Emergence* (London, Pearson) 71–75, 82–84.
[32] Romaniello, M (2007) 'The Russian Orthodox Church After the Conquest of Kazan', *Church History* 76 (3), 511–40; Huttenbach, H (1971) 'New Archival Material on the Anglo-Russian Treaty of Queen Elizabeth I and Tsar Ivan IV', *The Slavonic and Eastern European Review* 49 (117), 535–49; Grant, R (2011) *1001 Battles* (London, Penguin) 284.
[33] As noted in Vernadsky, G (ed) (1972), *A Sourcebook for Russian History*, Vol I (London, Yale University Press) 100.
[34] Selart, A (2013) 'Ivan the Terrible, Emperor for Livonia?', *Studia Slavica et Balcanica Petropolitana* 2, 181–200; Pavlov, A (2003). *Ivan the Terrible* (London, Pearson) 46–47, 89, 91, 94–95, 178–85; Paul, M (2004) 'The Military Revolution in Russia, 1550–1682', *The Journal of Military History* 68 (1), 9, 10–15.

Denmark (in 1560) and Sweden (in 1561) answered Livonia's call for help in what became a four-way struggle for the region. Poland-Lithuania, under the leadership of their new leader, Sigismund Augustus, also answered the call, and in 1561 concluded the *Treaty of Vilnius* with the Livonian authorities, under which it was agreed that all of the Livonian possessions in the non-Danish and non-Swedish parts of Livonia (with the exception of Riga, which would remain a free imperial city, but under the new umbrella) would be secularised, and would be ceded to Poland-Lithuania as a semi-independent Duchy.

The war then became more complicated when Ivan agreed the 1561 *Treaty of Novgorod* with Erik XIV, the autocratic King of Sweden. The 1561 agreement settled the border between Sweden and Russia, with Reval and a few castles in Livonia coming under Swedish rule but the rest belonging to Ivan. Although removing Sweden from the fight was good for Ivan (the Russian forces went on to capture Polotsk in 1562), it provoked a war between Sweden and Denmark (over status, trade and the fact that the deal Erik made involved territory, Estonia, the Danes believed was theirs by historic right) as well with as Poland-Lithuania (when Swedish forces advanced to claim what they had agreed with Ivan). The conflicts ended only when Erik XIV was deposed by Swedish nobles and his half-brother, John, in 1568. King John III introduced a constitutional monarchy that complemented the Polish-Lithuanian model, and then married Catherine Jagiellon, the sister of Sigismund Augustus. This marriage union between Sweden, Poland and Lithuania was accompanied by the *Treaty of Stettin* with Denmark, thus ending the war between Sweden and Denmark and allowing them to concentrate on their shared enemy, Ivan the Terrible, once more.[35]

Before they could make a united effort against Russia, since Poland-Lithuania was undergoing yet another succession process, Ivan IV decided to strike as hard as he could to finally overrun all of Livonia. The Russians advanced in 1575, attacking both Swedish and Polish areas, invading the entire country, except Riga and Reval, only for Poland and Lithuania to turn the tide, recovering Dvinsk in 1577, Wenden in 1578 and Polotsk in 1579. By 1581, Moscow had lost some 300,000 men in the war, Livonia was isolated from the east and the united forces were poised to invade Russia. Fearing an absolute disaster, Ivan was willing to give up everything in Livonia, except Narva, as this was his only point of access to the Baltic. In 1582, a 10-year armistice with Poland and Lithuania was agreed, under which Russia renounced all of her possessions in Livonia, retaining only Pskov, with the question of Narva left open. However, as this peace was being made with one of Ivan's enemies, the Swedes seized Narva. In the resultant *Treaty of Plussa/Narva* of 1583 with Sweden, a seven-year truce was awarded to Ivan in exchange for the loss of all of Estonia, Narva, Ivangorod, Yam, Koporé and

[35] Bonney, R (2012) *The European Dynastic States* (Oxford, Oxford University Press) 245, 257, 260, 262, 266; Stevens, C (2007). *Russia's Wars of Emergence* (London, Pearson) 85–95, 92–94; Frost, R (2000) *The Northern Wars 1558–1721* (London, Longman) 24–26, 30–35, 37, 44–45.

Korela. This allowed Moscow only a narrow passage to the Baltic. Russia thus lost not only all the lands it had conquered a few decades earlier, but also lands it regarded as traditionally Russian.[36]

D. Sigismund III Vasa

Sigismund III Vasa, the Catholic King of Poland and Grand Duke of Lithuania, was originally also the king of Protestant Sweden. He was helped in his election as the Polish-Lithuanian ruler in 1587, as his mother was the daughter of the Polish king, Sigismund the Old. His father was John III, the King of Sweden, who had been placed on the throne by Swedish nobles after deposing his half-brother, Erik XIV. Although Sweden was a constitutional monarchy akin to the model used in Poland-Lithuania, and also strongly Protestant, Sigismund III Vasa ascended to the Swedish throne easily in 1594, after the death of his father.

Sigismund III saw a weak Russia that was ripe for attack. Ivan IV had died in 1584 of natural causes, and was succeeded by his son, Feodor I Ivanovich. Feodor appears to have been a weak man who was only a nominal ruler, with his wife's brother and trusted minister Boris Godunov, acting as de-facto regent for Feodor for a land that was under stress in economic, political, social and military terms, with Feodor agreeing to resume Russia's payments to the khanate. This combination of considerations gave Sigismund the perfect opportunity to re-engage in Russia in 1590 at the end of the 1583 truce.[37] Feodor had no stomach, or ability, for the fight. He agreed to the *Treaty of Eternal Peace* with Sweden (of which Sigismund III was also in charge) in 1595. With this, Russia renounced all claims to Estonia, including Narva.[38]

Despite such victories against Russia, the difficulty that Sigismund III began to experience arose when he became increasingly devout in his support for Catholicism and the Counter-Reformation that would ultimately entangle him in the Thirty Years' War.[39] His marriage to Anne of Austria, the Catholic granddaughter of the Habsburg Holy Roman Emperor Ferdinand I, was the first inkling for many of problems to come. Although this union was overlooked by many of the Protestants within his realm, Sigismund's actions in the once relatively tolerant Poland-Lithuania could not be. With strong Jesuit support, discrimination against non-Catholics holding positions of power was followed by protests against non-Catholic worship and the closing of

---

[36] Moss, W (2005) *A History of Russia*, Vol I (London, Anthem) 135–37; Pavlov, A (2003) *Ivan the Terrible* (London, Pearson) 184–85; Greengrass, M (2015) *Christendom Destroyed: Europe 1517–1648* (NYC, Penguin) 175–76; Wernham, R (1968) *The New Cambridge Modern History: The Counter Reformation* (Cambridge, Cambridge University Press) 381, 391, 412.

[37] See page 192.

[38] Vernadsky, G (ed) (1972) *A Sourcebook for Russian History*, Vol I (London, Yale University Press) 180.

[39] See page 141.

Protestant churches in many areas, with towns and cities such as Krakow no longer having a Protestant church after 1593. Executions for blasphemy, although rare, followed in the coming decades. Sigismund's work on the *Synod of Brest* in 1596, to unite the Orthodox and Roman Catholic Churches in Poland-Lithuania, also was of great concern to many in the Orthodox community, who feared both for their faith and for their independence, as papal authority now stretched to the borders of Orthodox Muscovy. Rebellions in the Ukraine began by the end of the year, justified in terms of defending the Orthodox faith from Catholic subversion.[40]

The manifestations of disquiet against Sigismund III became most apparent in his homeland of Sweden. Here, in addition to his attempts to increasingly control the Swedish Parliament, such as by not letting it assemble without his consent, his overt support for Catholicism in Poland-Lithuania caused alarm bells to ring loudly in his Protestant homeland. When Sigismund returned to Sweden and tried to settle the matter first by diplomacy and then by force, he found himself and his forces defeated. He fled from Sweden back to Poland in 1598. The Swedish Parliament then decided to elect the leader of the rebellion, Duke Charles, the son of the earlier King of Sweden, Gustav I, to be their next monarch, Charles IX, in 1604. It was Charles's son, Gustavus Adolphus, who would go on to be one of the defining figures in the Thirty Years' War.[41] In the interim, the two sides, Sweden and Poland-Lithunania, continued to fight over disputed possessions around the Baltic, with battles such as that Kircholm, in 1605, leaving over 9,000 Swedish infantry dead on the field, crushed by the overwhelming Polish-Lithuanian hussars.[42]

E. The Time of Troubles

The 'Time of Troubles' was a period in Russia between 1598 and 1613, when perhaps five million people died. The Troubles were caused by a combination of starvation, economic collapse and conflict related to a dynastic dispute, which saw repeated civil wars and uprisings, which pulled in Sweden as well as Poland-Lithuania and, to some extent, Crimea. The Troubles began when Feodor I died in 1598 and a succession crisis ensued. As Feodor had no son, it had been assumed that his half-brother, Dimitrii, would inherit the throne upon Feodor's death. However, as the nine-year-old Prince Dimitrii had predeceased Feodor (his death in 1591 being unexplained), this meant that when Feodor died there was no obvious heir. The implications of this were massive,

---

[40] Bourdeaux, M (2000) 'Four Hundred Years of the Union of Brest', *The Journal of Ecclesiastical History* 51(2), 30–54; Hennel, T (2002) 'The Political, Social and National Thoughts of the Ukrainian Higher Clergy, 1569–1700', *The Harvard Ukrainian Studies* 26 (1), 97–152; Cooper, J (ed) (1970) *The New Cambridge Modern History: The Decline of Spain and the Thirty Years' War*, Vol IV (Cambridge, Cambridge University Press) 588–89.

[41] See pages 150–152.

[42] Davies, N (2005) *God's Playground: A History of Poland*, Vol I (Oxford, Oxford University Press) 135–37, 146, 328–40; Grant, R (2011) *1001 Battles* (London, Penguin) 313.

for it marked not just the death of a Tsar but the end of the entire Rurik dynasty. This created a dynastic gap in which foreign monarchs, in both Sweden and Poland, took a serious interest. Before they could act, Boris Godunov, the brother to Irina, the wife of Feodor and former de-facto regent for Feodor, ascended the throne with little difficulty. He did this with the consent of compliant nobles who voted him into power.[43]

The difficulty for Boris was that around the year 1600, Prince Dimitrii apparently reappeared, in good health and claimed the Russian throne. Many of the Russian population, refusing to believe that God would have allowed the favoured Rurik dynasty to disappear from history, accepted his story, especially as famine and economic collapse gripped the country, which many saw as divine punishment for the acts of Boris Godunov. From Poland-Lithuania, with some support from their king, Sigismund III, and even greater support from the papacy after the pretender Dimitrii secretly converted to Catholicism, an army of 4,000 Polish mercenaries and Cossacks (who would lend their support to different contenders) started to fight its way towards Moscow, gathering almost fanatical, quasi-religious (Orthodox) support en route. Before the pretender Dimitrii could reach Moscow, Boris Godunov died, possibly of natural causes, possibly not. As Boris's immediate family was murdered including his 16-year-old son and newly-crowned heir, Feodor II, the pretender Dimitrii ascended the throne in 1605. He then married the Polish noblewoman, Marine Mniszech, in 1606, but her Catholicism and links to Poland caused riots in Moscow, in which Dimitrii was killed.[44]

The leader of the riots causing the death of the pretender Dimitrii was Prince Vasily Shuisky, who was proclaimed Tsar by his supporters in 1606. As Vasily, a leading boyar but without a direct path to the Crown of Russia through either inheritance or election, was trying to solidify his position, in 1607 another pretender appeared, also claiming to be the lost Prince Dimitrii, provoking another uprising. Again, with tacit Polish support, a mercenary army battled its way to Moscow, at which point the Russians abandoned Tsar Vasily IV. He responded by fleeing and arranging an alliance with the Swedes, granting them a piece of north-western Muscovy in exchange for the loan of 5,000 Swedish troops to rescue his throne. The Poles took the Swedish intervention as a green light to get more involved in Russia. They crossed into Russia in 1609 to break the alliance with Sweden and elevate a new, Polish candidate to the Muscovite throne. At the Battle of Klushino that followed, more than 5,000 Swedish and Muscovite soldiers were destroyed by the superior Polish-Lithuanian forces.[45]

When Vasily Shuisky was deposed by a group of Russian nobles in 1610 (and sent to a monastery where he was finally assassinated in 1612), the boyars decided to turn

---

[43] The figure of 5 million is given in White, M (2011) *Atrocitology: Humanities 100 Deadliest Achievements*, (Melbourne, Text Publishing) 207; Kleimola, A (1975) 'Boris Godunov and the Politics of Mestnichestvo', *The Slavonic and East European Review* 53 (132), 355–69.

[44] Dunning, C (2009) 'Tsar Dimitrii's Bellicose Letter to King Karl IX of Sweden', *The Slavonic and East Euroepan Review* 87 (2), 322–36; Dunning, C (2001) 'Who Was Tsar Dimitrii?' *Slavic Review* 60 (4), 705–29; Thompson, A (1968) 'The Legend of Tsarevich Dimitrii', *The Slavonic and East European Review* 46 (106), 48–59.

[45] Stevens, C (2007) *Russia's Wars of Emergence* (London, Pearson) 118–19.

Moscow over to the Poles. Meanwhile, the second pretender Dimitrii was assassinated, thus leaving the throne of Russia vacant once more. It was at this point that King Sigismund of Poland-Lithuania struck an agreement with a number of Russian boyars in early 1610, whereby if he brought stability, law and order to Russia, and protected the Orthodox Church, they would accept his son, Wladyslaw, as their Tsar. A few months later, when the Polish forces reached Moscow, the boyars confirmed that 'Wladyslaw Sigismund ... shall be crowned sovereign of ... Moscow and all the great and glorious tsardoms of the Russian state with the tsar's crown'.[46] However, once the Polish troops and German mercenaries were in Moscow, Sigismund decided that he would be a better Tsar than his son. With this sudden change, in addition to concerns over the behaviour of the Polish and German soldiers and fears for the independence of the Orthodox Church, a revolt broke out.[47]

By this time, Russia was split into three parts. Novgorod and the north were held by the Protestant Swedes. They shared a treaty which promised, 'we shall not accept the Polish king, nor his male heirs, nor any Poles and Lithuanians, and we intend to resist them as our enemies in every way ... [I]nstead, we accept as protector and defender against our foes the most august king of Sweden ... [W]e, invite [him] or his male heirs, to become tsar and grand prince of Moscow [and Russia]'.[48] The problem was that Moscow and the western areas were, despite the growing uprisings, still held by the Catholic Poles. The rest of Russia belonged to anyone, such as the Cossacks, who could support (and had supported) different pretenders. With a real risk that the fight for the throne of Russia could turn into a full-blown international conflict, the Russians turned inwards to find a solution. This started when a self-organised, organic Russian militia from Nizhnii Novgorod drove out the forces occupying their town, and then became a nucleus for a national army that went on to drive the Poles out of Moscow, allowing the Russian people a brief window of time for the boyars from across Russia to gather in Moscow.[49]

The idea of electing their ruler sat uneasily with Muscovite traditions. Nonetheless, after two years of trying to work through what they desired, in early 1613 a national assembly of between 500 to 800 representatives of towns and regions throughout Russia, including elected representatives from different localities, clergy, richer and poorer nobles, and even some free peasants—a *Zemsky Sobor* (the Assembly of the Land)—met to elect a new Tsar. Although there were clear questions over the way the

---

[46] 'The Agreement Between Zolkiewski and the Moscow Boyars' in Vernadsky, G (ed)(1972) *A Sourcebook for Russian History*, Vol I (London, Yale University Press) 194; also 'Sigismund's Agreement with the Boyars, 1610', ibid, at 193.

[47] Orchard, E (1989) 'The Election of Mikhail Romanov', *The Slavonic and East European Review* 67 (3), 378–402.

[48] 'Novgorod's Treaty with Sweden' in Vernadsky, G (ed) (1972) *A Sourcebook for Russian History*, Vol I (London, Yale University Press) 200.

[49] Perrie, M (2006) 'Fugitive Tsars and Cossacks: The Development of a Seventeenth Century Stereotype', *Harvard Ukrainian Studies* 28 (1), 581–612; Havelock, H (1898) 'The Cossacks in the Early Seventeenth Century', *The English Historical Review* 13 (5), 242–60.

1613 *Sobor* operated, and it lost its authority after the 1620s (after the infrastructure around the Tsar managed to regain control), for a brief period, Russian practice was on par with some of the more progressive examples of democracy in Europe.[50]

F. Mikhail Romanov

As there was no obvious candidate for the Russian throne, it took a little time before attention came to focus on Mikhail Romanov. He was of Russian birth and of the Orthodox faith. His family and their work in the Troubles were popular with the Cossacks. He also had some connection with the Rurik dynasty, as his father was the nephew of one of the wives of Ivan IV, and first cousin to Feodor I. Furthermore, Romanov was not known for the sort of self-serving or collaborative behaviour that disqualified so many other candidates. The *Sobor* subsequently agreed that the 'best, most steadfast, and wisest man' to ascend the throne was Mikhail Romanov. Therefore:

> Mikhail Romanov should be tsar and grant prince and autocrat of all Russia; and that nei-ther the kings and princes or Poland, Lithuania, Sweden or any other kingdom, nor any men of Muscovite family, nor any of the foreigners serving in the Muscovite state, should ever become sovereign, but for Mikhail Romanov.[51]

With this support, Tsar Mikhail I started to regain control over the lower Volga from rebel Cossacks. However, in 1615, the Swedish king landed in Russia and laid siege to Pskov. Sweden, which continued to rule over some north-western lands, including Novogord, could not be easily dislodged. Only in 1617, with the 'eternal peace' of Stolbovo, did King Gustavus Adolphus agree to cede Novgorod and, most significantly, his claim to the throne of Russia. In exchange, Gustavus Adolphus received a 20,000 ruble indemnity and the right to retain Karelia and Ingria, thus keeping Russia back from the Gulf of Finland and away from becoming a power in the Baltic. Most impor-tantly for Gustavus Adolphus, it allowed him to concentrate on his other enemies in Poland-Lithuania, thus seeing decades of cordial relations develop between Sweden and Russia, with Sweden becoming the first county to establish permanent diplomatic representation in Moscow, in 1631.[52]

[50] Lapteva, T (2015) 'The Representative Bodies in Russia in the First Half of the Seventeenth Century', *Studia Historica* 37, 93–119; Keep, J (1957) 'The Decline of the Zemsky Sobor', *The Slavonic and Eastern European Review* 36 (86), 100–22; Kivelson, V (2002) 'Muscovite Citizenship: Rights without Freedom', *The Journal of Modern History* 74 (3), 465–89; for some of the work of the Sobors from 1619, 1634 and 1642, see Vernadsky, G (ed)(1972) *A Sourcebook for Russian History*, Vol I (London, Yale University Press) 211, 212 and 217.
[51] 'The Electoral Charter of Tsar Mikhail, 1613'in Vernadsky, G (ed) (1972) *A Sourcebook for Russian History*, Vol I (London, Yale University Press) 209; Cooper, J (ed) (1970) *The New Cambridge Modern History: The Decline of Spain and the Thirty Years' War*, Vol IV (Cambridge, Cambridge University Press) 113, 602–03.
[52] Moss, W (2005) *A History of Russia*, Vol I (London, Anthem) 155–59, 161–64.

Despite having peace with Sweden, Russia was still under attack by including Ukrainian Cossacks and the forces of Poland-Lithuania. Of the latter, although the son of Sigismund III, Wladyslaw, attempted to retake Moscow again in 1617 was roundly defeated, it was only when Sigismund III became distracted by other external threats, he agreed an armistice with Mikhail I in 1619. This *Truce of Deulino* brought Poland-Lithuania an appreciable amount of territory, as Moscow was forced to cede the districts of Smolensk and a broad belt of territory along her western border. Although Wladyslaw refused to surrender his claim to the Russian throne, the armistice gave Moscow a breathing space. More importantly for the Tsar, the truce led to the return not only of prisoners of war, but also of his father, Filaret, after eight years in Poland. Filaret went on to take up the position of Orthodox Patriarch. He was dogmatic in his dislike of Catholic Poland, and made his priority calls for the recovery of lands taken by the Poles in the Troubles.[53]

When Sigismund III of Poland-Lithuania died in 1632, just as the *Truce of Duelino* was due to expire, Moscow took advantage of the interregnum to try to undo the armistice. The *Sobor* promised Tsar Mikhail I that they would help to provide all the necessary funds 'to help the soldiers and to rescue the Orthodox Christian faith from the Polish and Lithuanian king'.[54] Despite their enthusiasm (and the hopes of an alliance with Sweden, which were unfulfilled), although the Russians managed to recover 20 towns before they laid siege to their main target, they could not capture Smolensk. After suffering heavy losses running to tens of thousands of men, Russia agreed to the 'eternal' *Peace of Polianovka* at the end of 1634. Russia had to pay Poland-Lithuania an indemnity of 20,000 roubles and abide by the territorial gains that Poland-Lithuania had made in the 1618 armistice. Wladyslaw, for his part, now abandoned his claims to the Romanov throne. Accordingly, the Tsar was finally free of foreign competition for his crown.[55]

Although Mikhail Romanov was now free from external threats, and had restored autocratic control over Russia, this was being achieved at a cost to the lower rungs of society. This became especially obvious after his son, Alexei Romanov, came to power in 1645, after the death of his father. Although slavery was rare in Russia, effective debt-slavery was widespread, and people being legally bound to the land, unable to move, as a form of serfdom, became common, rising sixfold between 1590 and 1650, with more than a quarter of the population in some regions being landless labourers.[56]

By the late 1640s, the management of and economic situation in many parts of Russia were dire. Gatherings in Moscow turned into riots in which thousands died, and the Kremlin, a sacred place for both Church and state, was stormed. The crowds then

[53] Moss, W (2005) *A History of Russia*, Vol I (London, Anthem) 161–62.

[54] 'The Sobor Enactment of 1634' in Vernadsky, G (ed) (1972) *A Sourcebook for Russian History*, Vol I (London, Yale University Press) 217.

[55] Lewitter, L (1948) 'Poland, the Ukraine and Russia in the 17th Century', *The Slavonic and East European Review* 27 (68), 157–71; Stevens, C (2007). *Russia's Wars of Emergence* (London, Pearson) 127, 133–34, 138–38 Frost, R (2000) *The Northern Wars 1558–1721* (London, Longman) 144–48.

[56] Greengrass, M (2015) *Christendom Destroyed: Europe 1517–1648* (NYC, Penguin) 84–85.

presented a petition, in the name of the 'common people of Russia' (not just Moscow) to the Tsar. In calling for a *sobor* to be gathered, they lamented:

> It has been brought to this: that they [the great ones] have stirred up Your Imperial Majesty against the people and the people against Your Imperial Majesty. So it now appears that such injustice has driven the entire population of the entire Moscow region and its adjoining provinces to revolt ... If you [Alexei] ... wish to avoid the punishment of God that now threatens your kingdom ... [l]et the unjust judges be rooted out; get rid of the incompetent; punish all bribery and injustice; the obstruction of justice and all unfairness. Delay and prevent the many innocent tears that fall. Protect the lowly and the weak from violence and injustice.[57]

Six hundred representatives from throughout Russia attended the *sobor* in 1649. The core of their work was agreement to a new code comprising almost 1,000 articles. In combination with tax reductions in some areas, ending privileged exemptions in others, Tsar Alexei created a compromise that satisfied most of the power-brokers, if not the rural poor. Although noblemen could not kill serfs, they could buy and sell them (and their families), move them around and trade them.[58]

4. Conclusion

Between the years 1400 and 1650, Eastern Europe saw the rise of one of the superpowers of the age, in the form of the union of Poland and Lithuania. This union, after establishing full independence from the Teutonic Order, went on to develop some of the most advanced forms of constitutional governance and religious tolerance (for the upper classes) of the age. The exception to these advances was the peasants, who were brutally suppressed throughout all of Eastern Europe, with all of their attempted uprisings coming to nothing.

The main opponent of Poland-Lithuania was Russia. This country slowly built itself up during the first part of the fifteenth century, adding to the importance and independence of the Orthodox Church, before Ivan the Great came to power and fully wrapped the legitimising power of the Orthodox Church around his own absolute authority as Tsar. In terms of warfare, he used the splitting of the Golden Horde into three separate parts to his advantage, playing divide and conquer, putting an end to the 'Tartar Yoke'. He also seized Novgorod, ending all of its internal republican structures and external independence, after it promised allegiance to Poland; and advanced into Lithuania. Peace treaties cemented by dynastic marriages could not hold Ivan back, who continued into Livonia at the turn of the sixteenth century, using the repeated justifications that the territory was once Russian and that it was necessary to protect the

---

[57] The Demands of the Rioters, as noted in Parker, G (2013) *Global Crisis: War, Climate and Catastrophe in the Seventeenth Century* (New Haven, CT, Yale University Press) 162.

[58] Moon, D (1996) 'Reassessing Russian Serfdom', *European History Quarterly* 26 (4), 483–526; Cooper, J (ed) (1970) *The New Cambridge Modern History: The Decline of Spain and the Thirty Years' War*, Vol IV (Cambridge, Cambridge University Press) 617.

interests of those of the Orthodox faith in these occupied lands. He only relinquished physical control after treaties guaranteed him some of the territory he had seized; and for the other parts, he was paid handsome rents.

The conflicts between Poland-Lithuania and Russia continued with the accession of Ivan the Terrible. Like his predecessors, he utilised the legitimising power of the Orthodox Church to buttress his conflicts, especially against the fragmented parts of the Golden Horde. As regards his own people, whom he controlled with absolute authority, he justified his use of force as being necessary for the survival of the Russian throne. His final war, to reacquire Livonia and gain strong access to the Baltic, was waged for breach of the earlier treaties (and non-payment of rent) and to reiterate that the area was once Russian land, and on the pretext that Orthodox subjects were being threatened by conflict between Protestants and Catholics in Livonia. This time, when Ivan invaded he triggered the intervention of Sweden, Denmark and Poland-Lithuania, who all came to the rescue of Livonia. All these forces were united enough to push Ivan out of the area, but by the turn of the seventeenth century they were no longer allies, with, in particular, Sweden and Poland-Lithuania waging war against one other over both dynastic issues and inter-Christian religious differences.

The breakdown of the relationship between Poland-Lithuania and Sweden saved Russia, as this occurred at the same time that Russia itself descended into civil war, following the end of the Rurik dynasty. This dynastic gap produced contenders from Sweden, Poland-Lithuania and within Russia itself, each willing to make alliances to achieve their position. The rivalry only ended when Mikhail Romanov was elected Tsar by a Russian assembly. Over the following decades, both the Swedes and the Poles were forced to relinquish the core Rus lands, and to withdraw their claims to the Russian throne (for which they were paid cash).

X

The New World

1. Introduction

THIS CHAPTER IS about the New World, as established in the northern, central and southern parts of the Americas. The causes of warfare in the central and southern regions of this area were founded on the fact that as had occurred with some parts of Africa in the second half of the fifteenth century, lands already occupied by other peoples could be gifted by the papacy to monarchs whom they approved of. Full and absolute obedience was owed by the indigenous peoples to these outsiders and their religious views. Failure to comply would, and did, give rise to repeated wars. The colonies in the north, especially as planted by the English, Dutch and French, adopted a view in which the benefits of European civilisation were the fruits the indigenous peoples would reap, religion being a secondary consideration. Moreover, in the north the colonists came to realise that they were sharing the land with indigenous groups who were anything but inferior to them, and whose only (fatal) weakness was that they were not unified as a political group. Accordingly, the colonists' survival, and eventual expansion, could be achieved by astute policies of divide and conquer. Although it was originally concluded that such indigenous peoples could be enslaved, opinion later changed and the enslavement of such populations, who were now considered citizens, was no longer an option. The same thinking did not apply to people torn from their homelands in Africa, with the vast majority of European religious, political and philosophical thinkers agreeing that such actions were lawful.

2. Precedents

The background to the thinking that came to dominate in the New World originated in the thinking that evolved in the precedents that appeared five decades before Europeans arrived in New World, when they were beginning to make headway in Africa. The basic assumption, as reflected by the explorers from Castile, was that as they were heirs to the Visigoth kingdom, which at one point covered North Africa, anything that they discovered in Africa was theirs. They threatened war against any other European countries, and especially Portugal, that might seek to explore and claim the same lands. Despite the obvious conflict that could arise between two Catholic countries, Pope Eugenius IV, in his *Rex regum* of 1443, remained essentially neutral in the disputes about ownership. However, eight years later, in 1455, the new Pope Nicholas V, in his bull *Dum diveras*, seeking to further the interests of Portugal (and support for his own papacy), recognised exclusive Portuguese title to those African 'provinces, islands, ports, districts and seas ... which have already been acquired and which shall be acquired in the future' and 'beyond towards that southern shore'. Nicholas V then granted the right to the King of Portugal:

> [t]o invade, search out capture, vanquish, and subdue all Saracens and pagans, whatsoever, and other enemies of Christ wheresoever placed, and kingdoms, dukedoms, principalities, dominions, possessions and all movable and immovable goods ... to apply and appropriate to himself and his successors ... [T]he right of conquest ... [which] we declare to be extended [from the north-west African coast] ... to Guinea, and beyond toward that southern shore ... belongs to King Alfonso, his successors... and not to any others.[1]

The following year, in 1456, the next Pope, Callixtus III, desperate to get support for his planned Crusade against the Ottomans, granted further privileges to the Portuguese monarchy in his Bull *Inter Caetera*, promising them the lands 'from Capes Bojador and Nam through the whole of Guinea and beyond its southern shore as far as to the Indians'.[2] A few decades later, the papacy would build on its strength in this area, helping settle disputes over ownership between two of the great seafaring nations of the day, regarding which country owned which new areas, with the 1479 *Treaty of Alcacovas*, confirmed by Pope Sixtus IV, settling the ownership issues between Castile and Portugal over the Canaries, Guinea, the Azores, Madeira and Cape Verde.[3]

3. THE NEW WORLD

Pope Alexander VI came to power at a time when both Spain and Portugal were making unprecedented discoveries of countries in which other peoples were already living. To the east, Vasco da Gama rounded the Cape of Good Hope and had his first sight of India. To the west, Christopher Columbus had inadvertently discovered what became known as the 'New World', on a voyage approved of and supported by the Spanish monarchs, Isabella and Ferdinand, in 1492, in a quest 'to see the said princes and peoples and lands ... and the manner in which may be undertaken their conversion to our Holy Faith'.[4] Columbus was promised titles and rewards if he was

[1] The Papal Bull Romanus Pontifex, 1455, as reprinted in Worger, W (ed) (2010) *African and the West: A Documentary History*, Vol I (Oxford, Oxford University Press) 15–17; Toews, J (1968) 'Formative Forces in the Pontificate of Nicholas V, 1447–1455', *The Catholic Historical Review* 261–84.

[2] The papal bull *Inter Caetera*, 1456, reproduced in Davenport, F (ed) (1917) *European Treaties Bearing on the History of the United States and its Dependencies to 1648* (NYC, Carnegie Institute) 27–33.

[3] The *Treaty of Alcacovas* is reproduced in Davenport, F (ed) (1917) *European Treaties Bearing on the History of the United States and its Dependencies to 1648* (NYC, Carnegie Institute) 33–48.

[4] Columbus, as noted in Sale, K (2006) *Christopher Columbus and the Conquest of Paradise* (NYC, Tauris) 11.

successful. In return, the land was to be claimed for the Spanish Crown. The Agreement under which Columbus set sail stated that he was authorised to 'discover and acquire islands and mainland in the Ocean Sea'.[5] Just over two months after setting sail, on 12 October 1492, land was sighted. As the ships anchored off an island in the Bahamas, Columbus declared that he had discovered the 'Indies', although they subsequently became known as the Americas, after the cartographer Amerigo Vespucci recognised them as *mundus novus*, a New World.[6]

Columbus landed and declared his lawful possession of the island. He named the island San Salvador, unfurled a banner and proclaimed the island the property of the Catholic sovereigns of Spain. He repeated this procedure of expropriation at least 60 times throughout the first voyage, claiming and naming each island he landed upon for the Spanish Crown, noting, as he did so, that he was 'not contradicted'[7] by the local indigenous peoples, although the first large-scale revolts against the Spanish colonialists would occur within three years of their arrival. Initially locals were recorded as living in a 'Garden of Eden', without clothing, weapons or organised religion. Columbus would then assure the Spanish monarchs that 'all of the men and women here, from this island especially, but also from the other islands, belong to Your Highnesses'.[8] He added that from these lands, the Spanish monarchy could be assured of acquiring lands for citizens, gold for coffers, and souls for faith. Ferdinand responded, acknowledging the work of Columbus and instructing him, 'by every means and ways possible … to persuade the inhabitants of said islands and mainlands to be converted to our holy Catholic faith'.[9]

Before such matters could proceed further, a large diplomatic disagreement arose when Columbus, returning from his first voyage, landed in Lisbon and described his discoveries to the King of Portugal, John II. Columbus found that King John believed that the lands discovered belonged to Portugal, as they were within his preserve, as promised by earlier papal bulls. The Spanish disagreed. The two kingdoms being at loggerheads, Pope Alexander VI was asked to rule on the matter, which he did, sending vicars and priests out to the new lands, and issuing three successive bulls confirming the Spanish title based on the discoveries of Columbus.[10] The bull of 1493, *Inter Caetera divinai*, declared that the lands discovered in the region belonged to the Spanish Crown,

---

[5] The 'Agreement of Columbus' in Parry, J (ed) (1968) *The European Reconnaissance* (NYC, Harper) 151.

[6] Elliot, J (2002) *Imperial Spain* (London, Penguin) 45–47.

[7] Columbus, 'Letter on the New World' in Cowans, J (ed) (2003) *Early Modern Spain: A Documentary History* (Philadelphia, PA, Penn State University Press) 29–31.

[8] Columbus, as quoted in Rivera, L (1992) *A Violent Evangelism* (Louisville, KY, John Knox Press) 11; also the 'Letter of Columbus to His Patrons', as reproduced in Cohen, M (ed) (2004) *History in Quotations* (London, Cassell) 324.

[9] Letter from Fernando, as recorded in Rivera, *A Violent Evangelism* (Louisville, KY, John Knox Press) 43; also Columbus, in Cowans, J (ed) (2003) *Early Modern Spain: A Documentary History* (Philadelphia, PA, Penn State University Press) 2–31.

[10] Russel, P (2009) 'Some Portuguese Paradigms for the Discovery and Conquest of Spanish America', *Renaissance Studies* 6 (3), 377–95; Jesse, C (1965) 'The Papal Bull of 1493: The First Vicar Apostolic in the New World', *Caribbean Quarterly* 11 (3), 62–71.

as Columbus had come upon a people 'undiscovered by others', and to the Pope's mind it was acceptable, important and pleasing that:

> the Catholic faith and Christian religion, especially in this our time, may in all places be exalted, amplified, and enlarged whereby the health of souls may be procured and the barbarous nations subdued and brought to the faith ... We greatly commend your godly and laudable purpose in our Lord and, we exhort you to ... bring the people of the said mainlands and isles to the Christian religion.[11]

The second bull was based on the realisation that more land might be available for discovery, and thus ownership needed to be agreed in advance. This bull, *Piis Fidelium*, began by recounting Spain's recent cleansing of Muslims from Spanish Granada,[12] which had enlarged and expanded the Catholic Church to the delight of the Pope. Thus:

> We therefore consider it as just and not undeserved by you, that we should concede to you ... the wherewithal by which you may be able to pursue your hold and laudable work [conversion] pleasant to immortal God ... and the expansion of Christian rule. ... These peoples inhabiting the said islands and lands ... seem well fitted to embrace the Catholic faith and to be imbued with good morals, and there is hope that were they instructed, the name of the Savior, our Lord Jesus Christ, could be easily introduced into these lands and islands ...[13]

Pope Alexander's third bull, *Dudum siquidem*, went even further, guaranteeing rights to lands not yet discovered to the Spanish Crown:

> We give, conceded and assign to you ... by the authority of Almighty God bestowed upon blessed Peter and by the Vicariate of Jesus Christ, which we discharge on earth—all the islands and mainlands, found or to be found, discovered or to be discovered, westwards or southwards by drawing and establishing a line running from the Arctic to the Antarctic Pole.[14]

The basic division of the New World between Spain and Portugal was then consolidated in the 1494 *Treaty of Tordesillas*.[15] This confirmed what Alexander had recently ruled, but slightly changed the geographical line, which was now about halfway between the Cape Verde Islands and Cuba. The land to the east of this line was to belong to Portugal, and the land to the west of the line to Spain. Spain thus secured virtually all of North and South America, leaving Portugal a fraction of the South

---

[11] The bull *Inter Caetera*, 1493, reproduced in Davenport, F (ed) (1917) *European Treaties Bearing on the History of the United States and its Dependencies to 1648* (NYC, Carnegie Institute) 56–65; Muldoon, J (1978) 'Papal Responsibility for the Infidel: Alexander VI's Inter Caetera', *The Catholic Historical Review* 64 (2), 166–84.

[12] See pages 251–253.

[13] *Piis Fidelium*, as in Williams, R (1990) *The American Indian in Western Legal Thought* (Oxford, Oxford University Press) 80–81.

[14] The bull *Dudum siquidem*, as reproduced in Davenport, F (ed) (1917) *European Treaties Bearing on the History of the United States and its Dependencies to 1648* (NYC, Carnegie Institute) 79–83; also Hector, A (2014) 'Pope Alexander VI, Slavery, and Voluntary Subjection', *The Journal of Ecclesiastical History* 65 (4), 738–60.

[15] The 1494 *Treaty of Tordesillas*, in Davenport, F (ed) (1917) *European Treaties Bearing on the History of the United States and its Dependencies to 1648* (NYC, Carnegie Institute) 84–100; McCourt, J (2010) 'The Treaty of Tordesillas, 1494', *Queensland History Journal* 21 (2), 88–102; Cohen, L (2015) 'The Events That Led to the Treaty of Tordesillas', *The Journal of the Society for the History of Discoveries* 47 (2), 142–62.

American continent, now constituted as Brazil. This rule of ownership meant that all future discoveries belonged to one or the other kingdom, even if the territory had not yet been discovered, regardless of whether it was found by Spain or Portugal. The treaty was confirmed by the papacy in 1506, although it was subsequently amended when further new lands were discovered.[16]

To begin with, France and England opted not to interfere with the arrangement. Although Henry VII granted the Italian John Cabot exploration rights in 1496, to 'occupy and possess all such towns, cities, castles and lands belonging to both heathens and/or infidels, getting unto us the rule, title and jurisdiction of the same', this only applied to journeys of discovery to lands 'unknown to all Christians'[17] that had not already been allocated by the papacy. Although Cabot may have landed in Newfoundland, as he and five ships subsequently disappeared, the matter was never pursued by either Henry VII or his son, Henry VIII. However, as early as 1503 the French tried to encroach on some of the new discoveries, crossing swords with the Portuguese in Brazil (the Portuguese explorer Pedro Alvares Cabral having landed on its coast in 1500), as a result of which the Portuguese king, John III, would later send armed fleets to drive off the French and settle and fortify the coastline. Although the French would initially accept this, King Francis I, before dispatching his own explorers to spread Catholicism and bring 'law and peace, by officers of justice so that they [the indigenous people] may live by reason and civility',[18] would later revisit the division of the world by the papacy, asking 'to see the clause in Adam's testament that excludes me from a share in the globe'.[19]

4. The Requirement

As the sixteenth century dawned, the Spanish authorities decided that the justifications for forthcoming wars in the New World needed to be set out clearly. The seeds

---

[16] When the Moluccas were visited in 1512, so as to avoid any confusion over which side of the demarcation line they belonged, Pope Leo X confirmed, in his bull *Praecelsae Devotionis* in 1514, that they belonged to Portugal, as did all of the territories in Africa, 'and all other places beyond the sea, acquired from the infidels'. The bull *Praecelsae Devotionis* is reproduced in Davenport, F (ed) (1917) *European Treaties Bearing on the History of the United States and its Dependencies to 1648* (NYC, Carnegie Institute) 112–15. However, this did not resolve all of the difficulties, and further treaties were signed between Portugal and Spain in 1524 and then in 1529 (updating the 1494 treaty), in which Charles V pledged all of his rights in the Moluccas to Portugal for 350,000 ducats in cash, and an arbitrary line of demarcation was fixed 15 degrees east of the islands. See the 1524 *Treaty of Vitoria*, reproduced in Davenport, ibid, at 118–30; the 1529 *Treaty of Saragoza*, in which the highly-prized Spice Islands were placed solidly under Portugal's jurisdiction, for an indemnity of 350,000 ducats, also reproduced in Davenport, ibid at 159–98. See also Gilmore, M (1952) *The World of Humanism* (NYC, Harper) 40–41.

[17] Reprinted in Commager, H (ed) (1968) *Documents of American History* (Upper Saddle River, NJ, Prentice Hall) 5–6.

[18] Commission of Francis I, as in Pagden, A (1995) *Lords of All the World: Ideologies of Empire in Spain, Britain and France* (New Haven, CT, Yale University Press) 33.

[19] Francis, as noted in Rivera, L (1992) *A Violent Evangelism* (Louisville, KY, John Knox Press) 30; also Williams, R (1990) *The American Indian in Western Legal Thought* (Oxford, Oxford Univeristy Press) 128–31.

of this thinking were evident in the royal decree issued by Queen Isabella of Spain in 1503, which explained that the Caribs had been sent many missionaries, with a view to converting them and incorporating them 'into the communion of the faithful and under our obedience'.[20] However, when they refused to grant missionaries entry on to their lands, attacked European and indigenous Christians converts, and then killed and ate their prisoners, it was decided 'to make war on the Caribs of the Islands ... make prisoners of them, and sell them and profit'.[21]

In 1511, Jamaica was settled and Cuba was conquered after the Spanish king, Ferdinand, had dispatched his explorers to see whether gold existed in these locations. On Cuba, the expedition, as led by Diego Velazquez and Hernan Cortes, found little opposition in the shape of the bows, arrows and slings of the native Tainos. They were no match for the Spanish armour, archers, artillery and long steel swords. Hundreds of native Cubans were slaughtered, and their leader was captured and executed; the indigenous population of Cuba would go on to fall from perhaps 300,000 down to 500 within a few decades. King Ferdinand also emphasised the importance of having the indigenous peoples instructed in the 'matter of our holy Catholic faith, since this is the principal basis for the conquest of those parts'.[22] A supplementary decree of 1511, issued to justify the use of force against the indigenous people of Boriquen, stated:

> Make your requirements formally, two or three times: and if after having done so they do not wish to submit and serve as do the Indians of Espanola, publicly declare war against them ... [Y]ou should try to take control of these miscreants so that they become our slaves or are subjected to hard labor in our mines.[23]

The following year, in 1512, the influential Spanish scholar Juan Lopez de Palacios argued:

> Supreme dominion, power and jurisdiction of these islands belong to the church whom the entire world, and all men, including infidels, have to recognise as owner and superior ... [I]f they refuse, the church could, either by itself or with the help of Christian Princes, bring them to subjection and expel them from their own lands.[24]

In 1513, as Florida and Puerto Rico were added to the Spanish holdings, the Spanish Crown instructed Rubios to draw up the *Requerimiento* (Requirement). This was the document that the authorities required to be read out to the first indigenous peoples they encountered in new territories, allowing the indigenous peoples to avoid bloodshed by

---

[20] Decree of Isabella, as recorded in Rivera, L (1992) *A Violent Evangelism* (Louisville, KY, John Knox Press) 33.

[21] The Cedula of 1511, as in Jesse, C (1963) 'The Spanish Cedula of December 23, 1511: On the Subject of the Caribs', *Caribbean Quarterly* 9 (3), 22–32.

[22] Letter from Fernando, 1511, to Diego Columbus, as in Rivera, L (1992) *A Violent Evangelism* (Louisville, KY, John Knox Press) 44; Wright, I (1921) 'The Early History of Jamaica', *The English Historical Review* 36 (141), 70–95.

[23] The Decree of 1511, as recorded in Rivera, L (1992) *A Violent Evangelism* (Louisville, KY, John Knox Press) 33.

[24] Rubios, as in in Rivera, L (1992) *A Violent Evangelism* (Louisville, KY, John Knox Press) 39; also Stannard, D (1992) *American Holocaust: The Conquest of the New World* (Oxford, Oxford University Press) 63–66.

their complete and immediate surrender. Aside from the absurdity of the assumptions in the document, or its delivery—being read out, untranslated, to the first person the explorers came across, or to empty huts (as occurred on a number of occasion)—the terms of what was official Spanish policy until 1556 spoke for themselves:

> Since the world was created, it was necessary that some men should go one way and some another, and that they should be divided into many kingdoms ... Of all these nations God our Lord gave charge to one man, called Saint Peter, that he should be lord and superior of all men in the world, that all should obey him, and that he should be the head of the whole human race ... One of these pontiffs ... made donation of these isles ... to the aforesaid king and queen [Ferdinand and Isabella] and to their successors, along with all that there is in these territories ... so their Highnesses are kings and lords of these islands by virtue of this donation ... [You must also] ... acknowledge the Church as the ruler and superior of the whole world ... [I]f you do so, you will do well ... But if you do not do this, I certify to you that, with the help of God, we shall powerfully enter into your country, and shall make war against you and in all ways and manners that we can, and shall subject you to the yoke and obedience of the Church and of Their Highnesses; we shall take you and your wives and our children, and shall make slaves of them, and we shall take away your goods, and the deaths and losses which shall accrue from this are your fault ...[25]

The *Requerimiento* was buttressed by the scholarship of Juan Gines de Sepulveda, who argued that the Spanish had a legal and moral right to enslave indigenous populations, as they were uncivilised, without reason and possessed no Christian faith. They could not possibly be said to be living a life of genuine 'political liberty and human dignity'.[26] Warfare against such people would be just, 'so that they may set aside their barbarism and be reduced to a more civilised life and the pursuit of virtue'.[27] He added that 'the force of terror' was legitimate to use, to 'break bad habits' if 'the salvation of many'[28] was the outcome.[29]

Although dominant, this view was not accepted by all the scholars of the age. Bartholomew de las Casas raised a lone voice in 1515 when he argued that

> there was never just cause or authorisation from princes to make war on innocent Indians, who were safe and peaceful on their lands and in their houses, we affirm that the conquests were, and are, null and lacking legality, unjust, evil, tyrannical and condemned by all the laws ...[30]

[25] Rubios, 'The Requirement' in Cowans, J (ed) (2003) *Early Modern Spain: A Documentary History* (Philadelphia, PA, Penn State University Press) 34–36; Faudree, P (2013) 'How to Say Things with Wars: Performativity and Discursive Rupture in the Requerimiento of the Spanish Conquest', *Journal of Linguistic Anthropology* 22 (3), 182–200.
[26] Sepulveda, as in Skinner, Q (1978) *The Foundations of Modern Political Thought*, Vol II (Cambridge, Cambridge University Press) 142.
[27] Sepulveda, 'Just War in the Indies' in Cowans, J (ed) (2003) *Early Modern Spain: A Documentary History* (Philadelphia, PA, Penn State University Press) 59–63.
[28] As in Rivera, L (1992) *A Violent Evangelism* (Louisville, KY, John Knox Press) 220.
[29] Brustetter, D (2011) 'Just War Against Barbarians: Revisiting the Debates Between Sepulveda and Las Casas', *Political Studies* 59 (3), 733–51; Fernandez, J (1975) 'Juan de Sepulveda on the Nature of the American Indians', *The Americas* 31 (4), 434–51.
[30] Casas, 'Thirty Propositions' in Cowans, J (ed) (2003) *Early Modern Spain: A Documentary History* (Philadelphia, PA, Penn State University Press) 64, 66; also, Orique, D (2014) 'The Life, Labor and Legacy of Las

For Casas, waging war against such peoples would only have been just if they had maliciously persecuted or disturbed the Christian faith, or without legitimate cause killed its preachers. Francisco de Vitoria followed suit, arguing that the fact that indigenous peoples were unbelievers was not sufficient to wage war against them, as they were rational. Warfare was only lawful against such peoples if they acted contrary to certain cosmopolitan values, such as allowing foreigners a right to travel, a right to trade, and/or a right to preach and declare the Gospel in their lands. He added that although many conquests in the New World were done wrongfully, since so many people had been baptised afterwards it would not be licit for the Spanish Crown to abandon the newly taken areas.[31] Francisco Suarez would later add to this argument, stating that it was legitimate to intervene militarily into other countries with repugnant cultural practices, such as human sacrifice, 'in order to recall those nations to a better way of living'.[32] He added that the Church, due to its obligation to pursue universal salvation, 'has a right and a special authority to preach the faith', and if this was not permitted, 'force [could] be used'.[33]

A. Hernan Cortes

As the scholars were debating, war was raging across the New World, with some missions being successful, whilst others ended in defeat, Spanish explorers coming to untimely ends and their troops being ejected from attempted settlements or incursions in both Florida and the Philippines, whilst in other areas long-lasting revolts occurred. Alongside these dramatic losses were near unimaginable victories against both the Aztecs and the Incas. The human cost for the indigenous population of Mexico over the following 50 years was a fall in population from perhaps 25 million to about 1.3 million. This accorded with the patterns of human loss throughout other parts of the region, such as the islands of the Caribbean and in Cuba, as well as in other parts of Central America and the western coast of South America, where millions of people lost their lives through war, colonial development and inadvertently introduced

Casas', *Peace Review* 26 (3), 325–33; Carman, G (1998) 'On the Pope's Original Intent: Las Casas Reads the Papal Bulls of 1493', *Colonial Latin American Review* 7 (2), 193–204.

[31] Vitoria, 'On the American Indians' in Pagden, A (ed), (1992) *Vitoria: Political Writings* (Cambridge, Cambridge University Press) sections 2.4, 3.5, Appendix A xiv; see also ibid, sections 2: 2–1.6 and 3: 1–4. Scott, J (1934) *Vitoria and his League of Nations* (Cambridge, Cambridge University Press) 106–07, 152, 164, 167; Salas, V (2012) 'Francisco de Vitoria on the Ius Gentium and the American Indians', *Ave Maria Law Review* 10 (2), 331–54.
[32] Scott, J (ed) (1944) *Selections from Three Works of Francisco Suarez*, Vol II (Oxford, Clarendon Press) 768 and 757–67.
[33] Scott, J (ed) (1944) *Selections from Three Works of Francisco Suarez*, Vol II (Oxford, Clarendon Press) 740–46; Lantigua, D (2015) 'The Freedom of the Gospel: Aquinas, Subversive Natural Law, and the Spanish Wars of Religion', *Modern Theology* 31 (2), 312–37; Courcelles, D (2005) 'Managing the World: The Development of Jus Gentium by the Theologians of Salamanca in the 16th Century', *Philosophy and Rhetoric* 38 (1), 1–15.

diseases from Europe, such as smallpox, measles and influenza, with population declines in excess of 90 per cent in some areas between the years 1500 and 1600.[34]

Hernan Cortes followed in the footsteps of other Spanish explorers in the region, who had by 1517 encountered another civilisation. The first encounter was not peaceful, the explorer Francesco Cordoba seeing over 20 of his men killed. Had Cordoba not managed to escape with his life, and some gold he had acquired, it is questionable whether the Governor of Cuba, Diego Velasquez, would have authorised another expedition. The second group of explorers suffered the same fate as the first. It was then that Cortes decided to undertake a third expedition. As agreed with Velasquez, this was meant to be orderly, for limited trading purposes, and involve fair treatment of the indigenous community. However, fearing that Cortes would not keep to the bargain, Velasquez attempted to revoke his authority, but it was too late, for Cortes sailed in early 1519 with 11 ships and 530 men, horses, dogs, gunpowder and steel weapons, with the goal, in the words of his companion, Bernal Diaz del Castillo, 'to serve God and the king, and also to get rich'.[35]

After landing at what is now known as Vera Cruz, and taking advantage of a resentment amongst the local tribes at the rule of the Aztecs (who called themselves 'Mexica'), as led by Montezuma II, Cortes made his way to the Aztec capital of Tenochtitlan. Cortes eventually met Montezuma. Cortes recorded that he, through the *Requerimiento*, threatened war and servitude for Montezuma and his people, if the Aztec leader did not pledge obedience to Christianity and the Spanish Crown. As Cortes explained to his king, Charles V:

> Through me, in your royal name, I required them … to have and adore only one God … and abandon all the idols and rituals they had until now … And that at the same time they would come to know how on earth it is to your majesty that the universe obeys and serves by divine providence; and that they had to submit and be under the imperial yoke … And if they did not do so, action would be taken against them.[36]

Cortes then recorded that in this meeting, due to Aztec prophecy, Montezuma gave, or donated, his kingdom to him. Very soon after, whilst still in a fortified section of the Aztec capital, he arrested Montezuma and began trying to order the kingdom through the voice of the king. There were frequent disagreements over Cortes' requests for gold, and especially regarding religion. As Cortes later explained, 'my principal motive in undertaking this war and any other one I should undertake, is to bring the natives to

---

[34] Livi, M (2006) 'The Depopulation of Hispanic America after the Conquest', *Population and Development Review* 32 (2), 199–232; White, M (2011) *Atrocitology: Humanities 100 Deadliest Achievements* (Melbourne, Text Publishing) 170–87; Stannard, D (1992) *American Holocaust: The Conquest of the New World* (Oxford, Oxford University Press) 73–85.

[35] Castillo, as noted in Elliot, J (2002) *Imperial Spain* (London, Penguin) 65; Raudzens, G (1995) 'Testing Military Superiority as a Cause of Europe's Pre-Industrial Colonial Conquests, *War in History* 2 (1), 87–104; Dodds, C (2007) 'Cortes and Montezuma', *BBC History* Nov 35–40.

[36] 'Cortes Description of Mexico' in Parry, J (ed) (1968) The *European Reconnaissance* (NYC, Harper) 200; Hill, E (2011) 'The New World Revealed: Cortes and the Presentation of Mexico to Europe', *Word and Image* 27 (1), 31–46.

the knowledge of our Holy Catholic faith'.[37] Cortes wanted to stop human all sacrifice, for the Aztecs to follow Christianity, to place an image of the Virgin on top of their great temple and to destroy all of their idols. Despite initial relative compliance with these demands, fearing a rebellion, he had a number of unarmed indigenous leaders killed. As the crowds turned against the Aztec king, he too was killed. This act sparked an overall rebellion, which forced Cortes to flee for the coast, losing hundreds of men (many of whom would be sacrificed) and thousands of allies to opposing angry tribes. He left little behind except smallpox. This disease, against which the indigenous people had no immunity, then did Cortes' work for him.[38]

When Cortes returned to this severely damaged land, his objective was war. With tens of thousands of supporting indigenous warriors, he surrounded the capital. Submission followed 80 days later, after the flow of food and fresh water had been stopped, and repeated skirmishing. Figures suggest that as a result of the smallpox epidemic, siege and warfare, the Aztecs lost 350,000 people. The Spanish lost nearly 850, plus 20,000 Tlaxcalan allies. This was the price paid by Spain for the empire of the Aztecs, with the blessing of both the papacy and the Emperor Charles V. Pope Clement VII, after accepting part of the booty taken from the Aztecs, issued a Bull of Indulgence in 1529, absolving any Spanish soldiers killed in the expedition from their guilt and sin. The Emperor Charles V forgave Cortes for the questionable start of the expedition, and made him the Governor of 'New Spain'. Cortes then oversaw further Spanish expeditions into other parts of the region, promising the Emperor Charles that he could 'call yourself emperor of this kingdom with no less glory than of Germany which your majesty already possesses'.[39] Charles V then reminded Cortes, in the laws of 1542, that the purpose was not just empire but also religion. Thus, 'our principal intent and will has always been and is the preservation of and increase of the Indians and that they be instructed and taught in the things of our holy Catholic faith'.[40]

B. Francisco Pizarro

Francisco Pizarro followed directly in the footsteps of Cortes. As the war in Mexico was reaching its climax, the Spanish in Panama began to explore the north-west coast

---

[37] Cortes, as recorded in Rivera, L (1992) *A Violent Evangelism* (Louisville, KY, John Knox Press) 48; also Folsem, J (1843) 'The Despatches of Hernando Cortes', *The North American Review* 57 (121), 459–90.

[38] Townsend, C (2003) 'No One Said it Was Quetzalcoatl: Listening to the Indians in the Conquest of Mexico', *History Compass* 1, 1–14; Almazan, M (1997) 'Hernan Cortes: Virtu vs Fortuna', *Journal of American Culture* 20 (2), 131–37; Stannard, D (1992) *American Holocaust: The Conquest of the New World* (Oxford, Oxford University Press) 77–79, 90–95, 102–07.

[39] Cortes, H, *Letters from Mexico*, trans, Pagden, A (London, Harvard University Press) 48; also Tibesar, A (1989) 'The King, the Pope and the Clergy in the Colonial Spanish-American Empire', *The Catholic Historical Review* 75 (1), 91–109; Hernan Cortez, 'The Conquest of Mexico' in Elton, G (ed) (1968) *Renaissance and Reformation* (London, Macmillan) 259–61.

[40] Charles V, as in Rivera, L (1992) *A Violent Evangelism* (Louisville, KY, John Knox Press) 45; Grant, R (2011) *1001 Battles* (London, Penguin) 249, 250, 261.

of South America. Pizzaro set sail in 1524 with 80 men into a four-year wilderness of hardship, searching for other, equally rich civilisations akin to what Cortes had found, but in what is now Peru. Contact was made in 1528 with indigenous groups, at which point Pizarro was able to ascertain that a second great civilisation existed, numbering perhaps as many as 10 million people. Before Pizzaro got to visit this peoples' capital, he returned to Panama and then to Spain, where he met both Charles V and Cortes. Upon returning to Panama, he obtained more men and was granted a licence 'to discover and conquer Peru'.[41]

The civilisation that Pizzaro came upon was the Incas. The Inca polity was far more organised that that of the Aztecs, its communications were better, the people were less warlike and human sacrifice had ended before the Spaniards had arrived. Despite these differences, before Pizzaro could return to the region in 1530, the Incas were struck down by smallpox and internal civil war based upon a dynastic challenge between two brothers, in which Atahualpa was victorious. When Pizzaro eventually met Atahualpa, the Inca ruler informed the Spaniard that he had no wish, nor need, for a pact of friendship. Pizzaro, undeterred, then had Atahualpa informed, in the form of a *Requerimiento* that had been forwarded to him by Charles V in 1533, that Atahualpa had to renounce the Inca gods for the Christian deity. As the chronicler of this meeting explained, Atahualpa declined to be the vassal of Charles V, and suggested the Pope was crazy to talk of giving away countries that did not belong to him. When Atahualpa was pressed to renounce his faith by a Catholic friar accompanying the Spanish, the Inca asked

> what authority he had for his own belief, and the friar told him it was all written in the book he was holding. The Inca then said, 'Give me the book so it can speak to me'. The book was handed up to him, and he began to eye it carefully and listen to it page by page. At last he asked, 'Why doesn't the book say anything to me?'[42]

Directly following this remarkable exchange, the order was given for the Spanish to attack. Atahualpa was then captured by Pizarro. Pizzaro explained:

> We came to conquer this land so that all may come to know God and the holy Catholic faith ... so that you will understand and abandon the diabolical and beastly life you lead ... And if you have been taken prisoner and your people scattered and killed, it is because ... you threw on the ground the book where God's words are.[43]

Thousands were killed and Athualpa was captured. He was then told he would only be released when the Incas had provided Pizarro with a room full of gold and silver.

---

[41] This licence is in Wood, M (2000) *Conquistadors* (London, BBC) 126; see also ibid, at 16, 42, 50, 57, 60, 63, 133. Also Culemans, J (1916) 'A Reevaulation of Early Peruvian History', *The Catholic Historical Review* 2 (2), 157–67.

[42] The Chronicle of the Meeting, as reprinted in Wood, M (2000) *Conquistadors* (London, BBC) 133; also Sowell, D (1993) 'Encounter at Cajamarca', *Juniata Voices* 1, 67–77; Hemming, J (1970) The *Conquest of the Incas* (London, Macmillan) 28, 37, 41–43, 130–32; Elliot, J (2002) *Imperial Spain* (London, Penguin) 72–75, 227–41.

[43] Pizarro, as recorded in Rivera, L (1992) *A Violent Evangelism* (Louisville, KY, John Knox Press) 208–09; also ibid, at 15, 90, 126.

Athualpa facilitated this, telling his people to help the Spaniards with what they requested. When this was done, Pizarro accused Atahualpa of treason and plotting against him, for which he was executed. Atahualpa's choice of baptism before his execution meant that he was rewarded by being strangled to death and buried in the grounds of a church, as opposed to being burned at the stake as a heretic. Pizarro then oversaw the placement of what he hoped would be a puppet king on the Inca throne at Lima, an entirely new capital. For this success, Charles V entrusted the northern part of the Inca Empire to Pizarro. From this seat of power, Pizarro put down two rebellions. The first, by the Incas in 1536, and the second, by colonists, in which Pizarro lost his life in a revenge attack in 1541, after which Peru descended into a type of anarchy. Order was re-established in the last decades of the sixteenth century, following a number of dedicated campaigns aimed at rooting out the Inca religion and putting an end to any consideration of shared forms of authority. These and similar military campaigns moving down the west coast of South America met with increasingly stiff resistance, with significant new settlements, such as at Santiago (from which Chile emerged), being hotly contested by local indigenous populations who did not welcome the European adventurers. Despite their resistance by force of arms, without resistance to the diseases the Europeans brought with them, along with the latter's advanced technology, the local tribes were brought to their knees. By 1650, millions of lives had been lost, to disease, colonial development and warfare, with population declines in some regions, such as Peru, recorded at an estimated 94 per cent since the arrival of Pizarro.[44]

5. England and the New World

Queen Elizabeth I could not agree with the Spanish or Portuguese claims that the oceans, and the new lands beyond them, could categorically belong to any one country by virtue of a papal edict. Elizabeth, who held (unproven) beliefs that her ancestors had successfully crossed the Atlantic 300 years before Columbus, insisted that she 'could not be convinced that [the Indies] were legitimately owned by Spain by decree of the pope in Rome, in whom I do not recognise any perogatives in any matters, much less that he can oblige Princes who do not owe him obedience'.[45]

Elizabeth did two things. First, she gave her subjects the right to trade and establish colonies in those parts of the New World in which the Spaniards had not settled.

[44] See Rice, P (2011) 'Order and Disorder in Early Colonial Peru', *International Journal of Historical Archaeology* 15 (3), 481–508; Julien, C (2007) 'Francisco de Toledo and his Campaign Against the Incas', *Colonial Latin American Review* 16 (2), 243–72; Hemming, J (1970) The *Conquest of the Incas* (London, Macmillan) 40–48, 64, 67, 77–81, 133, 162; Greengrass, M (2015) *Christendom Destroyed: Europe 1517–1648* (NYC, Penguin) 421.

[45] Elizabeth I, as noted in Greengrass, M (2015) *Christendom Destroyed: Europe 1517–1648* (NYC, Penguin) 155 and 156. See also Rivera, L (1992) *A Violent Evangelism* (Louisville, KY, John Knox Press) 30.

Sir Humphrey Gilbert was authorised, in 1578, 'to discover, search, find out, and view such remote heathen and barbarous lands, countries and territories not actually possessed of any Christian prince or people ... to have, hold, occupy and enjoy'.[46] Similarly, Sir Walter Raleigh was authorised to take, hold and own as a vassal of Elizabeth, 'remote, heathen and barbarous lands, countries and territories', so long as they were 'not possessed of any Christian prince, nor inhabited by Christian people'.[47] Raleigh did just this, planting the first colony of 107 English men, women and children as settlers on Roanoke Island on present-day North Carolina's Outer Banks around 1587. However, within a few years the settlers were all gone, dead from, probably, either starvation, or disease and/or violence from the local indigenous peoples.[48]

On the question of indigenous peoples, the English attempted to put forward a different justification for colonisation than the conquest approach espoused by the Spanish. Their thinking was based on the writings of the Italian-born but Oxford-based Protestant scholar, Alberico Gentili. Gentili was a great believer in the universal benefits of free trade, cosmopolitan views and the assumption that differences of religion were not a sufficient ground for the taking of land from indigenous peoples. Conquest and war were only justified against such peoples if they were 'rather like beasts than men'[49] (that is, cannibals), being common foes of humanity. The English promised that they would try to be more gentle in the bringing of the benefits of civilisation, technology and social betterment, and would not adopt the barbarity of the Spanish efforts. The English discourse was about promoting a more benign Christianity, utilisation of unused resources and the bringing of mutual benefit to both settlers and the indigenous communities. In reality, the expeditions lead by Gilbert to Newfoundland, and by Walter Raleigh to Virginia, were very similar to those of the Spanish, and violence became the norm once it became apparent that the indigenous populations did not welcome them. In the words of Richard Eden in 1555, 'merciful wars against these naked people'[50] were justified, as the planting of European civilisation was worth it for the indigenous populations in the long run.[51]

[46] The Charter given to Gilbert, as reproduced in Williams, R (1990) *The American Indian in Western Legal Thought* (Oxford, Oxford University Press) 156, 168–80, 185.

[47] The 'Charter of Sir Walter Raleigh' in Commager, H (ed) (1968) *Documents of American History* (Upper Saddle River, NJ, Prentice Hall) 6–7.

[48] Stahle, D (1998) 'The Lost Colony and Jamestown', *Science* 280 (5363): 324–30; Mires, P (1994) 'Contact and Contagion: The Roanoke Colony and Influenza', *Historical Archaeology* 28 (3), 154–67.

[49] Van-der-Molen, G (1930) *Alberico Gentili and the Development of International Law* (Amsterdam, Paris Printers) 9–14, 40, 185.

[50] Olesen, J (2009) 'Merciful Wars Against These Naked People: The Discourse of Violence in the Early Americas', *Canadian Review of American Studies* 39 (3), 235–53.

[51] MacMillan, K (2011) 'Benign and Benevolent Conquest? The Ideology of Elizabethan Atlantic Expansion Revisited', *Early American Studies* 9 (1), 1–22; Hodgkins, C (1997) 'Heathen Idolatry and Protestant Humility in the Imperial Legend of Sir Francis Drake', *Studies in Philology* 94 (4), 428–64; Pagden, A (1995) *Lords of All the World: Ideologies of Empire in Spain, Britain and France* (New Haven, CT, Yale University Press) 36 and 64.

6. THE COLONIES IN NORTH AMERICA

The beginning of the seventeenth century saw the signing of the 1604 *Treaty of London* between Spain and England. Part of this peace deal involved the Spanish agreeing to let the English enter those parts of the New World where the Spanish were not 'planted'.[52] Two years later, the *First Charter for Virginia* of 1606 was issued by King James I, and Jamestown, the first capital of the colony, was established in 1607. The *First Charter* reflected the 1604 Treaty, noting that Virginia was a colony upon land in part of America, 'which is not now actually possessed by any Christian Prince or people'.[53] Other outposts were planted by the French (with abortive colonies in Arcadia at the turn of the century, but success with Quebec in 1608), who constantly pressed inland, and the Dutch (New Amsterdam, later New York, from 1609). From these outposts, which were often caught up in the wider conflicts between their mother countries in Europe, two trends emerged, namely, growing political autonomy and relations with the indigenous peoples.[54]

In terms of growing political autonomy, despite the conservative nature of the new colonies, freedoms were developing that were not so readily available in the countries from which the colonists emerged. For example, although it was obvious that Virginia was an English colony, all three Charters in 1609, 1612 and 1621 gave it progressive, and considerable, degrees of autonomy, with the 1621 *Ordinance* beginning to turn the colonial council into a type of representative government, with the leaders to be 'chosen by the inhabitants' and matters '[to] be decided, determined and ordered by the greater part of the voices present'.[55] Even in Puritan Massachusetts (unlike the more righteous Pilgrim-founded Plymouth), despite its initially being more of a theological oligarchy than a democracy, evolved procedures by which views of non-Church 'freemen' had to be taken into account, along with their right to attend town meetings, courts and councils, as was their freedom from arbitrary punishment. Connecticut had no requirement for church membership, with authority coming from the people, and there was a limit on the term of office of the governor. Even Maryland, which looked more like a Crown fief than the others, came to pass its 1649 *Toleration Act*, promising free exercise of all forms of Christian religion. Others, such as the *Plantation Agreement at Providence* of 1640, provided for, inter alia, 'liberty of conscience',[56] whilst on Rhode

---

[52] The 1604 London Treaty Between Spain and Britain, as reproduced in Davenport, F (ed) (1917) *European Treaties Bearing on the History of the United States and its Dependencies to 1648* (NYC, Carnegie Institute) 246; Ungerer, G (1998) 'The Spanish and English Chronicles on the Anglo-Peace Negotiations', *Huntington Library Quarterly* 61 (3), 309–24.

[53] The 1606 'First Charter of Virginia' in Commager, H (ed) (1968) *Documents of American History* (Upper Saddle River, NJ, Prentice Hall) 8–9.

[54] Klein, S (2011) 'Boundary Negotiations in Anglo-Dutch Colonial Discourse', *Early American Studies* 9 (2), 1–14.

[55] The 1621 'Ordinance for Virginia' in Commager, H (ed) (1968) *Documents of American History* (Upper Saddle River, NJ, Prentice Hall) 13, 14.

[56] The 1640 'Agreement at Providence' in Commager, H (ed) (1968) *Documents of American History* (Upper Saddle River, NJ, Prentice Hall) 25.

Island, despite its originally being an outpost for religious zealotry, within a few decades the colonists had come to accept liberty of conscience and a separation of Church and state.[57]

With regard to the relationships that the colonies formed with indigenous peoples, the 1606 *Charter for Virginia* sought to bring the Christian religion to such people who

> [a]s yet live in Darkness and miserable Ignorance of the true Knowledge and Worship of God, and may in time bring the Infidels and Savages living in those Parts, to human Civility, and to a settled and quiet Government.[58]

This approach was different from that of the Dutch in their *Charter of Freedoms*, which established New Amsterdam (to become New York). The Dutch emphasis was not upon the rhetoric of puritan settlements, but rather upon security of tenure and private property, and it stipulated that 'whoever shall settle any colonies outside of the limits of Manhattan Island, shall be obliged to satisfy the Indians for the land they shall settle upon'.[59] The Dutch appear initially to have honoured this approach, with Peter Minuit purchasing Manhattan as a farming settlement from local Delaware chieftans and a fur-trading post at Fort Orange from the Mohawks. Having said that, their relationship with the indigenous tribes evolved over the coming decades into one where they picked sides to further their alliances. Although this ultimately worked out well for the Dutch, the fact that they had to build the Wall (thereafter the name of the well-known street in Manhattan), designed to keep the Indians out, testified to how tense early relationships were.

In Virginia, the colonists waged three wars with the Powhatan Indians. This was not expected, as violence had not been anticipated between the two groups. In large part this was because although the first English settlement was within the territory of the Powhatan, it existed with the tribe's consent and assistance. The exemplar of such thinking was found with the Pilgrims who settled at Plymouth in 1621 and co-existed alongside the local Squanto and Samoset tribes, who helped them plant crops and build houses. Their joint celebration of the harvest, at *Thanksgiving*, remains a key part of the modern American identity. With such realities, the English talked about such 'Indian people' as 'nations' from the start. They were clearly as fully human and rational as the colonists, and although there were obviously some assumptions that the colonists' Christian civilisation was superior to that of the Indians (who were often 'savages'), they was not based on clear ideas of racial superiority.[60]

---

[57] The 1632 'Charter of Maryland', the 1639 'Fundamental Orders of Connecticut' and the 1649 'Toleration Act' in Commager, H (ed) (1968) *Documents of American History* (Upper Saddle River, NJ, Prentice Hall) 21, 23, 31. See also Cooper, J (ed) (1970) *The New Cambridge Modern History: The Decline of Spain and the Thirty Years' War*, Vol IV (Cambridge, Cambridge University Press) 107, 129, 264–65, 672, 680, 683–85, 687.

[58] The 1606 'First Charter of Virginia' in Commager, H (ed) (1968) *Documents of American History* (Upper Saddle River, NJ, Prentice Hall) 8–9.

[59] Article 26 of the 1629 'Charter of Freedoms' in Commager, H (ed) (1968) *Documents of American History* (Upper Saddle River, NJ, Prentice Hall) 19–20.

[60] Rome, A (2014) 'Being Human in Early Virginia', *Renaissance Studies* 29 (5), 702–19; Thomas, G (1975) 'Puritans, Indians and the Concept of Race', *The New England Quarterly* 48 (1), 3–27.

Relationships turned sour in Virginia when the colonists began to strong-arm food from the Indians, when further land sales were refused and when lawless colonists acted with violence. Revenge and tit-for-tat actions escalated into indiscriminate attacks on each other, with the English colony teetering on the verge of extinction. Peace, and a resumption of trade, was achieved in 1614, with a marriage between the daughter of the chief and a notable colonist. However, unexpected massacres of colonists in 1622 triggered a second war, before a truce in 1626, followed by a third war in 1644. Although each time significant numbers of colonists were killed, they replenished their population with even greater numbers (as growing tobacco was now making the colony economically attractive, especially if more land could be obtained) and with increased firepower. At the same time, various diseases to which the indigenous peoples had little immunity continued to ravage their populations. The result was, in the case of Virginia, that the colonists managed to forge a peace after progressing deeper into new lands, which set a clearly delineated boundary between the English and the Indian settlements, which both sides were forbidden to cross. Although there were some areas set aside for loyal Indian tribes, the ideal, at this point, was separation, not assimilation.[61]

In Massachusetts, the colonists became involved in a war with the Pequot, due to a series of overlapping alliances related to securing monopolies on the fur trade, rogue European traders and lawlessness, and tit-for-tat killings. Specifically, following the death of some European traders, caused by allies of the Pequot, the authorities of Massachusetts ordered the killings to be avenged. This revenge killing and its spillover left the Pequot united in anger, and with their allies they attacked Connecticut. Connecticut first made peace with the Pequot allies, and then, with their Indian allies, the Mohawks, joined together in an unprecedented attack on a Pequot village, in which over 400 died in indiscriminate slaughter, which the Puritans justified as being sanctioned by God. Within a number of years, the Pequot had been destroyed as an independent political entity. This was confirmed in the 1638 *Treaty of Hartford*, under which the English settlers and the Indian allies that fought with them divided the booty (in terms of lands and captives, with many of the defeated sent off as slaves) between them. The significance lay not in the peace that followed, with the remaining defeated being resettled in special towns, but in the fact that the English were dealing with independent sovereign groupings.[62]

In some instances, such as with the Iroquois, the colonists were dealing not with one sovereign group but with several united into a confederation or league. This confederation of five autonomous and previously inimical Iroquoian tribal groups occupied adjoining territories spanning present-day New York State, with influences that

---

[61] Games, A (2014) 'Violence on the Fringes: The Virginia and Amboyna Massacres', *History* 99 (336), 504–29; Adams, L (2013) 'The Third Anglo-Powhatan War', *Native South* 6 (1), 170–92; Warrick, G (2003) 'European Infectious Disease and Depopulation', *Archaeology of Epidemic and Infectious Disease* 35 (2), 258–27; Lenman, B (2001) *England's Colonial Wars, 1550–1688* (London, Longman) 217–34; Fausz, F (1990) 'England's First Indian War, 1609–1614', *The Virginia Magazine of History* 98 (1), 3–56.

[62] Grant, D (2015) 'The Treaty of Hartford, 1638', *The William and Mary Quarterly* 72 (3), 461–98; Karr, R (1998) 'The Violence of the Pequot War', *The Journal of American History* 85 (3), 876–909; Katz, S (1991) 'The Pequot War Reconsidered', *The New England Quarterly* 64 (2), 206–24.

stretched up and down the east coast of North America. This league, perhaps comprising some 100,000 people, was made of up of the Mohawk, Cayuga, Oneida, Onondaga and later the Seneca. The members of this group were tied into a mutual peace and defensive alliance, which pre-dated the arrival of the Europeans, against other indigenous groups.[63]

It was an Top of these existing relationships that European influence, in terms of both being able to provide new technologies (firearms) and markets (for fur pelts that gave access to European goods) changed the nature and causes of war for some of the indigenous groups. This was most apparent with the French, who worked with the Hurons and the Algonquins, actually aiding them in some of their fights, and providing weapons against the Iroquois and their allies. The Iroquois, for their part, had good relations with the English and the Dutch, the latter providing them with firearms from 1614, which affected the balance amongst the tribes, the Iroquois going on to virtually destroy the Huron and Erie, enslaving a large number of Delaware. This in turn had a knock-on effect on the relationships between numerous Indian tribes and the colonists, with the Iroquois eventually going on to directly attack the French.[64]

7. SLAVERY

Slavery was common in Europe from the eleventh century onwards. People taken in wars were traded everywhere, with the great slaving routes running through what is modern-day Britain and France to Spain and Italy, whilst also linking to peripheral countries like Ireland, as well as Russia, Poland and Scandinavia involving perhaps 10,000 people each year. The word 'slav' and 'slave' are identical in most European languages (such as *esclave* in French, *esclavo* in Spanish and *sklave* in German), with them all having their roots in the Latin *sclavus*, maning a 'Slav' or person of Slavic descent. Only one voice in this epoch, that of Philippe de Beaumanoir at the end of the thirteenth century, argued against slavery as an institution. Conversely, the other great scholars of the age, such as Thomas Aquinas, viewed slavery as both a natural and a beneficial practice, due to the benefits that good Christian owners could give to slaves who were sinners. The only restriction upon slavery was that non-Christians, such as Muslims or Jews, were forbidden from owning Christians as slaves. Although uncommon, even inter-Christian slavery was legally possible, as clearly evidenced by a number of Popes, who threatened enslavement to dissident communities if they did

---

[63] Mohl, A (2007) 'The Rise and Fall of the Iroquois Confederacy', *The Journal of Psychohistory* 34 (4), 347–65; Kuhn, R (2001) 'Dating the League of the Iroquois', *American Antiquity* 66 (2), 301–14; Crawford, N (1994) 'A Security Regime Among Democracies: Cooperation Among Iroquois Nations', *International Organisation* 48 (3), 345–85.

[64] Blick, J 'The Iroquois Practice of Genocidal Warfare', (2001) *Journal of Genocide Research* 3 (3), 405–29; Starna, W (2004) 'From the Mohawk to the Beaver Wars', *Ethnohistory* 51 (4), 725–50; Carpenter, R (2001) 'Making War More Lethal: Iroquois vs Huron in the Great Lakes Region', *Michigan Historical Review* 27 (2), 33–51.

not act in accordance with papal edicts. The international law that existed upon the topic, including repeated treaties between Muslim and Christian countries, concerned the return of fleeing slaves who were seeking refuge in other countries.[65]

Until the fifteenth century, there was a relatively stable, albeit declining, supply of slaves in Europe. This began to change as Portuguese explorers began to discover a world previously unknown to them, including the islands of Madeira (1419), the Azores (1427) and Cape Verde (1456). The economic and imperialistic possibilities of these new territories filled the explorers' dreams, whilst the possible theological benefits excited religious leaders. However, when it became apparent that many of the rulers in these new countries, especially on mainland Africa, were ardent traders and willing to exchange or sell many items, including other human beings (they themselves being all too familiar with the institution of slavery), questions began to be asked, especially as the scale of the sales quickly began to escalate. The profits to be made, at up to 500 per cent, were exceptional, even if the process of enslavement itself was heart-breaking. As Gomes Eannes de Azurara recorded of the sale of 235 people who been snatched from fishing villages around the Arguin Bank (off Mauritania) to be sold in Genoa:

> But what heart could be so hard as not to be pierced with piteous feeling to see that company [of African prisoners]? For some kept their heads low and their faces bathed in tears, looking upon one another; others stood groaning ... But to increase their suffering still more there now arrived those who had charge of the division of the captives, who began to separate one from another, in order to make an equal partition of the fifths; and then it was needful to part fathers from sons, husbands from wives, brothers from brothers.[66]

Pope Eugenius IV spoke out in 1434 about such matters, prohibiting the sale of (indigenous) Christian converts from the Canaries. Moreover, despite the earlier allowance of Pope Clement 80 years earlier for Portugal to colonise the Canaries, Eugenius now banned all European Christians from the Canaries as a protective measure for both the converted and the pagan inhabitants. Duarte, the King of Portugal, appealed against the ban, arguing that although there was bloodshed on the islands, the papal ban was halting his noble work for the spread of both Christianity and civilisation. The king emphasised that there was no monetary gain for him, and that the salvation of souls

[65] Davis, D (2006) *Inhuman Bondage* (Oxford, Oxford University Press) 48–49, 80, 82; Meltzer, M. (1993) *Slavery: A World History* (NYC, Da Capo) 123; Carlyle, A (1906) *A History of Medieval Political Theory in the West*, Vol II (London, Blackwood, London) 34–38, 117–22, 130–35; ibid, Vol V, 21–24. Also Capizzi, J (2002) 'The Children of God: Natural Slavery in the Thought of Aquinas and Vitoria', *Theological Studies* 63 (1), 31–50. For the English laws, see 'The Laws of Stephen', reproduced in Rosenwein, B (ed) (2006) *Reading the Middle Ages: Sources from Europe, Byzantium and the Islamic World* (Ontario, Broadview) 241; for the international treaties, see Arts 4 and 8 of the Treaty between Al-Manur and Michael VIII Palaiologus of Byzantium of 1281, as reproduced in Holt, P (1995) *Early Mamluk Diplomacy (1260–1290): Treaties of Baybars and Qalawin With Christian Rulers* (Leiden, Brill) 122. Also the 1478 Peace Agreement between Ottoman Sultan Mehmed II and the Signoria of Venice, as reproduced in Rosenwein, B (ed) (2006) *Reading the Middle Ages: Sources from Europe, Byzantium and the Islamic World* (Ontario, Broadview) 498; and the 1535 'Treaty of Amity and Commerce', as reproduced in Foreign Office (1855) *Treaties Between Turkey and Foreign Powers* (London, Foreign Office) 169–74.

[66] Gomes, as reprinted in Cohen, M (ed) (2004) *History in Quotations* (London, Cassell) 315.

was his primary goal. In light of such justification, Eugenius revoked his initial ban, as the overall aim trumped his earlier concerns.[67] The pontiffs who followed, such as Nicholas V, then settled the official position of the Church in Rome. Thus, in the case of Portugal:

> We grant you [Alfonso V, King of Portugal] … with our Apostolic Authority, full and free permission to invade, search out, capture and subjugate the Saracens and pagans and any other unbelievers and enemies of Christ wherever they may be … and to reduce their persons into perpetual slavery.[68]

The justification for this was that such acts would be pleasing to God, as they 'may bring the sheep divinely committed to him into the one fold of the Lord, and may acquire for them the reward of eternal happiness, and may obtain pardon for their souls'.[69]

The Portuguese then began to consolidate the slaving relationships into commercial monopolies between them and African rulers, to the exclusion of other European powers. The first treaty, with Gambia, was made in 1456. The Portuguese progressed down the west coast of Africa, establishing forts and trading posts over the following decades, before they reached the Congo in about 1490 and encountered the Bantu people. The Portuguese made an alliance with the Bantu to trade in slaves, in exchange for European merchandise and military benefits. By the year 1500, some 150,000 slaves had already been shipped out of West Africa in Portuguese vessels, with a caravel able to carry as many as 150 slaves, and a three-masted vessel holding as many as 400. Slave mortality on voyages, mostly from dehydration, averaged around 15 per cent. Slave rebellions occurred on approximately 10 per cent of all slave ships, usually when they were still near the coast of Africa.[70]

The only further restrictions on slavery occurred at the end of the fifteenth century, with the arrival of Christopher Columbus in the New World, when he promised the Spanish monarchs that his discoveries would give them gold, spices and 'as many slaves as they shall order'.[71] Soon afterwards, on his third voyage, Columbus had his men capture 900 of the local population after they had begun rebelling against his policies, transporting them for sale as slaves back in Europe: only one-third of those captured

---

[67] Meredith, M (2014) *The Fortunes of Africa* (NYC, Simon & Schuster) 94, 118–25; Davis, D (2006). *Inhuman Bondage* (Oxford, Oxford University Press) 94, 100–01; Parry, J (ed) (1968) *The European Reconnaissance* (NYC, Harper) 33–35.

[68] See 'The Beginning of the Slave Trade' in Worger, W (ed) (2010) *African and the West: A Documentary History*, Vol I (Oxford, Oxford University Press) 5–14; Hay, D (1996) *Europe in the Fourteenth and Fifteenth Centuries* (London, Longman) 78–79, 403.

[69] The bull of 1455, in Worger, W (ed) (2010) *African and the West: A Documentary History*, Vol I (Oxford, Oxford University Press) 15–17; Ehler, S (ed) *Church and State Thought Through the Centuries* (NYC, Brown) 146.

[70] The bull of Sixtus, as in Davenport, F (ed) (1917) *European Treaties Bearing on the History of the United States and its Dependencies to 1648* (NYC, Carnegie Institute) 49–55; Saunders, A (1982) 'Trade as War as a Reflection of Portuguese Ideology and Diplomatic Strategy in West Africa, 1441–1456', *Canadian Journal of History* 17 (2), 100–25; Davis, D (2006) *Inhuman Bondage* (Oxford, Oxford University Press) 93; Rivera, L (1992) *A Violent Evangelism* (Louisville, KY, John Knox Press) 202–04.

[71] Columbus, letter, as reproduced in Rivera, L (1992) *A Violent Evangelism* (Louisville, KY, John Knox Press) 94.

survived the voyage.[72] This practice was stopped (in theory, not in reality), not by the papacy, which continued to condone slavery, but when Queen Isabella sought to forbid the actual enslavement of her new subjects in the New World, as they were no longer to be considered foreigners with whom she was at war[73]

As the Spanish authorities were rationalising how they could possess the lands of non-Christians, and that they could not actually enslave them, they realised that they had to establish a system for dealing with the indigenous communities. The system that was developed was the *encomienda* (or *repartimiento*). This was not new. It had long existed in Spain in connection with territory taken from the Moors, and also in the Canaries, with territory taken from the indigenous population. But in New World the system was given a more precise definition and found more extensive use. An *encomienda* was a native village, or part of one, or a group of villages, 'commended' to the care of an individual Spaniard—an *encomendero*—whose duty it was to protect the inhabitants, to appoint and maintain missionary clergy in the village(s), and to undertake military defence of the province. For the benefits of Christianity, 'civilisation', defence and colonial development, *encomenderos* were entitled to levy tribute from the villages in their care. Originally, tribute took the form of food, clothing or unpaid labour. There was not meant to be any cession of land. The villages were not meant to be feudal manors, nor were they estates worked by slaves. In theory, the Indians were free and their rights over their land were unimpaired.[74]

The problem was that the *encomienda* system became indistinguishable from the slavery it was meant to abolish, and it provoked unrest. Bartholomew de las Casas witnessed this, having arrived in the New World as a soldier to the Spanish Crown in 1502. Over the following 10 years, Las Casas performed an about-face, became a priest and was then appointed by the Spanish authorities as 'Protector of Indians'. Las Casas was inspired by the Dominican Antonio de Montesinos, who preached that the indigenous people were as rational as the Spaniards, for which they should be equally respected. Las Casas advanced this argument in both the New World and back in Spain in his *Defence of the Indians*, which was based on the supposition that 99 per cent of all of the indigenous peoples in the New World were endowed with the same reason as non-Indians, possessed political societies and were thus not, by nature, slaves. Therefore, equal rights and benevolent instruction in the ways of Christianity, not forced labour, should be the preferred approach to governance.[75]

---

[72] Sale, K (2006) *Christopher Columbus and the Conquest of Paradise* (NYC, Tauris) 64–69, 92–95, 130–37, 154–57, 178; Williams, R (1990) *The American Indian in Western Legal Thought* (Oxford, Oxford University Press) 82–84; Meltzer, M (1993) *Slavery: A World History*, Vol II (NYC, Da Capo) 6–12.

[73] Acalos, H (2014) 'Pope Alexander VI, Slavery and Voluntary Subjection', *The Journal of Ecclesiastical History* 65 (4), 738–60; Stannard, D (1992). *American Holocaust: The Conquest of the New World* (Oxford, Oxford University Press) 69–75.

[74] Batchelder, R (2013) 'The Encomienda and the Optimizing Imperialist: Spanish Imperialism in the Americas', *Public Choice* 156 (1), 45–60; Kirkpatrick, F (1939) 'Repartimiento-Encomienda', *The Hispanic American Historical Review* 19 (3), 372–79.

[75] Lantigua, D (2015) 'The Freedom of the Gospel: Aquinas and the Spanish Wars of Religion', *Modern Theology* 31 (2), 312–37; Skinner, Q (1978) *The Foundations of Modern Political Thought*, Vol II (Cambridge, Cambridge University Press) 171.

The Spanish Government, unlike many of the Spanish colonialists, was not, prima facie, opposed to the views of Las Casas and the need to bring some humanity to its government in the New World. It did not like the idea of a powerful aristocracy being constructed around a large-scale system of slaves from the local communities; it did not like the slave revolts that kept happening; and it was conscious that slavery was helping to kill off the indigenous populations, with an average life expectancy of only three to four months for each indigenous slave. Manumission was possible from 1522, and all slavery of indigenous populations in Spanish territories was prohibited in 1530. Pope Paul III concurred, and in 1537 issued his bull *Sublimis Deus*:

> The Indians are truly men ... capable of understanding the catholic faith ... they desire exceedingly to receive it ... [T]he said Indians and all other people who may later be discovered by Christians, are by no means to be deprived of their liberty or the possession of their property, even though they be outside the faith of Jesus Christ; and that they may and should, freely and legitimately, enjoy their liberty and the possession of their property; nor should they be in any way enslaved; should the contrary happen it shall be null and of no effect.[76]

In 1542, Emperor Charles V reiterated that slavery of the Indians 'because of war or any other cause' was prohibited. Similarly, the *encomienda* system was banned in 1549, following decades of failed attempts at reforming it to make it more humane.[77] The difficulty the authorities faced in trying to outlaw the slavery of indigenous peoples and associated systems of forced labour, was that the colonists pointed out that they required large numbers of workers to be successful in their ventures. Accordingly, a different source of human labour had to be found. That source, due to a belief that some humans were more suited to hard labour than others—not to mention the vast profits to be made—was slaves from Africa. Taking slaves from Africa was seen as no different from enslaving others, especially Muslims, who were taken as prisoners in times of war. The first African slaves arrived in the region in 1501, but the first real shipment, with the cargo going directly from Africa to the Caribbean, did not occur until 1518, when Charles V, in one of his first major acts, licensed and approved the slave trade from Africa to the New World. By 1540, thousands were being shipped per year, with about 900,000 African slaves having landed in the Americas by the year 1600.[78]

Only a few scholars, such as Luis de Molina and Bartholomew de Albornoz, openly declared the trade in any human beings repugnant. Important Protestant scholars, like Martin Luther, did not object to it, whilst John Calvin was ambiguous. Bartholomew de las Casas, who had argued so strongly against the enslavement of indigenous people, did not object to the enslavement of Africans and their transportation to work in the New World. The European powers were only concerned to the extent that it did not

---

[76] Paul III in Hanke, L (1937) 'Paul III and the American Indians', *The Harvard Theological Review* 30 (2), 65, 72.

[77] Goetz, R (2016) 'Indian Slavery: An Atlantic and Hemispheric Problem', *History Compass* 14 (2), 59–70; Rivera, L (1992) *A Violent Evangelism* (Louisville, KY, John Knox Press) 9–10, 16–17, 112 and 190–95.

[78] Salzmann, A (2013) 'On the Enslavement of Muslims in Renaissance and Enlightenment Europe', *Religions* 4, 391–411; Russell-Wood, A (1998) *The Portuguese Empire, 1415–1808* (Baltimore, MD, Johns Hopkins University Press) 58, 114–15.

become a trade monopoly. Thus, Queen Elizabeth I was happy for Sir John Hawkins to engage in slavery from the 1560s, challenging the Spanish dominance in this market, and she went on to order the deportation of all black people from England.[79] Even as regards the continent from which the slaves were traded, powerful rulers of the day, such as the Congo ruler Alfonso I, were content to provide slaves for export, provided it was a well-regulated system that did not ensnare their own free citizens.[80]

This near consensus of opinion was clearly reflected by the leading jurists of the period, such as Pyerino Belli, Baltazar Ayala and Alberico Gentili, who could all confidently proclaim that slavery was perfectly legal. As Gentili would explain, 'I have no hesitation in saying that the condition of slavery is a just one. For it is a provision of the law of nations ... slavery is really in harmony with nature'.[81] The Catholic scholar Suarez would add, in 1614:

> It is manifest that a division of property is not opposed to natural law ... The same is true with respect to slavery... for the very same reason that the man is the *dominus* of his own liberty it is possible for him to sell or alienate the same.[82]

The Protestant scholar Hugo Grotius refined this abstract line of argument in 1625. His progressive starting point was as follows:

> There is equal injustice in the desire of reducing by force of arms any people to a state of servitude, under the pretext of its being the condition for which they are best qualified by Nature. It does not follow that, because they are fitted for a particular condition, another has a right to impose it upon him ...[83]

Despite coming to the conclusion that slavery was not in accordance with laws of nature, Grotius did believe it to be consistent with positive law, especially in terms of the taking and selling of prisoners of war (although not Christian ones).[84] This view, buttressed by his strong belief in the sanctity of contracts and private property, meant that slavery was, in his mind, legal. With such strong support, there was an absence of any Dutch voice speaking out against slavery before the middle of the seventeenth century. Indeed, even when the Dutch captured part of Brazil from the Portuguese, and

[79] Bartels, E (2006) 'Deportation, Discrimination and Elizabeth I', *Studies in English Literature* 46 (2), 1–10; Dixon, L (2007) 'The Nature of Black Presence in England before the Abolition of Slavery', *Black Theology* 5 (2), 171–83.

[80] King Alfonso I, 'Letter to the Portuguese King', as reproduced in Worger, W (ed) (2010) *African and the West: A Documentary History*, Vol I (Oxford, Oxford University Press) 24–25; Green, R (2013) 'Africans in Spanish Catholic Thought, 1568–1647', *Black Theology* 11 (1), 96–116; Heywood, L (2009) 'Slavery and its Transformation in the Kingdom of the Kongo', *The Journal of African History* 50 (1), 1–22; Davis, D (2006) *Inhuman Bondage*, Vol II (Oxford, Oxford University Press) 10–12, 92–93, 96.

[81] This quote from Gentili is from his book, *De jure belli*, book III, ix. See Van-der Molen, G (1930) *Alberico Gentili and the Development of International Law* (Amsterdam, Paris Printers) 144–45.

[82] Scott, J (ed) (1944) *Selections from Three Works of Francisco Suarez*, Vol II (Oxford, Clarendon Press) 278–79.

[83] Grotius, H (1624) *The Rights of War and Peace* (1905 reprint, London, Dunne) 270.

[84] Ibid, 345–46. Also Watson, A (1993) 'Seventeenth Century Jurists, Roman Law and the Law of Slavery', *Chicago-Kent Law Review* 68, 1343–53.

could have secured their conquest by promising freedom to the slaves, they refused to consider this as a viable option.[85]

That the greatest Dutch legal scholar came to this conclusion was fortuitous for the United Provinces, as although many other European countries (in addition to Spain and Portugal) came to engage in the slave trade, it was the Dutch who dominated it. That is, the slave trade became the principal source of profits for the Dutch West India Company, and after the 1648 Peace of Westphalia, the Dutch went on to dominate the supply of slaves to the Americas, selling 10 times as many slaves as the English.[86] The rapid increase in demand and supply of slaves to the New World in the first half of the seventeenth century was because of the advent of the plantation system, in which the new commodities of tobacco, cotton and/or sugar (especially from Brazil, Barbados and the Caribbean, and Virginia in North America) were shipped to Europe in unprecedented amounts. These commodities required large amounts of labour, to furnish which the colonists looked to, the European overlords approved, the compliant African authorities provided and the entrepreneurs shipped. Thus, countries like Brazil saw the importation from Africa of at least 200,000 slaves to work in the sugar cane fields between the years 1600 and 1650.[87]

In the English colonies on the east coast of North America, in both Massachusetts and New England, there were no large-scale plantations. Accordingly, mass importation of slaves did not eventuate in these parts, unlike in Virginia, with the first black slaves arriving in 1619. Despite this growth, there was an uneasiness in some of the new colonies with the way in which the matter was proceeding. This was most evident in connection with the enslavement of Indians taken in war, unlike slaves from Africa, because it was felt that the latter were different (compared to the Indians), and in many instances their slavery could be justified on theological and biological (racist) grounds, as being people who were suited to servitude.[88]

Even with slaves of African origin, questions began to be asked from the 1640s. These questions arose as the civil war raged in England, Scotland and Ireland, and issues of oppression, privilege and freedom in the lands being fought over—and the colonies—came to the fore. Given that many of the new colonists had arrived as bonded labour (that is, they had obtained their passage across the Atlantic in exchange for a number of years of strict service, or as some of the thousands of prisoners of war deported after Cromwell's victories), there was an empathy for others who were bonded either for set periods, or in perpetuity (as slaves). It was from these concerns that the first laws restricting slavery emerged in North America. Specifically, in 1641,

[85] Vink, M (2003) 'Dutch Slavery and Slave Trade in the Seventeenth Century', *Journal of World History* 14 (2), 131–77.

[86] Rowen, H (ed) (1972) *The Low Countries in Early Modern Times: Select Documents* (London, Macmillan) 170.

[87] Blackburn, R (1998) *The Making of New World Slavery* (London, Verso) 168, 170–92, 210–14.

[88] Guasco, M (2007) 'The Paradox of Indian Slavery in Early Anglo-America', *Journal of Social History* 41 (2), 389–411; Peabody, S (2004) 'Missionaries and Racial Discourse in the Seventeenth Century', *Journal of Social History* 38 (1), 113–26; Vaughan, A (1989) 'The Origins Debate: Slavery and Racism in Seventeenth Century Virginia', *The Virginia Magazine of History* 97 (3), 311–54.

the colonists in Massachusetts prohibited bond-slavery between its citizens; and as regards slaves brought in from outside, the 'liberties of Christian and Christian usage which the law of God establishes in Israel'[89] were to apply. The colonists of Rhode Island went furthest, stating that 'black mankind or white' were not to be held for more than 10 years in servitude, or beyond the age of 24 if they had been acquired before the age of 14.[90]

8. CONCLUSION

The causes of warfare in the New World were based, originally, on the assumption that these lands, occupied by indigenous peoples in another part of the world, no longer belonged to those peoples. That is because they had been gifted by the papacy to both Spain and Portugal. Aside from the massive material benefits that would accrue to both realms, the justifications for the ownership of and subsequent wars in these lands revolved around the benefits that Catholicism and associated European values would bring to the indigenous peoples. There was no debate about independence or equality between civilisations. Full and absolute surrender of all political power and the abandonment of existing cultural practices were required. The alternative was war, which was resorted to repeatedly, and which, with European diseases, destroyed indigenous populations in South, Central and North America. In time, the Catholic view softened, with a number of their most important scholars arguing that indigenous peoples' being pagan was not sufficient, in itself, to justify war against them. Rather, greater abominations, such as cannibalism or refusal to accord rights to trade or preach, offered sufficient justification to kill and wage war. Either way, by the time some serious reflection had been undertaken, the conquests had been achieved, or the wars, especially in South America, had transmuted into ongoing conflicts, the beginnings and ends of which were hard to disentangle.

When the English, French and Dutch entered into the business of colonisation, and especially once the Reformation was underway, their emphasis was more on the values of 'civilisation', trade and exchange, although a strong Christian, albeit Protestant, gloss remained. The difference between the Catholic and the Protestant colonialism was that the massive conquests of the Aztecs or the Incas, recorded by the Spanish, were not replicated in North America. In the north, in the early years, the colonists were not in any way dominant, and the colonies' existence was promoted by treating the indigenous peoples more as equals, with their own legitimate cultural systems. The only reason the colonists in North America survived was because the indigenous groups that they were dealing with were not homogeneous. Rather, they comprised a

---

[89] This quote is from Blackburn, R (1998) *The Making of New World Slavery* (London, Verso) 239.

[90] Donoghue, J (2010) 'The English Revolution and the Atlantic Origins of Abolition', *The American Historical Review* 115 (4), 943–74.

multitude of tribes, with which the different colonial groups would make alliances and assist in war and trade, either directly or indirectly.

In all instances in the Americas, the colonists realised relatively quickly that the differences between themselves and the indigenous peoples, either (now) as citizens under the same monarch or as enemies taken in war, were not sufficient to justify the enslavement of such peoples. However, the same thinking did not apply to peoples taken from Africa, enslavement of whom the vast majority of European religious, political and philosophical leaders agreed was lawful, as being in accordance with either the laws of nature, or the laws of commerce and private property.

XI

The Muslim World

1. Introduction

THE WARS INVOLVING Islam during the period covered by this book were complex, and different from those involving other parts of the world. The most noticeable difference was the failure of independent political institutions to emerge, as they did in Western and Central Europe. Within dynasties, internal struggles were most likely to end in fratricide, as different male siblings fought each other for ultimate power. Inter-Muslim warfare between Sunni regimes was predicated on a drive for dominance, but wrapped in justifications such as that one was not fulfilling its duties, such as persecuting heretics or protecting pilgrims, as a leader of the faith. In the wars between Ottoman (Sunni) and Safavid (Shia) Iran, conflicts were commonly based on assertions that the other was a heretic, on restriction of movement and/or persecution of the faith of one in the territory of another, and/or fluid borders where local powers would commonly switch sides.

Muslim wars with Christian forces were much less nuanced. The causes for war, glossing over the underlying momentum and continual rhetoric of religion, were typically about the inability to control border areas, especially when local rulers were willing to swap allegiance from one side to another, often in exchange for greater degrees of autonomy, in religious and/or economic terms. Alternatively, the catalyst would be local forces' being blamed for attacks on the territory, people and/or commercial trade of the other. This was the pattern in Eastern Europe, the Western Mediterranean and North Africa, with the clear trend in all three areas being the advance of Muslim forces. These rapid advances, in part, were the catalyst for the decision of the new unified authorities in Spain to progressively remove any independent Muslim areas, and eventually peoples, from the areas they controlled.

2. Inter-Family Wars and Coups

Inter-family wars within Islam between 1400 and 1650 were primarily related to dynastic succession (as they were occasionally within the Mughal Empire, where sons tried to usurp their fathers' thrones, as did the occasional pretender) where there was more than one son to potentially inherit a throne, as a result of which violence was likely to ensue. As the Ottoman Sultan Mehmed II suggested in 1481, it was to be expected that his two sons, Bayezid II and Djem, would try to kill each other, 'for the sake of the good order of the world'.[1]

In this world there could only be one Sultan, with no competition for the throne. If there was competition, the stability of the Ottoman Empire would be at risk, such as occurred when one brother (Djem) fled for asylum to enemies of the Ottomans in Christian Europe, who put him forward as a pretender to the throne, thus holding further Ottoman expansion under Sultan Bayezid II in check.[2] In another instance, Sultan Ahmed I had decided not to execute his mentally impaired younger brother, Mustafa, but when Ahmed's son Osman was made Sultan and the Janissaries (the elite troops who formed the Sultan's personal guard) came into conflict with him (over a peace treaty made with Poland and challenges to their executive status), the Janissaries committed the first act of regicide in Ottoman history, putting the mentally impaired Mustafa on the throne in Osman's place before deciding that, as Mustafa was too damaged to rule, Osman's younger brother, Murad, would make a better leader. Once in power, Murad IV was determined not to make the same mistake, having his remaining three brothers executed, galvanising religious orthodoxy, and purging all and any within his administration whom he considered untrustworthy.[3]

In ideal situations, the inter-sibling killings would be effected quickly, with little collateral damage, such as when Sultan Mehmed III came to the throne in 1595, obtained the support he needed from the Janissaries and then ordered the execution of all of his 19 brothers. In less than ideal situations, opposing brothers would muster entire armies and battle each other for supremacy. This was most evident following the death of Sultan Bayezid I, when his five sons went to war against each other for eight years, before Sultan Mehmed I was victorious at the Battle of Camurlu in 1413, in which some 17,000 men clashed, with his opposing brother ending up being strangled. Mehmed then had to pursue one of his other brothers, who was eventually captured and then executed, on the orders of his nephew, in 1422.[4]

The second regicide within the period covered by this book occurred in 1648, when Sultan Ibrahim, another of Ahmed I's sons, took the throne after Murad IV failed to produce any heirs. This coup, highly reminiscent of the actions of the Praetorian Guard in ancient Rome, where the military controlled the ruler, saw the execution of

---

[1] As in Finkel, C (2005) *Osman's Dream: The History of the Ottoman Empire* (NYC, Basic) 71, and at 27, 165, 213; Parker, G (2013) *Global Crisis: War, Climate and Catastrophe in the Seventeenth Century* (New Haven, CT, Yale University Press) 47.

[2] Metin, K (2003) 'Sultan, Dynasty and State in the Ottoman Empire', *The Medieval History Journal* 6 (2), 217–23.

[3] Yasaroglu, H (2013) 'A Coup in the Ottoman Empire', *International Perioical for the Language, Literature and History of Turkey* 8 (7), 705–32; Baer, M (2008) 'Manliness, Male Virtue and History Writing at the Seventeenth Century Ottoman Court', *Gender and History* 20 (1), 128–48; Kinross, L (1976) *The Ottoman Centuries* (NYC, Quil) 191, 294, 305.

[4] Salgirli, S (2012) 'The Rebellion of 1416: Recontextualising an Ottoman Social Movement', *Journal of the Economic and Social History of the Orient* 55 (1), 32–77; Kastritsis, D (2007), 'Religious Affiliations and Political Alliances in the Ottoman Succession Wars of 1402–1413', *Medieval Encounters* 13 (2), 222–42; Flores, J (2004) 'The Shadow Sultan and Imposture in the Mughal Empire, 1628–1640', *Journal of the Economic and Social History of the Orient* 47 (1), 80–121.

Sultan Ibrahim after he refused the demands of the Janissaries and armed forces for the suppression of the sale of offices, the removal of favourites of the Sultana and the execution of the Grand Vizier. When they went to the Sultana, Ibrahim's mother, telling her that they wished to enthrone her other son, she was told that the jurists agreed that Ibrahim could be dethroned. The Grand Mufti explained to the Sultan, 'You are no longer [sultan], since you trample on justice and holiness and have ruined the world. You have wasted your years in play and debauchery; you have squandered the treasures of your Empire on vanities; corruption and cruelty have governed the world in your place'.[5] Thereafter, Sultan Ibrahim was executed, and his son, the seven-year-old Mehmed IV, was made Sultan of the Ottoman Empire.

3. Inter-Islam Wars: Sunni v Sunni

The first instance of inter-Muslim warfare in the period covered by this book, following on from his conquests against fellow Muslims at the end of the fourteenth century, involved the Sunni Muslim, Timur.[6] At the beginning of the fifteenth century, after the Mamluks had submitted to Timur's authority and agreed to be his vassals, the only remaining Muslim superpower was the Ottomans. Timur waged war against these fellow Sunni Muslims because they gave sanctuary to a rebellious Turkmen chief who had fled Timur's grasp, they would not hand over a castle in a region disputed between the two empires, and Sultan Bayezid I would not accept that Timur was the superior Muslim ruler. Timur's threat of 'the thunder of vengeance'[7] if Bayezid did not comply with his demands was answered by Bayezid in a letter that not only refused to fulfil Timur's requests, it also included both personal and diplomatic insults, Bayezid inscribing his own name in large letters of gold, with Timur's name written beneath it in small black letters. The resulting Battle of Ankara in 1402 saw Timur's army of 140,000 (including a number of disaffected emirs who resented Ottoman rule) destroy his opponent's force of some 85,000 men (including some Serbian vassals), with perhaps 30,000 men being killed on the field. Bayezid I was outmanoeuvered, outgeneraled, outfought and captured, and spent his last year of life, allegedly, being carried around in a specially built cage until he died in 1403. Thereafter, the Ottomans agreed to be vassals of Timur, settling all disputes with him, providing the people, tribute and territory he desired. Dispossessed local princes had their land returned to them by Timur, and Smyrna, the last Christian stronghold in the region, was captured after a mere two weeks of siege.[8]

Two years later, in early 1405, the most powerful man in the world, Timur, now in his mid-seventies, set off with 200,000 soldiers on what was to be his final campaign—the

[5] The Grand Mufti, in Kinross, L (1976) *The Ottoman Centuries* (NYC, Quil) 317.

[6] Gillespie, A (2017) *The Causes of War*, Vol 2: *1000 CE to 1400 CE* (Oxford, Hart Publishing) 224-227.

[7] Letter of Timur, in Kinross, L (1976) *The Ottoman Centuries* (NYC, Quil) 73.

[8] Milright, M (2011) 'Bayezid's Cage: A Re-examination of a Venerable Academic Controversy', *Journal of the Royal Asiatic Society* 21 (3), 239–60; Grant, R (2011) *1001 Battles* (London, Penguin) 213; Kinross, L (1976) *The Ottoman Centuries* (NYC, Quil) 73.

conquest of China. His goal, to 'perform some good action which may atone for the crimes of my past life' by making 'war on the infidels and exterminate[ing] the idolaters of China',[9] was never achieved, as a common cold progressed to a fever and Timur died. The massive empire achieved by Timur then quickly dissolved, as quarrels, coups and palace revolutions, backed by a tidal wave of resentment from all of the defeated populations, swept away everything Timur had achieved and new or original rulers reverted to their original positions.[10]

The second instance of inter-Muslim wars in which Sunni fought Sunni, involved Uzun Hasan. He was the leader of the Aq Qoyunlu, part of a Sunni tribal federation that ruled in present-day western Iran, Azerbaijan, Armenia, eastern Turkey and northern Iraq. Hasan was the grandson of the man appointed by Timur to rule the region, and through his own military acquisitions, he controlled almost as much land as the Ottomans. He put to death the last dynastic claimant from Timur in 1469, from which point he appeared to the world as the King of Persia. He then claimed to be the sole legitimate Islamic sovereign, suggesting that the Ottomans, and especially the Mamluks, were poor guardians of the Holy Places of Islam in Mecca and Medina, both of them failing to adequately protect the caravans sent on pilgrimage to these places. Therefore, warfare was justified. However, Hasan failed miserably in his quest for supremacy, defeated by joint Mamluk and Ottoman forces in 1472 at the eight-hour Battle of Erzinjan, after which Hasan fled. The Ottoman Sultan then spent three days on the battlefield, supervising the execution of prisoners. Hasan's territory was seized by the Ottomans and his son sought asylum at the Ottoman court, following which he married into the ruling family, thereby linking dynasties and providing a solid basis for his, and Ottoman, rule over the newly occupied territories.[11]

The third instance of inter-Muslim conflict in the period discussed in this book concerns the wars between the Sunni Ottomans and the Sunni Mamluks. The difficulties began when the remnants of Uzun Hasan's forces fled to the Taurus Mountains. This enemy was hard to pursue, because the Mamluks claimed a type of jurisdiction over the area. Eventually, the Ottomans crossed the border shared with the Mamluks in 1478, asserting that it was necessary to do because the area was lawless. Six years of inconclusive warfare followed, before the Mamluks were recognised as being the possessors of the disputed territory, but the revenues of the region had to be devoted to the sanctuaries and the protection of pilgrims going to Mecca and Medina. This treaty with the Mamluks, confirmed in 1490, also set the other boundaries between the two Sunni giants, especially since some of the territories, like Cyprus, which had been paying tribute to the Mamluks, had ended up being conquered by the Ottomans.[12]

---

[9] Timur, as noted in Marozzi, J (2005) *Tamerlane* (NYC, Harper) 347.

[10] Manz, B (2016) 'The Empire of Tamerlane as an Adaptation of the Mongol Empire', *Journal of the Royal Asiatic Society* 26 (1), 281–91; Gilmore, M (1952) *The World of Humanism* (NYC, Harper) 32.

[11] Melvin, M (2011) 'The Delicate Art of Aggression: Uzun Hasan', *Iranian Studies* 44 (2), 193–214; Grousset, R (2010) *The Empire of the Steppes* (New Brunswick, NJ, Rutgers University Press) 416, 465–68; Kinross, L (1976) *The Ottoman Centuries* (NYC, Quil) 133–34.

[12] Finkel, C (2005) *Osman's Dream: The History of the Ottoman Empire* (NYC, Basic) 64–66, 90, 108, 110–12, 119, 248.

Peace did not last. The spark came in 1512, when Sultan Selim I promised the locals in Albistan (in modern-day southern Turkey), who were estranged from the Mamluk regime due to high taxes and poorly controlled Mamluk soldiers, large degrees of autonomy. When the Mamluks demanded the return of this territory, Selim responded by saying that these demands gave him no choice but to invade Syria. It was added that although the Mamluks were not heretics themselves, because they had aided heretics (the Safavids, see below) in their fight against the Ottomans, they had lost any right to immunity that they may have had as Sunni Muslims. In the battle that followed, just outside of Aleppo in 1516, although the Ottomans lost 25,000 men, the Mamluks lost 65,000. Damascus and Jerusalem surrendered without a fight. Further battles outside Gaza and Cairo, in 1517, confirmed the conclusion that the gunpowder weapons of the Ottomans would always trump the bravery of the opposition. The final Mamluk leader, Tuman Bay II, was defeated in a battle near the Pyramids, captured and then executed. Cairo then surrendered, but was sacked without pity for four days as a reward for the soldiers. Baghdad, Medina and Mecca were occupied with minimal violence, after which the Abbasid Caliph swore allegiance to Sultan Selim and identified him as the rightful Sultan of the faithful. An Ottoman governor was then put in place to rule over Baghdad, whilst the Caliph was transferred to Istanbul, along with the relics of Muhammad, most notably his standard and cloak. The Sharif of Mecca recognised Selim as the defender of the Holy Cities of Mecca and Medina. With all of these titles, Sultan Selim could proclaim himself as the most powerful ruler in Islam.[13]

The fourth example of inter-Muslim (Sunni versus Sunni, and Sunni versus all others) warfare in this era involved India. At the turn of the fifteenth century, this geographical region was very complex. For example, at the top of modern-day India, Gurajat declared independence in 1407, as did Jaunpur in 1408. Several Rajput kingdoms appeared in Rajasthan, as the Sultanate of Delhi was in a continual process of political disintegration, struggling to maintain control, slipping between competing dynasties and locations, with divergent allegiances, such as the Sultanates of Gujarat and of Bijapur. The fragmented nature of India began to change when the forces of Zahir-ur din Muhammad Babur started to eye northern India. Babur, who was originally a refugee due to the actions of a coalition of Shia Safavids and Sunni Uzbegs (a Sunni-based confederation that had appeared in the wake of the collapse of Timur's regime and established control over Central Asia), took the title of *Ghazi* ('Warrior') and announced, 'for the sake of Islam I became a wanderer; I battled infidels and Hindus. Thank God I determined to become a holy warrior'.[14] Although Babur could not defeat the Uzbegs, and the two Sunni opponents spent their time insulting each other (the Uzbegs being called usurpers and Babur a heretic for his tolerance of non-Muslims), with occasional forays into each other's territories, he was able to make military progress in India. With the help of gunpowder and military reorganisation,

---

[13] Hodgson M (1974) *The Venture of Islam*, Vol II (Chicago, IL, Chicago University Press) 279–80; and ibid, Vol III, 20–25, 31, 35–40, 62–77, 104–09. Also Hess, A (1973) 'The Ottoman Conquest of Egypt', *The International Journal of Middle East Studies* 4 (1), 55–76; Grant, R (2011) *1001 Battles* (London, Penguin) 248.

[14] Babur, as noted in Gommans, J (2002) *Mughal Warfare* (London, Routledge) 46.

Babur managed to defeat significantly larger armies in Kabul in 1504 and the Delhi Sultanate in 1526, and then overcome a confederacy of Rajput kings at Kanua in 1527. His military prowess was buttressed by his political wisdom, as a result of which, although he cast himself as a Holy Warrior, he tried to govern his realm without 'religious bigotry', all faiths being protected, as 'the progress of Islam is better with the sword of kindness, not the sword of oppression'.[15]

Following the wars of his son, Humayun, Babur's grandson, Akbar, continued the Muslim conquests of India, ending the independent existence of the southern states and destroying the Hindu Vijayanagar kingdom in 1564, after striking with an army reportedly numbering hundreds of thousands of soldiers, when the kingdom was weakened by a succession struggle. He then conquered Gujarat in 1574, Bengal in 1576, and then Bihar and Orissa. When his half-brother Hakim died in 1585, Akbar's forces seized Kabul, advancing to the Hindu Kush, before agreeing with the Uzbeg monarch in 1587 that Hindustan would be the boundary between the Mughal and Uzbeg dominions. Like his grandfather before him, Akbar moved away from persecution of non-Sunni Muslims to a more tolerant regime, whereby if local authorities supported him both militarily and economically (ie in terms of levying taxes), they and their customs would be left in place (though not if they involved child marriage, forced conversion or *suttee*, ie the ritual burning of a wife on the death of her husband). This meant that Shia, Hindu, Jains and even Portuguese Catholics from Goa were not only all invited to Akbar's Hall of Worship to engage in public debates about the merits of their beliefs, they were also allowed to pursue their own religious practices. The revolt by orthodox Sunni in Mughal India caused by this tolerant approach had to be crushed with force. Akbar then made the rebels sign a declaration that they would repudiate the bonds of orthodox Islam and worship Allah directly, without intermediaries. In addition, whenever there were religious disputes (on which he would have the final word), he encouraged the opponents to debate the matters in public, rather than prohibit them as heretics.[16]

4. Inter-Islam Wars: Sunni v Shia

The wars between the Sunni and the Shia were most frequent, in the period covered by this book, following the rise of the Shia Safavids. The Safavids laid the foundations

---

[15] Babur, as noted in Black, A (2011) *The History of Islamic Political Thought* (Edinburgh, Edinburgh University Press) 240–41 and at 147, 163, 244, 256; Roy, K (2012) 'A Comparative Study of the Military Transition in the Mughal, Ottoman and Safavid Empires', *International Area Studies Review* 15 (2), 99–121; Grant, RG (2005) *Battle: 5000 Years of Combat* (London, DK) 136.

[16] Audrey, T (2015) 'Jain Responses to Theological Challenges at the Mughal Court', *Modern Asian Studies* 49 (5), 1311–44; Truschke, A (2012) 'A Sanskrit Vision of Mughal Conquests', *South Asian History and Culture* 3 (3), 373–96; Anooshshr, A (2006) 'Mughal Historians and the Memory of the Islamic Conquest of India', *The Indian Economic and Social History Review* 43 (3), 275–300; Talbot, C (2012) 'A Rajput Perspective on the Age of Akbar', *Journal of the Economic and Social History of the Orient* 55, 329–68; Farooqi, N (2004) 'Diplomacy and Procedure Under the Mughals', *The Medieval History Journal* 7 (1), 59, 64; Kulke, H (1996) *A History of India* (London, Routledge) 182, 200–02; Farooqi, N (1996) 'Six Ottoman Documents on Mughal-Ottoman Relations During the Reign of Akbar', *Journal of Islamic Studies* 7 (1), 32–48.

of modern Iran, taking control of the historic core of Persia. The Akkoynlu (White Sheep) dynasty, which was loyal to the Ottomans, was overthrown by Ismail I, who proclaimed himself Shah of Persia while still a teenager, after taking Tabriz in 1501. Ismail claimed direct descent from Mohammad's son-in-law, Ali, and thus leadership of the Shia faith. In so doing, Ismail mixed Sufi mysticism, conservative Shia Twelver philosophy, personal ambition and dynastic foundations, to cast himself as the legitimate spiritual leader of the entire global community. In Ismail's world, religious affiliation was a clear and inexorable marker of identity and status. Non-Muslims, such as Jews, Christians and Zoroastrians, were subject to frequent persecutions and, at times, forced to convert. Muslims of different denominations were threatened with Holy War. Western Iran was then secured, while the Uzbegs were defeated in the east after Khan Shaybani, the grandson of Genghis Khan, called upon Ismail to abjure the Shiite heresy and then attempted to invade, 'to convert him by the sword'.[17] Ismail repelled this invasion and then advanced to Merv in Turkmenistan, where the city, Shaybani and his army were destroyed. Most of what is modern-day Iran had been unified by 1509. Twelver Shiism was imposed as the official religion, which all subjects were obliged to profess within the Safavid theocratic state. Ismail warned his citizens that if they spoke against his theocratic rule, 'if the people utter one word of protest, I will draw the sword and leave not one of them alive'.[18]

Ismail continued to teach that the Sunni and Sufi faiths were mistaken, and then began to persecute these rival denominations when he found them within his realm and on his borders. The Ottomans did not take his words or actions lightly. The Ottomans had created a state-controlled religious system that closely supervised all forms of Islam, in which they claimed to be the sole repository of the 'right religion' for all Muslims. This system established a conservative religious body known as *Seykulislam*, which obtained its power by backing the absolute and dynastic regime of the ruling Ottoman Sultan. This group nearly always provided the theological arguments that the Sultan required to support his case. Thus, Fadl Allah Ibn Ruzbihan Khunji argued for Holy War against Ismail I and his Safavid state, because the Safavids were:

> unbelievers and heretics. Any who sympathise with them and accept their false religion or assist them are also unbelievers and heretics. It is a necessity and a divine obligation that they be massacred and their communities be dispersed.[19]

---

[17] Shaybani, as noted in Grousset, R (2010) *The Empire of the Steppes* (New Brunswick, NJ, Rutgers University Press) 483; Farhat, M (2013) 'Shi'i Piety and Dynastic Legitimacy', *Iranian Studies* 47 (2), 201–16; Savory, R (2003) 'Relations Between the Safavid State and its Non-Muslim Minorities', *Islam and Christian-Muslim Relations* 14 (4), 435, 440–46.

[18] Ismail, as noted in Black, A (2011) *The History of Islamic Political Thought* (Edinburgh, Edinburgh University Press) 233–34 and at 187–91, 202–05, 208–09; Matthee, R (2010) 'Was Safavid Iran an Empire?', *Journal of the Economic and Social History of the Orient* 53 (1), 233–65; Ashtiani, A (1989) 'Cultural Formation in a Theocratic State: The Institutionalization of Shiism in Safavid Iran', *Social Compass* 36 (4), 481–92.

[19] As in Finkel, C (2005) *Osman's Dream: The History of the Ottoman Empire* (NYC, Basic) 104 and at 97, 142–43, 172; Kunt, M (2003) 'Sultan, Dynasty and State in the Ottoman Empire: Political Institutions in the Sixteenth Century', *The Medieval History Journal* 6 (2), 217–30.

Tensions continued to rise as non-conforming Safavid followers were exiled from Ottoman territories or punished. Restrictions on travel to either Persia or the holy sites followed. When Ismail I began advocating for Ottoman citizens to rebel, (and called for the Ottomans to allow freedom of travel for the Shia from Iran), Sultan Bayezid wrote to Ismaíl (in 1504) warning him that good relations between the two regimes would be threatened if the persecution of Sunnis did not stop. Ismail did not stop. Rather, he sought (without success) to forge military alliances with the European powers against which the Ottomans were fighting, harboured pretenders to the Ottoman throne and supported further rebellions in the Ottoman territories. By 1508 the forces of Ismail had reached what is modern day Iraq. He was hailed as the Shah of that land, as the 'Shadow of God on Earth'[20] when he occupied Baghdad in 1510. He then proceeded to order the levelling of the tombs of Sunni saints in the city, as well as executing some of the city's leading Sunni figures. Ismail went on to send some gifts, consisting of a gold staff and a saddle, to Selim I, the new Sultan of the Ottoman Empire. In doing so, indirectly referencing the history of the Persian, as opposed to the Turkish, legacies, he warned:

> Ismail, great Sovereign of the Persians, sends to you Selim these gifts, quite equal to your greatness, as they are worth as much as our kingdom; if you are a brave man keep them well, because I will come and take them from you, together with your head and kingdom, which you possess against all right, as it is not proper that the offspring of peasants should bear rule over so many provinces.[21]

Regional authorities, in theory within the domain of the Ottomans in Anatolia, then attempted to break free from Istanbul, in revolts based on a combination of regional independence and Safavid teachings. The final spark for war was the new governor of Baghdad's act in offering submission to the Ottomans, rather than to the Safavids. Before Ottoman forces could come to his aid, he was murdered. This was all too much for the Sultan: Selim sent an army across Anatolia, which killed or imprisoned an alleged 40,000 adherents to the Shia faith, and preached a holy war against his Shia neighbours. Ismaíl responded by fielding 50,000 men and meeting Selim at the Battle of Chaldiran in 1514. Ismail was outnumbered and lost at least 10,000 men before fleeing the field. Although Selim pursued his opponent, the Ottoman troops refused to winter in the east, and so the Sultan returned to Constantinople.[22]

The Safavid Empire was saved because Selim turned his attention to the Mamluks, and the Safavids stayed neutral in that conflict. Their neutrality brought them an initial

---

[20] Rogerson, B (2010) *The Last Crusaders* (London, Abacus) 64, 67, 109, 175, 180–83; Barkey, K (2005) 'Islam and Toleration: Studying the Ottoman Imperial Model', *International Journal of Politics, Culture and Society* 19 (1), 5–19; Murphey, R (1999) *Ottoman Warfare: 1500–1700* (New Brunswick, NJ, Rutgers University Press) 14–18; Grant, R (2011) *1001 Battles* (London, Penguin) 246, 265.

[21] Ismail, in Marozzi, J (2015) *Baghdad: City of Peace, City of Blood* (Penguin, London) 175; Rahimi, B (2004) 'Between Chieftaincy and Knighthood: A Study of Ottoman and Safavid Origins', *Thesis Eleven* 76 (1), 85–102.

[22] Matthee, R (2015) 'Relations Between the Center and the Periphery in Safavid Iran: The Western Borderlands and the Eastern Frontier Zone', *The Historian* 17, 432, 445–45; Grant, RG (2005) *Battle: 5000 Years of Combat* (London, DK) 129, 524.

peace agreement with the Ottomans in 1530, under which the broad frontier between the two empires was agreed (and continues to define the modern-day border between Turkey and Iran). However, dynastic infighting following the death of Ismail proved too much of an opportunity for the Ottomans, who took advantage of the divisions within the Safavid world to support opposing factions, expel Shia merchants in the Ottoman territories and kill thousands of other Safavid sympathisers/heretics. The Ottomans then invaded the Safavid Empire in 1531, taking Bitlis and Tabriz (the Safavid capital) in 1532, and Baghdad in 1534. Despite these conquests, the Persians could not be subdued, and a further two decades of intermittent warfare followed.

A. The Treaty of Amasya

The opposing Muslim forces decided to stop killing each other in 1555, when the *Treaty of Amasya* was agreed between the two sides. This placed Baghdad and much of Mesopotamia in the Ottoman zone, and Azerbaijan in the Safavid realm, along with Tabriz, which was returned. Armenia and Georgia were divided equally between the two Muslim powers. The Ottomans also gave permission for Safavid subjects to visit the holy places of Mecca and Medina, as well as important Shia sites in Iraq. In exchange, the Safavids agreed to stop making inflammatory remarks around doctrinal matters, especially if preaching in Ottoman territories. Failure to comply could result in execution.[23]

The strength of the 1555 peace was displayed in 1561 when the Safavid authorities, for a large amount of gold, agreed to kill one of Sultan Sulieman's sons who had sought asylum with them, rather than keeping him as a pawn in the forthcoming succession challenge. However, when a Safavid succession dispute erupted in the 1570s, disgruntled vassals in the border zones, such as Georgia, restamped their authority over Anatolia and reoccupied Tiblis, as did the Uzbegs, plundering Khurasan. After declaring that the Safavid Shia were enemies of the true faith, the Ottomans also invaded. The invasion only stopped when Shah Abbas I regained control of the Safavid realm and agreed a peace with the Ottomans, under which he promised to stop his religious leaders cursing Sunni beliefs and established a border further to the east and north, ceding territories in Azerbaijan, Gangja, Georgia and Kurdistan. This peace allowed him to concentrate on ejecting the Uzbegs from Khurasan. In an attempt to strengthen the Safavid Empire, Shah Abbas began treaty relations pertaining to trade with European countries such as Russia, England and the Netherlands. He also became a little more tolerant (apart from the attempted forcible conversion of Christians in 1621) in his approach to non-Muslims.[24]

[23]   Stewart, D (2008) 'The Ottoman Execution of Zayn al-Din al-Amili', *Die Welt des Islams* 48, 289–347; Nabil, A (2007) 'Ottoman Iraq', *Journal of the Historical Society* 7 (2), 201–11; Panaite, V (2000) *The Ottoman Law of War and Peace* (NYC, Columbia University Press) 92.
[24]   Matthee, R (2014) 'The Ottoman-Safavid War of 1578–90: Motives and Causes', *International Journal of Turkish Studies* 20 (1), 1–17; Stewart, D (2009) 'Polemics and Patronage in Safavid Iran', *Bulletin of SOAS* 72 (3), 425–57; Savory, R (2003) 'Relations Between the Safavid State and its Non-Muslim Minorities',

The peace broke towards the end of the sixteenth century, and Abbas pushed the boundaries of his realm back across the territories ceded to the Ottomans in the 1590s. Basra fell to independent local dynasts around the year 1600. The Safavids took Erivan in Armenia in late 1604, and the following year seized large parts of Azerbaijan. Peace was achieved again in 1612 with the *Treaty of Nasuh Pasha*, which ceded all the lands the Ottoman Empire had gained in the war of 1578–90 back to Persia and reinstated the 1555 boundaries. In addition, Persia would send 200 loads of silk, annually, to Constantinople. When the silk failed to turn up the following year, war broke out again, raging for the following three years, before the peace made in 1612 was reconfirmed. Fighting was renewed over the next decade, as multiple regional governors (such as in Yemen, Egypt, Lebanon and the Barbary states) began to assert independence from Istanbul. This became a problem in what is today southern Iraq, in particular in Baghdad.[25]

Baghdad became the subject of internal disputes from the first decade of the seventeenth century, as Ottoman-authorised rulers tried to claim independence. Initially, Istanbul could bring these insurrections under control, until, in the 1620s, a further attempt by a Janissary captain resulted in his appealing to the Safavids for help, promising that they could be overlords, of which Shah Abbas was prepared to consider. When the Safavids arrived in Baghdad, the Sunni Muslims within the city were subject to fierce persecution. Sultan Murad IV was determined to reverse this trend of Safavid conquests, which he saws as the acts of heretics stealing his property. Although his forces could not hold Tabriz or Erivan, over the following 15 years the situation was slowly reversed, and in 1638, his forces took back Baghdad in a conflict that saw acts of extreme violence. Following the recapture of Baghdad, both the Safavids and the Ottomans came to terms in 1639 with the *Peace of Zuhab*, which 'dispelled the darkness of war and fighting with the light of quiet and happiness'.[26] The essence of the agreement was that Erivan and the adjacent territories would remain under Persian control, while Iraq was to be part of the Ottoman Empire. The resultant line dividing the Ottomans from the Safavids remains, largely intact, as the border between Iran and Iraq today.[27]

Islam and Christian-Muslim Relations 14 (4), 447–54; Floor, W (2000) 'Safavid Iran's Search for Silver and Gold', *International Journal for Middle Eastern Studies* 32, 345–68; Matthee, R (1994) 'Anti-Ottoman Politics and Transit Rights: The Trade in Silk', *Cahiers du Monde russe* 35 (4), 739–61; Elton, G (1968) *The New Cambridge Modern History: The Reformation*, Vol II (Cambridge, Cambridge University Press) 324–26, 510–12, 514–20, 524–32. The commercial treaties are in Hurewitz, J (ed) (1956) *Diplomacy in the Near and Middle East: A Documentary History* (Ottawa, Nostrand) 6–10, 15, 16, 18 and 20.

[25] Finkel, C (2005) *Osman's Dream: The History of the Ottoman Empire* (NYC, Basic) 210–13; Cooper, J (ed) (1970) *The New Cambridge Modern History: The Decline of Spain and the Thirty Years' War*, Vol IV (Cambridge, Cambridge University Press) 630.

[26] The 'Peace of Zuhab: Peace and Frontiers between the Ottoman Empire and Persia' in Hurewitz, J (ed) (1956) *Diplomacy in the Near and Middle East: A Documentary History* (Ottawa, Nostrand, 956) 21–23.

[27] Marozzi, J (2015) *Baghdad: City of Peace, City of Blood* (London, Penguin) 190–205; Murphey, R (1999) *Ottoman Warfare: 1500–1700* (New Brunswick, NJ, Rutgers University Press) 115–23; Kinross, L (1976) *The Ottoman Centuries* (NYC, Quil) 301.

5. MUSLIM AND CHRISTIAN WARS

A. The End of the Byzantine Empire

Sultan Murad II was only able to concentrate upon external enemies in 1422, after he had destroyed his family rivals for the throne of the Ottoman Empire. He would go on to personally lead 18 military campaigns, and direct a further 30. Although he fought continuously with the Turkish Emirates in Anatolia, it was in the West and the Balkans that his conquests were most expansive, where he alternated between truce and war with his multiple Christian enemies, including Venice, Genoa, Hungary and Byzantium. The process began when a treaty was made with Byzantium in 1424 after an unsuccessful siege of Constantinople was undertaken, after which the Emperor agreed to reinstate tribute and cede several pieces of Byzantine territory on the Black Sea, despite these areas having significant Orthodox populations. This deal was so humiliating that the Byzantine Emperor, Manuel II, then relinquished his position, seeking the solace of life as a monk in 1425, leaving his oldest son, John VIII, in charge of the once mighty Byzantine Empire, which was now reduced to Constantinople and its suburbs. Sultan Murad also made peace with Hungary in 1428, thereby ensuring that his next targets would get only limited assistance from outside. Macedonia was in the hands of the Ottomans in 1430, at the same time that the Venetian remnants in the Aegean, like Thessalonika (the capital of Greek Macedonia), were also being fought over. Venice could not hold the territories in dispute. The peace treaty of 1430 that followed recognised that Salonika no longer belonged to the Venetians, but they were allowed the right to trade throughout the Ottoman dominions, retaining without interference those islands and castles in the Peloponnese where they still had possessions.[28]

Sultan Mehmed II came to power in 1451. His primary goal was to capture Constantinople and destroy the Byzantine Empire. Constantinople was alienated from the West after attempts at theological reconciliation with Rome, although agreed at the Church Council in Florence in 1439 and endorsed by the Byzantine Emperor John VIII Palaiologos, were rejected (especially the idea that Rome would be superior on most theological matters) by the Orthodox authorities in Constantinople. Without this reconciliation, Pope Nicholas V could not agree to supply the substantial numbers of men or the arms needed for the defence of Constantinople.[29] Conversely, Mehmed II had no problems relating to theology and alliances. He ruled in a period when religious enthusiasm was running high, with Shia heretics being burned alive within his realm and calls for *jihad* ringing loudly. He justified his war against Byzantium in both

---

[28] Celik, N (2010) 'Black Sea and the Balkans under Ottoman Rule', *Karadeniz Arastirmalari* 6 (24), 1–27.

[29] Hibbert, C (1980) *The House of Medici* (NYC, Morrow) 67; Geanakoplos, D (1955) 'The Council of Florence and the Problem of Union Between the Greek and Latin Churches', *Church History: Studies in Christianity and Culture* 24 (4), 324–46; Norwich, J (2011) *Absolute Monarchs: A History of the Papacy* (London, Random) 240–44; Toews, J (1968) 'Formative Forces in the Pontificate of Nicholas V', *The Catholic Historical Review* 261–84.

religious (as a holy war against the infidels) and political terms (in that Byzantium often offered sanctuary to individuals fleeing the Ottomans). The spark he created was the execution of Byzantine envoys, who had come to complain about his building of a castle, just opposite Byzantine territory, that would secure him control of the Straits and provide him with a base for his projected siege of Constantinople. The last Emperor of Byzantium, Constantine XI, then wrote to the Sultan:

> As it is clear that you desire war more than peace, since I cannot satisfy you either by my protestations or sincerity, or by my readiness to swear allegiance, so let it be according to your desire. I turn now and look to God alone. Should it be his will that the city be yours, where is he who will oppose it? If he should inspire you with a desire for peace, I shall be only too happy. However, I release you from all of your oaths and treaties with me, and, closing the gates of my capital, I will defend my people to the last drop of blood.[30]

Outside the city, somewhere between 50,000 and 200,000 soldiers assembled under the Ottoman banners, including some Christian vassals of the Sultan. Opposing them was a force of about 6,000 Christians, with only Venice and Genoa providing some naval support and a few extra men, as did the papacy at the last minute, supplying 200 archers to Constantinople. It was not enough. After a siege shortened by the largest cannon ever built, on 29 May 1453, the walls of Constantinople were breached and an empire that had lasted 1,123 years came to an end. The new name given to the conquered city was *Istanbul*: 'abounding with Islam'.[31] The vow of an imperial officer on the eve of the fall of Constantinople:—'I would rather see the Muslim turban in the midst of the city than the Latin mitre'[32]—was fulfilled. This was especially so when Sultan Mehmed, astutely, appointed the greatest adversary of the union between Greek Orthodoxy and the Latin papacy to be the new Orthodox Patriarch within Istanbul. Moreover, although subject to the Islamic state and having to pay tribute, within the Ottoman Empire the Orthodox community was free to worship as it always had done.[33]

B. The Eastern Mediterranean and the Adriatic

The Ottomans' advance was multifaceted and long-drawn-out. In the years covered by this volume, their conquests in the eastern Mediterranean and around the Adriatic began when Sultan Murad partly subdued Albania after King Sigismund died in 1437,

---

[30] Constantine IX, as noted in Kinross, L (1976) *The Ottoman Centuries* (NYC, Quil) 102 and at 85–90, 97–98; also Nicol, S (1995) 'The Immortal Emperor Constantine Palaiologos', *The English Historical Review* 110 (437), 193–214.

[31] Hussey, J (1967) *The Cambridge Medieval History. The Byzantine Empire*, Vol IV (II) (Cambridge, Cambridge University Press) 44–45; Gabriel, R (2005). *Empires at War*, Vol III (London, Greenwood) 1012–15; Grant, R (2011) *1001 Battles* (London, Penguin) 224 and 226.

[32] Noted in Hay, D (1996) *Europe in the Fourteenth and Fifteenth Centuries* (London, Longman) 268, 311.

[33] Barkey, K (2014) 'Political Legitimacy and Islam in the Ottoman Empire', *Philosophy and Social Criticism* 40 (4), 169–477; Runciman, S (1965) *The Fall of Constantinople 1453* (Cambridge, Cambridge University Press) 7–10.

although the conflict with Albania reawakened Balkan dreams of independence. A point of contention was with Serbia, which had offered to be a Hungarian vassal rather than an Ottoman one, promising to give up territory if it received protection from the Hungarians. When assured that such protection would be forthcoming, Serbia stopped providing troops and tribute to the Ottomans when demanded, in response to which Sultan Murad laid siege to Smederevo in 1439, a fortress he had previously allowed the Serbs to construct on the Danube. The fortress fell after a siege of three months. Belgrade in northern Serbia was next, but it withstood a siege of six months in 1440. Murad then continued to authorise strikes into Hungarian territory on the other bank of the Danube. At this point, with strong support from Pope Eugenius IV, a crusade was launched against the Ottomans, with Poland at the forefront. Although Genoa helped the Ottomans with transport, Byzantium and Albania stayed neutral in the conflict, so as not to offend their Ottoman overlords. Nonetheless, volunteers flocked to the banner of the Polish king, Wladyslaw III, after Pope Eugenius endorsed the crusade, and supported Wladyslaw in his claim to the throne of Hungary (which was at that point engaged in a civil war).[34] The forces commanded by Wladyslaw then forced the Ottomans out of northern Serbia in 1441, and then in 1443 they defeated them again outside Sofia in Bulgaria. A 10-year truce between the two sides was then agreed in 1444, with the *Treaty of Edrine* and the *Peace of Szeged*. By this truce, northern Serbia and Wallachia were effectively freed from dependence on the Ottoman Empire, while the Hungarians agreed not to cross the Danube or to press claims in Bulgaria. The treaty was then sworn on both the Koran and the Bible.[35]

Cardinal Julian Cesarini decided that this 10-year truce was worthless and should not be ratified. To stop the ratification, he convinced Ladislaus, the child King of Hungary (and one of the parties in the Hungarian civil war) that he was absolved from any obligation to be bound by the treaty, as a 'rash and sacrilegious oath to the enemies of Christ' was not binding. Julian then said that the treaty was abjured in the name of Christianity and all of its saints, and the king was recommended to 'follow in the path of glory and salvation'.[36] Having convinced Ladislaus of this, he then also persuaded the King of Poland, Wladyslaw III, and the nobleman John Hunyadi that the 10-year truce with the Ottomans was invalid. When the Turkish delegation arrived to ratify the agreement, they were insulted and sent home.[37]

According to legend, when the Christian army of 30,000 men got to Varna (on the Black Sea coast of modern Bulgaria), they faced Murad, who had affixed the breached *Treaty of Edrine* and the *Peace of Szeged* to a pole held prominently aloft in front of his soldiers, praying 'O God, give the religion of Islam strength and bestow victory on the

---

[34] See page 6.

[35] Thaddeus, T (1949) 'Eugenius IV and the Crusade of Varna', *The Catholic Historical Review* 35 (3), 257–75; Turnbull, S (2003) *The Ottoman Empire* (London, Osprey) 26–29, 30–34, 37–39; Hussey, J (ed) (1966) *The Cambridge Medieval History: The Byzantine Empire* Vol IV (Cambridge, Cambridge University Press) 378–86, 552–53.

[36] Cardinal Julian Cesarini, as noted in Kinross, L (1976) *The Ottoman Centuries* (NYC, Quil) 91.

[37] Davies, N (2005) *God's Playground: A History of Poland*, Vol I (Oxford, Oxford University Press) 128–29.

religion of Islam out of respect for the light of Muhammad'.[38] His prayers appear to have been answered, as there were heavy Christian casualties accounting for two-thirds of the men fielded (including Wladyslaw III), whilst the Ottoman force of 60,000 suffered smaller losses. The Ottoman success continued in 1446, when Murad progressed through Greece, which ended with all parts accepting vassal status. Finally, in 1448, some 24,000 Hungarians, Poles, Italians, German and Wallachians, again under the leadership of John Hunyadi, were destroyed on the battlefield of Kosovo. Sultan Mehmet II then offered generous terms to the defeated, to obtain their neutrality as he faced Byzantium for the last time.[39]

Soon after Constantinople fell in 1453, Sultan Mehmet II turned his attention back to the eastern Mediterranean and the Adriatic. The Ottoman juggernaut only came to a halt when the forces of John Hunyadi stopped the Ottomans from taking Belgrade in 1456, an encounter in which the Ottomans lost at least 40,000 men and where Sultan Mehmed was wounded and carried unconscious from the field. The magnitude of this victory was so great that Pope Callixtus was convinced a miracle had occurred. However, it was only a pause, not the end of the Ottoman threat, as when Mehmed recovered, he went on to overrun the other parts of independent Serbia, making them tributary provinces under the direct administration of Istanbul. Mehmed then took Athens and Corinth in 1458, with the latter capitulating after a three-month siege, as part of a war that saw all of the Peloponnese consumed by 1460. The armies of Mehmed reached the southern shores of the Black Sea in 1461, with Trebizond falling in the same year after a six-week siege. The Sultan then conquered Wallachia in 1462, after it had stopped paying tribute. Once secured, as a punishment for its disobedience, its payments increased to 20,000 gold pieces per year, as opposed to the original 2,000. Bosnia was fully occupied the following year, 1463.[40]

At the end of the fifteenth century, Mehmed's son, Sultan Bayezid, played divide and conquer with Poland and Hungary. Truces were made with Poland in 1489, 1492 and 1494. Keeping Poland neutral meant that Bayezid could then target Hungary, after their truce, which had been agreed in 1483, came to an end in 1491. When succession disputes arose after the death of Matthias Corvinus, King of Hungary, Croatia and Bohemia, and Duke of Austria, in 1490, Ottoman forces swarmed over the border. At the Battle of Villach alone, some 10,000 Muslim and 7,000 Christian soldiers were said to have been slain. Repeated attacks in 1494 saw most of the Croatian nobility destroyed at Adbina. Peace was restored in 1495, when Bayezid, worried by what his brother Djem, who had found asylum in Italy, was planning, concluded a new truce

[38] 'Varna' in Lewis, B (ed) (1987) *Islam: From the Prophet to the Capture of Constantinople*, Vol I (Oxford, Oxford University Press) 143.

[39] Finkel, C (2005) *Osman's Dream: The History of the Ottoman Empire* (NYC, Basic) 40–47; Gabriel, R (2005) *Empires at War*, Vol III (NYC, Greenwood) 992; DeVries, K (1999) 'The Lack of a Western European Response to the Ottoman Invasions of Eastern Europe From Nicopolis to Mohacs', *The Journal of Military History* 63 (3), 539–59.

[40] Sahin, K (2014) 'Constantinople and the End Time: The Ottoman Conquest as a Portent of the Last Hour', *Journal of Early Modern History* 14, 317–54; Nisbet, B (1892) 'The Siege of Belgrade by Muhammad II, 1456', *English Historical Review* 7, 303–33; Johnson, L (1996) *Central Europe: Enemies, Neighbours, Friends* (Oxford, Oxford University Press) 55–57.

with Hungary for three years (and again in 1510 and 1513). The Poles decided to fight the Ottomans alone in 1497, attacking Moldavia, which was now a vassal of the Sultan. The Ottomans struck back, invading Poland in 1498, but met with disaster during a winter in the Carpathians. No further attempt was made, after the Polish king made peace with the authorities in Moldavia.[41]

The attempted conquest of Hungary began anew in 1519, when a truce was agreed with the Poles, under which, for the price of peace, they agreed not to oppose the Ottomans in the latter's other wars. This helped smooth the way for the Sultan, Suleiman, to advance and conquer Belgrade in 1521. Five years later, in 1526, Suleiman personally led an army of perhaps 100,000 men, armed with 300 cannon, north of Belgrade and invaded Hungary. King Louis II of Hungary and Bohemia (husband to Mary, the sister of Emperor Charles V) met this force at Mohacs in 1526 with an army numbering 35,000 men from his realm, as well as volunteers from across Christian Europe. Before the battle, Suleiman prayed for assistance for this 'powerless body of Muslims'.[42] This 'powerless body' then killed the Hungarian king, 1,000 nobles, 500 magnates, 13 lords of the lands and 17,000 common soldiers. Suleiman then occupied central Hungary, with defenceless Buda falling soon after. With King Louis II dead on the battlefield and leaving no heir to succeed him, a succession crisis loomed in a country that was now divided into three parts: Royal Hungary, under the Habsburgs, with Ferdinand I (later Holy Roman Emperor) taking the throne; an Ottoman-controlled province based around Buda; and Transylvania, under its own prince but now an Ottoman-controlled tributary, of which Suleiman gave the crown to John Zapolya. Sultan Suleiman then attempted to advance even further, to take Vienna in 1529 and 1532. The initial attempt involved over 300 pieces of artillery and 120,000 Ottoman troops. These attempts were defeated by Ferdinand, the brother of the Holy Roman Emperor Charles V, who successfully defended the city with only 30,000 men and 72 cannon.[43]

After his withdrawal from Vienna, Sultan Suleiman concluded matters in Hungary. John Zapolya agreed in 1533 to be Suleiman's vassal, to pay an annual tribute to the Sultan, place at his disposal every 10 years a tenth of the population of his realm and grant, in perpetuity, free passage for Ottoman forces through his territory. Suleiman proclaimed:

> [T]his realm belongs to me and I have set therein my servant … I have given this kingdom, I can take it back from him, if I wish, for mine is the right to dispose of it and all the inhabitants, who are my subjects. Let Ferdinand, therefore, attempt nothing against it.[44]

[41] Housley, N (2014) 'Christendom's Bulwark: Croatian Identity and the Response to the Ottoman Advance', *Transactions of the Royal Historical Society* 24, 149–69; Munsen, R (2005) 'Leadership and Patronage on the Fifteenth Century Ottoman Frontier', *Eastern European Quarterly* 39 (3), 269–95.

[42] 'Speech of Suleiman before Mohacs' in Cohen, M (ed) (2004) *History in Quotations* (London, Cassell) 260.

[43] Erler, M (1987) 'Suleiman's 1532 Vienna Campaign', *The Slavonic and East European Review* 65 (1), 101–12; Turnbull, S (2003) *The Ottoman Empire* (London, Osprey) 46–47.

[44] Suleiman, as noted in Elton, G (1968) *The New Cambridge Modern History: The Reformation*, Vol II (Cambridge, Cambridge University Press) 347, 523, 532–33; Benedek, P (2003) 'Hungary Overrun', *Moreana*. 40 (156), 17–40; Johnson, L (1996) *Central Europe: Enemies, Neighbours, Friends* (Oxford, Oxford University Press) 75–80; Hay, D (1967) *The New Cambridge Modern History: The Renaissance*, Vol I (Cambridge, Cambridge University Press) 393–94, 398–402, 410–11.

With the division of Hungary and the principle of non-interference in the realms of the other agreed, Suleiman promised peace with Ferdinand 'not for seven years, for twenty-five years, for a hundred years, but for two centuries, three centuries, indeed for ever if Ferdinand does not break it'.[45] The problem was that Ferdinand did not want this deal but another, which he sealed with Zapolya in 1538 with the *Treaty of Nagyvarad*, for the future division of Hungary with Transylvania breaking free from its Ottoman overlord. However, at the time of Zapolya's death in 1540, Emperor Ferdinand did not have the resources to try to take what he wanted, and Zapolya's son, John II, became the *voivode* of Transylvania with the Ottomans' assent, promising to be a loyal vassal to his Muslim overlord. When Ferdinand did strike in 1541, trying to retake Buda, he failed, and then lost the cities of Pecs and Esztergom to Suleiman in 1543. The conflict only came to an end in 1547, when a further treaty agreed that western Hungary should go to Ferdinand in return for an annual tribute (of 30,000 Hungarian ducats), Transylvania would be an autonomous state under Ottoman rule, whilst a large part of southern Hungary was annexed by Suleiman as a tributary principality. This did not end the conflict, after Emperor Maximilian II seized a series of towns that were meant to be under Ottoman control. This gave Suleiman the justification he needed to advance upon, and take, Szigetvar in 1568. Following this victory, Suleiman and Maximilian agreed the *Treaty of Adrianople*. This peace saw Maximilian II promise to pay an annual 'present' of 30,000 ducats for some new areas, whilst the Ottomans retained authority in Moldavia and Wallachia.[46]

War resumed in 1593, when Austrian-Hungarian forces advanced to regain disputed territory. The Ottomans responded, checking the Christian forces at the Battle of Keresztes in 1596, after both sides fielded armies that may have numbered in excess of 100,000 men, the Austrian-Hungarian losing over 20,000. Despite the scale of the killing, peace was not settled between them, meaning that in the seventeenth century, Sultan Ahmed I inherited the ongoing tension with the Habsburgs, evidenced by border skirmishes and/or the efforts of disgruntled Christian communities under Ottoman control to seek greater autonomy. Battles were waged over forts and territories, before the Ottomans, between 1604 and 1606, recaptured Pest and Vac, and then, with the help of the Prince of Transylvania, Stephen Bocskay, took Esztergom in 1605. Peace was finally achieved with the 1606 *Peace of Zsitvatorok*, which signalled the end of Ottoman expansion in Europe.[47]

The mechanisms of peace allowed for greater autonomy for Christian communities in Hungary within the direct Ottoman sphere of control, greater autonomy for Transylvania in the areas under indirect Ottoman control and the stabilisation of the

---

[45] Suleiman, in Kinross, L (1976) *The Ottoman Centuries* (NYC, Quil) 195; also ibid, at 168, 188, 220, 234, 240, 259, 289.

[46] Curtis, B (2013) *The Habsburgs: The History of a Dynasty* (London, Bloomsbury) 70–72, 87–89; Panaite, V (2000) *The Ottoman Law of War and Peace* (NYC, Columbia University Press) 168–71.

[47] The 1606 *Peace of* Zsitvatorok, as reproduced in Foreign Office (1855) *Treaties Between Turkey and Foreign Powers* (London, Foreign Office) 1–7. The renewals of the treaty are found ibid, at 7, 12, 20, 23, 26, 31, 34 and 35.

border regions. In exchange, the Habsburg ruler agreed to keep paying the Ottoman Sultan an annual tribute of 30,000 ducats. Sultan Ahmed accepted these terms because of revolts occurring within the Ottoman Empire, which were sparked by the levying of increasingly high taxes to provision his wars. The peace was extended in 1608, 1615, 1625, 1627, 1642 and 1649. The Habsburgs kept renewing it because they were in the middle of the Thirty Years' War; and the Ottomans kept renewing it because they were entering into a period of unstable government and needed certainty on the borders with their largest enemy.[48]

Sultan Ahmed also established peace with the Poland-Lithuania Commonwealth in 1617. Here, the causes of the conflict were the Cossacks, who raided repeatedly around the Black Sea, and Sigismund III Vasa of Poland, who tried to intervene in the affairs of Moldavia. After a short conflict, the *Peace of Buzra* of 1617 was concluded, by which it was agreed that Poland was not to interfere in matters relating to the government of Moldavia, and that measures should be taken, by both sides, to control the incursions of either Cossacks or (Muslim) Tatars. This peace did not endure, for three reasons. First, frontier disputes over slave and cattle thefts between the Sultan's vassals, the Crimean Tatars and the Cossacks of the Ukraine continued unabated along the frontiers. Secondly, Gaspar Gratiani, the *voivode* of Moldavia, was deposed from office on the orders of the new sultan, Osman II, and then sought aid from the Polish king, Sigismund III. Thirdly, and most significantly, Bethlen Gabor, the Prince of Transylvania and vassal of the Ottoman Empire, had taken part in the 1618 Bohemian uprising, supporting the rebels and going so far to help the rebels in their short siege of Vienna. Gabor was happy to do this as he had a terrible relationship with the Habsburgs, who believed that they (the Habsburgs) had an inherent right to rule over all of Hungary, including Transylvania. Sigismund III Vasa, in reply, wanted to wage war against Gabor, but his *sjem* denied him the resources he required. Accordingly, he had to fight and defeat him with mercenaries paid for out of his own pocket. His defeat caused Gabor to appeal to the young Sultan Osman II, to find an opportunity to attack Poland. After four weeks of fighting, Osman II decided to end hostilities with Sigismund III, with the *Peace of Pologne* of 1621. This followed the Battle at Khotyn, where the Ottomans lost 45,000 men out of a force of perhaps 100,000, whilst some 13,000 Polish-Lithuanian soldiers were killed out of a force of perhaps 50,000. The peace that followed was a reaffirmation of the *Peace of Burza* of 1617, and a return to the status quo by which Poland swore to restrain the Cossacks from interfering in Ottoman Hungary or the Ottoman vassal states of Transylvania, Moldavia and Wallachia. Likewise, the Ottomans promised to stop the Tatars from threatening Polish lands.[49]

[48] Tracey, J (2013) 'The Road to Szigetvar: Ferdinand I's Defence of His Hungarian Border', *Austrian History Yearbook* 44, 17–36; Murphey, R (2001) 'Suleiman I and the Conquest of Hungary', *Journal of Early Modern History* 5 (3), 197–221; Cooper, J (ed) (1970) *The New Cambridge Modern History: The Decline of Spain and the Thirty Years' War*, Vol IV (Cambridge, Cambridge University Press) 283.

[49] The '1621 Treaty of Peace of Pologne', as reproduced in Foreign Office (1855) *Treaties Between Turkey and Foreign Powers* (London, Foreign Office) 381; Kosary, G (1938) 'Gabriel Bethlen: Transylvania in the XVIIth Century', *The Slavonic and East European Review* 17 (49), 162–73;

Although the Cossacks linked to Poland-Lithuania were nominally under control, the Cossacks linked to Russia were not. This became problematic, as groups on both sides of the border were difficult to control, and often of mixed loyalty, to which one side or another claimed some type of primacy. This was evident when the forces of Sultan Selim II tried to take Astrakhan in 1569. The peace that followed in 1570 saw the Sultan acknowledged as sovereign over the Khanate of the Crimea, but he tacitly renounced any claims to Astrakhan. Peace broadly held for the following decades, until in 1637, Russian-linked Cossacks, on their own initiative, seized the formidable Ottoman fortress of Azov and executed the Ottoman envoy to Moscow, whom they had detained. This threatened to provoke a war which Moscow did not want. As the Ottomans' attention was focused elsewhere, it was 1641 before Sultan Ibrahim launched the long-expected counter-offensive. The Cossacks, outnumbered fifteen to one, fought with legendary bravery, forcing the Ottomans to retire. The Cossacks then offered Azov to Moscow. However, Moscow, not wanting a major war with the Ottomans, declined. Moreover, when the Cossacks were subject to reprisals, Moscow did not defend them.[50]

C. The Western Mediterranean

Within three months of the fall of Constantinople in 1453, the new pontiff, Callixtus III, had appealed to the Christian duty of all in Western Europe to unite against the Ottoman threat, and issued the bull *Turcorum*, announcing the fall of Byzantium and seeking funds for a new crusade. Churches everywhere were instructed to ring their bells daily to remind the faithful to pray for the success of a new crusade,[51] as a way to keep at bay what many believed was the Apocalypse. The problem was that, despite the unprecedented events, the leaders of Western Europe declined the Pope's invitation to attend a Congress to plan the crusade, and most of those who turned up were evasive or non-committal. Venice actually went in the opposite direction, agreeing a treaty in 1454 with the Ottomans, in exchange for commercial trading rights in their empire.[52]

The 1454 treaty between the Ottomans and Venice finally fractured when a Venetian boat in Athens gave sanctuary to a slave fleeing his Ottoman master, who governed Athens. The Ottoman authorities attacked a Venetian castle in the region in retaliation, for which Venice declared war on the Ottomans. Venice was joined by Genoa, which had already seen its remote territories disappearing. Although the allies could make some initial advances, the Ottomans forced them back, with the island of Euboea falling to the Ottomans in 1470, and all Genoese and Venetian colonies on the Black Sea gone by 1475. Moldavia was overrun in 1476, and thereafter became

[50] Finkel, C (2005) *Osman's Dream: The History of the Ottoman Empire* (NYC, Basic) 221.

[51] This would become the Angelus, the practice of ringing of church bells every day at noon.

[52] Moudarres, A (2013) 'Crusade and Conversion: Islam and Schism in Pius II and Nicholas of Cusa', *Modern Language Notes* 128 (1), 1–8; Rowe, J (1961) 'Pope Pius II: An Interpretation', *Church History* 30 (3), 288–313; Gilmore, M (1952) *The World of Humanism* (NYC, Harper) 15, 18–19.

entangled in a complicated set of dynastic, territorial and religious struggles. By 1477, the Ottoman army was within 22 miles of Venice. The Venetians reached for peace in 1478. This peace required Venice to hand over 100,000 gold ducats immediately, and 10,000 each year thereafter. It also included a swap of certain territory that both sides had recently acquired, although in substance Venice retained only a few toeholds in Greece and the Aegean, such as Crete, whilst Scutari, Croia and the islands of Lemnos and Negropont were placed in Ottoman hands. In exchange, the Venetians regained their rights to trade in Ottoman lands and retain the Venetian quarter in Istanbul.[53]

As soon as peace was reached with Venice, Sultan Mehmed II struck out against both Italy and Rhodes, the latter being a type of 'no-mans' land after being recaptured from the Turks in 1310 and occupied by the Knights Hospitallers of St John, who were a military order directly answerable to the Pope. The Ottoman attack against Rhodes, with 60,000 men of whom they lost perhaps 9,000, failed to achieve its objectives. Mehmed's other attack, which was undertaken at the same time, on Italy, resulted in the brief capture of the fortress town of Otranto in 1480. This resulted in Naples, Florence and the papacy in Rome all settling their differences to focus on the Ottoman threat, with the support of Pope Sixtus IV, who proclaimed a crusade against the Muslim invaders who now seemed ready to push up the Italian peninsula. Italy was saved not by their united effort but by the death of the Sultan, following which all the Ottoman forces returned to Istanbul, to discover which of the Sultan's sons would take power. As it was, the dynastic squabble turned into a civil war, which kept Istanbul fully occupied until one of the contenders, Sultan Bayezid, rose to the fore. Realising what was likely to occur, Pope Alexander VI organised the *Holy League* in 1495,[54] linked to the last crusading bull for the recruitment of Christian warriors to fight Muslim soldiers in 1496.[55]

Sultan Bayezid's first target was Venice, and he hoped that the Venetians would be too distracted by their Italian commitments to put up much of a fight. Bayezid was wrong. The Venetians recruited large numbers of mercenaries, although they were difficult to control, causing fights and disputes with the Ottomans before the formal declaration of war. As the Hungarians were engaged in a truce with the Ottomans, and the responses to Pope Alexander's pleas for a crusade were negligible, in 1499 Venice fought alone, as the two largest navies of the age, with over 350 ships and 60,000 men, clashed at the Battle of Zonchio. Although the sea battle was a stalemate, it was clear

[53] The 1478 'Peace Agreement between Sultan Mehmed II and the Signoria of Venice', as reproduced in Rosenwein, B (ed) (2006) *Reading the Middle Ages: Sources from Europe, Byzantium and the Islamic World* (Ontario, Broadview) 498; also Stern, S (ed) (1965) *Documents from Islamic Chanceries* (Cambridge, MA, Harvard University Press) 81–118; Stantchev, S (2010) 'The Venetian Response to Sultan Mehmed II in the Venetian-Ottoman Conflict of 1462–79', *Mediterranean Studies* 19 (1), 43–66; Panaite, V (2000) *The Ottoman Law of War and Peace* (NYC, Columbia University Press) 384–87.

[54] See pages 37–38.

[55] Mondola, R (2014) 'The Ottoman Capture of Otranto in 1480', *Studia Historica* 36 (1), 35–58; Crowley, R (2011) *City of Fortune* (London, Faber) 303–38; Finkel, C (2005) *Osman's Dream: The History of the Ottoman Empire* (NYC, Basic) 80–90; Karski, K (2012) 'The International Legal State of the Sovereign Military Hospitaller Order of Rhodes', *International Community Law Review* 14, 19–32.

that Venice was no longer the supreme maritime power, as the Ottoman navy came within 30 kilometres of the city walls. It was at this point that the French and Spanish offered some support to the Venetians. Although this helped stop the tide of Ottoman conquests, it could not turn it. Accordingly, in 1503, Venice agreed to a truce for seven years with the Ottomans. Only a few islands (Corfu, Crete and Rhodes) remained in Christian hands, albeit via payment of tribute in some instances. Further deals were made with the Ottomans in 1513 and 1517, whereby all of the tribute for Cyprus, some 10,000 ducats, which previously went to the Mamluks, was now sent directly to Istanbul, as the Ottomans had conquered the Mamluks.[56]

Sultan Suleiman then turned his attention to Rhodes. His justification for attacking the island was that Hospitaller vessels were behaving like pirate ships, attacking Muslim boats on the sea routes between Istanbul and the new Ottoman provinces of Syria and Egypt. The Hospitallers probably felt secure in their belief that the Christian countries of Western Europe would rush to their defence, as a united Christian front to fight the Muslims had been agreed with the *League of Cambrai* of 1508, the Fifth Lateran Council of 1512 and, in 1518, the *Christian League/Treaty of London*, in which 22 Christian powers agreed that 'it is the primary duty of Christian Powers to propagate the faith of Christ and to exterminate the enemies of the Christian name'.[57] In reality, none of these countries came to the island's aid, and Rhodes fell after a two-month siege. Although the defenders had lost only 3,000 of their men (out of 7,500), compared to the heavier Ottoman losses (25,000 out of 75,000), to avoid further killing they agreed that 'it would be a thing more agreeable to God to sue for peace and protect the lives of simple people, of women and children'.[58] An honourable exit for the Christian soldiers was agreed, who could freely move to Malta, and the Christian citizens of Rhodes were free to stay or go, their faith and churches being protected if they stayed, and a five-year tax holiday was proclaimed.[59]

Sultan Suleiman's next target was Italy. In what was considered to be the diplomatic coup of the sixteenth century, the Ottomans made a military alliance with Catholic France. This deal, which was concluded in 1535 (and renewed in 1569, 1581 and 1597), was for a 'valid, sincere and sure peace'.[60] The alliance was made by Francis I in an attempt to pursue a common enemy, the Emperor Charles V.[61] The King of France

---

[56] Guilmartin, J (2007) 'The Earliest Shipboard Gunpowder Ordnance', *The Journal of Military History* 71 (3), 649–69; Grant, R (2011) *1001 Battles* (London, Penguin) 228, 236.

[57] The Christian League, as in Reddaway, F (ed) (1930) *Select Documents in European History*, Vol II (London, Methuen) 32.

[58] The Council of Rhodes, in Kinross, L (1976) *The Ottoman Centuries* (NYC, Quil) 178; also ibid, at 174, 219, 265, 291.

[59] Castrillo, R (2007) 'The Ottoman Conquest of Rhodes', *Anaquel de Estudios Arabes* 18, 117–35; Brummett, P (1989) 'Foreign Policy and Defence of the Ottoman Empire in the Early Sixteenth Century', *The International History Review* 11 (4), 613–27; Brockman, E (1969) *The Two Sieges of Rhodes, 1480–1522* (London, Murray) 25–29, 67–76, 100, 167–75; Greengrass, M (2015) *Christendom Destroyed: Europe 1517–1648* (NYC, Penguin) 299.

[60] See the 1535 'Treaty of Amity and Commerce', as in Foreign Office (1855) *Treaties Between Turkey and Foreign Powers* (London, Foreign Office) 169–74; the 1569 treaty, ibid, at 174–85.

[61] See pages 47–51.

accepted 100,000 gold coins from Suleiman as a good faith payment, linked to the goal of a joint Ottoman/French alliance to attack the forces of Charles V in Italy between 1535 and 1537.[62]

Feeling emboldened by his alliance with Francis I, Suleiman tried to provoke a conflict by accusing Venice of plundering Ottoman vessels; and when an Ottoman ambassador was seized by mistake, this spark ignited a war. The Venetians joined with Genoa, Spain and the papacy in an alliance that resulted in nearly 200 galleys battling an Ottoman fleet of similar size (but without French support) at the Battle of Preveza in 1538. Although the Ottomans won the day (the *Holy League* lost half of their ships and over 2,500 men), their advance was slowed. Suleiman then pursued his French alliance, with a French artillery unit being dispatched to the war in Hungary and attached to the Ottoman army. However, the French–Ottoman alliance never really took off, despite Suleiman's marching a large army to the coast of Albania and landing it in Italy, near Otranto, just as Mehmed had done earlier. Francis I did not invade Italy from the opposite direction, as he had promised. Rather, he reconciled with the Holy Roman Emperor Charles V in 1538 in the *Truce of Nice*, and agreed to help Charles in his wars against the Ottomans. Upon hearing this, Suleiman withdrew his troops from Italy. However, the Christian offensive was piecemeal. Europe remain wracked by internal conflicts, and when Venice made an independent peace with the Ottomans in 1540 (whereby her last strongholds in the Morea, together with the last islands she controlled in the Aegean, were handed over as the price of peace), the collective response fragmented. This split widened in 1543, when the French alliance with the Ottomans resumed and the corsair Barbarossa and the French collectively attacked Nice. However, by 1544, the French–Ottoman alliance was off again.[63]

In 1558, Suleiman directed his fleets to attack the Balearic Islands, taking 4,000 Christians captive. In 1561, the Ottomans assaulted shipping around Naples, and in 1565 they made raids deep into Spain, again carrying off thousands of captives. Suleiman then turned his attention to Malta, held by the Knights Hospitaller. The spark for the war was the capture of one of the Sultan's merchant vessels and the placement of the Muslim crew as galley slaves. With this provocation, Suleiman advanced with 40,000 men against what was one of the bastions of the Mediterranean. Although the Hospitallers were left with only 600 men capable of bearing arms (out of an original force of 9,000), they destroyed over half of the opposition, and thus ended Suleiman's hopes of further expansion.[64]

---

[62] Heath, M (1989) 'Unholy Alliance: Valois and Ottomans', *Renaissance Studies* 3 (3), 303–15; Jensen, D (1985) 'The Ottoman Turks in Sixteenth Century French Diplomacy', *The Sixteenth Century Journal* 16 (4), 451–70; Vatin, N (2015) 'The Ottoman View of France From the Late Fifteenth Century', *French History* 29 (1), 6–14; Fuess, A (2005) 'Prelude to a Stronger Involvement in the Middle East: French Attacks on Beirut in 1403 and 1520', *Al-Masaq* 17 (2), 171–92.

[63] The 1540 'Capitulation, Peace and Commerce Treaty Between the Ottoman Empire and Venice' in Foreign Office (1855) *Treaties Between Turkey and Foreign Powers* (London, Foreign Office) 701–12.

[64] Bradford, E (1960) *The Great Siege* (London, Reprint Society) 18–20, 32–33, 220; Bonavita, H (2002) 'Key to Christendom: The 1565 Siege of Malta', *The Sixteenth Century Journal* 33 (4), 1021–43.

Sultan Suleiman was succeeded by his son, Selim, in 1566. Selim II ruled for only eight years. The most noteworthy event in his reign was his conquest of Cyprus, which had been under Venetian rule since 1489, even though the Venetians did pay tribute for it. It was, however, poorly governed, and the Cypriot population invited foreigners to rule over them. The problem for Selim was that Cyprus was ruled by Venice, with whom the Ottomans had just renewed their peace treaty in 1567.[65] Selim asked his grand mufti about whether it was permissible to break the treaty. The Sultan was advised that breaking the treaty with Venice was 'absolutely obligatory'.[66] Selim then informed the Venetians that despite the peace treaty, as the Ottomans now owned the former Mamluk possessions, Cyprus, once a Muslim land (in the eighth century) and later a Mamluk fief, actually belonged to the Ottomans. In addition, the *Signoria* of Venice was accused of failing to deal with a band of Christian pirates who were operating from Cyprus. Selim II then informed the Venetians, 'We demand of you Cyprus',[67] and dispatched 70,000 Ottoman troops to take the island in 1570, which they duly achieved. Five years later, Venice accepted the situation and formally ceded Cyprus to the Ottomans, in exchange for some war indemnities and renewed commercial privileges to re-engage in trade.[68]

Pope Pius V had hoped to save Cyprus with the formation of a new *Holy League*, which mustered 230 galleys, 50,000 infantry and 4,500 cavalry from Spain, Sicily, Florence, Genoa, Venice, Savoy and the papacy, as led by Don John of Austria, the illegitimate son of Charles V. Although they arrived too late to save Cyprus, the naval force engaged with 270 Ottoman galleys in the Gulf of Lepanto in 1571. Before the battle began, Pope Pius V's bull of general indulgence and absolution for all those who should happen to die in the battle against the infidels was read aloud on each of the League's ships. The Pope also blessed the image of the crucified Christ, which was placed on the mainsail of Don John's ship. Opposing him, Pasha Ali Mouezinzade flew under a banner inscribed 28,900 times with the name of Allah. The outcome of the battle, which was celebrated all over Europe as it was seen as a turning point in Mediterranean history, was that over 18,000 Muslims would be killed, with 3,000 taken captive. The Christian forces would lose 8,000 men and see over 20,000 wounded.[69]

[65] The 1567 'Peace Treaty between Venice and the Ottoman Empire' in Foreign Office (1855) *Treaties Between Turkey and Foreign Powers* (London, Foreign Office) 712–13; Stantchev, S (2010) 'The Venetian Response to Sultan Mehmet II in the Venetian-Ottoman Conflict of 1462–79', *Mediterranean Studies* 19 (1), 43–66.

[66] Newman, S (2007) 'Upwards Till Lepanto', *Historian* 96, 14, 17–19.

[67] Selim II, as noted in Cohen, M (ed) (2004) *History in Quotations* (London, Cassell) 296; also Wernham, R (1968) *The New Cambridge Modern History: The Counter Reformation* (Cambridge, Cambridge University Press) 352–53, 356–57, 360–62.

[68] The 1575 Peace Between Venice and the Ottoman Empire, as reproduced in Foreign Office (1855) *Treaties Between Turkey and Foreign Powers* (London, Foreign Office) 713–20; Bouwsma, W (1984) *Venice and the Defence of Republican Liberty* (London, California University Press) 190–91; Wernham, R (1968) *The New Cambridge Modern History: The Counter Reformation* (Cambridge, Cambridge University Press) 354.

[69] Capponi, N (2006) *Victory of the West. The Battle of Lepanto* (London, Macmillan) 153–58, 170–71, 263–64, 289; Hess, A (1972) 'The Battle of Lepanto and Its Place in Mediterranean History', *Past and Present* 57, 53–73.

The last time the Ottomans and the Christian countries in this part of the world waged war, in the period covered by this book, was towards the middle of the seventeenth century. The peace between Venice and the Ottomans finally unravelled when the maritime forces of Venice came into conflict with the corsairs of Algiers, Tunis and Tripoli. In 1639, when one of the corsairs that had recently been raiding Venetian territory took shelter in an Ottoman port, the Venetians gave permission for force to be used to take it. Although this disturbance was dealt with by the payment of compensation by Venice for the damage done when the Venetians seized the corsair, when a similar matter occurred in 1644, war broke out. In particular, a squadron from the Knights of Malta captured some Ottoman vessels filled with rich cargo. Although Venice had actively discouraged her subjects from having anything to do with the Knights of Malta, the squadron sailed its plunder to Crete. It was this harbouring of the Maltese vessels, contrary to the early agreement that no corsair vessels intent on, or guilty of, attacking the shipping of the other party would be given shelter, that the Sultan used as his justification to attack Crete, launching a war that would last for quarter of a century.[70]

D. North Africa

North Africa was a complicated region at the beginning of the fifteenth century. Following the Portuguese capture of the city of Ceuta in Morocco, the area had been divided between the Hafsid (around Tunisia), Marinid (around Morocco) and Zayyanid (north Algeria) dynasties. As these dynasties often fought each other, new lines appeared (such as the Wattasid dynasty), and all were willing to seek military alliances with each other and/or Christian Portugal or Spain to secure their ends. This pattern remained consistent into the sixteenth century, with many of the territories within the region toggling back and forth between different overlords. The Spanish and Portuguese poured men and resources into the areas they held both directly and indirectly, supporting local Muslim authorities hold power, in exchange for ultimate suzerainty over an area. Other Muslim rulers preferred to get their support not from Christian Europeans, but rather supporters of the Ottomans, such as the famous corsairs, the Barbarossa brothers. For example, the Barbarossa brothers were asked by the Hafsid dynasty to expel the Spanish and their supporters from their lands, after which the Zayyanid ruler (who kept switching his allegiance between the Hafsids and Aragon) fled from Tunis. The future Emperor Charles V responded by directing a force of 15,000 Spanish troops into the area in 1516, returning the deposed sultan to the Zayyanid throne and recovering some territory, but he could not reclaim Algiers. Portugal also began to lose the territory it possessed around modern-day Morocco after the local Wattasids

---

[70] Finkel, C (2005) *Osman's Dream: The History of the Ottoman Empire* (NYC, Basic) 226–27; Kinross, L (1976) *The Ottoman Centuries* (NYC, Quil) 315.

reconciled with the Muslim forces in southern Morocco (the Saadis) via their 1527 *Treaty of Tadla*. This degree of stability allowed them, together, to force the Portuguese back, as evidenced most clearly in 1541 with the fall of Santa Cruz.[71]

In turn, the Hafsids were themselves toppled by the Barbarossas on the pretext that a fugitive prince from the same dynasty was better suited to rule, especially since the Hafsid Emir, Muley Hassan, had decided to become a Spanish ally. Charles V responded in a similar way as previously, seeking to reinstate Muley Hassan with the backing of 60,000 soldiers from Germany, Spain, Portugal and the papal states. This assault resulted in the sack of Tunis, which led to the killing of perhaps 20,000 soldiers but allowed the city to be returned to Muley Hassan. The grateful Emir promised to allow a Spanish base in the territory, not to allow corsairs into his harbour, and to pay an annual tribute to the Emperor Charles and to release any Christian slaves in his territory. Charles attempted a similar action in 1541, trying to recapture Algiers with 37,000 men, but failed, leaving 12,000 dead. Tripoli was wrest from Spanish hands in 1551, and then Oran, the last of the Spanish forts in Algeria, garrisoned with 12,000 men, was overrun. The following year, a force that had captured the Tunisian fortress of Djerba was in turn besieged and then destroyed, with a total loss of 27 Spanish galleys and at least 10,000 men. The only area where disaster was not recorded was in Morocco, when the Wattasid dynasty was destroyed at the 1554 at the Battle of Tadla, after which the new dynasty of Saadian Sharif emerged. Although the Portuguese forces were expecting the worst from this newly unified regime, Sharif, in 1551, did the opposite of what was expected and sent 30,000 men into Western Algeria, to attack the Ottoman forces, and began exploring the possibilities of alliances with the Spanish and Portuguese.[72]

Tunis changed hands again in 1569 and once more in 1573, when an Austrian force recaptured it and returned it to a loyal Hafsid ruler. However, it was lost again the following year, when the Ottomans returned and pushed the Christian forces out once more, with the last Caliph of the Hafsids brought to Istanbul and publicly executed due to his collaboration with the Christians. With a compliant ruler back in place in Tunis, and in Algiers and Tripoli, the Ottoman rule along the coast of North Africa was now extensive.[73]

Five years later, in 1578, the Portuguese king, Sebastian, answered a call to help Sultan Muhammad Al-Muttakawil, who had been deposed from his kingdom in Morocco by

[71] Coleman, D (2013) 'Forms and Functions of Coastal Raiding on Both Sides of the Western Mediterranean, 1490–1540', *Medieval Encounters* 19, 167–92; Gurkan, E (2010) 'Ottoman Cooperation with the North African Corsairs in the Sixteenth Century', *Turkish Historical Review* 1, 125–63; Salvadore, M (2010) 'The Ethiopian Age of Exploration: Prester John's Discovery of Europe', *Journal of World History* 21 (4), 1–19; Meredith, M (2014) *The Fortunes of Africa* (NYC, Simon & Schuster) 114–15, 148–50.

[72] Lower, M (2009) 'Sultan of Tunis and Would Be Christian Convert', *Mediterranean Historical Review* 24 (1), 17–27; Grant RG (2005) *Battle: 5000 Years of Combat* (London, DK) 133; Bonney, R (2012) *The European Dynastic States* (Oxford, Oxford University Press) 137, 242–44.

[73] Curtis, B (2013) *The Habsburgs: The History of a Dynasty* (London, Bloomsbury) 64–66; Rogerson, B (2010) *The Last Crusaders* (London, Abacus) 194, 199, 227, 295–300; 312, 380–87, 400–20; Turnbull, S (2003) *The Ottoman Empire* (London, Osprey) 58–61, 84.

an Ottoman-backed coup. Dreams of glory and prestige, coupled with the advantage of having a loyal Muslim vassal to act as a staging post for Portugal's growing interests in East and West Africa, seemed sufficient justification to get involved. The venture was, however, a disaster for Sebastian. He perished with his army of nearly 17,000 men (divided between Portuguese and local forces), after being outnumbered three to one. This not only created a succession crisis in Portugal (to the benefit of King Philip II),[74] but the victory and its momentum also spilled over the borders into the African Songhai Empire (encompassing much of modern Mali and West Africa) a dozen years later, when this West-African empire, was toppled by 5,000 men with gunpowder weapons, trumping an opposing force four times that size, without gunpowder.[75]

E. Spain

Spain was the one country in Western Europe that had a significant Muslim population. After the reconquest had occurred,[76] a type of balance had been achieved. This disintegrated following the fall of Constantinople in 1453 and the continual expansion of territory and power by the Ottomans. The Spanish response was to commence military action against the last-remaining, autonomous and independent Muslim kingdom of Granada, after Henry IV of Castile resumed the *Conquista* in 1455. Six large-scale military incursions were made into Granada between 1455 and 1457, but they achieved nothing of importance. The idea then fell into abeyance for a decade, until the marriage of Ferdinand of Aragon and Isabella of Castile united Spain in 1469.[77] The marriage concessions made by Ferdinand explicitly stated that once the two kingdoms were joined, inter alia, 'we will be obliged to wage war on the Moors, enemies of the holy Catholic faith, as the other preceding Catholic monarchs have done'.[78]

Granada, although always punctual about paying about 25 per cent of its annual revenue as tribute, as demanded, now faced a unified Spain. At the same time, dynastic disputes began to fragment the Emirate of Granada, these being actively fanned by Ferdinand and Isabella, who encouraged dissidents in the Muslim kingdom. The Emir of Granada, Abu al-Hassan, for his part, hosted Christians who fled the reign of the new Spanish monarchs. Abu al-Hassan also tried to reach an accord with Sultan

---

[74] See pages 94–96.

[75] Trim, D (1997) 'The Campaign of Alcazarquivir, 1578', *Small Wars and Insurgencies* 8 (1), 1–34; Meredith, M (2014) *The Fortunes of Africa* (NYC, Simon & Schuster) 154–58; Fernandez-Armesto, F (2011) *1492: The Year Our World Began* (London, Bloomsbury) 68–73; Grant, RG (2005) *Battle: 5000 Years of Combat* (London, DK) 140–41; Kinross, L (1976) *The Ottoman Centuries* (NYC, Quil) 272–76.

[76] Gillespie, A (2017) *The Causes of War*, Vol 2: *1000 CE to 1400 CE* (Oxford, Hart Publishing) 72–74, 99–100.

[77] See pages 39–41.

[78] 'Ferdinand's Marriage Concessions', as reproduced in Cowans, J (ed) (2003) *Early Modern Spain: A Documentary History* (Philadelphia, PA, Penn State University Press) 8–9; MacKay, A (1977) *Spain in the Middle Ages* (London, Macmillan) 58–59, 63; O'Callaghan, J (2003) *Reconquest and Crusade in Medieval Spain* (Philadelphia, PA, Pennsylvania University Press) 2–3, 23, 47–56, 87, 95,103, 139–46.

Bayezid of the Ottoman Empire, but no offer of military assistance was forthcoming. No assistance came from the Muslim communities in North Africa either.[79]

When Abu al-Hassan realised that the Muslims in Granada were both alone and about to be attacked, he provoked the war. First, he refused to pay the tribute he was obliged to provide, stating, 'the palaces in Granada where they used to strike the coins to pay tribute are now being used to forge lance-heads to prevent it ever being paid again'.[80] His forces then seized one of two border fortresses at Zahara, forcing hundreds of Christians into slavery. These acts allowed Ferdinand and Isabella to declare that they would now 'wage war against Moors on every side'.[81] The son of the Emir, Boadbil, then sought to further his father's claims, and his own prestige, by invading Castile, but failed miserably, being taken prisoner. He only obtained his freedom by consenting to hold Granada as a tributary kingdom under the Catholic monarchs, and not to intervene in their ongoing battles against his father, and later his uncle El Zagal, the latter going on to take the title of Emir of Granada. This claim of El Zagal to the emirate, and the willingness of Boadbil to accept the loss of Granada's independent sovereignty, led to a civil war within the Muslim community of Granada. As the civil war raged, some 10,000 Christian horsemen and 50,000 foot soldiers proceeded to overrun the territories of Granada bit by bit.

When the last Muslim enclave outside the city of Granada fell in late 1489, El Zagal submitted to Ferdinand and Isabella. Although sovereign independence would be lost, El Zagal would retain some power in managing Granada. It was at this moment that Boadbil, unhappy with his share of the rewards of the reconquest, tore up his agreement with Ferdinand and Isabella and proclaimed his determination to fight for what Muslim territory remained, namely, the city of Granada. This act spurred Ferdinand and Isabella to finish the matter once and for all. Writing to the Pope, they explained their goals as those whereby 'the holy Catholic faith may be spread and Christendom quit of so unremitting a menace as abides here at our gates'. They then suggested that it was necessary that 'these infidels of the kingdom of Granada are uprooted and expelled from Spain'.[82]

Despite his earlier bravado, after an eight-month siege of the city, when Boabdil recognised that outside Muslim help was not going to arrive and the risk of total destruction of his community of 53,000 Muslims at the hands of the 60,000 men massed outside the walls, he opted for a negotiated surrender, even though it meant the end of the independent emirate, which had existed for over 500 years. The terms of surrender were generous. Ferdinand and Isabella promised 'love, peace and goodwill' in

---

[79] Castaner, L (2005) 'Mamluks, Ottomans and the Fall of the Kingdom of Granada', *En la Espana Medieval* 28, 299–316; Robinson, F (ed) (2009) *The Islamic World* (Cambridge, Cambridge University Press) 36–37.

[80] Abu al-Hassan, as noted in Rogerson, B (2010) *The Last Crusaders* (London, Abacus) 122.

[81] Isabella, as noted in Rogerson, B (2010) *The Last Crusaders* (London, Abacus) 122; also ibid, at 17–19, 30–33, 40–41, 56–61, 140, 375.

[82] Letter to the Pope, as in Fernandez-Armesto, F (2011) *1492: The Year Our World Began* (London, Bloomsbury) 29, 30–34; also, Rodriguez, E (2010) 'The Military Orders and the War of Granada', *Mediterranean Studies* 19 (1), 14–42.

67 articles designed to protect the property, faith, mosques and legal traditions of their new Muslim subjects. It was spelt out that 'no Moor shall be forced to become a Christian against his will'. This was in addition to a tax holiday lasting three years, a general pardon for all acts of the war and the release of prisoners.[83]

The terms of the peace were not observed. Fears of revolt, which could be actively fuelled by Muslims offshore, led to the development of inducements for unhappy Muslims to emigrate to North Africa, an offer that Boabdil accepted in 1493 along with 6,000 others. In 1497, Portugal expelled all Muslims, and the following year, in 1498, the city authorities in Granada divided the city into two zones—one Christian, one Muslim. Subsequently, in 1499, Archbishop Cisneros of Toledo, in direct contravention of the surrender agreement, started to undertake a policy of forcible conversions and mass baptisms. He was unapologetic in his approach, declaring, 'if the infidels couldn't be attracted to the road to salvation, they had to be dragged to it'.[84] The first mosques were forcibly converted into churches, and some Muslim libraries were consigned to the flames around 1498. Prominent Muslims were also tortured and cajoled into accepting public baptisms. When the Muslims of the Alpujarra mountains took to arms again to protect their rights as guaranteed by the 1491 treaty, the Spanish Crown declared the treaty suspended. In 1501, all mosques and shrines were converted to Christian settings. The rebellious regions were then dealt with one by one, their only option, if their inhabitants wished to remain in Spain, being to convert to Christianity. The Andalusian Muslims who would not convert were formally expelled in 1499, after further revolts broke out in southern Spain. Similar edicts, offering baptism or exile, were issued in 1501 and 1502, whilst Isabella's dying request to her husband in 1504 was that he devote himself 'unremittingly to the conquest of Africa and to the war for the Faith against the Moors'.[85]

The conversion, forced or voluntary, of the once Muslim populations never fully satisfied the Spanish authorities of their loyalty. Suspicions became heightened in the following decades, especially following raids in 1565 and 1566 by Muslim corsairs along the coast of Granada. Philip II, the King of Spain, Naples, Sicily and the Netherlands, buoyed by the fervour of the Counter-Reformation, yet fearful that the power of the Ottoman Empire could link up with disaffected Muslims in Spain, decided to tighten his grip by strictly enforcing all of the earlier regulations, with restrictions on Moorish culture, language and practices. When a revolt of up to 45,000 local fighters and 4,000 foreign Muslim volunteers broke out in 1568, fuelled by apocalyptic prognostications and leading to the quick and indiscriminate killing of at least 3,000 Christians, the Spanish authorities responded with force, crushing the rebellion within two years.

---

[83] The 'Surrender Treaty of the Kingdom of Granada, 1491' in Cowans, J (ed) (2003) *Early Modern Spain: A Documentary History* (Philadelphia, PA, Penn State University Press) 15–19.

[84] Cisneros, in Carr, M (2009) *Blood and Faith: The Purging of Muslim Spain* (NYC, New Press) 58; also ibid, at 19–24.

[85] Isabella, as noted in Elliot, J (2002) *Imperial Spain* (London, Penguin) 53. Sover, F (2008) 'The Expulsion of the Muslims from Portugal', *Al-Masaq* 20 (2), 34–54; O'Callaghan, J (2003) *Reconquest and Crusade in Medieval Spain* (Philadelphia, PA, Pennsylvania University Press) 2–3, 23, 103, 133.

Philip II offered his troops extra motivation, allowing them to loot and enslave at will, even absolving them from the customary one-fifth of the spoils that were meant to go to the Crown. He then decided to disperse over 50,000 Moors throughout Castile, bringing in 50,000 Christians to resettle the vacated places.[86]

Eventually, in 1609, King Philip III made the decision that his father had refused to take. Despite their conversion, the former Spanish Muslims' persistent use of Arabic customs and speech, coupled with a fear that they were continuing to practise Islam in secret and were conspiring with Spain's enemies, led to his expelling some 275,000 people (mostly to the Muslim countries in North Africa) and confiscating their lands. The Spanish king explained:

> A few days ago many learned and noble men addressed me, urging me to take swift measures that good conscience requires to placate our Lord, who is so offended by these people, assuring me that one could without any scruples punish them in their lives and property, for the continuation of their crimes … of heresy, apostasy, and actions of divine and human treason … [I decree] … [f]irst, that all the Moriscos of this kingdom, men and women, with their children, within three days of the publication of this decree … must leave going to the place where the authority … orders them … They will take with them that movable property that they can carry on their persons … If, at the end of the three days … any of the Moriscos are found outside of their proper place … [they should be captured] … [I]f they resist, they may be killed.[87]

F. India

The final example of Muslim and Christian conflict, followed by relative peace, involved the Portuguese after they had reached the west coast of India in 1498, in search of a direct route to the very lucrative spice market, following Vasco da Gama's rounding of the Cape of Good Hope in a small fleet of four vessels with about 170 men, his silken banner embroidered with the Crusading Order of Christ. Da Gama's standards were given under the authority of King Manuel I, who had financed, organised and licensed the expedition, wanting to benefit from trade and strike a blow at the Muslims at the same time. After sailing along the coasts of West and East Africa, demanding that the local trading cities pay him tribute or face European military technology, Vasco da Gama eventually reached the destination that Columbus had failed to find, arriving

---

[86] Green, M (2013) 'Messianism, Apocalypticism and Morisco Rebellion in Late Sixteenth Century Spain', *Medieval Encounters* 19 (1), 193–220; Borreguero, E (2006) 'The Moors Are Coming, the Moors are Coming!', *Islam and Christian-Muslim Relations* 17 (4), 417–32; Hess, A (1968) 'The Moriscos: An Ottoman Fifth Column in Sixteenth Century Spain', *The American Historical Review* 74 (1), 1–25.

[87] The 'Decree of Expulsion of the Moriscos' in Cowans, J (ed) (2003) *Early Modern Spain: A Documentary History* (Philadelphia, PA, Penn State University Press) 145. Also Waite, G (2013) 'The 1609 Spanish Expulsion of the Moriscos', *Journal of Early Modern History* 17 (2), 95–123; Carr, M. (2009) *Blood and Faith: The Purging of Muslim Spain* (NYC, New Press) at 233; see also ibid, at 120–35, 150–64, 176, 220–32; Johnson, M (2007) 'The Expulsion of the Moriscos from Spain in 1609–1614: The Destruction of an Islamic Periphery', *Journal of Global History* 2 (2), 195–212.

on the west coast around the centre of India, at Goa. It was his good fortune that he arrived in a land that lacked unity. In this complicated world, the locals were surprised by, suspicious of, or hostile to the European interlopers. Only a few wanted to secretly trade with Vasco da Gama, meaning that when he left Calicut in 1498, he did not have a lot to show for his adventure. When he returned in 1500, he was accompanied by 13 vessels and 1,500 men, whom he believed would open the market through force of arms and create a monopoly over the spice trade. This venture was not a success, and after negotiations turned bad and misunderstandings abounded, 48 Portuguese were killed in Calicut. In return, the town was bombarded before Vasco da Gama sailed for home in 1501.[88]

His third visit in 1503 began with da Gama's finding allies in India against Calicut. Forts were built, tribute was collected and the desired monopoly was established, before opposing forces began to come together in 1507 and 1509, when a Mamluk fleet arrived to help the Gujarat and Bijapur sultanates force the Portuguese interlopers out of the area. This attempt was ultimately unsuccessful, as the technologically superior and better commanded Portuguese squadron of 18 ships, with help from some local Hindu corsairs, returned, meeting the combined fleet of over 100 Gujarat, Bijapur and Mamluk vessels, which was comprehensively destroyed, leaving over 6,000 Muslim sailors dead. The Portuguese admiral, Afonso de Alburquerque, then wrote to the King of Portugal, informing him that 'once Goa was conquered, everything else was at our command'.[89] Within a short space of time, the Portuguese would have 100 vessels and 8,000 men stationed on the west coast of India, in areas acquired from the Sultan of Gujarat, who now preferred to deal through negotiation rather than violence. Mangalore was occupied in 1526, Daman in 1531, Bombay in 1535 and Diu in 1535. Portuguese forces attacked and seized Aden, the Yemeni port that stands just south of the Red Sea (which they held until 1538, when the Ottomans secured the port and Yemen in full, although it was difficult to govern), then in 1515 they seized control (for a short time) of Ormuz, at the entrance to the Persian Gulf.[90]

By this stage, Muslim India was no longer fragmented, having been unified by the Mughals. Luckily for the Portuguese, the Mughals, who had ambivalent relations with the other great Muslim powers, such as the Ottomans, tolerated their presence, accepting their traders, their diplomats and their cultural practices. In this world, the bigger threat to the Portuguese was not the Muslim Mughals but the Protestant English and

[88] Elton, G (1968) *The New Cambridge Modern History: The Reformation*, Vol II (Cambridge, Cambridge University Press). 595; Gommans, J (2002) *Mughal Warfare* (London, Routledge) 1519; Richards, J (2008) *The Mughal Empire* (Cambridge, Cambridge University Press) 6–8, 20–40, 80–90; Nossov, K (2006) *The Rise and Fall of the Delhi Sultanate* (London, Osprey) 4–5; Grant, R (2011) *1001 Battles* (London, Penguin) 201, 242, 256, 268, 269, 272.

[89] Afonso de Albuquerque, in Cohen, M (ed) (2004) *History in Quotations* (London, Cassell) 318.

[90] Martinez, A (2012) 'Conquistadores, Mercenaries and Missionaries: The Failed Portuguese Dominion of the Red Sea', *Northeast African Studies* 12 (1), 1–28; Subrahmanyam, S (2007) 'The Birth-Pangs of Portuguese Asia: 1498–1509', *Journal of Global History* 2 (3) 261–80; Hair, P (2002) 'Before Vasco da Gama', *Bulletin of Spanish Studies* 79 (1), 54–65; Blackburn, R (1979) 'The Collapse of Ottoman Authority in Yemen', *Die Welt des Islams* 19 (4), 119–76.

Dutch, who both worked hard to squeeze the Portuguese out of their zones of occupation in India, making alliances with the Mughals, promising them even greater benefits from alliances than Portugal could offer. In response to these offers, permissions (not treaties) were granted to the English to stay and trade through the English East India Company, which was operating in India with Mughal consent, from 1617.[91]

6. Conclusion

The wars involving Islam during the period covered by this book were complex and different from those involving other parts of the world. The most noticeable difference was the failure of independent political institutions to emerge, as they did in Western and Central Europe. The exception to this was in the Ottoman Empire in the seventeenth century, where two coups were staged, as in ancient Rome, the military enthroning compliant (but dynastically legitimate) favourites. However, for the vast majority of the time, internal struggles within ruling Muslim dynasties were much more likely to lead to fratricide, as different male siblings fought each other for ultimate power.

Inter-Muslim warfare was common between different Sunni regimes, with the typical justification being that one was not fulfilling its duties, such as persecuting heretics or protecting pilgrims, as a leader of the faith. The degree of tolerance exhibited in each of these regimes was relative. Some, such as the Ottomans, were relatively tolerant towards non-Muslims, while others, such as the Mughals, at times showed remarkable tolerance towards all faiths. Peace between competing Sunni regimes was possible, but the tendency was towards struggles for dominance, especially when their borders brushed up against each other.

A close proximity of borders was especially difficult with regards to other Muslims who were not Sunni. This was most evident with the emergence of Safavid (Shia) Iran. Wars with the Safavids were commonly based around assertions that the other side was heretical, on the imposition of restrictions on movement and/or persecution of the faith of one side in the territory of another, and on fluid borders along which local powers would commonly switch sides. Peace was possible, but only when no clear military victory could be claimed, there were strict borders, and when promises of non-abuse of the opposition and non-support for uprisings in each other's territories were given by both sides.

Muslim wars with Christian forces were much less complicated. The Ottomans were excellent at playing divide and conquer, fighting on different fronts, consuming small pieces at a time, after obtaining truces with one enemy, allowing them to concentrate on others. This policy became particularly easy as the coherence of Christian Europe fragmented. The most spectacular loss was Constantinople, although the Ottoman advances through the western Mediterranean and south-eastern Europe were equally

---

[91] Farooqi, N (2004) 'Diplomacy and Procedure Under the Mughals', *The Medieval History Journal* 7 (1), 59, 74–75; Greengrass, M (2015) *Christendom Destroyed: Europe 1517–1648* (NYC, Penguin) 158.

impressive. The causes of war, although given the gloss of the underlying momentum and continual rhetoric of religion, were about the inability to control border areas, especially when the local rulers were willing to swap allegiance from one side to another, typically in exchange for greater degrees of autonomy, in religious and/ or economic terms. Alternatively, the catalyst might be local forces' being blamed for attacking the territory, people and/or commercial trade of the other. Peace, at least for short periods, could always be achieved by acknowledging recent conquests in terms of either territory or local authorities' swapping overlords, and a through the revitalisation of trading rights. This was the pattern in Eastern Europe, the western Mediterranean and North Africa, with the clear trend in all three areas being the advance of Muslim forces. These rapid advances were part of the catalyst for the new unified authorities in Spain to progressively remove any independent Muslim areas and finally eject all Muslim inhabitants, as they feared that the latter could not be trusted in a region that demanded complete uniformity of faith.

XII

Asia

1. INTRODUCTION

THIS CHAPTER IS about war in Asia. At the beginning of the period covered by this book, in 1400, the dominant power in the region was Ming China. At the end of this period it was Qing China. Over the same time, Vietnam became more independent, while Korea drew closer to China's orbit. Japan started to become unified, and when this process was complete, for the first time in its history projected its power outwards, invading Korea with a view to conquering China. The external wars were about honour, power and the acquisition of the territories of others. The internal wars sought to bring stability, order and virtue back to failing states. Religion, in the form of Buddhism, was only a minor catalyst in all of these countries, although its legitimising power for successful rulers was lost on no one.

2. THE MING AND THEIR NEIGHBOURS

The start of the fifteenth century saw civil war in China, when Zhu Yuanzhang, first Emperor of the Ming dynasty, passed his power on to his grandson, Zhe Yumen, only for the latter to be usurped by his uncles in a three-year conflict that started in 1399, known as the Jingnan rebellion. From this conflict, the third Ming ruler, the Yongle Emperor, Zhu Di, came to power in 1402, after winning comprehensive victories against enemies in his own family, who had to be 'pacified' after they had fallen into 'evil ways' through the misguidance of self-serving officials. Then, copying the example of his grandfather, he executed tens of thousands of his own officials, to ensure that their loyalty could be relied upon.[1] A similar pattern repeated itself when Emperor Zhu Qizhen was captured by the Mongols, whom he was battling, on the other side of the Great Wall in 1449. Although he was eventually released in 1457, after befriending his captors, he discovered that in his absence he had been replaced by his younger brother, who had no intention of giving up the imperial throne. The military sided with Zhu Qizhen, and thereafter his brother died in mysterious circumstances, while all of

---

[1] Ditmanson, P (2007) 'Venerating the Martyrs of the 1402 Usurpation', *T'oung Pao* 93, 110–56; Brooke, T (2010) *The Troubled Empire: China in the Yuan and Ming Dynasties* (Cambridge, MA, Harvard University Press) 92–93, 96–97, 170–71.

the conspirators who had put him on the throne, or who had refused to recognise Zhu Qizhen's legitimacy, were purged.[2]

Aside from the dynastic challenges, the Ming in the fifteenth century enjoyed a relative stability that allowed them to focus on more external considerations. Notably, seven large naval expeditions between 1405 and 1431, each with up to 27,000 men in 50 or more ocean-going junks, visited the East Indies, Malacca, Siam, Ceylon, India, Ormuz in the Persian Gulf, the Red Sea and the east coast of Africa. Some of these missions involved actual or threatened violence, as the Ming believed they had unified the seas and continents, and that all countries beyond the horizon and at the ends of the Earth, and all of those now contacted, had become Chinese subjects. In reality, the Ming expeditions faded as quickly as they appeared, and it was only in those areas that were geographically more accessible that they really projected long-term power. Even in some connected areas, such as Tibet, the Ming had little interest in occupation (allowing local dynasties to jostle for position), seeking only acknowledgement that they were the imperial suzerain in the region.[3]

In other instances, such as with Korea and Vietnam, the Ming synchronised their expeditions with regime change. In the case of Vietnam, Le Quy Ly seized power and reorientated northern Vietnam towards Ming China, introducing a new-Confucian approach and relinquishing the influence of Buddhism, along with many other changes designed to strengthen central administration and end peasant uprisings. When Le Quy Ly was threatened, the Ming invaded, annexed northern Vietnam and even changed the country's name from Dai Vet to Dai Ngu, to reflect the change of leadership. The north Vietnamese would not accept this occupation, and by 1428 all of the Ming forces all been ejected and the name Dai Vet reinstated, but at the cost of the deaths of up to 7 million people. Within five decades, Dai Vet would go onto crush, and incorporate, the territories of the Champa in south Vietnam, due to their failure to accept that the Dai Vet were superior, their attacks against Dai Vet soldiers and their unjustifiably harsh policies against their own citizens, in terms of both taxation and labour. Further Dai Vet advances into what are now Laos and northern Thailand were possible, as much of this area was in a state of turmoil, as Ming forces were advancing into adjoining areas, soon to make them permanent parts of China. Their progress was greatly aided by the collapse of the Khmer Empire around the same period, with Angkor finally being abandoned in 1430.[4]

[2] Lorge, P (2005) *War, Politics and Society in Early Modern China* (London, Routledge) 120–24.

[3] Weirong, S (2007) 'Accommodating Barbarians From Afar: Political and Cultural Interactions Between Ming China and Tibet', *Ming Studies* 56, 37–93; Schaik, S (2013) *Tibet: A History* (New Haven, CT, Yale University Press) 90–91, 117–20; Wade, G (2008) 'Engaging the South: Ming China and Southeast Asia in the Fifteenth Century', *Journal of the Economic and Social History of the Orient* 51, 578–638; Finlay, R (2008) 'The Voyages of Zheng He: Ideology, State Power and Maritime Trade in Ming China', *The Journal of the Historical Society* 8 (3), 327–47.

[4] Nguyen, T (2002) 'From Indra to Maitreya: Buddhist Influence in Vietnamese Political Thought', *Journal of Southeast Asian Studies* 33 (2), 225–41; Whitmore, J (1970) 'Vietnamese Historical Sources for the Reign of Le Thanh-tong', *The Journal of Asian Studies* 29 (2), 373–94; White, M (2011) *Atrocitology: Humanities 100 Deadliest Achievements* (Melbourne, Text Publishing) 154; the 1470 'Edict on Champa', as reproduced in Dutton, G (ed) (2012) *Sources of Vietnamese Tradition* (NYC, Columbia University Press) 139–41.

The country with which the Ming had the strongest relationship in the fifteenth century was Korea. The Koreo dynasty had come to an end in 1392. It had staked its own survival on the Yuan dynasty's beating the Ming in China. The opposing faction in Korea, the Choson, as led by General Yi Songgye, came to power via a coup in which the General defied orders to attack Ming forces in China and decided to overthrow the Koreo instead, in support of the Ming. Thereafter, Korea became known to many as 'little China', due to its provision of tribute and the strong similarities in its political, philosophical and military goals, which all overlapped with those of 'big China'. The name 'Choson' (meaning 'Morning Serenity') was approved by the Ming Emperor. In taking power, the General's *Founding Edict* proclaimed that the previous Koreo ruler was

> [c]onfused and broke the law, causing many people to rebel and even his own relatives to turn against him, and he was incapable of preserving and protecting the ancestral shrines and institutions. How could anyone restore what Heaven had abandoned? The ancestral shrines and institutions should only be entrusted to one who is worthy, the throne must not be left vacant for long. People's minds are all looking [at my] meritorious achievements and virtue, and [I] accepted the throne to rectify the situation, thereby satisfying the people's desire ... I declined the offer of the throne repeatedly. But I am told that the people's wishes Heaven's will is clearly manifested [that I should rule] and that no one should refuse the wishes of the people, for to do so, is contrary to the will of Heaven.[5]

Yi Songgye moved the capital of Korea to present-day Seoul, as a way to signify the complete break with the old regime. After a decade of civil war between the princes, the royal power was consolidated under his third son. Thereafter, Korea saw a remarkable period of cultural, social and economic stability. Particular emphasis was laid on ending corruption and pursuing equity, including the redistribution of land. The Choson philosophy, like the Ming's, adopted a neo-Confucian approach, with occasional outbursts against both Buddhists and the literati, for their wealth, impropriety or inability to contribute usefully to society.[6]

The last country to consider in fifteenth-century Asia is Japan. Civil war over succession disputes ended in 1392, with Ashikaga Yoshimitsu emerging as the shogun, the military dictator of Japan. He ended the imperial schism that had split the country, and dispatched ambassadors to the Ming court in 1395, laden with tribute, where a successful trade agreement with China was agreed. Six years later in 1401, the Ming court recognised Yoshimitsu as the 'king of Japan'.[7] Despite this achievement and

[5] 'The Founding Edict', as reproduced in Lee, P (ed) (1997) *Sources of Korean Tradition*, Vol I (NYC, Columbia University Press) 272; Ji-Young, L (2013) 'Diplomatic Ritual as a Power Resource: The Politics of Asymmetry in Early Modern Chinese Korean Relations', *Journal of East Asian Studies* 13 (2), 309–36; Weiguo, S (2012) 'An Analysis of the "Little China" Ideology of Choson Korea', *Frontiers of History in China* 7 (2), 101–32; Bohnet, A (2011) 'Ming Loyalism and Foreign Lineages in Late Choson Korea', *Journal of Early Modern History* 15, 477–505.

[6] Duncan, J (1994) 'Confucianism in the Late Koryo and Early Choson', *Korean Studies* 18, 77–102; the 'Anti Buddhist Memorial from Pak Chó', as reproduced in Lee, P (ed) (1997) *Sources of Korean Tradition*, Vol I (NYC, Columbia University Press 1997) 212.

[7] See the 'Chronicle of the Great Peace' in de Bary, B (ed) (2001) *Sources of Japanese Tradition*, Vol I (NYC, Columbia University Press) 284–86; Huffman, J (2010) *Japan in World History* (Oxford, Oxford University Press) 50–51.

the stability that Yoshimitsu created, by the 1450s many of the provinces of Japan were in a state of rebellion against centralised authority. A further succession dispute within the Ashikaga family, which began in 1467, provoked a decade-long war that resulted in the destruction of most of Kyoto, helping to lead to five more decades of conflict and disorder, known as the Age of War. Even leaders of Buddhist monasteries ordered their adherents, or mercenaries, to attack rival Buddhist factions, whilst associated warriors-cum-warlords continued to battle on, with highly significant cultural areas, such as the Kanto plain, where modern Tokyo now lies, changing hands several times.[8]

3. The Imjin War

The sixteenth century in China began with civil unrest after Emperor Zhengde came to power in 1504. In 1510, he had to wage war against his great-great uncle, the Emperor's victory being followed with a purge of his own administration. Further rebellions within his realm arose, in which banditry and opportunism proliferated, only to be crushed by mass executions and the replanting of difficult areas with more loyal subjects.[9] At the same time, new regulations restricted foreign envoys, private trade was curbed, maritime trade supervisorates (*shibosi*, often called trading-ship offices) were closed down, and all large ocean-going ships were ordered to be dismantled. The Portuguese request to trade with China was declined in 1521, and the traditional maritime ban in China, 'that all the foreign ships and bays and all the foreigners who have secretly entered and reside there shall be expelled, that non-official interactions be prohibited',[10] was reinstated.

This approached was reversed when Zhu Houcong took the throne, allowing more licenced foreign trade, with the Portuguese receiving permission to establish their trading station in 1557. When Emperor Wanli took power in 1572, he continued this open approach, allowing the Spanish limited trading rights in 1575. Wanli also dealt with some regional rebellions, made peace with the Mongols and intervened in border disputes in Burma. Most notably, he kept the semi-nomadic steppe people, known as the

---

[8] de Bary (ed) (2001) Sources of Japanese Tradition, Vol I (NYC, Columbia University Press) 420–21; Friday, K (2004) *Samurai, Warfare and State in Early Medieval Japan* (London, Routledge) 24–28; Grant, R (2011) *1001 Battles* (London, Penguin) 231, 268.

[9] Israel, L (2008) 'The Prince and the Sage: Concerning Wang Yangming's Effortless Suppression of the Ning Princely Establishment Rebellion', *Late Imperial China* 29 (2), 68–128; Shin, L (2006) 'The Last Campaigns of Wang Yangming', *T'oung Pao* 92 (1), 101–28.

[10] The edict from the Emperor in Fujitani, J (2016) 'The Ming Rejection of the Portuguese Embassy of 1517', *Journal of World History* 27 (1), 87–102; Wade, G (2008) 'Engaging the South: Ming China and Southeast Asia in the Fifteenth Century', *Journal of the Economic and Social History of the Orient* 51, 578–638; Russell-Wood, A (1998) *The Portuguese Empire, 1415–1808* (Baltimore, MD, Johns Hopkins University Press) 7–10, 22–23, 44, 61. See 'Portuguese Embassy to China' in Parry, J (ed) (1968) *The European Reconnaissance* (NYC, Harper) 122–42.

Jurchen (who had created the Jin dynasty centuries earlier) from Manchuria, in today's north-east China, and later the Qing, in check.[11]

In Japan, the last Ashikaga shogun was forced from Kyoto by the warlord, Oda Nobunaga. The justifications given by Nobunaga for these actions in 1572, in which vassals overthrew those who were once deemed to be socially superior, were that the shogun had become unjust, niggardly, greedy, blinded by favouritism, underhand, disregarding of legality, obstinate, vindictive and extortionate on pecuniary matters, displaying 'improper' and 'outrageous'[12] behaviour. Nobunaga achieved his goal by enlisting not hundreds of traditional but expensive Samurai warriors, but thousands of common foot-soldiers, armed with copies of the firearms that the Portuguese had brought to the country. Brigades of 3,000 men were rotated in three ranks, making it possible to fire a volley every 10 seconds. At the Battle of Nagashino, over 10,000 of the opposition were killed, including 54 of the 97 Samurai leaders. When the fighting was over, the prisoners and the Buddhist priests who had legitimised the shogun were executed, and the Enryakuji temple, which had been built in 785 CE, which was the very symbol of orthodox Buddhism's entrenched power in Japan, was destroyed. With such victories, Nobunaga had his personal seal engraved to read, 'the realm subjected to military power'.[13]

When Oda Nobunaga was assassinated, he was succeeded by Toyotomi Hideyoshi, a man with no traceable provenance. Hideyoshi completed the subjection of all of Japan. In 1585 he conquered the island of Shikoku with a musket-led army of 150,000 men. In 1587, Kyushu was taken by an army of nearly 250,000 men, and in 1590 Hideyoshi destroyed the independent power of the Kanto region. He then secured his reign by denying the non-military populace the right to hold any weapons. He also sought to stop the foreign influence of Westerners in Japan, ordering all Christians to leave in 1587. Although he never enforced the order, 26 Christians were crucified, including six European priests, after Hideyoshi heard rumours of a Spanish attempt at conquest.[14]

After completing the conquest of Japan, Hideyoshi set his sights on Ming China. His justification was set out in a letter to King Seonjo of Korea in 1590:

> As far away and foreign regions and distant islands, all is now in my grasp. ... As a result of this miracle, anyone who turned against me was automatically crushed. Whoever I fought, I never failed to win; wherever I attacked, I never failed to conquer. Now that the realm has

[11] Kung, J (2014) 'Autarky and the Rise and Fall of Piracy in Ming China', *The Journal of Economic History* 74 (2), 509–34; Laichen, S (2003) 'Military Technology Transfers from Ming China', *Journal of Southeast Asian Studies* 34 (3), 495–517; Pei, H (1990) 'New Light on the Origins of the Manchus', *Harvard Journal of Asiatic Studies* 50 (1), 239–82.

[12] The 'Remonstrance of 1572', as reproduced in de Bary (ed) (2001) *Sources of Japanese Tradition*, Vol I (NYC, Columbia University Press) 442.

[13] The motto is reprinted in Hawley, S (2014) *The Imjin War* (NYC, Conquistador) 11, 22–23; Clulow, A (2015) 'European Military Power in Early Modern Asia', *History Compass* 13 (3), 148–57; Grant, R (2011) *1001 Battles* (London, Penguin) 271, 285, 287, 290.

[14] The 1588, 'Disarmament of the Populace', as reproduced in de Bary (ed) (2001) *Sources of Japanese Tradition*, Vol I (NYC, Columbia University Press) 458–59; also Huffman, J (2010). *Japan in World History* (Oxford, Oxford University Press) 56–65.

been thoroughly pacified, I caress and nourish the people, solacing the orphaned and deso-
late. My subjects live in plenty ... I shall in one fell swoop invade the Great Ming. I have in
mind to introduce Japanese customs and values to the four hundred and more provinces of
that country and bestow upon it the benefits of imperial rule and culture for the coming hundred million years ... even if this is a distant land of little islands in the sea ... I have no other
desire but to spread my fame throughout the Three Countries ...[15]

Hideyoshi's thinking was that now that Japan was unified, he wanted a national goal
on which to focus the country's attention, rather than going back to traditional feuding.
His vassals, old and new, would thrive on the rewards of conquest. His own aggran-
disement was the icing on the cake. The difficulty was that, to get to China, Hideyoshi
first had to go through Korea. The relationship between Korea and Japan was poor.
Trade, despite earlier being positive, had officially been discontinued in 1548, due to
clashes and lawlessness in the trade zones. In addition, piracy, especially that based in
Japan, was a real concern (though one that Hideyoshi promised to, and did, control).
The bigger difficulty for Hideyoshi was that Korea, although independent, had a close
relationship, in both political and cultural terms, with Ming China.[16]

When Korean envoys visited Japan to express their congratulations on Hideyoshi's
consolidation of power in 1590, Hideyoshi demanded that Korea send tribute to him
as a sign of its obeisance, and that King Seonjo should himself come to Japan to pay
the necessary respects. He made similar demands of both Taiwan and the Spanish-
ruled Philippines. Whilst the authorities in the Philippines and Taiwan could choose
to ignore these demands, the Koreans, who were Japan's near neighbours, could not.
The Choson Government of Korea, which knew almost nothing of Hideyoshi, was
dumbstruck. It found Hideyoshi arrogant, rude and completely lacking in diplomatic
protocol and the appropriate humility, which was not surprising, given his former lack
of social standing. The Choson Government found it very easy to refuse to send tribute to him. Hideyoshi then explained to the Korean ambassador that his goal was not
to attack Korea but to attack China: 'I shall go by way of Korea and if your soldiers
will join me in this invasion you will have shown your neighbourly spirit'.[17] When
Hideyoshi pushed further for an alliance against China, King Seonjo responded:

We shall certainly not desert 'our lord and father nation' [China] and join with a neighbouring nation in her unjust and unwise military undertaking. Moreover, to invade another nation
is an act of which men of culture and intellectual attainments should feel ashamed. We shall
certainly not take up arms against the supreme nation ... your proposed undertaking is the
most reckless, imprudent and daring of any of which we have ever heard.[18]

---

[15] 'Letter from Hideyoshi to the King of Korea', as reproduced in de Bary (ed) (2001) *Sources of Japanese Tradition*, Vol I (NYC, Columbia University Press) 466–67.

[16] Swope, K (2009) *A Dragon's Head and a Serpent's Tail* (Norman, OK, Oklahoma University Press) 37–40; Robinson, K (2000) 'Centering the King of Choson: Aspects of Korean Diplomacy, 1392–1592', *The Journal of Asian Studies* 59 (1), 109–25; Robinson, K (1992) 'Border Security and Border Control in Early Choson', *Korean Studies* 16, 94–115.

[17] Hideyoshi, as recorded in Hawley, S (2014) *The Imjin War* (NYC, Conquistador) 83.

[18] The Korean Response, as reproduced in Hawley, S (2014) *The Imjin War* (NYC, Conquistador) 88.

Following this rejection, a well-disciplined army of 158,000 Japanese, many armed with muskets and supported by cannon, landed in Korea. The capital city, Seoul, fell after three weeks of fighting, as did Pyongyang. The successive defeats forced King Seonjo to flee northwards towards the Chinese border, as the Japanese forces advanced up through Korea, all the way to the Yalu and Tumen rivers, taking about four-fifths of its taxable arable land. At this point, the Koreans asked for military help from the Ming Emperor Wanli, who was emerging, successfully, from a sequence of battles in China waged in order to consolidate his authority, as a result of which his military and leadership were strong. Wanli realised that as his country was the ultimate target, it made more sense to fight the Japanese in Korea rather than in China. In providing weapons, economic assistance and some 167,000 Chinese troops to help fight the Japanese in Korea, he argued:

> If the military force of Korea would cooperate with our imperial army and attack those atrocious creatures from both sides, we should be able to exterminate them ... [T]hose insignificant and malignant brutes have dared to come forward and overrun your country ... [T]he day will come soon when that whale-like monster Hideyoshi must submit his head and be slain.[19]

The military support of China was matched by a growing national identity in Korea, which sought to throw out the foreign invader. For example, Sosan Taesa, the leader of the Buddhist community, despite suppression under the Choson, called upon all able-bodied monks to fight, of whom more than 8,000 heard the call:

> Hold your banners high, and arise, all you monk soldiers of the eight provinces! Who among you have not been given birth in this land? Sacrificing oneself for a just cause and suffering in the place of the myriad souls is the spirit of Bodhisattvas ... Put on the armour ... Hold in hand the treasured sword to fell the devil, and come forward ... [to] do your duty. Let the aged and weak pray in the monastery. Let the able-bodied come out with their weapons to destroy the enemy and save the land.[20]

The cumulative result was that the Japanese advance was halted, and they were forced to retreat south. In 1593 there were battles at sea (Hansando, 9,000 Japanese dead) and on land (Byeokjegwan, with losses of 8,000 on both sides; Haengju, with 24,000 Japanese killed; Jinju with a total 60,000 dead). In the stalemate that followed, Hideyoshi tried to make peace with China, proposing that Korea should be divided between them and the two countries linked by imperial marriages. The Chinese would not accept these proposals, being willing to agree to peace only if Japan submitted to being a vassal of China, withdraw all Japanese troops from Korea and pledged never to invade Korea again. Hideyoshi responded to the Chinese proposals by reigniting the war and launching another invasion force, numbering an additional 40,000 men, into Korea in

---

[19] The Wanli emperor, Hawley, S (2014) *The Imjin War* (NYC, Conquistador) 247; Hasegawa, M (2016) 'War, Supply Lines, and Society in the Sino-Korean Borderland', *Late Imperial China* 37 (1), 109–52; Swope, K (2005) 'Military Technology Employed During the Sino-Korean War', *The Journal of Military History* 69 (1), 11–41.

[20] Sosan Taesa, as noted in Hawley, S (2014) *The Imjin War* (NYC, Conquistador) 279.

1597. The Ming responded by sending a further 75,000 men into Korea. The results for Japan were bad. The Japanese were defeated at sea by the Koreans (losing 10,000 men and 31 ships), and were then forced to retreat even further. When Hideyoshi died of natural causes in the middle of 1598, the decision was made to evacuate all of the Japanese forces from Korea. In the course of their retreat, they were attacked unrelentingly. In the final evacuation from Korea, some 450 of the 500 Japanese ships involved were destroyed at Noryang, resulting in the deaths of thousands.[21]

The reverberations were felt even further in Japan when, 18 months later in 1600, civil war broke out amongst the five rulers left to govern in the power vacuum left following the death of Hideyoshi. Out of this conflict, Tokugawa Ieyasu rose to the fore. Tokugawa was the regent Hideyoshi had appointed for his son. However, he preferred to take power for himself, sparking (by occupying the castle of Hideyoshi's son) and then winning, the civil war that followed. Once victorious in this internal conflict, Tokugawa founded his shogunate, which would rule Japan until 1868.

Relations with Korea recommenced with the 1609 *Treaty of Kiyu*, which allowed limited trade but restricted the right of Japanese envoys to go further than Pusan. Such limitations were reflected in Japan, as the shoguns forbade all emigration and prohibited the construction of large ships. Other than this, there was no settlement like the *Treaty of Westphalia* in Europe to end the conflict between the three powers, and the relationships and geographical territories settled back into their earlier patterns. Finally, although the shoguns were initially tolerant of Christians as a counterbalance to too much Buddhist influence, they sought to stop their missionary work. Soon after, the Jesuits were ejected, allowing the much more business-orientated Dutch to fill the gap left by their departure. However, they were restricted to doing business on some specified off-shore islands. For the rest of Japan, from 1635 the so-called *Sakoku* (Closed Country) decrees came into force, forbidding all contact with the outside world. Japanese citizens were forbidden, on pain of death, to travel or trade abroad.[22]

4. The Qing

The Qing dynasty came to eclipse the Ming. Records of what happened, between 1635 and 1662, when perhaps 25 million people perished, are patchy. Nonetheless, it is possible to assert that if there was one particular cause for the collapse of the Ming dynasty, which is commonly recognised as representing the height of traditional Chinese cultural achievements, it was not a lack of resources (as the dynasty was wealthy, powerful

---

[21] Lorge, P (2005) *War, Politics and Society in Early Modern China* (London, Routledge) 130–36; Swope, K (2009) *A Dragon's Head and a Serpent's Tail* (Norman, OK, Oklahoma University Press) 88–92, 99–103, 151–54, 227–30; Grant, R (2011) *1001 Battles* (London, Penguin) 300, 301, 302, 305, 307, 308.

[22] Myongsob, K (2014) 'Why No Westaphalia Like Peace Order After the Hidyoshi War in Korea?', *Korea Observer* 45 (1), 117–43; Parker, G (2013) *Global Crisis: War, Climate and Catastrophe in the Seventeenth Century* (New Haven, CT, Yale University Press) 71; Swope, K (2009) *A Dragon's Head and a Serpent's Tail* (Norman, OK, Oklahoma University Press) 290–94.

and had a technological advantage in foreign weapons) but the absence of leadership and, ultimately, morale. Those in charge were unable to deal with successive waves of peasant uprisings that started to break out in the 1590s and multiplied throughout the coming decades, as local populations repeatedly challenged the status quo as they were worn down by population growth, epidemics, bad harvests (connected to drought and floods), poor infrastructure management, inequitable distribution policies, burdensome tax structures and lawlessness. People turned to violence as a strategy to survive in a world of diminishing resources, as a short-cut to power or to right grievances.[23]

Emperor Wanli had been a brilliant leader, engaging in the external war with Japan in Korea and in internal wars in China, suppressing rebellion, which required armies of over 150,000 men under his direction. However, in the last two decades of his reign, from 1600 to 1620, he became progressively uninterested in leadership. He virtually stopped meeting with his officials after reaching what appears to have been a type of stalemate with his own government. The subsequent Tianqi Emperor, who ruled from 1620 to 1627, followed the same path. In the vacuum that expanded around the Emperors who would not lead, where those who were critical of the government risked execution, a bureaucracy developed that was corrupt, factional, self-serving and conflicted. As a consequence, the morale and direction of the vast Ming forces slowly imploded.[24]

The dynasty that succeeded the Ming was the Qing dynasty, whose roots lay in the Manchus, a Jurchen people from the area known as Manchuria in today's north-east China. The Manchus lived and fought as horse archers, similar to the Mongols. In then recent history, they were neither hostile nor friendly to the Ming. They had worked for them in places and taken some Ming titles, but were largely independent. The founder of what became the Qing dynasty, Nurhaci, grew up in the household of a Ming general in the Yalu region. He went on to be the Ming-designated commander of the region, as well as leader of his own Jurchen tribe. In 1593, he consolidated four Jurchen tribes into one confederation, after starting a conflict with one of them over a vendetta relating to the death of his father. His military achievements were supplemented by his policies to reduce tax but increase revenue via enhanced trade.

---

[23] Jingyun, Z (2014) 'How Climate Change Impacted the Collapse of the Ming Dynasty', *Climatic Change* 127 (2), 48–65; Struve, L (1989) 'Early Qing Officials as Chroniclers of the Conquest', *Late Imperial China* 10 (1), 1–26; White, M (2011) *Atrocitology: Humanities 100 Deadliest Achievements* (Melbourne, Text Publishing) 223; Wakeman, F (1986) 'China and the Seventeenth Century Crisis', *Late Imperial China* 7 (1), 1–25; Parsons, B (1970) *Peasant Rebellions of the Late Ming Dynasty* (Tuscon, AZ, Arizona University Press) 1–21, 26–29, 68–75, 81–82.

[24] Han, L (2014) 'History, Fiction and Public Opinion: Writings on Mao Wenlong in the Early Seventeenth Century', *Journal of the American Oriental Society* 134 (1), 69–88; Jia, L (2011) 'Conflicts Between Monarch and Ministers', *Chinese Studies in History* 44 (3) 120–36; Yuan, L (2011) 'The Ming Emperor's Practice of Self Examination and Self Blame', *Chinese Studies in History* 44 (3), 6–30; Struve, L (2007) 'Dreaming and Self Search During the Ming Collapse', *T'oung Pao* 93 (1), 159–92; Wakeman, F (1977) 'Rebellion and Revolution: The Study of Popular Movements in Chinese History', *The Journal of Asian Studies* 36 (2), 201–31; Hacker, B (1977) 'The Weapons of the West: Military Technology and Modernisation in China and Japan', *Technology and Culture* 18 (1), 43–55.

He also imported foreign fighters and their weapons. Finally, he developed social policies to record Manchu as a separate language and develop a strong and independent culture.[25]

In 1616, Nurhaci proclaimed his regime to be the 'Latter Jin', after he had destroyed or incorporated most of the remaining Jurchen and the Mongolian tribes within his reach. He moved them away from tribal-based systems and towards a structure known as the 'Eight Banners'. This structure was critical for the development of Qing ideology, as it moved away from ethnic-based identities as the foundation of social policy, to a type of hereditary aristocracy based exclusively around the military. Although each of the Eight Banners signified a fighting unit, and was identified with distinct (and sub-divided) national groups (Manchus, Mongols and Chinese), the importance of the Banners lay in their elite status and loyalty to the regime, not in their ethnic backgrounds, which were becoming a pretext for conflict at the end of the sixteenth century, with the traditional Chinese versus Barbarian idea resurfacing.[26]

Nurhaci proclaimed his *Seven Grievances* before attacking the Ming in early 1618. These accused the Ming, inter alia, of killing his family members without reason; playing favourites amongst the ethnic groups of the region; not honouring territorial agreements; and permitting the abuse of power by some regional governors. Nurhaci then pushed outwards, taking the city of Fushun in 1618. In the following years, in addition to defeating Ming armies sent to crush him, he expanded his realm. He took Tieling, Shenyang and Liaoyang. In each instance, by offering generous terms, he encouraged Ming soldiers to defect and join his rebellion.

Zhu Youjian, the so-called Chongzhen Emperor, was the last ruler of the Ming dynasty, coming to power in 1627. His first challenge was to deal with Zhang Xianzhong, a bandit who became active in 1628. Zhang came to control much of the inland valley of Sichuan by coercing, coopting or cooperating with other rebel groups in the region. Next, Chongzhen had to get to grips with Nurhaci's successor, his son Hong Taiji, who started raiding Ming territory in 1629 after defeating other family contenders for his father's power, and then centralising, reorganising and reinforcing the military forces under his command. Hong Taiji also established a chancery and six administrative boards, modelled on earlier Chinese examples, to ensure more efficient management of the territories under his control. This was supplemented by orders for scholars to produce works showing when bad Chinese rulers had been justifiably overthrown. He then advanced his forces, which breached the Great Wall and occupied four cities on the central plain. When some of his commanders treated the defeated badly, he had them executed, for fear of losing the hearts and minds of his new subjects. This action was supplemented by his recruitment of officials and soldiers of Han ethnicity.

---

[25] See Pei, H (1990) 'New Light on the Origins of the Manchus', *Harvard Journal of Asiatic Studies* 50 (1), 239–82.

[26] Xiangyu, H (2013) 'A New Perspective on Legal Privilege for Bannermen', *Asia and Pacific Studies* 34 (2), 1–16; Lorge, P (2005) *War, Politics and Society in Early Modern China* (London, Routledge) 141–43; Waley, J (2014) *The Culture of War in China: Empire and the Military under the Qing Dynasty* (London, Tauris) 18; Swope, K (2003) 'All Men Are Not Brothers: Ethnic Identity and Dynastic Loyalty', *Late Imperial China* 24 (1), 79–129.

He also publicly accepted Buddhism (especially to get the support of the Tibetans and the Mongolians), despite being personally scathing of its value and practices.[27]

In 1632 the armies of Hong Taiji brought Inner Mongolia under Manchu control, and five years later, in 1637, Korea was added. Although Choson Korea was closely linked to the Ming dynasty, for the sake of its own survival, it swapped allegiance to support the newly emerging Qing. The Manchus concentrated on settling this area before progressing deeper into China, to ensure that the Korean flank was neutralised. Despite the fact that many of the Choson considered the Qing to be barbarians, they continued to provide tribute, three times each year, to the new dynasty. Although they remained, in theory, subservient to the Qing, they obtained much more autonomy than they had possessed under the Ming. With such advances, Hong Taiji felt confident enough not only to change the ethnic designation of Jurchen to Manchu, but also to change his dynasty's name to 'Qing' (instead of 'Latter Jin') in the middle of 1636. The name 'Qing' was associated with water, and thus was the element that would destroy the 'brightness' or 'fire' of the Ming.[28]

The difficulties for the Chongzhen Emperor multiplied when Li Zicheng, a Ming army officer, mutinied in 1634 after some of his men had been executed for crimes they had committed. Li Zicheng, who cooperated with Zhang Xianzhong, ended up being virtually the sovereign of large areas adjacent to the Tibetan plateau, stretching from the Yangtze to the Great Wall. He took measures to alleviate the suffering of the poor, promoting measures of social justice. He seized Luoyang in 1638, and later tried to starve out Kaifeng in 1642 (only 30,000 of the 370,000 citizens surviving). He took Beijing in 1644, with the Chongzhen Emperor inside it, the latter killing himself. The most capable Ming general of the day, Wu Sangui, appealed to the Qing for help, and returned to Beijing to pursue Li Zicheng, who had not only breached the capital but had also killed Wu Sangui's parents. Li Zicheng fled to the Jiugong region, where he was eventually killed by locals in September 1645.[29]

The efforts by Li Zicheng and Zhang Xianzhong created the perfect opportunity for the Manchus to topple the Ming dynasty. The new leader of the Manchus, following the death of Hong Taiji in 1643, was his son and successor, Fulin. However, given that he was young, Hong Taiji's brother, Dorgon, acted as regent. It was Dorgon who destroyed Zhang and his forces, as well as mopping up the surviving Ming forces. Dorgon justified his military drive by explaining that the 'Great Qing Dynasty' had long sought harmonious relations with the Ming, 'hoping for perpetual peace', and had only invaded when their letters were ignored. Meanwhile, bandits had taken control and chaos was endemic. Accordingly:

> We have pledged not to return until every bandit is destroyed. In the countries, districts and locales that we pass through, all those who are able to shave their heads and surrender,

---

[27] Parker, G (2013) *Global Crisis: War, Climate and Catastrophe in the Seventeenth Century* (New Haven, CT, Yale University Press) 124.

[28] Bohnet, A (2011) 'Ruling Ideology and Marginal Subjects: Ming Loyalism and Foreign Lineages in Late Choson Korea', *Journal of Early Modern History* 15, 477–505.

[29] Lorge, P (2005) *War, Politics and Society in Early Modern China* (London, Routledge) 146–47, 153.

opening their gates to welcome us, will be given rank and reward, retaining their wealth and nobility for generations.[30]

He then ordered that several unpopular taxes be ended, reduced the land tax by one-third for all areas that submitted to the Qing, and promised all former bureaucrats an instant one-grade promotion if they came back to work with shaved heads and Manchu dress, and worked for new paymasters. Such offers were persuasive to many, if not most, of the occupied people. In 1645, two crucial Ming generals, including Wu Sangui, formally swapped sides (being rewarded with fiefdoms in the new Qing territories), taking tens of thousands of troops with them. Defection followed defection, and defended areas remaining on the southern side of the Yellow River had the choice of either surrender (like Nanjing) or destruction (like Yangzhou, where somewhere between 30,000 and 800,000 were killed). The last surviving member of the Ming royal family fled to Burma, where his plea for sanctuary was ignored. He was handed over to Wu Sangui, and executed in 1662. This made all future claims to be flying the banner of Ming resistance tenuous or moot. In the ensuing chaos, some rebels/traders/pirates from the coastal regions also broke free and established themselves on Taiwan, after ejecting Dutch forces that had tried to plant themselves there, before they, in turn, were toppled a few decades later, and Taiwan was brought back into the Qing realm in 1683. The Qing were now undisputed masters of all of China proper.[31]

The biggest challenge for those who fought the Ming was how to govern the core Chinese populations under their control. In practice, the Qing takeover, once the battles were won, was easy. Local militia, dismayed at the incompetence of the former Ming administration, handed over their localities to the new Qing officials. This was no surprise when it became obvious that the Qing had sought an accommodation with the local gentry in all regions. Unlike the Ming, who had come to power with a strong social justice ethos, the Qing had little enthusiasm for seizing large plots of land and redistributing it. Although areas were taken for military purposes, the Qing's primary intention was to respect existing ownership rights and help landowners displaced by the peasant rebellions to reclaim their property. This meant that the interests of landlords and the ruling class were very closely bound and mutually reinforcing.[32]

The easy transition to the Qing dynasty was challenged when established cultural practices were violated. It had long been a concern of the Manchus that 'old ways' would be lost to the 'Chinese ways'. As early as 1636, Hong Taiji had decreed:

> All Han [Chinese] people—be they official or commoner, male or female—[in] their clothes and adornment will have to conform to Manchu styles ... Males are not allowed to fashion wide collars and sleeves; females are not allowed to comb up their hair or bind their feet.[33]

[30] Dorgon, as noted in Parker, G (2013) *Global Crisis: War, Climate and Catastrophe in the Seventeenth Century* (New Haven, CT, Yale University Press) 137.

[31] Rowe, W (2009) *China's Last Empire: The Great Qing* (Cambridge, MA, Harvard University Press) 12, 17, 26–30; Grant, R. (2011) *1001 Battles* (London, Penguin) 341.

[32] Wiens, C (1980) 'Lord and Peasant: The Sixteenth to the Eighteenth Century', *Modern China* 6 (1), 3–39.

[33] The Edict of 1636, as reproduced in Parker, G (2013) *Global Crisis: War, Climate and Catastrophe in the Seventeenth Century* (New Haven, CT, Yale University Press) 124.

Above all, males had to shave the front part of their head and wear the rest in a long pig-tail, or queue, like the Manchus. Failure to do so meant that the offenders 'will be considered treasonous bandits and will be heavily penalised'.[34] Taiji, and subsequently Dorgon, may have underestimated the degree of rage that this demand aroused amongst Han men, who saw it as a direct insult, since their hair was part of their cultural identity and to do what the Manchus demanded was intolerable. The revolts that followed in support of the continuation of traditional practices relating to hair were brutally suppressed, the Qing insisting, 'Keep your head, lose your hair; keep your hair, lose your head.'[35] This extreme push for cultural conformity only slowed when Fulin came of age and took power as Shunzhi, the third emperor of the Qing, upon Dorgon's death in 1650.[36]

In his short reign, Shunzhi undid many of Dorgon's controversial policies, going to great lengths to avoid his dynasty's being labelled as 'barbarian' and therefore ripe for challenge. Allowing the Han to arrange their hair in their own style produced the compromise needed to stop the rebellion. Moreover, Shunzhi made fighting corruption his priority, and sought to end influence of the Manchu nobility. Most notably, he pushed hard to revive many of the Chinese-styled institutions that had been either abolished or marginalised in the years following the Qing military victories. Shunzhi adopted Chinese ways of governance to embed the Qing dynasty. New laws, taxes, offices, governing councils, administrative structures and efficiencies followed. In addition, at the top level, dual appointments of Manchus and Chinese was the rule, while at the local levels, Chinese dominated.[37]

It was in this period that Shunzhi invited the Dalai Lama of Tibet to visit him. This meeting reflected the status of the Qing Emperor as patron of Buddhism, and of the other as cleric and servant of the Emperor. The end result was that not only did it keep the hugely influential Dalai Lama and Tibet in check, it was also an important stamp of legitimacy that mattered to the Chinese, and especially the Mongolians (who had officially adopted Tibetan Buddhism as their religion in 1640, owing spiritual, if not political, allegiance to the Dalai Lama). This is not to suggest, at all, that the Qing were strongly religious. Rather, they identified religion as a tool. They used the Tibetan-Buddhism connection to help legitimise their rule, not create a competing ideology that could become autonomous. In the same way, within their direct realm, although religious activity was not banned, anyone who claimed a special relationship with spirits risked contravening the law and would be punished.[38]

---

[34] Dorgon's Edict, in Rowe, W (2009) *China's Last Empire: The Great Qing* (Cambridge, MA, Harvard University Press) 22–23.

[35] As noted in Parker, G (2013) *Global Crisis: War, Climate and Catastrophe in the Seventeenth Century* (New Haven, CT, Yale University Press) 53.

[36] Zarrow, P (2004) 'Anti-Manchuism and Memories of Atrocity', *History and Memory* 16 (2), 67–107.

[37] Xiang, G (2013) 'Expounding Neo-Confucianism: Choice of Tradition at a Time of Dynastic Change', *Social Sciences in China* 34 (2), 105–33; Guy, K (2010) 'Ideology and the Organisation in the Qing Empire', *Journal of Early Modern History* 14, 355–77; Kessler, L (1969) 'Ethnic Composition of Provincial Leadership in the Qing Dynasty', *The Journal of Asian Studies* 28 (3), 489–512.

[38] Kohle, N (2008) 'Patronage, Pilgrimage and the Place of Tibetan Buddhism at the Early Qing Court', *Late Imperial China* 29 (1), 1–28; Waley, J (2014) *The Culture of War in China: Empire and the Military under the Qing Dynasty* (London, Tauris) 52–54; Kang, D (2014) 'Why There Was No Religious War in Premodern Asia?', *European Journal of International Relations* 20 (4), 965–86.

5. Conclusion

The dawn of the fifteenth century saw Ming China, with its high culture, neo-Confucian outlook, and oscillation between inward-looking and outward-looking policies, entrench its position as the pre-eminent power in Asia. Within China, purges following dynastic struggles were the pattern in an age when there were initially few contenders against Ming influence. As regards its neighbours, Korea became a carbon copy of China, whilst Vietnam broke free of its Ming overlords, making the most of the breakdown of many similar regimes in the area. Chaos also reigned in Japan, as regions, families and even Buddhist sects all fought for autonomy and/or dominance.

It was only when the chaos ended that a single warlord emerged as absolute ruler in Japan. Here, the feuding warlords, who kept the country splintered for nearly two centuries, were finally brought under the yoke when Oda Nobunaga, and then Toyotomi Hideyoshi, subdued all of their rivals. Hideyoshi then determined to keep feeding his war machine by attacking Ming China, with the purpose of gaining glory for himself and spreading the benefits of Japanese culture to mainland Asia. When the Korean Government refused him the right of passage to achieve this goal, Hideyoshi attacked Korea first. Despite initial successes, the Japanese were forced out when the Koreans found their fighting spirit and the Ming joined forces with them.

This loss did not result in a Peace of Westphalia-type of deal, and Japan entered into a further sequence of civil wars following the death of Hideyoshi and the struggle for power that followed. Even more unsettling was the collapse of the Ming dynasty, eclipsed by the Qing. The factors that ultimately led to the latter's success were the lack of direction and morale of the Ming, as a result of which lawlessness and the inability to deal with uprisings took hold. The new regime pragmatically swung back towards more support for Buddhism, and after a short but provocative period of trying to force the Chinese to adopt different cultural practices, reverted to the adoption of Ming bureaucracy, albeit it with greater support for the wealthy classes and for law and order.

XIII

Conclusion

THE CAUSES OF war between the years 1400 and 1650 were in many instances a continuation of the patterns discussed in the previous volumes of this series. This was especially so in the case of Europe and wars relating to monarchs. Here, war was caused either by those wanting to be, or to remove, the existing monarch, and/or by monarchs seeking to expand their realms by military force. The exemplars of these are the Hundred Years' War, the Wars of the Roses, the wars for the expansion of France and the Italian Wars. Warfare waged to topple kings who were tyrants, incompetent or simply unable to govern was also seen in Germany, France and England. None of this removal from power was carried out by constitutional agents, with the exception of England at the end of this epoch, where the king lost his head at the direction of a purged Parliament. Before this point, although a weak Parliament existed in England, the *Cortes* in Spain and shades of the Three Estates in France, none of these bodies had sufficient power to seriously challenge the monarchy and what were becoming increasingly autocratic forms of government. The only region in which constitutional structures really came to serve as a counterbalance to the absolute power of the monarch was Poland-Lithuania. In all of the other instances, the trend was towards greater, if not absolute, power for the ruler, given a gloss of legitimacy either by the Church and/or by some form of constitutional body. In the case of England, this meant that the Parliament, from the time of Henry V through to Henry VII, remained flexible, providing the stamp of legitimacy to anyone who had the military power to demand it.

Once secure, the tendency for most sovereigns was to meddle, via marriages and military alliances, in the counterbalances, or families, of their largest neighbours. For France, the counterbalance they held against English power was Scotland. For England, it was Burgundy and Brittany. For as long as those areas two were independent, both were threatened. France escaped this threat with Burgundy being split between France and Germany, and Brittany, after a war, being sequestrated via both marriage and occupation into the territorial solidarity of France under the clear rule of one king. There were no longer semi-autonomous regions, and all English influence was ejected from the Continent.

In the 60 years of war that followed French intervention in Italy, war was fought over dynastic considerations and to seize power within a very complicated landscape of semi-independent polities. Peace was achieved only when the French were fully ejected, except that this time, the ejection was effected by the Habsburgs, who eventually acquired full power over all of Italy. Any vestiges of independent republics, in addition to a powerful papacy, disappeared beneath the succession of treaties that ultimately reflected the fact that what had become a dynastic competition for power in Italy between Spain and France, had been won by Habsburg Spain.

War in Eastern Europe also broadly followed the patterns of earlier centuries, with the notable difference that everything was getting bigger, most notably the rise in power and prestige of both Russia and Poland-Lithuania. The union of Poland and Lithuanian, after they established full independence from the Teutonic Order, went on to see some of the most advanced forms of constitutional governance and religious tolerance (for the upper classes, not the peasants) of the age. The main opponent of Poland-Lithuania was Russia. This country slowly built itself up during the first part of the fifteenth century, adding to the importance and independence of the Orthodox Church and the absolute authority of the Tsar. In terms of warfare, the splitting of the Golden Horde into three separate parts was to Russia's advantage, enabling it to play divide and conquer, as was the slow acquisition of semi-independent areas, such as republican Novgorod. Peace treaties cemented by dynastic marriages could not hold the Tsars back, and they continued to wage war in Livonia at the turn of the sixteenth century, using repeated justifications, such as that the territory was once Russian and that it was necessary to protect the interests of those of the Orthodox faith in these occupied lands. Future Tsars continued on the same trajectory, utilising the legitimising power of the Orthodox Church, galvanising absolute authority and trying to hold Livonia to gain strong access to the Baltic. The difference by the seventeenth century was that the Russian invasions now triggered the intervention of Sweden, Denmark and Poland-Lithuania, who all came to the rescue of Livonia. Russia was only saved by the breakdown of the relationship between Poland-Lithuania and Sweden. This fracture between Protestant Sweden and the increasingly Catholic Poland-Lithuania occurred at the same time as Russia itself descended into civil war, following the end of the Rurik dynasty. This dynastic gap produced external contenders from Sweden and Poland-Lithuania, and from within Russia itself. The contest only ended when Mikhail Romanov was elected by a Russian assembly. Over the following decades, he fought both the Swedes and then the Poles, to force them to abandon the core Rus lands and withdraw their claims to the Russian throne.

Where the changes were most pronounced, in terms of differences from earlier centuries, was where the causes of war were based on inter-Christian hatred and the inability of different faiths to coexist. Inter-Christian differences as a cause for war went from being a relatively minor consideration at the beginning of the sixteenth century, to the dominant paradigm at the end of that century. The background to the wars based around inter-Christian hatred began in the fifteenth century, when all of the elements of theological challenge—national discontent and a loosely-held-together Holy Roman Empire—were present. The Western Schism and the absolute power of the Pope began to cause disquiet. This was evident with the Hussite wars, in which direct disagreement with Rome overlapped with a strong drive for national autonomy. Martin Luther built on all of these concerns, which were multiplied by the Italian Wars and the increasingly extreme actions of the papacy, both in its theological beliefs and in political meddling. Luther's teachings, in essence that the intercession of the Catholic Church between Christians and God was not required, split Western Europe. However, before this split became apparent, the Peasant Wars occurred in Germany. These wars, again showing the discontent of the age, were driven by a desire to end serfdom and improve the status and rights of the poorest people. They failed to achieve any lasting success, but were notable in the sense that Luther came to support the established princes, not the peasants. Thus the revolution that Luther fathered was about a change in theological, not political, direction.

The splitting of Europe on theological grounds was assisted by temporal rulers, who sought to use religion to advance their own power. Most notably, warfare came to cover the countries we know today as Germany, Switzerland, France and the Netherlands, and then Germany again as the Thirty Years' War reached its climax. Peace was ultimately achieved through sovereign independence and/or the abandonment of the ideal of an absolute and universal type of Christianity. In terms of sovereign independence, the foremost example of this period was the rise of the Dutch Republic. The Dutch broke free from their Spanish Habsburg overlords, using the justification that they were fighting against tyranny, as their overlords were heavy-handed in their attempts to control the Dutch and would not allow them to practise the considerable degrees of autonomy they had long possessed and which had been guaranteed to them, as part of which the issue of practising their own Protestant faiths came to the fore. Accordingly, the Dutch abjured the right to be ruled by others.

Where new countries could not emerge and warring communities were forced to remain within a union, peace was achieved not by outright domination, but by learning to tolerate different religious views in different regions. Such tolerance was based more upon pragmatic necessity, in that neither side could defeat the other at this point of time. Neither faith was intrinsically tolerant of any teaching that was different from its own. In Germany, peace was achieved by broadly agreeing to the principle that the ruler of each realm could determine the religion to be followed. In France, peace came after four decades of warfare, agreement being reached regarding freedom of religious belief in all areas when practised in private, but public demonstrations of a different faith being tolerated only in those areas where that faith was dominant. When war broke out over the same issue in Germany, it led to the start of the Thirty Years' War. This conflict, although it began as a war ostensibly about religion, ended up being largely a dynastic struggle between the Catholic Habsburgs and the Catholic Bourbons, with the latter making alliances with the Protestant countries of the Dutch Republic, Denmark and Sweden. The support for this alliance grew as religious intolerance increased. The war that destroyed much of Germany was only brought to an end at Westphalia in 1648. Peace was agreed and the Habsburgs survived, although bruised, after agreeing to several principles. Notably, territory changed hands, then money was paid over to demob the armies and make reparations, and finally the sovereign autonomy of all members of the Holy Roman Empire was increased, including the issue of religious tolerance, via a somewhat extended understanding of the earlier agreement that the ruler of each realm could determine the religion to be followed.

Even countries like England, which managed to avoid being pulled directly into the wars of religion, were strongly influenced by them, fundamental changes to theological leanings and constitutional governance occurring. Here, what started out as the expression of Henry VIII's ego—breaking free from the influence of Rome—gained momentum as his descendants tried to maintain, reverse and then get back on to Henry's path to independence. In the event, although religious violence in England was relatively rare (compared to what was happening elsewhere), the changing currents would pull England into a marriage alliance with Spain, and then into war, with conflicts raging from Ireland to the Netherlands. Peace was achieved between Spain and England only with the accession of new monarchs, both of whom promised to stop supporting religious factions to the detriment of the other.

Where the matter got out of hand, and led to actual civil war in England, Scotland and Ireland, was where questions of religion became mixed with, and ultimately subsumed within, questions about who was the dominant power in the land—the king, Parliament or the military. When the English Parliament failed to act decisively against a king whom many saw as the root of the difficulties, it was purged by elements linked to the military. Those surviving the purge directed two events. First, they ordered the execution of the king, on grounds of tyranny and treason against his own people. Secondly, they determined that the revolution would not be too radical. That is, their goal was to turn Parliament into a republican body for the propertied elite, not a popular franchise for all. In one of the most remarkable acts of the age, the king lost his head, and all of the power of the sovereign was placed into the hands of a collective in the shape of the English Parliament, albeit one which was very vulnerable to manipulation by the military.

The last big noticeable difference, in terms of the causes of war as evidenced between 1400 and 1650, was the developments in the New World, as seen in the northern, central and southern parts of the Americas. The causes of war here were originally based on the premise that the lands occupied by indigenous peoples no longer belonged to them because they had been gifted by the papacy to both Spain and Portugal. Aside from the material benefits that accrued to the colonists, the justifications for seizing ownership of these lands, and the wars that followed, revolved around the benefits that Catholicism and the associated European values would bring to the indigenous peoples. There was no debate about independence or equality between civilisations. Full and absolute surrender of all political power and abandonment of existing cultural practices were required. The alternative was war, which was waged repeatedly, and which, along with European diseases, significantly decimated indigenous populations in all areas.

When the English, French and Dutch got into the business of colonisation, and especially once the Reformation was under way, their emphasis was more on the values of 'civilisation', trade and exchange, although a strong Christian, albeit Protestant, gloss remained. The difference between Catholic and Protestant colonialism was that the massive conquests of the Aztecs or the Incas, recorded by the Spanish, were not replicated in North America. Fundamentally, this was not because of religious differences but because, in the north, in the early years, the colonists were not in any way dominant, increasing their chances of success by treating the indigenous peoples more as equals, with their own legitimate cultural systems. Nonetheless, the only reason the colonists in North America survived was because the indigenous groups were not a homogeneous mass. Rather, they comprised a multitude of tribes, with whom the different colonial groups would make alliances and help in war and trade, either directly or indirectly.

The Muslim wars covered by this this book were similar to those in earlier centuries, but also exhibited certain differences. Compared to Europe, the Muslim world failed to see independent political institutions emerge as counterbalances against the power of rulers. The exception to this was in the Ottoman Empire in the seventeenth century, where two coups were staged, akin to those in ancient Rome, in which the military elected compliant favourites as the supreme rulers. Where Muslim wars in this epoch differed from those in the past was that inter-Muslim wars became much more common, predicated on a drive for dominance but wrapped in justifications such as that one dynasty was not fulfilling its duties to persecute heretics or to protect pilgrims visiting the holy places, or was itself heretical. The degree of tolerance in each of these regimes was relative. Some, such as the Ottomans, were relatively tolerant towards non-Muslims, whereas others, at times, such as the Mughals, showed remarkable tolerance towards all faiths. Tolerance between different Muslim regimes, much less faiths, was much more difficult. Peace between competing Sunni regimes was possible, but the tendency was towards struggles for dominance, especially when their borders brushed up against each other. This close proximity was especially difficult following the Sunni/ Shia split, as evidenced by the emergence of Safavid Iran. Peace between the theologically opposed Muslim faiths was possible, but only when no clear military victory was likely. Thereafter, strictly defined borders and promises of non-abuse of the opposition and non-support for uprisings in each other's territory could bring an end to the killing.

Muslim wars with Christian forces were much less nuanced. The Ottomans were excellent at playing divide and conquer, alternating between different fronts, consuming small pieces at a time after obtaining a truce on one front, allowing them to concentrate on others. This policy became particularly easy as the coherence of Christian Europe fragmented. The most spectacular loss was Constantinople, although the Ottoman advances through the western Mediterranean and south-eastern Europe were equally impressive. The causes of war, glossed over with the underlying momentum and continual rhetoric of religion, were typically about provocations that followed on from the inability to control border areas, where local forces would be blamed for attacking the territory, people and/or commercial trade of the other, and/or about seeking greater autonomy or benefits from one side or the other. Peace, at least for short periods, could always be achieved by acknowledging recent conquests in terms of either territory or local authorities' swapping overlords, and through the revitalisation of trading rights.

Finally, the patterns of warfare in Asia were broadly similar to those in the previous centuries, with the exception that at the beginning of this period, in 1400, the dominant power in the region was neo-Confucian Ming China. At the end of this period it was Qing China. The key to the Qing's success, and the dynasty's justification for war, was the Ming's lack of direction, bad faith and inability to deal with uprisings that occurred from the beginning of the seventeenth century. The new regime pragmatically swung back towards more support for Buddhism and, after a short but provocative period of trying to force the Chinese to adopt different cultural practices, reverted to the adoption of Ming bureaucracy, albeit with greater support for the wealthy class and for law and order.

In terms of other countries in the region, Korea became a carbon copy of ruling Chinese dynasties, whilst Vietnam broke free from its Chinese overlords, making the most of the breakdown of many similar regimes in the area. Chaos also reigned in Japan, as regions, families and even Buddhist sects all fought for autonomy and/or dominance. It was only when the chaos ended that a single warlord emerged as absolute ruler in Japan. He then introduced a novel concept, deciding to keep feeding his war machine by attacking Korea and China, with the purpose of gaining glory for himself and spreading the benefits of Japanese culture to mainland Asia.

Index

Francis I (King of France, 1515–1547), 46–48,
  50–52, 58
  alliance with Protestants, 78
  alliance with Suleiman the Magnificent, 245–46
  Treaty of London, 48
  Treaty of Madrid, 79–80
Francis II (Duke of Brittany, 1458–1488), 30
Frederick III (King of Germany, 1440–1493)
Frederick III (Holy Roman Emperor, 1452–1493),
  26–28, 65–66
Frederick V (Elector Palatine, 1610–1623), 141–44
Frederick the Wise (Elector of Saxony,
  1486–1525), 70
Freud, Sigmund, 2

Gentili, Alberico (b. 1552–d. 1608), 213, 222
George of Kunštát and Poděbrady (King of
  Bohemia, 1458–1471), 64, 65
Germany, 64, 77–80
  see also Bohemia; Hussite wars
Glyndŵr, Owain (Prince of Powys, Wales,
  1404–c.1415), 10
Glyndŵr Rising, *see* Welsh Revolt
Golden Horde (1465–1481), 184–85, 187, 191,
  199–200, 272
Granada, *see* Emirate of Granada
Grand Remonstrance (1641), 168–69
Great Horde (1465–1481), 187–88
Great Privilege (1477), 28, 127–28
Gregory XIII (Pope, 1572–1585):
  excommunication of Elizabeth I, 102–03
Grotius, Hugo (b. 1583, d. 1645):
  slavery, 222
  Thirty Years' War, 159–60, 161
Grunwald/Tanneburg, battle of (1410), 181
Guinegate, battle of (1479), 29
Gustavus Adolphus (King of Sweden, 1611–1632),
  148, 150–51

Haengju, battle of (1593), 263
Hansando, battle of (1592), 263
Heilbronn League, 152–53
Henri II (King of France, 1547–1559), 56, 79–80
Henri III (King of France, 1574–1589), 120–23
Henri IV (King of France, 1589–1610), 118, 119,
  122–24
  Edict of Nantes, 124–25
  St Bartholomew's Day Massacre, 119–20
  Treaty of Lyons, 125
  Treaty of Vervins, 124
  Triple Alliance, 124–25
Henri of Navarre, *see* Henri IV (King of France)
Henry Bolingbroke, *see* Henry IV (King of
  England)
Henry IV (King of Castile and Léon, 1454–1474),
  250
Henry IV (King of England, 1399–1413), 8–11

Henry V (King of England, 1413–1422), 11–14,
  57–58
Henry VI (King of England, 1422–deposed 1461),
  14, 18, 20–22, 57
Henry VII (King of England, 1485–1509), 24–25,
  30–31, 57
Henry VIII (King of England, 1509–1547),
  113–14
  accession, 45
  Act of Supremacy (1534), 85–86
  Anne Boleyn, 84
  Catherine of Aragon, 44–45, 84–85
  Defender of the Faith, 83
  dissolution of the monasteries, 86–88
  excommunication, 85, 87
  France, 45–46, 55–56, 59, 88–89
  Ireland, 51, 87–88
  James V (King of Scotland), relationship with,
    88–89
  Julius II (Pope) and French throne, 44–45
  More, 83, 86
  Peace of Crépy, 55–56, 59, 89
  Scotland, 51, 88–89
  Second Act of Annates (1534), 85
  support for Catholic Church, 45, 83
  Third Act of Succession, 93
  treaty of alliance with Charles V, 51–52
  Treaty of Perpetual Peace, 45–46
  Treaty of Westminster, 45
Henry Tudor, *see* Henry VII (King of England)
hereditary rights of monarchs, 8–9, 20, 24, 36
Hideyoshi, Toyotomi (b. 1535, d. 1598):
  attempted submission of Korea, 262–64
  Byeokjegwan, battle of (1593), 263
  conquest of Japan, 261
  death, 264
  Haengju, battle of, 263
  Hansando, battle of, 263
  Jinju, battle of, 263
  Treaty of Kiyu, 264
  unification of Japan, 260–61
Holy League of Venice (1495), 37–38, 244
Hong Taiji (b. 1592, d. 1643), 267
  concern about old ways, 268–69
Huguenots:
  Catherine de Medici, 116–18
  Edict of Amboise, 118
  Edict of Chateaubriant, 116
  Edict of Compiègne, 116
  Edict of Ecouen, 116
  Edict of Fontainebleau, 116
  Edict of Saint-Germain, 117
  Edict of Toleration, 117
  Elizabeth I, support from, 117–18
  Francis I, 116
  Henri II, 116
  Louis XIII, 146–47